W9-BJR-839

Property of
FAMILY OF FAITH
LIBRARY

CONTENTS

Copyright © 1965 by American Book Company
New York   Cincinnati   Atlanta   Dallas   Millbrae

Manufactured in the United States of America. All rights reserved. No part of this book protected by the copyright hereon may be reprinted in any form without written permission of the publisher.

1   3   5   7   9   11   13   15   EP   16   14   12   10   8   6   4   2

Family of Faith Library

Teacher's Guide and Key for

MODERN GRAMMAR

AND

COMPOSITION 2

David A. Conlin
George R. Herman

AMERICAN BOOK COMPANY

Introduction to the
MODERN GRAMMAR
AND
COMPOSITION SERIES

In the *Modern Grammar and Composition Series,* we present to you and your students something fresh and new in the study of language and composition. In grammar, we have tried to bring into the classroom the ideas and methods that have developed from the extensive and intensive study of language during the past thirty years. In composition, we have presented a complete program of study, from planning a simple theme to creative writing. The coverage is traditional, but the method and the approach are modern and stimulating.

The series is developed in four volumes. The treatment of subject matter in both grammar and composition is sequential. The student will not be bored by constant repetition, for he moves forward from chapter to chapter and from book to book. Yet there is ample provision for review and reinforcement in the consistent return to the study of the sentence and to the problem of improvement in sentence structure. It is here that much of what is learned in the study of grammar may be related to written composition and to its improvement.

The title *Modern Grammar and Composition* implies that in this series grammar has been brought up to date. Step by step, we believe that this is exactly what has been accomplished:

Step 1: We have recognized, first of all, that speech and writing are two different forms of communication. Each form uses a different set of symbols. Speech is reinforced by intonation, by voice qualifiers, by gestures, and even by repetition. Written language consists of cold graphic symbols that appear on a page with almost no reinforcement. Speech is learned early and well, and the learning is highly motivated in the security of the home. Written English is learned in the schoolroom in an entirely different kind of environment. The implications for the teacher, then, are that written English—since it lacks the reinforcement of speech—has to be that much more effective in order to communicate clearly and adequately. Furthermore, in learning to write, the student must be led to full exploitation of his familiarity with the structure of spoken English.

Step 2: In the *Modern Grammar and Composition Series,* the teaching process is inductive rather than deductive. Learning then becomes a process of observation and discovery instead of a study of definitions and rules along with the endless application of these rules and the detailed analysis of their various exceptions. The inductive process is consistent with the modern study of language. Generalization is made when possible, but it comes only after observation of the language forms. In the basic study of the sentence, for example, the student observes the various physical characteristics of the English sentence: initial capital and end punctuation, subject and predicate, finite verb, word order, and the drop or rise in pitch at the end with a fading off of the voice. The older subjective definition ("a statement of complete thought") is thus replaced by the application of objective criteria.

Step 3: As a corollary to the inductive approach, we have emphasized the objective signals of language as clues to meaning. In the study of the four main form, or word, classes—nouns, verbs, adjectives and adverbs—we help the student observe the characteristics of form that serve as signals to the identification of these words in communication. We note the way in which these words are used in a sentence, observing their functions in determining meaning. We note the variety of positions in which these words are used, observing that syntax in English is determined largely by this position.

Step 4: We have separated the concepts of grammar and usage. In the modern approach, grammar is thought of as the study of the structure of English as it is used; usage is thought of as the choice of language forms depending on the factors of time, place, and the degree of formality. The *Modern Grammar and Composition Series* develops the concept of standard written English and its restrictions on usage. The series further emphasizes the importance of the knowledge of the structure of grammar in meeting these requirements.

Step 5: Finally, each book of the series introduces material that relates the study of intonation to the problems of sentence structure and punctuation. Furthermore, each book of the series applies in detail the study of English sounds, or phonemics, to the reduction of spelling difficulties.

In written composition (comprising Part II of the first three books of the series), the emphasis is on the writing assignment—whether it is writing a paragraph, a theme, a research paper, an editorial for a newspaper, or a short story. We have tried to develop provocative and challenging assignments related to the specific problems inherent in the writing process. We have provided experiences for the student in the important areas of thinking critically, building word power, using the dictionary, and using the library.

Throughout the first three books of the series, we have contributed to the continuity of movement from chapter to chapter with two features. At the beginning of Chapter 1, the student will find "A Look Forward," which gives a capsule impression of the ground covered by the chapter. After the first chapter, this opening guide becomes "A Look Back and A Look Forward," relating what has been offered so far with what is to come. The second transitional feature of each of the first three books is the summary either at the end of each chapter or at an appropriate break within the chapter. The summaries reemphasize the most significant points in the chapter. Transitional devices of this kind are especially helpful in planning reviews.

Other novel features of the first two books in the series include end-of-chapter tests, a "Grammar Workshop," a "Composition Workshop," and a section called "The Structure of Your Language," which provides supplementary study for the student whose interests carry him beyond the basic requirements of the text.

Although the first two books of the *Modern Grammar and Composition Series* consistently apply the structure of grammar to the sentence, the paragraph, and the theme, the grammar in *Modern Grammar and Composition 3* is more obviously student-writing centered. The application of the structural approach to the writing problems of the classroom is effected by having the student analyze his own writing and the writing of others for errors and shortcomings that cut down on the effectiveness of communication.

Like the first two books in the series, *Modern Grammar and Composition 3* includes a flexible two-part supplementary test that provides sufficient material for a mid-year and end-of-year test. The first three books in the series also include a substantial glossary of terms ("The Language of Grammar") in which descriptions and explanations are reinforced with examples. The easy-to-find, easy-to-understand entries actually comprise a brief course in modern grammar.

Resources for Modern Grammar and Composition, the fourth book of the series, has been set up as a three-part guidebook to better Expression (Part I) and to an increased understanding of the Structure (Part II) and Convention (Part III) of language. The arrangement of this final book in the series is such that it can be used either in the classroom as a teaching tool or independently as a handbook.

In presenting the *Modern Grammar and Composition Series* to the high school English teacher, we do so in the belief that it meets the present urgent need for a subject-matter approach to language study and to written composition. We have tried to adapt the best of the materials currently available in linguistic research to the development of these four texts, bearing firmly in mind that the background and training of the high school teacher and of the high school student are largely traditional. We have also kept in mind that the change from the old to the new must be gradual. We believe that the *Modern Grammar and Composition Series* represents a step in the direction of a more effective study of grammar and of its application to improved written composition.

Introduction to
MODERN GRAMMAR
AND
COMPOSITION 2

As its title states, the grammar in this text is modern. The modern grammar in Part I, however, has been built on a foundation of concepts that are largely traditional and of nomenclature that is essentially conventional. The method of study is inductive and objective. Definitions and arbitrary rules have, for the most part, been abandoned. *Modern Grammar and Composition 2* emphasizes that the study of grammar is the study of language structure and that this structure may be described in terms of physical characteristics and verifiable statements. New terms and new concepts have been introduced only where there is a definite need—such as in the development of phonemes and graphemes in the discussion of the relation between sound and spelling.

Chapter 1 is largely a review of sentence structure supplemented by the detailed observation of the physical characteristics of the sentence. Chapter 2 works in detail with the expansion of the basic sentence patterns, developing the many combinations of headwords and modifiers present in the noun cluster, the verb cluster, the adjective cluster, and the adverb cluster. Chapter 3 examines the basic functions of the sentence, stressing the significance of function and the importance of the characteristics of form and explaining the relationship between the two. The student is thus provided with a basis for understanding the principle of functional shift and the nature of English as an analytic language. This separate development and mastery of the basic concepts of form and function prepare the way for the study of verbals in Chapter 4. The study of appositives and absolutes in Chapter 5 completes the study of syntax. In Chapter 6, the student works with the subject-predicate relationship and with those complications of usage that most frequently lead to errors in agreement. In Chapter 7, the student works with pronouns, subordinators, and determiners as substitute words and, again, examines those complications of usage that lead to error. Chapters 8 and 9 continue the study of punctuation and spelling. The relation of the sounds of English to the problem of spelling is further developed, and word lists of special difficulty are provided. The final chapter in Part I works with the student in helping him to eliminate the structural errors to which high school students are most susceptible.

Part II of *Modern Grammar and Composition 2* is designed to advance the principles and techniques of writing set forth in the first book of the series. While Book 2 is constructed to approach the assignments from a different direction, the material is basic and the method inductive; therefore, Book 2 does not rely on Book 1 to clarify its design or its purpose. Its explanations are brief and well illustrated; above all, it is rich in practice material.

The focus moves from smaller to larger units of expression. Chapter 1 ("Using the Dictionary") explores the magic of words; Chapter 2 ("Looking at Sentence Structure") considers the ways in which a writer may develop sentence power and variety; Chapter 3 ("Organization and Outlines") suggests methods for dividing and arranging larger bodies of material; Chapters 4 and 5 ("Description and Narration" and "Exposition and Argumentation") offer ways to write for particular purposes. Finally, in Chapter 6 ("Newspaper Writing"), all the approaches to the writing process so far examined are applied to the various types of composition required in journalistic writing.

In Chapter 1, the dictionary is examined as both a wordbook and a world book. It is explained as a guide to definitions, synonyms, antonyms, etymology, language skills, standards of usage, and finally as a clarifier of allusions and a book of knowledge.

In Chapter 2, the effects of various structural variations are explained and practiced. Different patterns of sentence length and word order are evaluated. The communicative power of parallel structure, of balanced sentences, and of loose and periodic sentences is demonstrated.

The theory and practice of outlining are developed in Chapter 3. Informal divisions of material are discussed as a prelude to presentation of the conventional outline form. Outlining is approached from two directions: first, as an analytical device used to describe the writing of another person; second, as a dynamic process that guides one's own construction of a written assignment.

Word pictures and the recording of other sense impressions are initial concerns of Chapter 4, which then explores another approach to imaginative writing—the narrative. Narrative writing is examined and practiced as a presentation of a selected sequence of events—arranged, begun, and concluded to create the most compelling effect.

Chapter 5 is devoted largely to the study of writing which explains—which conveys information. Several techniques of presenting a body of knowledge are distinguished. These include informing through (1) defining terms, (2) partitioning the subject matter, (3) comparing or contrasting points of information, (4) classifying parts of the whole, (5) explaining a process, and (6) developing causes and effects. Following this detailed approach to expository writing, some characteristics of effective argumentation are suggested and illustrated.

Chapter 6 offers practice in writing news stories, features, editorials, and columns; it is not committed to an assumption that any of the students will eventually study journalism or become newspaper writers. Rather, it is designed to encourage wider interest in and reading of current events. But above all, in this chapter we wish to direct all that has been practiced (the study of words and sentences; the concern for descriptive, narrative, expository, and argumentative techniques) to the writing which touches masses of people involved in real events—newspaper stories, features, editorials, columns.

Throughout the grammar and composition sections of *Modern Grammar and Composition 2*, the special features of the *Modern Grammar and Composition Series* are continued: the transitional introductions and summaries ("A Look Back and A Look Forward," "Summary," and "Summing Up"); the "Grammar Workshop" and the "Composition Workshop"; and the "Supplementary Tests."

FLEXIBILITY OF ORGANIZATION

The content of *Modern Grammar and Composition 2* can be presented effectively in a variety of ways:

1. *All of Part I (Grammar) may be taught first, followed by Part II (Composition).*

   In Part I, the structure of grammar is consistently applied to the sentence. As a result, the student who works his way through Part I brings to Part II an understanding of basic sentence structure that will serve as a foundation for the composition skills developed in Part II.

2. *The chapters in Part I (Grammar) may be interwoven with the chapters in Part II (Composition).*

   The transitional devices within the text ("A Look Back and A Look Forward," the chapter "Summary," and "Summing Up") make it practical to interweave one or more chapters from Part I with material from Part II.

3. *Chapters from Part II (Composition) may be taught first as indicators of the needs and interests of your students.*

   The same transitional devices make it practical to begin with Part II and to teach the grammar of Part I as the needs and interests of your students become apparent.

Guide

PART I

CHAPTER **1**   *The Structure of the Sentence*
                 pages 13-42

AIM

The purpose of Chapter 1 is to present an overall picture of the structure of the sentence as developed in *Modern Grammar and Composition 1*. Since the treatment in the series is sequential, it is especially important that students who did not use the first book in the series master the fundamentals of sentence structure before attempting the more advanced work presented in later chapters in Book 2.

PROCEDURE

Review the six characteristics of the sentence as outlined on pages 14-17. The presentation here supplements the more limited treatment of the preceding book. By this time students who used Book 1 will be familiar with the basic sentence patterns (pp. 17-18) as well as with the basic sentence elements (pp. 18-22). A review of the formal characteristics of nouns and verbs (pp. 23-33) will pave the way for the material in the next several chapters. Coordination and subordination (pp. 33-35) are reviewed in relation to expanding basic sentence structures.

The twelve exercises and the end-of-chapter tests should provide ample practice in building sentences as well as in analyzing sentences. For a thorough review, all the exercises should be completed with whatever supervision is needed.

Students having difficulty with certain concepts or encountering these concepts for the first time may require even more intensive study. If possible, material from *Modern Grammar and Composition 1* should be made available to such students. Mastery of the fundamentals of grammar is essential before any of your students attempt the next chapter.

CHAPTER **2**   *Headwords and Modifiers*
                 pages 43-64

AIM

The aim of this chapter is the expansion of basic sentences by means of modifiers, coordination, and subordination. In Chapter 1, we have discussed coordination and subordination and have had some practice in constructing sentences. Now we will consider how sentences can be expanded by means of both single-word modifiers and word-group modifiers. We will examine the structures that result in terms of the headword about which modifiers group themselves as well as in terms of the nature of the modifiers themselves.

PROCEDURE

Headword is a new term in grammatical discussion. Its choice is particularly appropriate for two reasons: (1) In speech, words (a noun or verb with its modifiers) group themselves by sound patterns (intonation) into units of syntax (meaning). Therefore, from the standpoint of grammatical study, the observation and analysis of such a group is of prime importance. (2) The important word in a group of this kind (sometimes called a noun cluster or a verb cluster) is the word about which the modifying words and word groups gather. This is called the *headword.* It is the head of the group (the nucleus), the most important word in the group from the standpoint of meaning.

Single-word modifiers include adjectives and adverbs (pp. 48-51), noun adjuncts (p. 51), and possessive nouns (pp. 51-54). Word-group modifiers include prepositional phrases (p. 55), clauses (p. 55), and verbal phrases (pp. 56-59). These pages review characteristics of form as well as the ways in which words function, or communicate, within the sentence. Thus in Chapters 1 and 2 the students review (or learn) all the form classes: nouns and verbs as primary elements of communication and adjectives and adverbs as secondary elements of communication.

The exercises help the student understand the grammatical principles and fix the concepts firmly in mind. Again, practice in writing sentences is of great importance, since the student is practicing the skill in a usable manner. Constructing sentences according to grammatical requirements provides the student with the opportunity of using his knowledge of structure in the development and improvement of sentences themselves. Thus transfer of training becomes deliberate.

CHAPTER **3**   *Form and Function*
pages 65-80

AIM

So far we have discussed factors of form—inflection, characteristic derivational suffixes, and certain prefixes. We have reviewed nouns, verbs, adjectives, and adverbs as form classes. We have discussed the functions of these words as they are used in the sentence in communication. The aim of Chapter 3 is to show the importance of the characteristics of form and the significance of function and then to explain the relation between the two. This chapter reveals English as a truly analytic language. It also provides the student with the incentive and the opportunity to build sentences in which he uses a given word in a variety of functions as well as a variety of words and word groups in a given function.

PROCEDURE

The important functions of the English language as it is communicated in sentence structure are subject, predicate, complement, and modifier. We find that a given word may often be used in two or more of these functions (pp. 66-69). This grammatical phenomenon is called *functional shift* (pp. 69-72). Thus, we find that in any one of the given functions, a variety of forms may be used (pp. 73-76), resulting in great flexibility in communication.

This chapter emphasizes the fact that position determines function. The position of a word may be reinforced by inflectional changes. It may be reinforced by certain function words—as determiners for nouns, auxiliaries for verbs, and intensifiers for adjectives and adverbs. But position, above all, is the determining factor in syntax.

Completion of the exercises will indicate how thoroughly the concepts of this chapter have been mastered.

CHAPTER 4   *Verbals*
pages 81-100

AIM

This chapter was designed to clarify the meaning and use of verbals. Verbals frequently give difficulty for two reasons: (1) students do not understand the principle of functional shift and the underlying concepts of form and function; (2) they do not perceive the predicating power (in communication) of the verb form as it takes on modifiers and often a complement. Confusion also results from the traditional classification in which form and function are used inconsistently.

PROCEDURE

We suggest you begin with the "Form of Verbals" (p. 82)—the *to* verbal, the *-ing* verbal, and the *-ed* and *-en* verbals—and follow with "Verbal Phrases" (pp. 82-83). "Functions of Verbals" (pp. 83-93) then shows how the three kinds of verbals are used; that is, the functions of each form within the sentence. Traditional nomenclature may be retained (as it has been in this text) as long as these names are not used at the outset. It would be wise to begin with form (three classes) and proceed to function. The illustrative material makes this arrangement easy to grasp, and the exercises give practice in identification and in sentence building. Students should have no difficulty with "Recognizing Verbals" (pp. 94-96) and the practice involved.

CHAPTER **5** *Appositives and Absolutes* *pages 101-110*

AIM

The aim of Chapter 5 is to complete the study of English syntax with the consideration of apposition and absolute structure. These rather common grammatical devices provide the writer with great flexibility of expression, although they present the student of grammar with additional complexity of structure.

PROCEDURE

Appositives are fully covered in "The Appositive Structure" (pp. 102-106). After presenting a variety of forms used in apposition—nouns, noun clauses, and infinitive phrases—exercises are provided for practice and discussion. Many students have difficulty in distinguishing between restrictive and nonrestrictive appositives as well as in punctuating sentences that include such appositives. These concepts are clearly explained and illustrated.

Little space is needed for "The Absolute Structure" (p. 107), which is fully illustrated in a variety of forms. The exercise material will be helpful to the student in his comprehension of these structures.

CHAPTER **6** *Agreement*
pages 111-126

AIM

The fact that we have agreement, or concord, in Modern English is the result of vestiges of inflections inherited from the synthetic language of the Anglo-Saxon period. The fact that concord is incomplete is the result of the changes of the past 1500 years during which our language has changed from a synthetic structure to an analytic structure. We no longer depend on inflected forms as the important signals of syntax.

In modern grammar, the student observes his language and generalizes where it is possible. If we observe our language carefully, we find that subject-verb agreement is limited to relatively few situations. It is the business of the student of grammar, in describing language, to know the conditions under which agreement may be found, as well as to become familiar with the limitations of concord. The aim of Chapter 6 is to present the facts of concord clearly and completely—to call attention not only to those structures that do involve agreement but also to those that do not.

PROCEDURE

In "Subject-Predicate Relationship" (pp. 112-118), we present many examples of agreement between the noun and the verb as well as between the pronoun and the verb (or auxiliary). Exercises 1 and 2 on pages 114-115 should reveal just how thoroughly the student has grasped these concepts. The material on structures that do not involve agreement presents no problems.

With "Complications of Agreement" (pp. 119-124), difficulties are likely to develop. Sometimes intervening structures obscure the close relationship between the subject and the verb. Then, too, many students are confused by the inverted sentence pattern or by a sentence with a compound subject. The problem of usage is also complicated by noun substitutes, nouns ending in *s* in the subject position, agreement in a subordinate clause, and contractions. In all these matters, the illustrations and the abundant exercise material should prove helpful to the student in clarifying these facts of concord and in promoting the consistent use of standard English forms in oral and written communication.

CHAPTER **7**   *Substitution*
                 pages 127-146

AIM

Our language is rich in grammatical resources. There are the devices for expanding basic sentences—modification, coordination, subordination, apposition, and the use of absolute structures. There is the principle of word order which gives stability to our sentence structure but which allows for some manipulation that produces unique effects in communication and subtle changes in emphasis. There is the fact that English is an analytic language which permits the phenomenon of functional shift with the result that a variety of forms can be used in the different functional positions of a sentence. The aim of this chapter is to show how we can communicate effectively with an economy and a precision of words by substituting one word for another.

PROCEDURE

When we think of substitution, we think first, of course, about pronouns (pp. 128-133). Traditionally, the pronoun is the foremost substitute word, particularly the personal pronoun. That the personal pronoun is a very useful substitute word is supported by the fact that it is highly inflected, with twenty-three different forms representing changes for person, number, gender, and case.

The study of the subordinators *who, which,* and *that* (pp. 133-135) goes beyond their use as connectives. These words are substitute words with antecedents, and they also function within their own subject-predicate word group, a fact often confusing to students. The subordinator *who,* which in traditional grammar is called a relative pronoun, is also inflected, with three forms representing changes in case. Its case form will depend on its function within its own word group. Students will have little trouble with *who* and *whom* if this fact is clearly understood.

The use of pronouns as substitute words creates problems for the young writer (pp. 137-143). We might call these problems of usage; their solution depends on a knowledge of grammar. There are problems of reference, of agreement, of case forms, of consistency. The student is frequently careless of his usage of pronouns in speech. He readily transfers his speech habits into writing. Actually, if his speech is nonstandard, he will have to change his speech habits in order to correct his written English.

We suggest that considerable time be spent with the inflected forms of pronouns. To be satisfied with something less than mastery of English inflections will create problems in the students' composition work. Both spoken language drills and written language drills should be practiced.

CHAPTER **8** *Punctuation*
pages 147-170

AIMS

In Chapter 8 we return to the study of punctuation. Our aims here are to review the material discussed in previous chapters and to introduce supplementary material to complete the treatment of the subject.

PROCEDURE

A knowledge of grammar is the basis of effective punctuation. The problem of the writer is to help his reader to understand what he has written by separating his material into meaningful word groups. These are the units of syntax which determine meaning.

Since, in speech, the patterns of intonation (pp. 148-150) group words into meaningful units, these patterns should be helpful to the writer when faced with punctuation problems. Sensitivity to intonation then becomes an asset to the writer, especially in helping him mark off the larger units of syntax such as the sentence and other subject-predicate word groups.

"Relation Between Intonation and Punctuation" (pp. 151-155) explains the correlation in detail, with a variety of illustrations. By mastering this material, the student will avoid the commonest of all errors in their themes: run-together sentences, sentence fragments, and the comma fault.

"Punctuation Review" (pp. 155-159) outlines the uses of the comma, the apostrophe, the semicolon, italics, and quotation marks—matters of form or of sound. The completion of Exercise 4 (pp. 158-159) will show how familiar the students are with these common marks.

"Conventions of Punctuation" (pp. 162-166) presents marks that have been developed by writers and printers and accepted as matters of custom: the colon, the dash, the ellipsis, the exclamation point, and the single quotation mark as well as the placement of double punctuation marks. In their composition work, the students in all probability will have occasion to employ most of these marks.

CHAPTER **9** *Phonemes and Graphemes in English*
pages 171-192

AIM

This chapter is essentially a spelling chapter. The aim is to emphasize the relationship of the sounds of English to the graphic representation of these sounds in the written language.

PROCEDURE

There are forty-four common sounds in our spoken language. There are only twenty-six letters in the alphabet. Certain letters and digraphs represent several different sounds. Conversely, many sounds are spelled in a variety of different ways. The /th/ sound in *think* is one of the two sounds spelled in only one way. The /sh/ sound in *shine* is spelled in thirteen ways, the maximum variety of spellings for a single sound.

The basis for a productive study of sound and spelling is the mastery of the sound system. The sounds of English should be studied systematically and mastered. The sound symbols—either phonemic symbols or the pronunciation symbols developed in the dictionary (pp. 176-177)—should be mastered and used in practice. The student should then be directed in the building of word lists for each different spelling of each sound ("Developing Graphemic Word Lists," pp. 177-178).

Word lists presenting special difficulties for the writer are given in this chapter ("Words with Silent Letters," pp. 180-182; "Homonyms and Other Words Often Confused," p. 184; "Words with the *ie* and *ei* Graphemes," p. 186; "Other Words Frequently Misspelled," p. 188). Concentration and work on these words should be effective for the student. Improvement in spelling is largely a matter of hard work.

Here for your convenience are dictation sentences for the diagnostic and mastery tests referred to in the note on text page 191.

Diagnostic Test

1. Dick's **absence** from the basketball game was unavoidable.
2. The Harrison Hotel can **accommodate** at least 750 guests.
3. Noisy, loud-mouthed people always **aggravate** me.
4. We enjoyed watching the **amateur** hour on TV.
5. The $3000 estate was divided **among** eighteen heirs.
6. How would you **analyze** this news report?
7. It was **apparent** that Virginia had misunderstood my question.

8. The first **appearance** of the leading man was greeted with lengthy applause.
9. What **argument** can you give in favor of the proposition?
10. Great **Britain** includes England, Wales, Scotland, and Northern Ireland.
11. Both the ancient Egyptians and the Mayas developed a fairly accurate **calendar.**
12. The **cemetery** has beautiful magnolias and Japanese cherry blossoms in the spring.
13. You never know what to expect from a person with a **changeable** disposition.
14. What is the most important **characteristic** of hydrogen?
15. A girl who makes her own **clothes** can dress well on comparatively little money.
16. Walter hopes to participate in **collegiate** football next fall.
17. The social **committee** will meet today to plan the party.
18. We must **congratulate** Judy on her new honor.
19. If you're a **connoisseur** of modern art, tell me what you think of this abstract.
20. Strive to make your actions **consistent** with your beliefs.
21. Water flowed over the dam **continuously.**
22. Stop to see us when it's **convenient.**
23. Only constructive **criticism** is helpful.
24. Never **criticize** others unnecessarily.
25. Our school **curriculum** offers a variety of courses.
26. Here is an interesting **description** of an orbital flight.
27. "Now watch the rabbit **disappear,**" said the magician.
28. Are you an **efficient** window cleaner?
29. We're learning to **eliminate** wordiness from our writing.
30. Ken is **especially** anxious to do well in math this year.
31. Age is no advantage unless it is combined with **experience.**
32. Are you **familiar** with this type of adding machine?
33. A spellbinder has the ability to **fascinate** his listeners.
34. After a long debate the Senate **finally** passed the measure.
35. As the forest fire approached, the dogs yelped **frantically.**
36. Ted **generally** walks instead of taking the school bus.
37. There is no **guarantee** that this watch will run indefinitely.
38. What kind of **heroes** do you like best in plays and movies?
39. We can't explain Stan's **hesitancy** to join our club.
40. I won't go if I'll be more **hindrance** than help to the group.
41. Uncle Jim mentioned **incidentally** that he was flying to Tokyo.
42. It seems **incredible** that Roger would pass up a chance to eat.
43. Binoculars are **indispensable** to the bird watcher.
44. What an **ingenious** way to mend a broken racket!
45. Kay spent three hours in the **laboratory** dissecting a frog.
46. Are refreshments for committee meetings considered a **legitimate** club expense?
47. Henry made many trips to the **library** in search of material for his term paper.
48. We were thrilled to visit a **medieval** castle in France.
49. Singers Marian Anderson and Leontyne Price are both **Negroes.**

50. There was a **noticeable** lack of fresh air in the auditorium.
51. A heavy coat is a **nuisance** on such a warm day.
52. The hero of the story overcame one **obstacle** after another.
53. Have you **paid** your club dues yet?
54. It's not **permissible** to interrupt the speaker.
55. You **probably** wish you could take a trip to the moon.
56. The parade **proceeded** to the reviewing stand before disbanding.
57. Pat's ambition is to become a **professor** of aeronautics.
58. A forgiving spirit will help to avoid a **quarrel.**
59. Each argument in a debate should be **relevant** to the main issue.
60. The Bible sets forth the **religious** principles of the Hebrew and the Christian.
61. Shakespeare's plays were written during the English **Renaissance.**
62. Jerry has a talent for getting into **ridiculous** situations.
63. Most parents have to **sacrifice** for their children's education.
64. The **separation** of church and state has become a controversial issue.
65. Joe was promoted to the rank of master **sergeant.**
66. Two people may be **similar** in appearance, but they are never exactly alike.
67. David's sister is a **sophomore** at Northwestern College.
68. Did your brother **succeed** in making the varsity baseball team?
69. The most **successful** people are those who are the most helpful.
70. These new math books will **supersede** the old ones.
71. Do you know how to **suppress** a sneeze?
72. An expensive car is often a **symbol** of wealth or position.
73. A neurotic person has an extremely nervous **temperament.**
74. Out of the dozen eggs I bought, this makes the **twelfth** bad one.
75. You would **undoubtedly** accept a free trip around the world.
76. "It's entirely **unnecessary** to have a chaperon," said Peggy to her small brother.
77. "Wait **until** I get up to bat!" bragged Sammy.
78. The panoramic view of the mountains and **valleys** was breathtaking.
79. The bushes we transplanted look **vigorous** enough.
80. "You **villain,** you!" shouted the hero of the old-time movie.

Mastery Test

1. The **absence** of recreational facilities is a contributing factor in juvenile delinquency.
2. Old people often find it difficult to **accommodate** to new conditions.
3. Be careful not to **aggravate** your wound.
4. I'm an **amateur** as far as speechmaking is concerned.
5. Barbara was fortunate to be **among** the winners of the $5000 scholarships.
6. Dr. Shaw is going to **analyze** this medicine to see if it is harmful.
7. The **apparent** reason for the death of all the fish was the disposal of chemicals from a factory upstream.
8. It is best to avoid the **appearance** of evil as well as the evil itself.
9. Homer can always put up an **argument** when someone suggests that he get to work.

10. Often the entire British Commonwealth is called **Britain**.
11. Does your new **calendar** show the holidays in red?
12. We visited the **cemetery** at Arlington.
13. Jane's spring coat is lined with **changeable** silk.
14. With **characteristic** good humor Peter joined in the laughter at his own expense.
15. It is not **clothes** but character that makes a man.
16. Sally thinks her new outfit will make her look truly **collegiate**.
17. The legislature voted to refer the bill back to the education **committee**.
18. Terry is always quick to **congratulate** a successful opponent.
19. A book critic must be a **connoisseur** of all types of literature.
20. A good theme has a **consistent** viewpoint throughout.
21. A scout should be **continuously** alert to opportunities for helpfulness.
22. The station will be a **convenient** place for us to meet.
23. The happiest people have learned to accept **criticism** gracefully.
24. If you wish to make enemies, **criticize** people's motives.
25. Conversational Spanish has been added to our elementary school **curriculum**.
26. On the streets of a big city you will see people of every **description**.
27. How long ago did the Alaska caribou **disappear**?
28. An **efficient** student gets down to work immediately.
29. Efficiency experts often **eliminate** useless jobs.
30. We need your presence at the meeting, **especially** if Betty and June can't be there.
31. The bus ride on icy roads was a harrowing **experience**.
32. This book of **familiar** essays is thoroughly enjoyable.
33. Did W. H. Hudson's *Green Mansions* **fascinate** you as much as it did me?
34. At midnight we **finally** located a motel room.
35. Tommy **frantically** waved a red flag at the approaching train.
36. It is **generally** true that boys read more science fiction than girls do.
37. I'll **guarantee** that once you start this book, you won't be able to put it down.
38. Roy likes to read stories of Revolutionary **heroes**.
39. "I feel a somewhat natural **hesitancy** in expressing an opinion on that particular subject," Gene replied tactfully.
40. The boys found that their heavy packs were a **hindrance** in walking.
41. The speaker touched **incidentally** on the enjoyments of an ocean voyage.
42. The juggler's abilities were almost **incredible**.
43. A good pitcher is **indispensable** to a winning baseball team.
44. An inventor must be persevering as well as **ingenious**.
45. Thomas A. Edison practically lived in his **laboratory**.
46. The king didn't regard the peasants' grievance as **legitimate**.
47. Andrew Carnegie gave the money for this **library**.
48. The serfs in **medieval** times were bound to the land.
49. A number of major-league baseball players, such as Jackie Robinson, have been **Negroes**.
50. Jane's lack of enthusiasm was quite **noticeable**.
51. What a **nuisance** a puppy can be when you're trying to dress!
52. The **obstacle** race was fun for both the participants and the spectators.

53. I **paid** for my football equipment myself.
54. Parking in front of a hydrant is not **permissible.**
55. Since we're having our picnic tomorrow, it will **probably** rain.
56. After winning the title role in the play, Frank **proceeded** to learn his part.
57. Our next-door neighbor is a geology **professor** at the university.
58. My sister and I rarely **quarrel.**
59. Be sure that every sentence in the paragraph is **relevant** to the topic sentence.
60. Army chaplains help soldiers with their problems and also conduct **religious** services.
61. The **Renaissance** period was marked by great activity in art, literature, exploration, and science.
62. The little dog looked **ridiculous** in its bright red sweater and bonnet.
63. Staying home with her sick brother was a real **sacrifice** for Linda.
64. After their **separation** the twins developed quite different personalities.
65. Mr. Vincent is a **sergeant** on the police force.
66. The cats are **similar** except that Tippy has a white tail.
67. A **sophomore** is supposed to be wiser than a freshman.
68. Freddy didn't **succeed** in annoying his sister, though he tried hard.
69. To be happy, one must be **successful** in some worthwhile endeavor.
70. In which decade did the automobile **supersede** the horse?
71. Once the secret was out, it was impossible to **suppress** it.
72. The **symbol** for the schwa resembles an upside-down *e*.
73. Joanna has a truly artistic **temperament.**
74. What is one to the **twelfth** power?
75. "You will **undoubtedly** climb to the top of the Washington Monument," suggested Uncle Ed.
76. Biting sarcasm is always **unnecessary.**
77. You never know what you can do **until** you try.
78. From a plane, it is hard to tell where the **valleys** are.
79. You won't feel so **vigorous** after you've walked fifty miles.
80. Bob made a wonderful **villain** in the class play.

CHAPTER 10   *Effective Sentence Structure*
pages 193-212

AIM

The aim of this chapter is to help the student eliminate some of the common errors in sentence structure found in most student themes.

PROCEDURE

The most blatant errors are, perhaps, the comma fault and the run-together sentences (pp. 194-197). The illustrations on these pages are from actual high school themes. If the students understand the reason for the illustrated corrections, Exercise 1 should present no difficulties.

"Excessive Coordination" (pp. 197-202) is often responsible for ineffective communication. The solutions to the problems posed on pages 198 and 199 should help in eliminating errors of this nature.

"Illogical Subordination and Incoherence" (pp. 202-205) involves relationships of clauses to sentences. Again, the examples should prove valuable in teaching this concept.

Ridiculous sentences are created by "Dangling Modifiers and Misplaced Modifiers" (pp. 205-207). The completion of Exercise 7 will show how well the students have grasped the importance of avoiding dangling constructions.

Other common errors are incorrect verb forms and shifts in tenses (pp. 208-210). This section is amply illustrated, preparing the way for Exercise 8.

Notice that the terms used in this chapter are the old familiar ones. The problem here is merely to relate the students' knowledge of language structure to sentence improvement. Teaching must be directed to this end. Discussion, review, and a great deal of writing practice will help most students to correct their mistakes of form.

In discussing sentence structure and suggested revisions, the use of an opaque projector would be helpful in displaying themes (without corrections). The suggestions could then be recorded and used when revising the papers. If a projector is not available, a number of themes might be duplicated and discussed. The theme under discussion might then be revised by each member of the class and the revisions finally analyzed.

Grammar Workshop
pages 213-218

The purpose of this section is to help the student evaluate his own progress in the study of the structure of language. The workshop is so arranged that the student turns the page for an immediate answer to the particular exercise. In the introduction to this section, the student is directed to the Index as a tool in finding additional information in those areas where he has not yet achieved mastery.

The Language of Grammar
pages 365-404

This section is designed to serve as a ready reference for grammatical terminology and nomenclature. It should prove especially helpful to students and teachers making the transition from traditional to modern grammar. There are 170 terms explained and illustrated in this section. They are arranged alphabetically and described in a concise manner with pertinent illustrations.

This section may be used not only for reference but for review. Terms which have already been studied in the text may be assigned periodically for study and the class then tested for mastery. This practice may well serve as a diagnosis of difficulty and of the need for review and renewed study.

SUGGESTED READING   PART I

Books

BLOOMFIELD, LEONARD, *Language*, New York, Holt, Rinehart and Winston, Inc., 1933.

BROWN, DONA W., BROWN, WALLACE C., AND BAILEY, DUDLEY, *Form in Modern English*, New York, Oxford University Press, 1958.

GLEASON, H. A., JR., *An Introduction to Descriptive Linguistics*, New York, Holt, Rinehart and Winston, Inc., 1961.

HALL, ROBERT A., JR., *Linguistics and Your Language*, Garden City, Doubleday & Company, Inc., 1960.

LLOYD, DONALD J., AND WARFEL, HARRY R., *American English in Its Cultural Setting*, New York, Alfred A. Knopf, Inc., 1956.

MARCKWARDT, ALBERT H., *American English*, New York, Oxford University Press, 1958.

MYERS, L. M., *Guide to American English*, 3rd ed., Englewood Cliffs, New Jersey, Prentice-Hall, Inc., 1963.

POOLEY, ROBERT C., *Teaching English Grammar*, New York, Appleton-Century-Crofts, 1957.

ROBERTS, PAUL, *Patterns of English*, New York, Harcourt, Brace & World, Inc., 1956.
——— *Understanding Grammar*, New York, Harper & Row, 1954.

SAPIR, EDWARD, *Language*, New York, Harcourt, Brace & World, Inc., 1921.

TRAGER, GEORGE L., AND SMITH, HENRY LEE, JR., *An Outline of English Structure*, Washington, D. C., American Council of Learned Societies, 1951.

Articles

"Growing Pains in Grammar," *The English Journal,* vol. XLVII (April 1958). (This issue includes a variety of articles devoted to this topic.)

"New Perspectives in English," *College English,* vol. 23 (March 1962). (This issue includes a variety of topics that may be applied to literature and composition as well as to language.)

"Symposium on Structure," *College English,* vol. 24 (May 1963). (In this issue, a series of articles relates structure to thought, language, and literature.)

Guide

PART II

CHAPTER 1 *Using the Dictionary pages 221-252*

AIM

This chapter was developed in the hope that it might increase your students' fascination with the English language. It is based on the premise that a current, reputable dictionary is the most practical record readily available to describe our language as it is used today. If this is true, then practice in the use of the dictionary may motivate the students to study, to appreciate, and to expand their use of the English language.

PROCEDURE

The dictionary is first considered as a guide book to a language that is constantly changing in order to describe a world that is continually in motion. It is then discussed as a guide to the meaning of words in specific contexts as well as to the formal definition of words.

After the dictionary is examined for information about the history of our language (pp. 222-223) and as a guide to meaning (pp. 224-234), it is explored in these areas: as an aid in problems of spelling (pp. 239-240); pronunciation (pp. 241-243); grammar (pp. 243-244); prefixes, suffixes, and combining forms (pp. 244-245); capitalization (pp. 245-246); abbreviations (p. 246); expressions from other languages (pp. 246-247); and usage (pp. 247-248). Finally, the dictionary is regarded as a reference book for interpreting allusions, figures of speech, and even whole poems (pp. 248-252). Almost every prominent distinction the text makes is supported by at least one exercise.

While the students' responses to most of the exercises will vary depending on the particular dictionary available for reference, this point can be directed to your advantage for the way in which it demonstrates how dynamic language is. The exercises that could be handled in a manner consistent with most dictionaries have been included in the key. A useful class project might involve working out keys for the remaining exercises—taking into account inevitable variations.

Exercise 1 (pp. 224-225) was designed to show how context determines whether a word will be included in a dictionary; and if so, how it will be handled. Thus a dictionary editor is a compiler of contexts from which he develops his dictionary entries (by a process which may be somewhat interpretive, of course). Above all, this exercise shows that when a word can have several different referents, only its use in some specific context can distinguish among the many possible meanings. This multiplicity of mean- ings of a word is further explored in Exercise 3 (p. 228), while Exercise 2 (pp. 226-227) should give your students some insight into the complexity of a lexicographer's work.

Exercise 4 (pp. 228-229) is the first in this chapter that calls for sum- marizing. These summaries of changes in meaning of words may involve short paragraphs of unified sentences, or even longer passages, if more extensive dictionaries are used as sources. As with most of the exercises in this chapter, far more work has been suggested than any one student could reasonably complete; the exercise is set up to enable your assignment of a different word to each student. The changing nature of language will probably be more evident to a student who has written one *thorough* discussion of a word than it will be to one who has completed superficial summaries of several words.

If students respond well to Exercise 4, you may find it useful to investigate the two phenomena referred to, *specialization* and *generalization* of mean- ing, and present your findings to the class. At this time suggest that they compile lists of words that illustrate each of the processes.

Exercise 5C (pp. 231-232) provides an opportunity for you to point out that many desk dictionaries do not include synonyms, not simply because of space limitations, but because many pairs of words can be used synony- mously in one context but cannot be interchanged in others. Is it not likely that in a desk dictionary the synonym relationship is pointed out only when two words may be interchanged successfully in a majority of their contexts?

Exercise 5D was designed to suggest that synonyms may convey a com- mon core of information that may be enlarged upon in some particular direction if one chooses appropriately from among several relatively syn- onymous terms.

After the students have completed Exercise 6 (pp. 233-234), they might be encouraged to pool their responses and compile lists of words in each category, supplying you with a master list—one that will grow, of course, as subsequent classes cover this material. The list of prefixes and suffixes, too, should grow as the students discover similar activity in other words they know. Then it might be appropriate to point out some words that only *look* as though they should fit these lists, such as *instinct* and *unctuous*, but, of course, have no place here.

In many exercises in this chapter, Exercise 8 (p. 235) for example, some of the words refer to such recently discovered or recently popularized terms as *antibiotics, streptomycin, cyclotron,* and *trampoline.* The purpose of their inclusion is to show again how our words reflect the world we live in; as our world changes, our language adjusts. To be effective, a dictionary must acknowledge these changes with each new edition.

You might ask the students to name recent discoveries, inventions, concepts, and terms that have been coined to enable discussion of these new topics. Then compile a list of these terms—terms almost every well-read American has heard, read, or perhaps even used but too new to be found in any dictionary. Such compilation may bring home to them the difficulty of the lexicographer's tasks and the dynamic nature of words in a changing world. Furthermore, it may permit you to consider with your students how each of us is his own dictionary compiler, carrying a record of words and word associations around to use as needed.

Where two dictionaries conflict on some point in these exercises, the question of *authority* may arise. If the point is a matter of something which logically changes with the passing of time, then the most recent reputable dictionary may be given the edge, or no resolution sought. If students can understand that, because of the changing nature of language, an honest difference can exist between two reputable dictionaries, both compiled in good faith, then the matter should not baffle them. Such a resolution need not deny or destroy the idea of "authority" in language matters; it suggests, however, that neither you nor anyone else knows everything about anything, surely not a phenomenon as complicated as our language. Yet your broader study and experience with language probably qualifies you as an authority, relative to those you teach.

The dictionary as "A Guide to Other Language Skills" (pp. 238-248)— spelling, pronunciation, grammar—is not treated in depth, since the students have probably used the dictionary for many years in these functions. Several related activities may be appropriate in connection with Exercise 14C (pp. 242-243). First, rhyming offers a rather painless way of studying and practicing word sounds, one which permits the subject of pronunciation to be treated without involving diacritical marking. At the same time, rhymes might be used to introduce or review the study of the written symbols that represent the basic sounds in English. Furthermore, since this part of the text is devoted to composition, the study of rhyming words could logically lead into some student writing of simple verse. This original work could in turn lead to the study of poetry.

Exercise 15 (p. 244) should offer you the opportunity both to review *functional shift* and to encourage composition of imaginative sentences. Refer students who have difficulty with Exercise 16 to the "Contents" and the "Using Your Dictionary" section of *Webster's New Students Dictionary,* © 1964 by G. & C. Merriam Co.

Exercise 17 (p. 245) touches upon an area that could easily be expanded in your classes: the study of combining forms. The final term in the exercise, for example, is offered here without subtlety for two reasons. First, it is said to be the longest word in recent editions. This uniqueness may fascinate some students, and that fascination for one word might spread to others, or to the language in general. Secondly, the word illustrates that today's words are built from the words and ideas of yesterday's world. This word is a fine example because the fragments from which it is constructed are still intact. When each of the fragments is looked up, it is not difficult to understand that the combination labels "a disease affecting the lungs associated with particles of a particular kind of silicon dust which (particles) are too minute to be observed through an ordinary microscope."

Exercise 17, therefore, is designed to open the way for an independent study of all combining forms as shortcuts to meaning, since to know a few dozen common combining forms may lead to understanding hundreds of terms without the aid of a dictionary. But of even more value is the way understanding of combining forms helps us to remember the words we do look up and expect to use.

The cautions at the top of page 248 against inappropriately informal usage need not incline you toward requiring in themes language that is *unnaturally* formal for your students. To get some students to express themselves at all, it may be necessary to encourage them to "say it in your own words," at least in the first draft. Somewhere along the way you may then introduce them to the idea of *degrees of formality* in words, and lead them toward choices that are appropriate for standard written English—formal or informal—depending on the specific occasion, but standard in either case.

The use of the dictionary in the study of poetry can easily be expanded if this sample proves fruitful. Important historical documents such as "The Gettysburg Address" and the "Declaration of Independence" may become clearer to students through such analysis.

CHAPTER 2 *Looking at Sentence Structure* *pages 253-270*

AIM

In Chapter 2, we return to the important subject of sentence structure. This structure is the essential link between grammar and effective writing. Our specific aim here is variety in sentence structure.

PROCEDURE

The achievement of variety in sentence structure is the mark of maturity in written composition. The craftsman who uses both long and short sentences (pp. 254-256), who employs such devices as coordination and subordination (pp. 256-259), who uses verbal phrases (pp. 259-262), who manipulates the delicate balance of word order (pp. 262-265), who exploits the communicating power of parallel structure (pp. 265-267), who writes both loose and periodic sentences (pp. 268-270) is demonstrating his mastery of the structures of his language. The variety of expression he gains is the result of this mastery.

Briefly, then, the study of sentence variety is a review of the structural resources employed in shaping good sentences. Grammar now becomes functional. We not only observe and study the writings of others for their effective value; we also direct our own practice, using the resources that we have studied to gain the same ends.

Although the emphasis is again on form, we must not lose sight of the importance of content. It is suggested that much of the practice in revision be done on themes that are worth rewriting—themes in which the student definitely has something worthwhile to communicate but is handicapped by his lack of effectiveness in developing sentences of power and beauty.

CHAPTER 3 *Organization and Outlines* *pages 271-288*

AIM

Our purpose now is to approach the matter of organizing material as honestly and realistically as possible. We would not pretend that every professional writer works out on paper an outline of the manuscript he hopes to produce; at the same time we might suggest that such a writer may have trained himself to take mentally some of the steps of the process we suggest to students.

PROCEDURE

Our first consideration is the division of the material into logical groups that can stand in some reasonably equal relationship to each other. Next we introduce the outline and offer the conventional outline form. Then we point out some differences between (a) outlining what someone else has constructed and (b) outlining as a prelude to one's own work. In regard to the latter, a number of approaches are discussed. These include outlining (a) according to random associations, (b) according to logical divisions, (c) from a central idea, and (d) by anticipating questions. Finally, there is an essay to be outlined, one which is above the level of writing your students will probably do, yet one which is not over their heads in subject matter, one especially designed for this exercise.

You may find the game called "Twenty Questions" (pp. 272-273) useful in many ways, once your students get the hang of it. It is the sort of exercise that can profitably fill the last few moments of a class for which your planned lesson has run a bit short. But it is also a study in many things besides factual information. First, it offers practice in dividing and grouping. Furthermore, it provides experience in handling classifications. But above all, it dramatizes the fact that subdividing in this way is usually quite arbitrary, neither "right" nor "wrong" but instead "logical" or "illogical" in terms of purpose and direction. Your best students will even begin to recognize patterns of questions which will suggest an *order* that may be carried over from one game to the next.

In conjunction with conventional outlines on page 276, you might encourage students to recognize the distinctions between topic outlines and sentence outlines by suggesting they begin with one kind and convert (translate) to the other: from topics to sentences, from sentences to topics. They should then be able to see for themselves what is lost or gained in the transfer.

The last sentence before the exercise on page 276 mentions the *thesis statement,* but not by name. Exercise 3 (pp. 278-279) and Exercise 5 (pp. 279-280) call for the *central idea.* Finally, the issue of developing a central idea is faced directly on page 284. We have attempted to reach this matter as gradually and as naturally as possible, but the several references may reflect our view: that along with the concept of the *topic sentence* in paragraph development, the *central idea* or *thesis statement* in theme development is of utmost importance in any study of organization in written composition. Any additional devices, exercises, or drill that you can devise to strengthen the students' awareness of this concept should prove valuable, since *unity* and *coherence* greatly depend on well-handled topic sentences and a strong, well-developed central idea (thesis statement).

Some practice in devising outlines from someone else's completed copy (pp. 280-282) might prove useful if the selections you ask the students to outline are well organized, well developed, and not so difficult in subject matter as to confuse the interrelationships of ideas. A student could apply this kind of activity to his schoolwork in such related activities as reviewing text material, preparing a report of such a piece of writing, or taking notes for research.

On the other hand, if Johnny is asked to struggle over outlining a professional writer's passage which is either very complex or poorly organized, he may become convinced that outlining has no practical value—that success may be achieved without it.

Furthermore, an overdose of outlining what someone else has written may sour Johnny on the process and thus discourage his attempts to write from outlines. The two activities are distinguished in the text (p. 280) for just this reason: so that although Johnny may develop a dislike for outlining sections of his history text, he will recognize the basic distinction and not carry his dislike over to outlining as a prelude to composition.

As suggested on page 284, the several methods of developing an outline may be combined in a single effort if a central idea is the primary unifying device. Once the commitment is made to a thesis, then free association of ideas, logical divisions of subject matter, and answers to anticipated questions can all be examined as they bear on the thesis statement.

A useful review of this chapter could easily be timed to coincide with one or more future theme assignments. Depending on the nature of the assignment, one or more of the suggested methods of approach might come under particular scrutiny. For the writing that class work will demand— essay examinations, research papers, and so forth—the *central idea* method of organization may be a profitable area of regular reconsideration.

CHAPTER 4 *Description and Narration*
pages 289-310

AIM

In this chapter and the next, we have made some rather arbitrary, however traditional, classifications of types of prose writing. We have distinguished what we might call "imaginative" prose from "expository" or "intellectual" prose in the largest sense of the word. We have distinguished writing whose appeal is to the imagination and the emotions from writing whose appeal is to the intellect. Furthermore, we have subdivided the first category into *description,* which gives us word pictures and other sense-oriented impressions, and *narration,* which entertains us with its relation to a sequence of events.

While these divisions are useful, it is important to remember that they are only *patterns* we have abstracted, not exclusive categories into which any piece of prose writing can be placed. For example, we can argue (Chapter 5) through the use of word pictures (description), and we can explain (Chapter 5) through reporting a sequence of events (narration). A skilled writer might interweave all these characteristics into a single presentation, without heed to the distinctions we make.

Briefly, the aim of Chapter 4 is to help your students distinguish between (a) word pictures (other sense impressions) and (b) imaginative sequences of events.

PROCEDURE

Under the heading "Why Do You Write?" (pp. 290-291), you may be able to motivate students by helping them see that writing practice in the classroom is not designed as an end in itself, but rather as a skill whose usefulness must not be disregarded. Practice in the writing of grocery lists, memorandums, and notes to the milkman is certainly unnecessary. However, there are hundreds of specific applications that life demands of our writing skill, and one can hardly practice all of them. Therefore, we practice basic forms: the sentence, the paragraph; basic types: descriptive, narrative, expository writing. The lessons learned in the practice of these basic procedures should carry over to the almost infinite range of writing tasks demanded of us.

The distinction between *description* and *explanation* of common items is difficult for some students to make ("Description," pp. 293-294). There is a common approach to this confusion that skirts for the time being the question of "What is description?" or "What is explanation?" One solution is to have each student describe in writing one object only as that object confronts his senses—as it stands before him (or can be imagined). He must write as though what he is describing is a unique object, not one of a *class* of similar items. For the purpose of descriptive writing, Johnny must tell about *his* 1960 V-8 as though it were the only such object made; he must describe it in terms of the way *his* senses would record the object. If he lapses into a discussion of 1960 V-8's in general, or begins telling how his 1960 V-8 is similar to or different from other 1960 V-8's, then Johnny is explaining, not describing. He is relating in terms of details abstracted intellectually—not in terms of what his senses record. Once a student has settled on a very specific, perhaps very personal, title and subject, he may avoid explaining class characteristics: not "Frogs," but "My Frog," or "Alvin, My Pet Frog."

Notice that on page 295 we encourage observations based on *all* the writer's senses and make appeals to *all* the reader's senses. We make distinctions between *impersonal* and *more personal* impressions and between sharp, specific impressions and more general ones.

The directions for Exercise 2 (pp. 295-296) introduce with some subtlety what may be a very important distinction—the difference between more *objective* and more *subjective* records of what our senses pick up. If you could arrange to have a visitor, unknown to your students, spend several minutes in your classroom, you could test both the students' powers of observation and their ability to distinguish between objective and subjective impressions. After your visitor has left the room, you could ask either the class, orally, or the individual students (in writing) to give you a typical police-bulletin description: approximate age, sex, height, weight, hair color, eye color, build, kind of clothing, color of clothing, and distinguishing characteristics.

Then you might ask students for their *personal* reactions to the visitor. What sort of person is he? What does his face express? Were their reactions positive, negative, or indifferent? What sort of occupation would they associate with him? What personal qualities: hard? easygoing? strong willed? Does he have a sense of humor? In all the foregoing, it would be desirable, but not essential, for the students to describe some act, expression, utterance, or mannerism on which they based their reactions.

This activity should clearly differentiate two quite distinct kinds of sense impressions. Class discussion will surely accentuate the points of more general agreement on the first kind of picture than on the second. If your visitor is a person you can discuss freely (as he would almost have to be— a visiting relative, perhaps, whom your students are never likely to meet), you could give them factual information by which they could verify (or contradict) *both* kinds of information they had compiled. They might then wish to reject the subjective kind of description. However, they can probably be shown how much more interesting and exciting the subjective description can be to us—granting its greater margin of error—than the police-bulletin statistics.

In visual descriptions, the *spatial* relationships are held important, while the *dominant impression* technique is applied in cases where both *external* and *internal* evaluations are encouraged (pp. 297-298).

Students cannot describe what their senses are not recording; thus at least some consideration might be given to "Observing and Selecting Detail" (p. 299). The suggested activity will test visual alertness.

Another demonstration can easily show the students something about their sense of hearing. Ask the class to be quiet and attentive, watching your hands. Busy yourself turning and displaying some common object at the front of the room. Suspecting another test of *visual* alertness, they will doubtless watch you very closely and ignore the sounds that can be heard outside almost any classroom. After a minute or so, ask them what they heard during the test. In all probability, they will have little to report. Now ask them again to be completely quiet, while you point out various sounds that were present but not recorded a minute earlier—sounds of leaves rustling, birds chirping, children playing, trucks rumbling, and so forth. This experience should demonstrate how our powers of observation can be directed by concentration and developed with practice.

An interesting experiment with the sense of touch might be made by asking several students to face the class while you place in their hands, held behind their backs, some small object—a coin, a lipstick, or anything small enough to be held out of sight. Then, with direct questions, ask what their sense of touch tells them about the object. The purpose would not be to identify it but to demonstrate how much information about it could be transmitted through touch alone.

If these experiments prove fruitful for eliciting descriptive writing or enthusiasm for description, some blindfold tests could be devised to observe reactions to tastes and scents. In these experiments with touch, taste, and smell, physical limitations might make it necessary to restrict the actual participants, but the class as a whole could make observations since the experiments should be handled on a class basis, rather than individually as in the case of the visual test.

The distinction might be reemphasized between (a) words that actually describe and (b) words that merely sound descriptive (function as adjectives) but in effect pass judgments that tell more about the describer than they do the thing described. Such words as these fit this category (unless they are clarified in a context): *fine, cute, beautiful, ugly, glorious, clever, keen.*

You may have some success if, after a student has used such a term in his description, you draw from him a report of the observations upon which he based his judgment. For example, if Tom says that Joe is "clever," ask him how he knows. If he becomes resentful at your doubting his word, he should eventually realize that you ask only for the purpose of searching his past experience for the specific acts, words, or other evidence to support his evaluation of Joe. If he is able to report what incidents and experiences led him to his conclusion, you might pose this question: "If you really want to describe Joe and convince a stranger about the kind of person he is, which is the better approach—to say he is clever or to offer an account of the evidence (report of incidents, experiences) that convinced you?" You might finally agree that *both* the label "clever" *and* the specific evidence, in combination, give the strongest picture. The distinction is another example of the difference between "showing" and "telling," discussed under "Record or Story?" (pp. 308-309) in narration.

Character sketches (pp. 301-302) have many uses because they deal with people—a universally fascinating subject. You might use the character sketch when you study literature, asking students to review a book or story and assemble the details surrounding one person. Their impressions of a certain literary figure might be revealing. The device is also useful when you call for biographical data on names that crop up in your classes. Finally, the character sketch can be well applied to your students' favorite characters, themselves.

In the study of narration beginning on page 302, the *sequence of events* is of major importance. Since no one could have insight into all happenings, any narrative must involve a *selection* of events in a sequence. Once committed to the idea of a selection, the question arises: who selects the events and on what basis?

In relation to "A Selected Sequence of Events" (p. 303), any further demonstrations you devise may be used to show students how one event flows into another. Thus a sequence we report is at best only a sequence of events we noticed; there will always be omitted details, if only because we did not "see" them. In other words, our senses are selective.

The importance of this point appears when a student insists on cluttering up his narrative with sentences of deadly, insignificant details which merely cloud or bury the main line of action in which readers may have an interest—all because that student feels that he must "tell everything that happened" lest his account lack "honesty." If he can be shown that selective judgment always enters the reporting of any event, he may be willing to sacrifice insignificant and unimportant detail to the principal narrative sequence, all in good faith, of course.

You may wish to relate some of the observations about narratives to works of literature your class has covered, or you might find a review of this material advantageous when you take up biographical narratives later in the school year.

In this connection, you might also point out how much more freedom of selection the writer of *fiction* has, since he is not committed to reporting "what *really* happened." (This difference between factual and fictional narrative will be considered more thoroughly, however, in an appropriate chapter of *Modern Grammar and Composition 3.*)

The "Order of Events" (p. 305) can be illustrated very readily through references to stories all the students have studied. The *chronological order* will be familiar; however, to show how writers suspend the normal order of happenings, you might make specific references to stories you know they have covered. The *flashback* technique could be especially meaningful if illustrated in this manner.

As long as the students' narratives are first-person accounts of their own experiences, the question of "point of view" (pp. 306-307) need not be emphasized, unless you wish to make references to stories in literature that you have covered. As a technique your students might normally use, point of view (beyond simple first person) is not essential unless they undertake fictional narratives—and even then the first-person point of view should suffice. If you do wish to have your students practice third-person point of view, it might simplify matters for them to relate an actual incident from their own experience, merely translating the "I" to "he." After studying the effects of this change, they might move more easily to the handling of complicated points of view. However, while delving this deeply could challenge accelerated students, it might needlessly antagonize and confuse those who are not predisposed to it.

Regarding "Thinking About Beginnings and Endings" (pp. 307-308), you may find that your students often begin their sequence of events too far ahead, chronologically, of the dramatic highpoint on which they wish to close. The result is page after page of rambling detail whose purpose is not clear and whose end is not foreseeable.

With or without further explanation of the *flashback* technique, you could encourage your students to *get to the point* of their narrative. Buried under tons of insignificant detail is often a line that would have made a fast, suspenseful opening. In such case you might suggest that they rewrite the narrative beginning with the buried line.

Suddenly Uncle Jack leaped to his feet . . .

My father was shocked when I phoned him from the police station . . .

"A mouse!" shrieked Aunt Clara . . .

The men at the bus stop turned around suddenly and started walking our way—all together . . .

In personal letters we often relate *what happened* to us since our last communication with our correspondent. You might profitably combine some practice in letter writing with narrative techniques.

The use of dialogue for dramatizing the events of a narrative is illustrated on page 309.

Finally, "Kinds of Narratives" (pp. 309-310) relates the material of this chapter to a wide number of kinds of written expression which rely heavily on the narrative approach: history, biography, journals.

CHAPTER **5** *Exposition and Argumentation*
pages 311-326

AIM

In this chapter we are continuing the delineations set forth at the beginning of Chapter 4. Whereas we then considered the appeal writing makes to the imagination, we propose now to elaborate on the appeal made to the intellect. It must be remembered that these are rather arbitrary distinctions, the validity of which rests on recurring *patterns*, not on mutually exclusive categories into which every sample of writing must neatly fall.

PROCEDURE

Any one of the patterns for developing expositions may be applied to a subject, the usefulness of such an application depending, however, upon what the anticipated reader wants to know and how much he already knows.

In the closing pages of the chapter, expositive writing is distinguished from argumentative on the basis that while the former involves explaining a subject (usually in noncontroversial terms), the latter involves advancing one's own point of view—usually in the face of an opposing or at least neutral position.

You may find that in writing extended definitions your students can get through the *verbalizing* (the verbal definition), but cannot extend the definition to its application in the lives and experience of their prospective readers. They might be encouraged to include illustrative examples— hypothetical examples, if necessary—to point up each distinction raised in the purely verbal definition. A student may supply a verbal definition of a "true sports car"; but he should further be able to say whether Sam's car is a "true sports car," and if not, where its characteristics fall short of those limited by the definition. In other words, part of an extended definition involves relating the *words* to the world of nonverbal men and events.

Short expository themes that can be developed through partition (pp. 316-317) may be helpful in practicing organization. At this stage of their development, a five- or six-paragraph theme may be about what you can expect of your students. Therefore, a topic that suggests a three- or four-part partition would fit such assignments.

After an introductory paragraph, the body of the theme might quite logically contain the three or four parts in the partition, with a paragraph allotted to each. Then, after a closing paragraph, the assignment would be complete, the organization natural and logical.

You may know from past experience that students tend to handle comparison or contrast (pp. 317-318) quite naturally, or at least in a manner that is recognizable, whether or not they have earlier studied expository patterns. The clear-cut division that often characterizes such parts of the analysis may fit well with our past experiences quite apart from composition exercises. You may find two common weaknesses, however. First, if not directed otherwise, students may choose their battlegrounds carelessly. They may choose items that are almost impossible to compare: a rose with an anvil, a sailboat and a deep-sea fishing reel. Or they may choose to compare vast classes of things (sharks with goldfish or bombers with fighter planes), rather than two reasonably comparable, specific objects which they know thoroughly enough to discuss in detail. In the second place, given fairly comparable items, students often concentrate so hard on likenesses that they ignore differences, or *vice versa*. Sometimes, however, the question which prompts the discussion will stipulate whether *differences,* *similarities,* or *both* should be included. (*See* Exercise 4, item 1, page 318.)

There are several classroom exercises that might make classification (pp. 318-319) more useful and meaningful. The "Twenty Questions" game (p. 272) has a direct application in this matter. It can be used to encourage students to regard a subject in terms of the stratification of its structure; quite possibly it can serve to indicate which students have difficulty thinking in terms of such structural patterns.

Another way to demonstrate the classification process is to ask each student to classify himself, preferably in some relationship that has not been touched upon by an earlier respondent. After a few labels have been suggested, you may have to help out, of course. Students may offer descriptive terms for class labels: "I am young," a boy might say, instead of classifying himself as a "teen-ager," a "minor," or an "adolescent." A distinction might be made here between more personal, subjective classifications— "patriot," "friend," "nice guy"—and formal labels which our society officially imposes on us for some actual purpose: "taxpayer," "voter," "veteran," "licensed driver," "student." (Just because our society has classified us in these terms, however, it does not necessarily follow that such terms are any more permanent, absolute, or magical than the other, more personal, labels.)

In the range of expository processes—patterns by which we tell what we know to others—classification (and subclassifying within larger classes) has a particular usefulness. The students may find that this pattern is one by which we can convey information about *basic structure:* in other words, classifying and subclassifying show the overview, the big picture. The graphic (pictorial symbols instead of verbal symbols) counterpart of this kind of explanation is the organizational chart of a corporation or a bureau or an army. Therefore, if a person wants to know how professional football operates in the United States, or something about the organizational structure of the Olympic games, or how various countries participate in exploration of the Antarctic, the *classification* pattern may serve this purpose well.

Explaining through a process (pp. 319-320) should be one of the most natural and directly applicable ways of conveying information that your students face in expository writing, since they are familiar with how-to-do-it books and since they have been asking each other and their elders almost since birth, "How did you do it?" Therefore, your task may not have to include much by way of explaining this approach or motivating its use. Two stumbling blocks may appear, however.

The first is one of organization. A student who is proficient in the performance of some skill may be both incapable of breaking the flow of actions he performs into meaningful steps and inept at introducing his discussion of those steps in the best order to provide information without creating confusion.

The second possible obstacle is one of point of view. A person who has mastered an operation must project himself (imaginatively) into the shoes of the learner; otherwise, he may explain on such a level that only another master of the process could understand. But if he explains in terms of the limitations of his audience, his chances of success are likely to improve. How often, for example, have you, a stranger in a city, asked directions, only to be given precise instructions, delivered, however, in terms of land-marks—buildings, parks, towers, rivers, bridges—that only a resident of that city could possibly recognize and follow. In the process development, especially, it is important to be aware of and sympathetic to the ignorance of an audience.

Only your best students may write good cause and effect themes (pp. 320-321), but some practical discussion of the subject might be in order, since (1) the development may seem simple and natural even though extremely complicated, and (2) we do have an amazing tendency to think and talk in terms of cause and effect relationships, often without regard for the highly *interpretive* nature of the process (the major role subjective interpretation plays in many assignments of *causes* or *effects*). It is possible that each of us sees himself as an expert on "How?" "Why?" and "What would happen if . . . ?"

Your students might be fascinated by an article in *Harper's Magazine*, September, 1957, by Beirne Lay, Jr., called "The Jet That Crashed Before Take-off." It illustrates in a very suspenseful way how highly complex (and arbitrary) is the task of assigning causes and predicting effects.

As a pattern for *conveying information*, cause and effect discussions must be confined to areas where these relationships have been so often demon-strated by experience that we can state them rather dogmatically. In this manner we can discuss the effects of Sabin or Salk vaccine for polio, the laws of gravity, the characteristic effects of deep water on divers and weightlessness on astronauts. When our assignments of causes or effects are challenged, however, they become subjects for argumentation. This observation might provide you with a useful transition to the second part of Chapter 5, "Argumentation" (p. 322).

Before leaving these patterns for explaining what we know, however, we might consider the possibility that the patterns discussed often occur in combination, when an actual person seeks information from another actual person. Furthermore, there is the possibility (which your ablest students might appreciate) that these patterns may occur in sequence. As we move from ignorance to knowledge, there may be stages at which our curiosity seeks certain answers. Having these answers, we may be prepared to seek others. If you overhear someone say, "I like weelinkniks for break-fast," you might ask the following questions—in about the order they appear here:

What are *weelinkniks?* (Definition)

What is in *weelinkniks?* (Partition—its composition)

How are *weelinkniks* different from sausage, then? (Comparison or contrast)

Who eats them? (Classification)

How are they made? (Process)

What are the effects of eating *weelinkniks?* (Cause and effect)

In this light, the arbitrary patterns we have described for developing expositions become simply different ways of focusing attention on a subject as well as different ways of telling others what we know.

In the second section of Chapter 5, we turn from the consideration of writing that is primarily informative to writing designed primarily to advance a point of view. Not much space has been given to "Argumentation" (pp. 322-326); nevertheless, you may find it an area for assignments that your students will be strongly motivated to write. What they may lack in background information they may compensate for with strongly held opinions upon which you can draw for their written assignments. They must be trained to realize, however, that despite the fervor of their convictions, their points of view need strong support. But even so, enthusiasm for a point of view may be an important motivating force which will lead to (a) the writer's informing himself on the subject and (b) the writing of the argument.

In conjunction with the material on argumentation, several related language studies might logically follow. Condensing the argumentative statements of others, either through the use of summaries or of outlines, seems definitely in order. Such questions as these might help students draw out their summaries or outlines:

What is the principal point of view being advanced?

What evidence does the writer offer to prove that he is seriously concerned about the state of affairs?

What specific details—examples, statistics, opinions of authorities—are offered in support of the point of view?

Is the author concerned with changing your thinking only, or does he want you to act? If the latter, what is the nature of the act he calls for?

Such analyses may offer useful practice in summarizing and outlining. If you wish to take the matter further, however, you can use these condensations as springboards for the writing of counterarguments or refutations by your students. In these the student may either begin his counterargument with the capsule of the original, or he may introduce the original argument one point at a time, refuting it as he goes—point for point.

In your deliberations over this subject with advanced students, you may wish to touch upon a pair of other distinctions within the broad area of argumentation:

Through studying many samples of argumentation, your students may distinguish those that stop after promoting a certain intellectual position from those that call not only for a certain attitude in the reader, but expect the reader who adopts the new attitude to adjust his actions accordingly; in other words, such samples call the reader to action. Advanced students may wish to practice writing themes in which they demonstrate their awareness of the distinction under discussion.

An even more subtle analysis for advanced students might involve the study of many classical and popular samples of argumentation in search of *emotional appeals.* Once isolated, these appeals could be studied together with the more rational appeals upon which all expository writing, especially argumentation, rests so strongly.

CHAPTER 6 *Newspaper Writing* *pages 327-354*

AIM

The study of newspaper writing begins inductively with a look at several different newspaper items, at which time some of the particular features of each are pointed out through questions. In this way we propose to show the characteristics of news stories, feature stories, editorials, and columns.

Following a study of types through analysis of professional samples, the emphasis shifts to your students as they prepare to write newspaper items of their own.

PROCEDURE

In all phases of the study of this chapter, it might be helpful to gather ample current newspaper material for direct reference. When discussing the samples (pp. 329-336), you might then call for similar items to be chosen from among the major offerings of a newspaper. Perhaps your school library subscribes to a nationally published news magazine. If so, you might use it to supplement the study of this chapter.

Since the news story is the common starting point for a reporter, the specific focus moves to reporting the news. "Writing for the Newspaper" (p. 336) introduces the practical work, once analysis of the sample newspaper items has been completed. Nothing could be further from the truth than a possible suspicion that all the rest of this chapter relates only to those who are studying journalism or expect to go into newspaper work. Granted, this may provide good practice for such students, and who can say with complete certainty that he will not be engaged in such an occupation someday? (Have the students poll their parents to learn how many of them had chosen their life's work before their graduation from high school.)

"The Reporter as a Fact-Finder" (p. 337) summarizes the task of the news-story writer. A useful experiment might be in keeping with this topic. Try to arrange to have your class confronted with a single shared experience. Then ask them to report what they saw, heard, smelled, and felt. If a planned excursion such as a walk around the block is impractical, perhaps your class will meet some day following an assembly, a pep rally, a fire drill, or some other occurrence that might lend itself to reports of observations on the spur of the moment.

Whatever the circumstances, your students should observe everything possible of the events (sights, sounds, smells) occurring around them, taking brief notes if they wish. On their return to class, they might summarize their observations. The principal revelation could come through comparing their reports with those of their classmates. In this comparison, such important considerations as completeness, objectivity, and degree of agreement with other reporters would arise naturally to be contemplated.

"Probable Sources of News" (p. 337) suggests, of course, places where events interesting to the public are most likely to occur. At this point the term *beat* is explained.

In the process of "Recognizing Newsworthy Events" (pp. 338-339) and rating events according to their news value, the matter of individual *taste* may present itself for fruitful discussion. Just as different newspaper items appeal to various persons, the appeal of particular news reports may vary from person to person. Discussion may lead your students to recognize how one's taste in these matters can be affected by external circumstances—one's age, sex, physical makeup, mental abilities, formal education, personal interests and ambitions, cultural background. These considerations may help the students evaluate the general newsworthiness of events, even though they themselves recognize that their own tastes do not incline toward their choices at this time. They should now be prepared to answer the questions beginning at the bottom of page 338.

Exercise 2 (p. 339) is designed to promote discussion of the *relative* significance of events for a particular audience of newspaper subscribers. Clearly, the validity of a student's choices will rest on the soundness of his reasoning. If your city is fortunate enough to support more than one daily newspaper, it would be appropriate to bring to class a copy of each paper on a particular day and compare the handling of a single occurrence—size of headline, prominence of position, number of details, interest of the lead, and so forth.

As an example of relative significance of events, notice items 1 and 7 of Exercise 2. The latter is clearly a more serious accident than the former— more persons involved and more damage. But it occurred miles away to persons who were probably unknown locally, and the injured were taken to another town, further removing the event from your scene.

"Distinguishing Fact from Opinion" (pp. 340-341) points out the importance of recognizing the difference between personal evaluations and verifiable facts. Such distinctions will be useful when your students are asked to seek information from outside sources (research). Even though formal research writing is not covered here, the most informal report may be enhanced if the writer (researcher) has distinguished verifiable data from opinions, furnishing names, titles, offices, and affiliations of the persons offering the opinions.

You might discover a few students who confuse verbal concepts: thus where "facts" are distinguished from "opinions," such students might assume that facts are to be accepted and approved, while opinions are to be rejected. If it can be done without belaboring the issue, you may be able to help them realize that the distinction does not demand an either/or response, that both facts and opinions are highly valuable in our lives if we can recognize them and use them appropriately. A sample passage from a history book might serve to illustrate the point.

A student who equates "fact" with "truth" may be inclined to identify "opinion" with "falsehood." You may be able to clarify some of this confusion without becoming ensnared in verbal concepts.

Within the study of "The Structure of the News Story" (pp. 341-344), such specific matters as the lead, the paragraph structure, the style in general, and the achievement of suspense are discussed and practiced in exercises. Finally, "Writing a News Story" (pp. 344-345) brings all these concerns together into the culminating activity.

In the discussion of the feature story beginning on page 345, a hypothetical student-written sample is offered for comparison with the professionally written features on pages 331-333. "Writing a Feature Story" (pp. 347-350) lists specific steps to follow. Also, the handling of both the opening and the central idea in feature stories is discussed in detail at this time.

Student-written editorials are approached in both "Preparing to Write an Editorial" (pp. 350-351) and "Writing an Editorial" (p. 351), followed by appropriate exercises. This aspect of newspaper writing serves as a follow-up to editorial writing discussed and practiced as argumentation in Chapter 5.

"Preparing to Write a Column" and "Writing a Column" (p. 352) complete the practice in the various newspaper-writing assignments.

However beside the point it might be, the sample newspaper column on page 335 offers several possibilities for language review motivated by this interesting item. The study of the item itself can easily provide a review of diction, figures of speech, clichés, folk etymologies, and dead metaphors.

It can prompt a search by the students for other news or magazine stories about their language. It might also suggest the compilation of a list of such expressions from the experience of the students. From (a) a review of the structures involved, (b) a study of newspaper or magazine articles, or (c) the usage lists, some interesting theme assignments should present themselves.

The writing practice suggested should enhance your students' skill in many other kinds of writing. A skilled recorder of his observations is a valuable asset in innumerable professions; practice in reporting news stories can provide apprenticeship for investigators, adjusters, assessors, surveyors, doctors—men in any occupation who must write for others to read what they themselves saw, heard, felt. By the same token, practice in feature writing may be comparable to practice in expository writing—skill in bringing words to life on the page. Editorial and column writing are typical of much reporting that is personal—that reflects the personality of the writer and advances a personal point of view. Any person who runs for public office would profit by this practice—and who can say what future officeholder is not now a member of your class?

A variety of short research projects closing the chapter might be assigned those students interested in further exploration in the field of journalism.

Composition Workshop
pages 355-360

This section is a carefully planned review of the areas that have been explored in Part II of the text. The review questions developed on one page are answered on the turnover page. The Workshop may be used for reinforcement after the students have completed Chapter 6. If the review indicates the need for additional instruction, return to the appropriate chapter for extra study.

Supplementary Tests
pages 361-364

These flexible two-part supplementary tests should provide you with sufficient material for a mid-year and end-of-year test. These tests may also be used for practice or as diagnostic and review tests.

SUGGESTED READING PART II

Books

BROOKS, CLEANTH, AND WARREN, ROBERT PENN, *Modern Rhetoric*, 2nd ed., New York, Harcourt, Brace & World, Inc., 1958.

BRYANT, MARGARET M., ED., *Current American Usage*, New York, Funk & Wagnalls Company, Inc., 1962.

DRESSEL, PAUL L., AND MAYHEW, LEWIS B., *Handbook for Theme Analysis*, Dubuque, Iowa, Wm. C. Brown Company, 1956.

HAYAKAWA, S. I., *Language in Thought and Action*, 2nd ed., New York, Harcourt, Brace & World, Inc., 1964.

MACRORIE, KENNETH, *The Perceptive Writer, Reader, and Speaker*, New York, Harcourt, Brace & World, Inc., 1959.

MYERS, L. M., *Guide to American English*, 3rd ed., Englewood Cliffs, New Jersey, Prentice-Hall, Inc., 1963.

PERRIN, PORTER G., *Writer's Guide and Index to English*, 3rd ed., Chicago, Scott, Foresman and Company, 1959.

Articles

BATEMAN, D. R., "More Mature Writing through a Better Understanding of Language Structure," *The English Journal*, vol. L (October 1961), pp. 457-460.

CHRISTENSEN, FRANCIS, "Notes Toward a New Rhetoric: Sentence Openers," *College English*, vol. 25 (October 1963), pp. 7-11.

DALE, J., "Sequential Procedures in the Teaching of Written Composition," *Journal of Secondary Education*, vol. 39 (January 1964), pp. 14-19.

DUSEL, WILLIAM J., "How Should Student Writing Be Judged?" *The English Journal*, vol. XLVI (May 1957), pp. 263-268.

EVANS, BERTRAND, "Writing and Composing," *The English Journal*, Vol. XLVIII (January 1959), pp. 12-20.

EVANS, W. H., "Composition, Reading, and the Conant Report," *The High School Journal*, vol. 46 (May 1963), pp. 268-278.

HACH, CLARENCE W., "Needed: A Sequential Program in Composition," *The English Journal*, vol. XLIX (November 1960), pp. 536-547.

KEAVY, HUBBARD, "The Simpler Sentence: Key to Better News Writing," *The English Journal*, vol. XLVIII (November 1959), pp. 462-465.

KLEIN, A. L., "Expository Writing for Amateurs," *The English Journal*, vol. LIII (January 1964), pp. 16-22.

LEVINE, I., "Teach Students to Be Their Own Lay Readers," *High Points*, vol. 46 (February 1964), pp. 21-37.

MADDEN, EDGAR, "Evolution of a Writing Program," *The English Journal*, vol. LIII (January 1964), pp. 34-39.

MARCKWARDT, ALBERT H., "Dictionaries and the English Language," *The English Journal*, vol. LII (May 1963), pp. 336-345.

WONNBERGER, CARL G., "Writing—A Way of Life," *The English Journal*, vol. XLVIII (February 1959), pp. 66-73.

Key

PART I

ABBREVIATIONS USED IN THIS KEY

abs	absolute structure	na	noun adjunct
adj	adjective	n cl	noun clause
adj cl	adjective clause	nm	noun-modifier
adj m	adjective-modifier	obj	object
adv	adverb	oc	objective complement
adv cl	adverb clause	pa	predicate adjective
adv m	adverb-modifier	part	participle
agr	agreement	phrase m	phrase-modifier
app	appositive, apposing	pl	plural
attrib	attributive	poss	possessive
comp	complement	pp	participial phrase
coord	coordination, coordinator	ppr	personal pronoun
dtr	determiner	pred	predicate, predicative
do	direct object	prep	preposition
funct	function	prep p	prepositional phrase
ger	gerund	refl	reflexive pronoun
gp	gerund phrase	sent m	sentence-modifier
HW	headword	sing	singular
inf	infinitive	sub	subordinator, subordination
inf m	infinitive-modifier	subj	subject
io	indirect object	vb	verb
ip	infinitive phrase	vi	intransitive verb
lvc	linking-verb complement	vt	transitive verb
mod	modifier, modifying	vm	verb-modifier
n	noun	v	verb

CHAPTER 1 *The Structure of the Sentence*
pages 13-42

Exercise 1   p. 15:   **1.** The shoes should have been ready today.   **2.** The gifts are being sent overseas to the boys for Christmas.   **3.** The packages are to be mailed early.   **4.** The troops are to go by plane to Germany.   **5.** Nancy will return before Sunday.

Exercise 2   p. 18:   **1.** The Dutch settled in the Hudson River Valley. Did the Dutch settle in the Hudson River Valley?   **2.** Oxygen is a life-giving gas. Is oxygen a life-giving gas?   **3.** The saguaro cactus is found in the great deserts of the Southwest. Is the saguaro cactus found in the great deserts of the Southwest?   **4.** Mother has gone to Chicago to visit Aunt Belle. Has Mother gone to Chicago to visit Aunt Belle?   **5.** Sarah will attend the State University. Will Sarah attend the State University?   **6.** The soccer game has been postponed. Has the soccer game been postponed?   **7.** The hurricane caused great loss of life in the West Indies. Did the hurricane cause great loss of life in the West Indies?   **8.** Helen has the chicken pox. Does Helen have the chicken pox?   **9.** Dad parked the car behind the grocery store. Did Dad park the car behind the grocery store?   **10.** Mrs. Kelly has fourteen boarders. Does Mrs. Kelly have fourteen boarders?

Exercise 3   pp. 19-20:   **1.** non-sentence (no finite verb)   **2.** Mountain streams carry rich soil. From . . . plains—non-sentence (no subj and pred)   **3.** question   **4.** non-sentence (signal of sub with normal word order)   **5.** non-sentence (signal of sub with normal word order)   **6.** Then the band began to play some cheerful music. (A verbal functions as the sentence complement.) Which . . . enjoyed—non-sentence (signal of sub with normal word order)   **7.** non-sentence (no subj and pred)   **8.** Wherever you go, you will meet friendly people.   **9.** non-sentence (no subj and pred)   **10.** The coach plans to give the boys a day off.   **11.** inverted   **12.** The car overturned, injuring all of the occupants.   **13.** non-sentence (signal of sub with normal word order)   **14.**

                                      N   V

Because Germany is not rich in natural resources, the Germans must rely on hard work and technical skill to produce wealth from their raw materials.   **15.** non-sentence (no finite verb)   **16.** Serving as a short cut between two oceans, the

N   V

Big Ditch weaves across the Isthmus of Panama.   **17.** non-sentence (no finite

              N   LV   ADJ

verb)   **18.** Thus Captain Hornblower was able to rout the enemy without any

                N   LV   N

casualties.   **19.** <u>That you will graduate with honors</u> must be a source of pride to your parents. (A clause functions as the subject.)   **20.** non-sentence (no finite verb)   **21.** non-sentence (signal of sub with normal word order)   **22.**

         NS   V   N   N

The wind having let up, we decided to start for home.   **23.** The night shall be

V   N   V

turned into music.   **24.** Tecumseh served in the War of 1812 as a brigadier

                             NS   V

general.   **25.** Whenever I hear that song, I think of that summer at Camp

                   N   V   N

Twintrees.   **26.** In 1961, Roger Maris hit 61 home runs in 164 games.   **27.** non-sentence (no finite verb)   **28.** non-sentence (no subj and pred)   **29.** A

     N   V   N

rolling stone gathers no moss.   **30.** non-sentence (no subj and pred)

Exercise 4   *p. 21:*   **1.** Henry was the best pinch hitter on the bench.   **2.** Mountain streams carry rich soil from the highlands to the flood plains.   **4.** We'll go whenever you're ready.   **5.** The rain had stopped and the sun was shining once more.   **6.** Then the band began to play some cheerful music which we all enjoyed.   **7.** I enjoy a good book, a warm fire, and the smell of steak broiling over the coals.   **9.** He has nothing to look back on with pride and nothing to look forward to with hope.   **13.** Because you had gone to the trouble of painting the porch furniture white, Dad decided to paint the trellis.   **15.** We grant, of course, that what the witness said is true.   **17.** We hoped but did not expect to win the free trip to Texas.   **20.** We peeked into the dimly lighted room but did not see anyone there.   **21.** When you are on your way to the theater, you think about the wonderful evening ahead of you.   **27.** We did not realize what dangers were ahead of us.   **28.** This is the kind of cake that Mother used to make.   **30.** Very little was to be seen from the portholes.

Exercise 5   *pp. 21-22:*   (The pattern labels N and V indicate the headword in the subject and the headword in the predicate. The complement is identified in

            N   V   N

parentheses.)   **1.** Pitcairn Island / belongs to Great Britain.   **2.** The bill of

           V   N   N   V

the pelican / can hold several quarts of water. (do)   **3.** Prince / barked

                   N   LV   N

fiercely at the intruder.   **4.** Thomas Edison / was a productive inventor. (lvc)

                   N   V   N
5. The family across the street / left for Europe this morning.   6. Anne /
LV   ADJ   N   V
looks beautiful in her new coat. (lvc)   7. The neighbor's cat / has eaten our
N   N   LV   ADJ
canary. (do)   8. Kathy / seemed nervous during the first act. (lvc)   9.
            N   V   N
The taxes on our home / have been raised again this year.   10. The horses /
V   N
raced wildly through the mountain pass.   11. The girl who lives next door /
V   N   N   V   N   N
won a scholarship to Vassar. (do)   12. The boys elected Henry captain of the
                            N   V   N   N
soccer team. (do, oc)   13. Mother / told the children the legend of Pecos
         NS LV   N
Bill. (io, do)   14. This is your last opportunity to see the circus. (lvc)   15.
      N   V
The painting / was sold to Mrs. Rumkin who lives on Pine Street.   16. The
N   LV   ADJ
crowd / became angry because the referee stopped the fight. (lvc)   17. The
N   LV   N   NS   LV   ADJ
Pecos River / is a branch of the Rio Grande. (lvc)   18. We / 'll be very happy
                                   N   V
when this day is over. (lvc)   19. The children / were not at home when the
           NS   V   N
fire started.   20. We / ate a buffet supper in the club house after the game was
             N   V   N
over. (do)   21. Jean Riccard / made a stratospheric ascent of almost 58,000
                       N   V
feet in 1934. (do)   22. Mrs. Smathers / had to dash out to the grocery store
because there was very little food in the freezer. (*had to* functions as an auxiliary)
          N   V   NS   N
23. The butcher / sold her a side of beef although it was very late. (io, do)
       NS   V
24. We / went down to the harbor to survey the storm damage in the morning.
              N   V   N
25. The Shawnee Chief / refused the offer of General Harrison. (do)   26.
   N   V   N
Maybelle / likes the heavyset boy who plays left end for the Rams. (do)   27.
                                                          N   V
inverted sentence   28. inverted sentence   29. The construction boss / handed
N   N
Cassidy a shiny new shovel. (io, do)   30. question   31. question   32.
        N   V
The girl in the white dress / slipped into the seat which the usher found for her.
                                                         N   V
33. inverted sentence   34. inverted sentence   35. Charley / didn't wait
for the bad news.

Exercise 6   *p. 25:*   1. analyses   2. editors-in-chief   3. wolves   4.
children   5. alumni   6. deer   7. mice   8. princesses   9. torpedoes
10. quizzes

Exercise 7   *pp. 26-27:*

A. Navajo's   church's
children's   hero's
horses'   Socrates'
Cortez'   boss's
Doris'   lady's
month's   river's
brother-in-law's   ship's
alumnus'   duchess'
money's   patient's
ally's   crowd's

C.

Singular	*Plural*	*Sing Poss*	*Plu Poss*
man	men	man's	men's
ally	allies	ally's	allies'
child	children	child's	children's
fox	foxes	fox's	foxes'
mouse	mice	mouse's	mice's
tomato	tomatoes	tomato's	tomatoes'
wife	wives	wife's	wives'
boss	bosses	boss's	bosses'
information	————	————	————

D.   oxen *also* ox, geese, curriculums *or* curricula, buses or busses, alleys, alumnae, deer, knives, women

Exercise 8   *pp. 27-28:*   **Line 1**—story, survival   **Line 2**—sea, environment   **Line 3**—two-thirds, Earth's, surface, depth   **Line 4**—mountains, volume   **Line 5**—miles   **Line 6**—region, man's   **Line 7**—doorstep, exploitation   **Line 8**—cause, equipment   **Line 9**—diver's, movement   **Line 10**—team, surface, hydrographers, oceanographers   **Line 11**—biologists   **Line 12**—wealth, waves, oil, coal   **Line 13**—minerals, life   **Line 14**—source, food   **Line 15**—achievements, man, directions   **Line 16**—tops, mountains   **Line 17**—space, man, progress, conquest   **Line 18**—sea, development   **Line 19**—apparatus, aqua lung   **Line 20**—attitude, career, salvage   **Line 21**—information   **Line 22**—scientists, engineers, equipment   **Line 23**—diver, movement, exploration   **Line 24**—sea's, secrets   **Line 25**—movement, diver   **Line 26**—achievements, submarine, diving bell   **Line 27**—bathyscaphe, craft   **Line 28**—valleys, oceans   **Line 29**—shield   **Line 30**—link, man, sea   **Line 31**—vehicles, use   **Line 32**—headquarters, locks   **Line 33**—divers, astronauts   **Line 34**—space ships   **Line 35**—analogy, space, scientists   **Line 36**—fields, problems, pressure, respiration   **Line 37**—endurance, adaptation, years   **Line 38**—money, effort, research   **Line 39**—hope, returns   **Line 40**—fruits, exploration   **Line 41**—effort [More advanced students may include these noun adjuncts (see text p. 51):   **Line 10**—support   **Line 11**—marine   **Line 13**—animal   **Line 20**—marine   **Line 21**—marine   **Line 32**—pressure   **Line 38**—space. Note also that in line 20, *diving* is a verbal (see text p. 88) and that in American usage *aqua lung* (line 19) and *space ships* (line 34) are usually written solid.

***Exercise* 9   *p. 32:*   1.** sat   **2.** got *or* gotten   **3.** slew   **4.** lying
5. threw   **6.** burst *or* bursted   **7.** sprung   **8.** bound   **9.** swum
10. woven   **11.** swore   **12.** laid   **13.** forbade *or* forbad   **14.** waked
or woke   **15.** shaken   **16.** slunk

Exercise* 10   *p. 33:   See Chapter 4, *Modern Grammar and Composition 1,* for
a comprehensive listing of irregular verbs.

Exercise* 11   *pp. 36-37:   (The connectives are underlined.)   **1.** compound,
and   **2.** complex, since . . . work—adv cl, vm   **3.** complex, who . . . work—
adj cl, nm   **4.** complex, who . . . day—adj cl, nm   **5.** complex, when . . .
ready—adv cl, vm   **6.** compound, but   **7.** complex, whoever . . . store—
n cl, subj; where . . . kept—n cl, do   **8.** compound, or   **9.** complex, that
. . . ounces—adj cl, nm   **10.** complex, what . . . mean—n cl, do   **11.** compound-complex, yet; that . . . successful—n cl, do   **12.** compound, but   **13.**
complex, If . . . noon—adv cl, sent m   **14.** complex, who . . . chances—adj
cl, nm; that . . . pay—n cl, do   **15.** compound-complex, and; when . . . camp—
sent m (*or* modifier of the predicate adjective *exhausted*)   **16.** compound without a connective   **17.** compound-complex, but; after . . . out—adv cl, sent m
18. complex, whose . . . bright—adj cl, nm   **19.** complex, where . . . signed—
adj cl, nm   **20.** complex without a subordinator, he . . . Circleville—n cl, do
21. complex, where . . . been—n cl, do   **22.** complex, that . . . bought—adj
cl, nm; that . . . Lake—adj cl, nm   **23.** complex, whatever . . . say—n cl, subj
24. complex, that . . . yesterday—n cl, app   **25.** complex, Whenever . . .
Regina—adv cl, sent m; where . . . trained—adj cl, nm

Exercise* 12   *pp. 37-38:   **1.** The car that Father just bought is a 1937
Plymouth.   **2.** The fighter knew that he would be beaten.   **3.** Taxes will
be raised again unless the public protests.   **4.** The driver must slow down, or he
will get a ticket. He will not take medicine, nor will he consult a doctor. The family
is wealthy, yet they live in a modest home. We were late, so we took a taxi.   **5.**
The outboard motor stalled; nevertheless, the boys managed to row back to camp.
(Other conjunctive adverbs: *however, therefore, moreover, then, consequently,* and
so forth.)   **6.** They found the man who had been lost in the desert.   **7.**
What children want most is frequently not the best for them.   **8.** The store-
keeper was angry when the lady dropped the bottle of catsup.   **9.** He bragged
about what he had done.   **10.** Henry Banks is a fellow who will work hard.
11. This vacation is just what Henry has always wanted.   **12.** A law that
sixteen-year-old boys cannot operate scooters has been passed in this state.   **13.**
A helicopter crew found the plane that had crashed, but rescuers were unable to
reach the wreckage.   **14.** The crowd left the stadium when the game was over,
but several hundred people milled around the players' entrance.   **15.** The sun
rose in a flaming red sky, and we knew that still another hot, dry day lay ahead
of us.   **16.** The question that the interviewer asked was difficult, but the appli-
cant was able to give a satisfactory answer after he had given it some thought.

17. The troops crossed the river, <u>but</u> it was dark, <u>and</u> the enemy forces could not be seen. **18.** The old fisherman knew <u>that he had lost the struggle</u>.

Chapter Test, Form A *pp. 39-40:* **1.** b, c, d, e, and g **2.** wolves, churches, alumni, data, moose, pliers, potatoes, oxen *also* ox, women **3.** Agnes', children's, uncle's, wives', mother-in-law's, friends' **4.** The team fought well in the second half. The team has usually fought well. **5.** (a) swum (b) sworn (c) borne (d) shrank (e) ridden **6.** (a) n cl, subj (b) adv cl, adj m (c) n cl, do (d) adj cl, nm (e) adv cl, vm

Chapter Test, Form B *p. 40:* **1.** a, c, d, f, and h **2.** wives, curriculums *or* curricula, mice, children, no plural, tornadoes *or* tornados, teeth, trousers, boxes **3.** Morris', aunt's, wolves', brother-in-law's, Mr. Alden's, brethren's **4.** Tommy has drunk all the milk. The milk was drunk. This milk should have been drunk first. **5.** (a) lain (b) drunk (c) woven (d) sprang *or* sprung (e) wrung **6.** (a) coord N-V pattern (b) adj cl, nm (c) coord N-LV-ADJ pattern (d) n cl, lvc (e) adv cl, sent m

CHAPTER **2** *Headwords and Modifiers* *pages 43-64*

Exercise 1 *p. 48:*

1. Lines[N] had been planted[V]

Headword	Lines
<u>Modifier</u>	<u>of chestnut trees</u>
Headword	had been planted
<u>Modifier</u>	<u>along the strip of lawn . . . center</u>

2. yacht[N] has sailed[V]

Headword	yacht
<u>Modifiers</u>	<u>white</u>
	<u>that was . . . yesterday</u>
Headword	has sailed
<u>Modifier</u>	<u>for a cruise . . . Delaport Point</u>

3. $\overset{\text{N}}{\text{girl}}$ $\overset{\text{V}}{\text{scraped}}$ her $\overset{\text{N}}{\text{elbow}}$

Headword	girl
Modifiers	little
	in the blue dress

Headword	scraped
Modifier	when she fell . . . swing

Headword	elbow
Modifier	her

4. $\overset{\text{N}}{\text{father}}$ $\overset{\text{LV}}{\text{is}}$ the $\overset{\text{N}}{\text{architect}}$

Headword	father
Modifier	His

Headword	architect
Modifiers	noted
	who designed . . . group

5. $\overset{\text{N}}{\text{woman}}$ $\overset{\text{V}}{\text{gave}}$ the mischievous $\overset{\text{N}}{\text{boys}}$ a penetrating $\overset{\text{N}}{\text{look}}$

Headword	woman
Modifiers	elderly
	standing in the bus stop

Headword	boys
Modifier	mischievous

Headword	look
Modifiers	penetrating
	that instantly . . . . them

6. $\overset{\textbf{N}}{\text{bowerbirds}}$ $\overset{\text{LV}}{\text{are}}$ $\overset{\text{N}}{\text{architects}}$

Headword	bowerbirds
Modifier	of Australia and New Guinea

Headword	architects
Modifiers	skilled
	who . . . decorations

Exercise 2   *p. 52:*   1. grave, *pa;* patient's, *nm*   2. anxious, *nm;* patiently, *vm*   3. well, *vm;* last, *nm*   4. whole, *nm;* unhappy, *pa*   5. Jimmy's, *nm;* dazzlingly, *adj m;* white, *pa*   6. faster, *vm*   7. barely, *phrase m*   8. early, *adv m;* yesterday, *vm*   9. south, *na;* lush, *pa*   10. balmy, *nm;* steadily, *vm*   11. certain, *pa;* suitable, *nm*   12. farther and farther, *vm*   13.

hard, *vm* 14. happy, *oc* 15. south, *vm* 16. weary, *pa;* slowly, *vm*
17. chocolate, *na;* temptingly, *adj m;* delicious, *pa* 18. carefully, *adj m;*
arranged, *nm* 19. slow, *vm;* parking, *ɳm* 20. stumpy, *nm;* sideways, *vm*

Exercise 3 *pp. 52-53:* See text pages 49-51.

Exercise 4 *pp. 53-54:* **Line 2**—private, *attrib;* strong, *attrib* **Line 5**—
curious, *attrib;* upright, *attrib* **Line 6**—individual, *attrib;* half-proud, *attrib;* half-
comic, *attrib;* Prussian, *attrib* **Line 9**—tall, *pred;* broad, *pred* **Line 10**—
moody *pred;* good-humored, *pred;* original, *pred* **Line 13**—well-cut, *attrib;*
white, *attrib;* long-sleeved, *attrib* **Line 14**—elegant, *pred;* old-fashioned, *pred*
Line 15—graceful, *pred;* debonair, *pred* **Line 16**—preliminary, *attrib* **Line
20**—dumpy, *pred* **Line 21**—skinned, *attrib;* severe, *attrib* **Line 22**—slight,
attrib **Line 23**—soft, *attrib;* attractive, *attrib* (both in apposition) **Line 24**—
red, *attrib*

Exercise 5 *p. 54:* 1. **Line 1**—out **Line 2**—once **Line 3**—again and
again **Line 4**—even **Line 5**—so **Line 7**—off **Line 9**—strongly, first
Line 11—even **Line 12**—unerringly **Line 13**—Now **Line 14**—little
Line 17—sensibly **Line 20**—little **Line 23**—prettily **Line 25**—down
Line 26—back, methodically 2. **Line 14**—Oxford **Line 17**—tennis **Line
22**—female **Line 24**—tennis

3. *Nouns as headwords*	*Modifiers*
thrill	private
	strong
	of pride . . . him
pride	that had moved . . . him
time	she had known him
walk	curious
	upright
	individual
	half-proud
	half-comic
sergeant	Prussian
	drill
	on . . . off
Sunday	his
	off
mixture	of amusement . . . him
	that . . . met
distance	of . . . yards

crowd	of people
trousers	well-cut white
shirt	long-sleeved Oxford
shirt	tennis
handkerchief	around her head
appearance	skinned severe
twinge	slight of female regret
regret	female
Eleanor Burns	soft and attractive in . . . dress with . . . hair
dress	prettily cut tennis

4. *Verbs as headwords*   *Modifiers*

walked	out onto the court behind her husband
felt	once more
moved	again and again in the time . . . him
married	six years
stride	before her in that . . . walk like a Prussian . . . off
felt	even so as she . . . off
touched	so strongly when they . . . met
met	first
pick out	unerringly
hit	in the . . . rallying
dressed	sensibly in shorts . . . shirt

imprisoned	in a bandanna
	so that . . . eyes
get	into her eyes
had	when she looked . . . hair
looked	across the net
concentrated	on keeping . . . ball
	as Mr. Croker . . . her
sliced	back
	methodically

5. *Adjectives as headwords*   *Modifiers*

elegant and . . . old-fashioned	among . . . players
old-fashioned	little
graceful and debonair	as he hit . . . rallying
dumpy	little

6. *Adverbs as headwords*   *Modifiers*

more	once
so	even

Exercise 6   *p. 57:*   **1.** running . . . touchdown, *pp* (Bill Bunch)   **2.** at . . . window, *prep p* (teller)   **3.** sitting in the first row, *pp* (gentleman); in . . . row, *prep p* (sitting); from . . . County, *prep p* (assemblyman)   **4.** breaking . . . sand, *pp* (waves); over the sand, *prep p* (breaking); of the hurricane, *prep p* (arrival) **5.** to watch . . . race, *ip* (horse); in this race, *prep p* (to watch)   **6.** of money, *prep p* (plenty); to spend . . . Fair, *ip* (money); at . . . Fair, *prep p* (to spend)   **7.** to go . . . church, *ip* (ready); to church, *prep p* (to go)   **8.** from Pittsburgh, *prep p* (traveled); to play . . . pirates, *ip* (traveled)   **9.** Walking along . . . Street, *pp* (Uncle Thatcher); along Main Street, *prep p* (Walking); to greet . . . friends, *ip* (stopped)   **10.** around my neck, *prep p* (wound); licking . . . tongue, *pp* (kitten); with . . . tongue, *prep p* (licking)   **11.** to the surface, *prep p* (rose); to point . . . carrier, *ip* (rose); at the carrier, *prep p* (to point) **12.** After the flash flood, *prep p* (found); running . . . ranch, *pp* (river); through the ranch, *prep p* (running)

Exercise 8   *p. 59:*   **1.** The farmer ploughed the <u>fertile</u> <u>south</u>^{HW} field <u>where he plans to plant early potatoes.</u>   **2.** The farmer <u>quickly</u>^{HW} ploughed the field <u>after it had dried out from the rains.</u>   **3.** The cashier gave the <u>young</u> lady^{HW} <u>in the blue dress</u> her change.   **4.** The <u>young</u>^{HW} cashier <u>in the grocery store</u> <u>who came</u>

here from Germany gave the lady her change.   **5.** Fire damaged the basement
of the <u>old</u> house <u>which Mrs. Brown had just bought.</u>   **6.** Father became
<u>extremely</u> angry <u>when the waitress burned his toast.</u>   **7.** <u>My father, who is very
nervous,</u> became extremely angry when the waitress <u>accidentally</u> burnt his toast
<u>because she did not understand the mechanism of the new toaster.</u>   **8.** The fire
<u>in the basement</u> <u>which had been ignited by an overheated furnace</u> spread rapidly.
9. The boy ran up the hill <u>so</u> quickly <u>that he had difficulty catching his breath.</u>

Chapter Test, Form A   *p. 61:*   **1.** (a) Mother became <u>very</u> anxious <u>when
her sister did not arrive.</u>   (b) The little boy was running <u>excitedly up and down
the walk.</u>   (c) The <u>old</u> house <u>on Bank Street</u> <u>which has been vacant so long</u> burned
down last night.   (d) Our cat Missy caught the <u>big</u> gopher <u>which had damaged
our lawn.</u>   (e) Miss Sweet is the <u>new</u> <u>English</u> teacher <u>in North High</u> <u>who
comes from Rock Glen.</u>   **2.** (a) The Cranfords have bought a <u>beautiful</u> <u>new</u>
Oldsmobile.   (b) The little boy ran <u>crying to his mother.</u>   (c) The <u>pretty</u> waitress <u>in
Smogg's Cafe</u> spilled the coffee.   (d) The groom seemed nervous <u>standing alone
at the altar.</u>   (e) <u>Waiting for his mother,</u> the <u>little</u> boy <u>in the blue suit</u> smiled when
I gave him some candy.   **3.** (The headwords are in **boldface.** The modifiers
are <u>underscored</u> and identified in parentheses.)   (a) The rain **came** <u>down</u> (adv)
<u>in torrents</u> (prep p).   (b) Father **remained** <u>in the city</u> (prep p) <u>for the night</u>
(prep p).   (c) The coach was <u>greatly</u> (adv) **pleased** <u>when the team won its first
game</u> (adv cl).   (d) The <u>young</u> (adj) **man** <u>who lives across the street</u> (adj cl)
is shoveling our driveway. (<u>across the street</u> is a *prep p* modifying **lives**)   (e) We
drove <u>quickly</u> (adv) <u>to the **field**</u> (prep p) <u>where the game was to be played</u> (adj
cl).   (f) The first **group** <u>to leave</u> (ip) was the **delegation** <u>from Oklahoma</u> (prep p).
(g) The **man** <u>in the blue suit</u> (prep p) <u>casually</u> (adv) **tipped** his hat <u>to mother</u>
(prep p) <u>as he walked by</u> (adv cl).   (h) This is the <u>young</u> (adj) **lady** <u>who has
just completed her first concert tour</u> (adj cl).

Chapter Test, Form B   *pp. 61-62:*   **1.** (a) Father seemed <u>highly</u> nervous
<u>as he checked the repair bill.</u>   (b) The <u>old</u> car <u>belonging to Jim</u> was wrecked.   (c)

Mother baked a banana cake with pistachio frosting. (d) Mr. Jones is a former naval officer who retired after service in the Pacific. (e) The dog was barking

_{HW}
excitedly at the mailman. 2. (a) The dog gulped his supper greedily in less
_{HW}   _{HW}
than a minute. (b) The good-looking young man smiled. (c) Helen is the girl
_{HW}
in blue who is smiling at the audience. (d) We saw a huge bear on a chain
_{HW}
begging for food. (e) Father was reading quietly when Jane trooped in with all her boy friends. 3. (The headwords are in **boldface**. The modifiers are
_N
underscored and identified in parentheses.) (a) The **wind** blowing from the north-
_V   _N   _N   _V
east (pp) **piled** the snow in great drifts (prep p). (b) The corn will not **grow**
_N
well (adv) unless the ground is fertilized (adv cl). (c) The new (adj) **car** in our
_V   _N
driveway (prep p) **belongs** to Mr. Scott (prep p). (d) The young (adj) **lady**
_{LV}   _N
who is sitting on the platform (adj cl) is the **speaker** who will tell us about the Peace Corps (adj cl). (on the platform is a *prep p* modifying **sitting**; about the
_N   _{LV}   _{ADJ}
Peace Corps is a *prep p* modifying **tell**) (e) Father became **angry** when the
_N   _V
waitress served him bluefish (adv cl). (f) The car had **stopped** on the bridge
_N   _V
(prep p) because the tank was empty (adv cl). (g) Mother bought a new (adj)
_N
dress which was made in Mexico (adj cl). (in Mexico is a *prep p* modifying **made**)
_N   _V
(h) The **sailor** in the neat white suit (prep p) **smiled** gallantly (adv) at Hilda (prep p) when she stumbled over the winch (adv cl). (neat and white are *adj* modifying **suit**; over the winch is a *prep p* modifying **stumbled**)

The Structure of Your Language   pp. 62-64:

1. Headword sun
   Modifier looking . . . valley

   Headword valley
   Modifier white-curtained

   Headword outcasts
   Modifier dividing . . . meal

   Headword store
   Modifiers slowly decreasing
              of provisions . . . meal

   Headword dividing
   Modifier for . . . meal

Headword	decreasing
Modifier	slowly

Headword	meal
Modifier	morning

2.
Headword	gentlemen
Modifiers	on the grass
	at a distance

Headword	sat
Modifiers	under . . . trees
	while . . . green

Headword	trees
Modifier	great

Headword	dress
Modifier	crimson

Headword	bit
Modifier	of color

Headword	color
Modifier	amid . . . green

Headword	green
Modifiers	fresh
	rich

3.
Headword	wheel
Modifier	of the world

Headword	swings
Modifiers	through . . . phases
	again . . . again

4.
Headword	One
Modifier	of the soldiers

Headword	soldiers
Modifier	who . . . him

Headword	came
Modifiers	stealthily
	round . . . corner

(Note: *Suddenly* is a sentence-modifier.)

5.
Headword	below
Modifiers	Far
	on . . . river

Headword	river
Modifier	black

Headword	stars
Modifiers	spaced
	red and white

Headword	tugs
Modifier	slow-moving

Headword	lights
Modifiers	faint
	splintered . . . rain

Headword	splintered
Modifier	in the rain

Headword	hinted
Modifier	at the city

(Note: The introductory phrase and the adverb *beyond* are sentence-modifiers.)

6.
Headword	purchased
Modifier	from . . . them

Headword	newsdealer
Modifier	in the cubbyhole

Headword	cubbyhole
Modifier	beneath them

Headword	magazine
Modifier	next month's

Headword	month's
Modifier	next

Headword	paper
Modifier	tomorrow morning's

Headword	morning's
Modifier	tomorrow

Headword	walked
Modifier	with . . . arm

Headword	these
Modifier	tucked under . . . arm

Headword	arm
Modifier	plump

7.
Headword	dawned
Modifiers	cold and clear
	across . . . nation

Headword	most
Modifier	of the nation
Headword	thousands
Modifier	of . . . worshippers
Headword	worshippers
Modifier	sunrise
Headword	feast
Modifiers	Christianity's
	joyous
Headword	greeted
Modifier	with . . . flurries
Headword	collars
Modifiers	coat
	turned . . . flurries
Headword	breezes
Modifier	stiff
Headword	flurries
Modifier	snow

8.

Headword	lay
Modifier	in . . . green fields
Headword	midst
Modifier	of a checkerboard
Headword	checkerboard
Modifier	of . . . farms
Headword	farms
Modifier	with . . . orchards
Headword	fields
Modifier	of grain
Headword	hillsides
Modifier	of orchards
Headword	orchards
Modifier	where . . . green fields
Headword	clouds
Modifiers	white
	of bloom
Headword	drifted
Modifier	above . . . fields
Headword	fields
Modifier	green

9. Headword   turned
    Modifiers   sadly
                from . . . visage

    Headword   shrewdness
    Modifiers   wrinkled
                of . . . visage

    Headword   visage
    Modifier   sordid

    Headword   gazed
    Modifier   up . . . soul

    Headword   valley
    Modifier   where . . . soul

    Headword   distinguished
    Modifiers   still
                amid . . . sunbeams

    Headword   mist
    Modifiers   gathering
                gilded . . . sunbeams

    Headword   sunbeams
    Modifier   last

    Headword   features
    Modifiers   glorious
                which . . . soul

    Headword   impressed
    Modifier   into . . . soul

10. Headword   backed
    Modifier   up to . . . house

    Headword   sidewalk
    Modifiers   wooden
                before . . . house

    Headword   house
    Modifiers   naked
                weather-beaten
                frame

    Headword   group
    Modifiers   same
                composite
                ill-defined
                that . . . siding

    Headword   stood
    Modifier   upon . . . siding

| Headword | siding |
| Modifier | station |

| Headword | huddled |
| Modifier | about the gate |

11. | Headword | Moby Dick |
    | Modifiers | Resuming . . . attitude |
    | | churning . . . wake |

| Headword | attitude |
| Modifier | horizontal |

| Headword | wake |
| Modifier | vengeful |

Headword	swam
Modifiers	swiftly
	round . . . crew

| Headword | crew |
| Modifier | wrecked |

12. | Headword | highway |
    | Modifier | concrete |

| Headword | edged |
| Modifier | with . . . grass |

| Headword | mat |
| Modifier | of . . . grass |

Headword	grass
Modifiers	tangled
	broken
	dry

| Headword | heads |
| Modifier | grass |

| Headword | heavy |
| Modifier | with . . . coat |

Headword	beards
Modifiers	oat
	to catch

| Headword | to catch |
| Modifier | on . . . coat |

| Headword | coat |
| Modifier | dog's |

CHAPTER **3**   *Form and Function* *pages 65-80*

Exercise 1   *p. 71:*   (The functional labels given are based on *Webster's New Practical School Dictionary*, © 1964 by G. & C. Merriam Co.) move, *vb, n;* plane, *vt, n, adj;* brave, *adj, vt, n;* out, *adv, vi, adj, prep, n;* ready, *adj, vt, n;* far, *adv, adj;* call, *vb, n;* round, *adj, adv, prep, n, vb;* near, *adv, prep, adj, vb;* below, *adv, prep;* down, *n, adv, adj, prep, n, vb;* top, *n, vt, adj*

Exercise 2   *pp. 71-72:*   **A.** desk, *n;* book, *n, vb, adj;* climb, *vb, n;* prepare, *vb;* carve, *vb;* foundation, *n;* educate, *vt;* breeze, *n, vi;* knuckle, *n, vb;* furnish, *vt;* finish, *vb, n;* carelessly, *adv;* cement, *n, vb;* consciousness, *n;* intelligent, *adj;* careless, *adj;* abbreviate, *vt;* abbreviation, *n;* nail, *n, vt;* complex, *adj, n;* often, *adv;* religious, *adj, n;* backward, *adv, adj;* away, *adv, adj;* reform, *vb, n;* style, *n, vt;* unhealthy, *adj;* water, *n, vb*   **B.** In English, a given word is often used in a number of functions.   **C.** desk, carve, foundation, educate, furnish, carelessly, consciousness, intelligent, careless, abbreviate, abbreviation, often, unhealthy   **D.** English words do not have an absolute identity or classification. What a word is—noun, verb, adjective, adverb, function word—depends on the context in which it is used.

Exercise 3   *p. 72:*   1.   The lawyer will <u>petition</u> for a new trial.   2.   Aunt Ida gave most of her money to the <u>poor.</u>   3.   <u>Walking</u> is a healthful exercise.   4.   The New York *Times* publishes a <u>daily.</u>   5.   He picked up <u>his</u> books and stalked out of the room.   6.   Mr. Gilman is a <u>science</u> teacher.   7.   <u>What you decide now</u> will affect your future.   8.   A sharp tongue is the only edged tool <u>that grows keener with constant use.</u>   9.   Scamp always barks <u>when he hears a car door close.</u>   10.   We watched the birds <u>splashing in the fountain.</u>

Exercise 4   *p. 75:*   1.   comp   2.   pred   3.   subj   4.   mod   5.   comp   6.   mod   7.   mod   8.   mod   9.   mod   10.   subj   11.   subj   12.   pred   13.   pred   14.   mod   15.   mod   16.   comp   17.   mod   18.   subj   19.   comp   20.   comp   21.   mod

Exercise 5   *p. 76:*   1.   (a) it   (b) money   (c) liberally   2.   (a) swimming   (b)   tennis   3.   (a) new   (b) leather   4.   (a) conscientious   (b) chemistry   5.   (a) soon   (b) green   (c) Monday   6.   (a) around   (b) pale   7.   (a) worker   (b) diligent   8.   (a) mystery   (b) interesting   (c) Hemingway's   (d) his   (e) these

Exercise 6   *p. 76:*   1.   (a) <u>Nobody</u> volunteered to do the dishes.   (b) <u>What this family needs</u> is a top sergeant.   (c) <u>Washing</u> dishes can be fun.   2.   (a) Harvey wants <u>something.</u>   (b) Mary knows <u>what I have in the bag.</u>   (c) Helen likes <u>dancing.</u>

Chapter Test, Form A   pp. 77-78:   1. (a) momen<u>tous</u>, *adj;* occas<u>ion</u>, *n;* arriv<u>ed</u>, *v* (b) atten<u>tion</u>, *n;* direct<u>ed</u>, *v;* immediate<u>ly</u>, *adv;* conduc<u>tor</u>, *n*   (c) play<u>ing</u>, *v;* game<u>s</u>, *n*   (d) farm<u>er</u>, *n;* walk<u>ed</u>, *v;* home<u>ward</u>, *adv;* field<u>s</u>, *n*   (e) guest<u>s</u>, *n;* <u>sat</u>, *v;* captain<u>'s</u>, *n*   2. (a) comp (b) pred (c) subj (d) mod (e) comp (f) mod (g) subj (h) mod (i) comp   3. We usually <u>walk</u> to school. Have you shoveled the <u>walk</u>?   4. His <u>work</u> is done. He will <u>work</u> tomorrow. He studied the <u>work</u> sheet.   5. The <u>dance</u> will be in the Fire House. They will <u>dance</u> the tango. He asked for her <u>dance</u> program.   6. The boys climbed <u>up</u> the cliff. The passenger cars moved <u>up</u> to make more room on the ferry. Life has many an <u>up</u> and down.   7. The <u>good</u> child is seen and not heard. The <u>good</u> are often unappreciated.   8. He usually has a <u>ready</u> answer. They will <u>ready</u> our room when the other guests leave.   9. (a) <u>All</u> is lost. (b) <u>What will be</u> will be. (c) The <u>meek</u> will inherit the earth. (d) <u>Painting</u> is hard work.   10. (a) The car was driven <u>south</u>. (b) He bought a car <u>that he admired</u>. (c) Father repaired the <u>kitchen</u> sink. (d) The crew abandoned the <u>sinking</u> ship.

Chapter Test, Form B   pp. 78-79:   1. (a) dread<u>ful</u>, *adj;* accid<u>ent</u>, *n;* occur<u>red</u>, *v* (b) inten<u>tions</u>, *n;* <u>were</u>, *v;* obvi<u>ous</u>, *adj*   (c) farmer<u>'s</u>, *n;* milk<u>ing</u>, *v;* cow<u>s</u>, *n* (d) direc<u>tor</u>, *n;* walk<u>ed</u>, *v;* slow<u>ly</u>, *adv*   (e) princip<u>al</u>, *n;* come<u>s</u>, *v;* partie<u>s</u>, *n*   2. (a) mod (b) subj (c) subj (d) comp (e) mod (f) subj (g) mod (h) mod (i) pred   3. We'll <u>climb</u> to the peak this afternoon. It was a difficult <u>climb</u>. 4. The <u>play</u> was delightful. Let's <u>play</u> Monopoly. The children changed into <u>play</u> clothes.   5. The <u>team</u> played a good game. We will <u>team</u> up for a game of tennis. The <u>team</u> play was exceptionally good.   6. We walked <u>down</u> the long road. He decided to jump <u>down</u>. The fighter should <u>down</u> his opponent in the third round.   7. The <u>ambitious</u> student graduated with honors. The rewards usually go to the <u>ambitious</u>.   8. He took a <u>long</u> look at his partner. The boys often <u>long</u> for pancakes and syrup.   9. (a) The winner will take <u>all</u>. (b) The loser will get <u>what is left</u>. (c) The family likes <u>eating</u> at the beach. (d) Helen wants <u>to go to the movies</u>.   10. (a) Herman <u>elbowed</u> his way through the crowd. (b) We hope that Frank will <u>better</u> the record. (c) The little craft will soon <u>near</u> the shore. (d) The dealer <u>upped</u> the price of cars.

The Structure of Your Language   pp. 79-80:   1. poor   2. dance   3. Tomorrow   4. Traveling   5. Driving all the way   6. To spread   7. What our plans will be   8. attention   9. dig   10. him   11. calling 12. aged   13. ambitious   14. when   15. to go home

CHAPTER 4   *Verbals*
pages 81-100

Exercise 1   p. 83:   1. **worn**—out, *adv;* by . . . work, *prep p*   2. **to build** —on . . . side, *prep p;* school, *comp*   3. **Playing**—on . . . pavement, *prep p;*

hopscotch, *comp* 4. **to be seen**—in . . . coat, *prep p* 5. **to go**—to . . .
camp, *prep p;* next summer *n* as *adv* 6. **to eat**—before bedtime, *prep p;* fudge,
comp 7. **to move**—forward, *adv;* at daybreak, *prep p* 8. **to make**—for the
party, *prep p;* cake, *comp* 9. **Rowing**—easily, *adv;* over . . . lake, *prep p*
10. **Chilled**—by the wind, *prep p* 11. **washing**—car, *comp* 12. **Cheer-**
ing—wildly, *adv*

Exercise 2 *pp. 86-87:* 1. to be . . . sailor, *do* 2. to fail . . . examination, *subj* 3. to translate, *adj m* 4. to open . . . door, *object of prep*
5. to leave tomorrow, *do* 6. to play tennis, *vm* 7. to advance . . . woods,
lvc 8. to erect . . . house, *subj* 9. to drive . . . city, *app* 10. to drive
slowly, *nonfinite pred* 11. to wear . . . dress, *vm* 12. to leave . . . tomorrow, *do* 13. To be sure, *abs* 14. to be played tonight, *nm* 15. to see
. . . St. Louis, *vm* 16. to see . . . mother-in-law, *adj m* 17. to wash . . .
wedding, *do* 18. to be receding rapidly, *lvc* 19. to buy . . . broom,
nonfinite pred 20. hide Tom's ice skates, *nonfinite pred* 21. To put . . .
briefly, *abs* 22. to be solved, *nm* 23. to be allowed . . . wife, *app;* to see,
do 24. to buy the car, *adj m* 25. to know . . . happened, *lvc*

Exercise 3 *pp. 87-88:* See text pages 83-86 for sentences illustrating the
various functions of the infinitive.

Exercise 4 *pp. 89-90:* 1. Descending . . . ocean—subj; miles, *adv comp* 2.
giving . . . paint—object of prep; it, *io;* paint, *do* 3. baby-sitting . . . night—
app 4. sorting . . . fruit—lvc; culls, *do* 5. cultivating . . . orchids—lvc;
varieties, *do* 6. chewing . . . grass—object of prep 7. catching . . . trout
—object of prep; quota, *do* 8. rising . . . breakfast—comp 9. Raising
sandworms—subj; sandworms, *do* 10. squeezing . . . corners—object of prep
11. being suspicious—object of prep; suspicious, *lvc* 12. Feeding . . . animals
—subj; animals, *do*

Exercise 5 *pp. 92-93:* 1. water, Abe 2. C 3. anchor, we 4.
C 5. Kasimars, thrilled . . . barbecue, 6. C 7. dogs, whimpering
. . . terror, 8. trail, Doc 9. truck, swerving . . . corner, 10. C

Exercise 6 *p. 93:* 1. Dancing is fun. 2. We watched the crowd leaving the grandstand. 3. Walking along the boardwalk, the delegates enjoyed
the cool ocean breeze. 4. Mother enjoys playing bridge. 5. He is thinking of buying a new car. 6. This table seems broken beyond repair. 7. Her
job is teaching the fifth grade. 8. They found Helen bored. 9. The job,
answering the phone for six salesmen, did not appeal to Janice. 10. He thought
of his brother, working in the coal mine.

Exercise 7 *pp. 94-95:* 1. Walking with Agnes—gp, subj 2. Strolling
down the road—pp, mod (I) 3. strolling . . . suit—pp, mod (William) 4.

no verbal   **5.** going . . . supermarket—gp, object of prep   **6.** Shaken . . .
panic—pp, mod (Herman)   **7.** aching with misery—pp, mod (Julie)   **8.**
photographing hummingbirds—gp, lvc   **9.** talking in assembly—gp, do   **10.**
no verbal   **11.** sitting . . . bench—pp, mod (woman)   **12.** Pushing and
shoving—pp, mod (boys)   **13.** amused . . . lights—pp, mod (baby)   **14.**
doing his job—gp, object of prep   **15.** putting out the cat—gp, app (job)
16. growing . . . asparagus—gp, do   **17.** excited . . . news—pp, lvc   **18.** no
verbal   **19.** Sleeping—gp, subj   **20.** no verbal   **21.** Running . . . stairs
—pp, mod (boy)   **22.** built . . . century—pp, mod (castle)   **23.** shattered . . . hand—pp, mod (vase)   **24.** Having finished their work—pp, mod
(painters)

Exercise 8   ***pp. 95-96:***   **1.** willing, *vb;* to buy, *inf*   **2.** served, *part*   **3.** to
play, *inf*   **4.** Winking, *part;* walked, *vb*   **5.** promised, *vb;* to finish, *inf*   **6.**
looking, *ger;* boarded, *vb*   **7.** asked, *vb;* to run, *inf*   **8.** walked, *vb;* feeling, *part*
9. contended, *part*   **10.** painting, *ger*   **11.** to demolish, *inf*   **12.** flagged,
vb; standing, *part*   **13.** standing, *vb;* approaching, *part*   **14.** excited, *vb;*
blowing, *part*   **15.** granted, *vb;* to hold, *inf*   **16.** Rowing, *ger*   **17.** written, *part;* sent, *vb*   **18.** walking, *part* (In this sentence, a participle functions
as a verb-modifier. Earlier in the history of our language, this construction took the
form of a gerund: *go on walking.*)   **19.** milking, *ger*   **20.** milking, *vb*
21. ordered, *vb;* covered, *part;* buried, *part;* whipped, *part*   **22.** to stay, *inf;*
shouting, *ger*   **23.** found, *vb;* bruised and broken, *part*   **24.** collecting, *ger*
25. collecting, *vb*

Chapter Test, Form A   ***p. 98:***   **1.** (a) Henry Adams, whistling a merry tune,
breezed into the living room.   (b) Hortense enjoys picking out tunes on the guitar.
(c) It is time to go to bed.   (d) Grandma's hobby is painting murals.   (e) Mrs.
Oddfellow looks charming in her new ensemble.   (f) A defendant is foolish to
argue his own case.   (g) He spoke of resigning his commission.   (h) To get to
Manchester tomorrow is impossible.   (i) He spoke about all the children suffering
from malnutrition.   (j) Father asked Joe to wash the car.   **2.** (a) Diving and
striking—pp, mod (hummingbirds); to rout . . . size—ip, comp   (b) camping . . .
mountains—gp, subj; to spend . . . vacation—ip, mod (way)   (c) to go . . . school
—ip, do   (d) to beat . . . election—ip, mod (man)   (e) frozen in rich cream—
pp, mod (strawberries)   (f) buying . . . car—gp, object of prep   (g) painted . . .
barn—pp, mod (sign); baking—participle, mod (powder)   (h) to go—ip, mod
(ready)   (i) to fight . . . fire—ip, mod (came)   (j) terribly frightened . . . storm
—pp, lvc

Chapter Test, Form B   ***pp. 98-99:***   **1.** (a) Walking briskly before breakfast
is invigorating.   (b) He scrambled over the fence to get away from the goat.
(c) Alice Adkins has a new hobby, collecting bottle tops.   (d) You will have to
be there early to obtain good seats.   (e) They found the boy curled up on the
back seat.   (f) They considered his conduct annoying beyond forgiveness.   (g)
Grandpa wants to play checkers again.   (h) The plan is to leave Prescott early in

the morning.   (i) <u>Groping his way across the darkened room,</u> the intruder suddenly stumbled over a footstool.   (j) The principal requested <u>everybody to remain
seated.</u>   **2.**   (a) grazing . . . river—pp, mod (cattle)   (b) hiking . . . mountains—gp, do   (c) to ski . . . Death—ip, lvc   (d) to own . . . eagle—ip, app (it)
(e) roasted . . . hour—pp, mod (corn)   (f) playing . . . band—gp, lvc   (g) playing—gerund, do   (h) men to advance . . . highway—subj-inf structure   (i) Seizing
. . . hand—pp, mod (woman)   (j) to win—ip, mod (plays)

The Structure of Your Language   **pp. 99-100:**   **1.** Playing in the sandbox
in kindergarten, little Mike was lonesome for his mother.   **2.** Seated on our
front porch, we could see the moon rising over the distant hills.   **3.** I dislike
dogs when they are barking.   **4.** While driving recklessly on the thruway, Herman was flagged down by an officer.   **5.** Around his neck he wore a scarf tied
with two intricate knots.   **6.** The leather-bound books on the desk belong to
Helen.   **7.** On the wall, Mrs. Prince hung a picture painted by Rembrandt.
8. The minister ate a piece of Mother's delicious apple pie, topped with ice cream.

CHAPTER **5**   *Appositives and Absolutes*
pages 101-110

Exercise 1   **pp. 102-103:**   **1.** gorilla (Herbert, *subj*)   **2.** Robert Frost
(poet, *subj*)   **3.** Bob Hornblower (friend, *comp*)   **4.** cell (cell, *lvc*)   **5.**
trader (Hiram Scott, *object of prep*)   **6.** college (William and Mary, *object of
prep*)   **7.** one (St. Louis, *subj*); river (Mississippi, *object of prep*)   **8.**
Robinson Crusoe (novel, *object of prep*)   **9.** fish (barracuda, *object of prep*)
10. trip (prize, *comp*)

Exercise 2   **p. 105:**   **A.** **1.** descriptive   **2.** identifying   **3.** identifying   **4.** descriptive   **5.** descriptive   **6.** descriptive   **7.** descriptive (2)
8. identifying   **9.** descriptive   **10.** descriptive   **B.** **1.** all—funct word
app subj (girls)   **2.** to mixing . . . and spreading—inf app adv m (to frosting)
3. one—funct word app subj of inf (members)   **4.** to listen—inf app subj (To
hear)   **5.** instructing—gerund app subj (Teaching)   **6.** that . . . traps—n
cl app do (truth)   **7.** to . . . Italy—prep p app vm (to Europe)   **8.** Jenny
Mae and I—app funct word as subj (Two)   **9.** of . . . industry—prep p app
nm (of . . . cities)   **10.** that . . . waves—n cl app funct word as subj (It)
11. to dismiss . . . fantasy—ip app funct word as subj (It)   **12.** that . . .
humanity—n cl app subj (fact)

Exercise 3   **pp. 105-106:**   **1.** James Stewart, the office <u>boy,</u> has just received
a raise.   **2.** Father just bought a new stallion, a handsome <u>thoroughbred.</u>   **3.**

They moved to Albany, the capital of New York.   **4.** My brother Donald will graduate in June. The fact that you're so sensitive isn't helping matters any. I myself will prepare the posters. We will all go.   **5.** William James, a freshman Senator, will address the assembly. Bud is eager to overhaul his engine, to get everything in working order. The computer accurately predicted the outcome, that the state would vote Republican. The Goldens, all ten of them, are coming for dinner.   **6.** They have a cottage at the shore, at Rockaway Beach.   **7.** Speaking in public, addressing a large audience, is good experience for the young student of politics.   **8.** Henry wants to go home, to visit his parents in Alabama.   **9.** The story, that Uncle Sean has gone to Ireland, is not true.   **10.** Joe finally mastered the theorem that the sum of two sides of a triangle is greater than the third side.   **11.** It is undoubtedly true that man has descended from the anthropoids.   **12.** It is a sin to tell a lie.

Exercise 4   p. 106:   Henry James, a subway conductor, worked every night from four until midnight. The subway in which he worked was in New York City, probably the busiest city in the world. ¶ One night during the winter, while the train was heading south from 183 Street, a station on the East Side in the Bronx, Henry saw a little girl who was all alone and in tears. He asked her what was wrong. ¶ "I've lost my mother," she sobbed. "She got off at one of the stations back there and left me." ¶ Henry looked at the child, a thin little waif who seemed half-starved. She was wearing a skimpy coat that just about buttoned across her chest. It was evident that she was quite poor. Henry James, an old man who had seen difficult times, thought he was hardened to life. But now the plight of the little girl, her tears and her poverty, filled him with pity. "We'll find your mother," he said. "Just leave it to old Henry."

Exercise 5   p. 107:   **Line 1**—The weather being mild   **Line 3**—As a matter of fact   **Line 5**—Breakfast over   **Line 6**—the kitten; His . . . satisfaction   **Line 10**—Careful . . . is   **Line 12**—To be sure   **Line 13**—Too . . . quickly   **Line 15**—In my opinion   **Line 16**—His face . . . embarrassment

Chapter Test, Form A   pp. 108-109:   **1.** (a) The poet Milton wrote *Paradise Lost*. (b) Mrs. Prawn has bought a new home, a bungalow in Seaside Park. (c) It is unfortunate that Stella has the measles. (d) It is dangerous to drive fast on narrow roads. (e) The weather being fair, we all went for a walk. (f) Jim, the tallest boy on the team, was named captain. (g) I gave the keys to Miss Crooks, the new English teacher. **2.** (a) capital—nonrestrictive app (b) *The Return of the Native*—restrictive app (c) The services over—abs (d) scholarship—nonrestrictive app (e) all—restrictive app (f) choice—nonrestrictive app (g) that you . . . speaker—restrictive app (h) her face . . . smiles—abs

Chapter Test, Form B   p. 109:   **1.** (a) Mother invited my roommate Jim Wilson. (b) The champion, a native of Australia, can run a mile in four minutes. (c) The lawyer disclosed the fact that the accused was a minor. (d) He had made a special plea, <u>to go to see his ailing mother.</u>   (e) They boarded the schooner, a rum <u>runner</u> from Malago.   (f) They arrested my cousin <u>Aristides.</u>   **2.**   (a) his appetite . . . speed—abs   (b) capital—nonrestrictive app   (c) a . . . cup and a trip . . . —nonrestrictive app   student—nonrestrictive app   (d) all—restrictive app   teacher—nonrestrictive app   (e) decision—nonrestrictive app   (f) that . . . governor—restrictive app   (g) to become . . . nurse—nonrestrictive app   (h) Teeth chattering—abs

The Structure of Your Language   *p. 110:*   **1.**   Father hired a new accountant, a recent graduate of the University of California.   **2.**   Margaret Mitchell, a native of the South of Irish parentage, is famous for having written *Gone with the Wind*, a singularly popular novel.   **3.**   The common law of England, a mighty instrument of freedom's growth, also forms the basis of American law and justice.   **4.** Mr. Wilson, a chemical engineer, lives next door to us.   **5.**   During the night, a heavy rain, a total of four inches in three hours, washed out the roads.   **6.** Nathaniel Hawthorne wrote *The Scarlet Letter*, the story of Hester Prynne.   **7.** The voters rejected the bond issue for a new sewer system, an unfortunate choice for a rapidly growing city.   **8.**   Valparaiso, one of Chile's most progressive cities, is also an important manufacturing center.   **9.**   Valentine's Day, once a pagan feast, is celebrated today as a festival of romance and affection.   **10.**   Temperature affects viscosity, that property of a fluid that causes it to resist flowing.

CHAPTER **6** *Agreement*
pages 111-126

Exercise 1   *pp. 114-115:*   **1.**   goes (1)   **2.**   play (1)   **3.**   looks (1) **4.**   look (1)   **5.**   am (3)   **6.**   are (3)   **7.**   is (2)   **8.**   was (4)   **9.** are (2)   **10.**   writes (2)   **11.**   write (2)   **12.**   belongs (1)   **13.**   belong (1)   **14.**   has (5)   **15.**   have (5)

Exercise 2   *p. 115:*   **1.**   go   **2.**   lives   **3.**   are   **4.**   leaves   **5.**   was **6.**   does   **7.**   are   **8.**   were   **9.**   hate   **10.**   has

Exercise 3   *p. 118:*   **1.**   cows / were driven (5)   **2.**   children / attend (1)   **3.**   he / leaves (2)   **4.**   I / plan, *no agr*   **5.**   men / are coming (5) **6.**   club / will meet, *no agr*   **7.**   She / sweeps (2)   **8.**   Miss Garve / likes (1)   **9.**   We / can see, *no agr*   **10.**   You / were, *no agr*   **11.**   We / are planning (5)   **12.**   information / must fall, *no agr*   **13.**   He / gave, *no agr*   **14.**   cameras / are designed (5)   **15.**   trees / grow (1)   **16.**   She / is (2)   **17.**   telephone / has been ringing (5)   **18.**   orange / tastes (1) **19.**   You / are, *no agr*   **20.**   man / was rushed (5)   **21.**   Jim / keeps trying (5)   **22.**   boys / kept nagging, *no agr*   **23.**   I / am planning (5)   **24.** foundation / is being poured (5)   **25.**   people / are (1)

Exercise 4   *pp. 122-123:*   1. come   2. is   3. are   4. are   5. want   6. are   7. makes   8. was   9. go   10. object   11. am   12. are   13. deals   14. were   15. is   16. Were   17. is   18. doesn't   19. is   20. takes

Exercise 5   *pp. 123-124:*   1. The petunia and the sunflower are Mother's favorite flowers.   2. Mr. Thew and his wife are leaving for Siberia next week.   3. There are the women who are the mainstays of our organization.   4. None of the chops are fit to eat.   5. Where is the boy who is looking for a summer job at Camp Walden?   6. Mr. Tewksbury, along with his seven motherless children, is moving to Rainbow Springs.   7. Helen is one of those girls who always want something to eat after a movie date.   8. Neither the history test nor the French exams were especially difficult.   9. Neither James nor I have been invited to Rosemarie's party.   10. Both are usually ravenously hungry.

Chapter Test, Form A   *p. 125:*   1. (a) The old lady paints very well.   (b) The horses ran across the field.   (c) I attend classes at Harvard.   (d) He likes spinach.   (e) The children were all there.   (f) He is my brother.   (g) The dog is barking.   (h) The dogs are barking.   (i) Jaybird, with her two cousins, is spending the summer on her uncle's ranch.   (j) Here come my mammy and my pappy.   2. (a) has   (b) is   (c) is   (d) have   (e) is   (f) go   (g) refuse   (h) am   (i) come   (j) is   (k) are   (l) was   (m) is   (n) doesn't   (o) Weren't

Chapter Test, Form B   *pp. 125-126:*   1. (a) The horses run wild over the desert.   (b) The man painted the barn.   (c) I walked to the village in fifteen minutes.   (d) He writes well.   (e) The boy was ill.   (f) He is the winner.   (g) The salesmen have gone to Utica.   (h) The salesman has gone to Utica.   (i) The table, as well as the chairs, was stained a deep mahogany.   (j) There are your books.   2. (a) come   (b) deals   (c) were   (d) keeps   (e) participate   (f) is   (g) is   (h) come   (i) are   (j) Were   (k) doesn't   (l) were   (m) takes   (n) are

CHAPTER 7   *Substitution*
pages 127-146

Exercise 1   *p. 131:*   1. their—third, pl, poss (Doris and Mae)   2. I —first, sing, subj; your—second, poss   3. her—third, sing, feminine, poss (Mrs. Leman); my—first, sing, poss   4. his—third, sing, masculine, poss (Henry); her—third, sing, feminine, obj (mother); his—third, sing, masculine, poss (Henry)   5. Our—first, pl, poss; its—third, sing, neuter, poss (car)   6. he—third, sing, masculine, subj (Paul); her—third, sing, feminine, obj (Martha); him—third, sing, masculine, obj (Paul)   7.   We—first, pl, subj; you—second, subj; our—first, pl, poss   8.   I—first, sing, subj; your—second, poss; mine—first, sing, poss   9. us—first, pl, obj   10.   me—first, sing, obj; her—third, sing, feminine, poss (Mary Jane); her—third, sing, feminine, obj (Mary Jane)   11.   she—third, sing, feminine, subj (Mrs. Smith)   12.   its—third, sing, neuter, poss (mongrel); it—third, sing, neuter, subj (mongrel)   13.   them—third, pl, obj (boys); their—third, pl, poss (boys)   14.   It—third, sing, neuter, subj (book); my—first, sing, poss (Bobby); his—third, sing, masculine, poss

Exercise 2   pp. 131-132:   1.   She—third, sing, feminine, subj (Mrs. Sullivan)
2.   him—third, sing, masculine, obj (mailman)   3.   He—third, sing, masculine, subj (Jack)   4.   They—third, pl, subj (the Andersons)   5.   you—second, subj   6.   I—first, sing, subj   7.   them—third, pl, obj (boys)   8.   his— third, sing, masculine, poss (Mr. Brown)   9.   my—first, sing, poss   10.   it— third, sing, neuter, subj (tire)   11.   We—first, pl, subj (Jack and I)   12. me—first, sing, obj   13.   ours—first, pl, poss   14.   my—first, sing, poss   15. its—third, sing, neuter, poss (ship)

Exercise 3   pp. 132-133:   1.   <u>We</u> live on Broadway.   2.   He nodded politely to <u>us</u>.   3.   When Alice came home, we gave <u>her</u> the letter.   4.   The boys ate <u>their</u> dinner hurriedly.   5.   She wants <u>me</u> to take her to the prom. 6.   When John came in late, the teacher looked at <u>him</u> sharply.   7.   When the Carsons return, Mother will invite <u>them</u> to dinner.   8.   The dog wagged <u>its</u> tail. 9.   John said that the coat was <u>his</u>.   10.   When Kathy heard the phone, <u>she</u> was sure the call was <u>hers</u> and rushed downstairs before <u>her</u> father could answer.   11. <u>I</u> want <u>my</u> pay.   12.   I have invited <u>you</u> to go with me, because I know that <u>you</u> enjoy music.

Exercise 4   p. 137:   1.   that, *sub;* their, *ppr*   2.   My, *ppr;* I, *ppr;* our- selves, *refl*   3.   All, *dtr;* my, *ppr;* I, *ppr*   4.   This, *dtr;* my, *ppr;* yours, *ppr* 5.   my, *ppr;* that, *sub*   6.   We, *ppr;* who, *sub;* his, *ppr*   7.   You, *ppr;* your, *ppr*   8.   he, *ppr;* his, *ppr;* us, *ppr*   9.   herself, *refl;* her, *ppr*   10.   This, *dtr;* my, *ppr;* that, *dtr;* my, *ppr*

Exercise 5   pp. 138-139:   1.   me   2.   me   3.   We   4.   he   5.   she 6.   I   7.   he   8.   me   9.   he   10.   me   11.   me   12.   He

Exercise 6   p. 140:   1.   that *or* which   2.   that   3.   whom *or* that 4.   whose   5.   who   6.   whose   7.   that *or* which   8.   whom   9. who   10.   that *or* which

Exercise 7   pp. 142-143:   1.   Bud Ellis challenged Jody Baker to a game of chess when they met at the Recreation Center.   2.   When the roof sprung a bad leak, all the clothes stored in the attic were ruined.   3.   According to this morn-

ing's paper, Route 4 can't be used until the flood damage is repaired.   **4.**   Patricia
reported that Ellen's essay on fire prevention won first prize in the Kiwanis contest.
5.   Dad pointed out the ragged seat covers and the rusty tire rims, but the dealer
insisted on asking a thousand dollars for the used car.   **6.**   When Mrs. Ames
drove into Tillamook last week, Mother had lunch with her.   **7.**   Whitey said,
"Yogi, where is my (*or* your) baseball gear?"   **8.**   The center outmaneuvered
his guard and crammed the ball through the basket for two points.   **9.**   We
visited Buckingham Palace where we watched the changing of the guard.   **10.**
Mike told Kevin to ask Dad for the car keys.

Chapter Test, Form A   pp. 144-145:   **1.**   See page 128.   **2.**   (a) his—third,
sing, masculine, poss   (b) us—first, pl, obj   (c) Your—second, poss   (d) My—
first, sing, poss; her—third, sing, feminine, poss   (e) It—third, sing, neuter, subj;
it—third, sing, neuter, subj; ours—first, pl, poss   **3.**   (a) The teacher gave the
book to me.   (b) The Bensons drove their boys to camp.   (c) She told me to go
home.   (d) Mother gave them a good dinner.   (e) Jimmy claims the book is his.
4.   (a) himself   (b) me   (c) he   (d) which   (e) who   (f) whom   (g) me   (h)
his   (i) We   (j) I   **5.**   (a) Henry saw his girl at the Snack Shop with Bill.
(b) Mr. Grodsky mows the lawn by hand because he claims the exercise keeps him
physically fit.   (c) Who is the boy that ran the ball for a gain of twelve yards?

Chapter Test, Form B   pp. 145-146:   **1.**   See text page 128.   **2.**   (a) her
—third, sing, feminine, poss; she—third, sing, feminine, subj   (b) they—third, pl,
subj   (c) them—third, pl, obj   (d) Your—second, sing, poss   (e) it—third, sing,
neuter, obj   **3.**   (a) We will dine with the Bunches tomorrow.   (b) The teacher
gave her the prize.   (c) You will all go to the cafeteria for lunch.   (d) The canary
sang its little song.   (e) When Jim raised his hand, the teacher called on him.
4.   (a) herself   (b) me   (c) his   (d) himself   (e) whom   (f) that   (g) us   (h)
whom   (i) me   (j) I   **5.**   (a) The picket fence around our house needs
painting.   (b) Because his father is a doctor, Fred wants to make medicine his
profession.   (c) Joe is a fishing enthusiast; however, he never likes to clean the fish.

The Structure of Your Language   p. 146:   **1.**   Walking home from church
with Sally Jones was exhilarating.   **2.**   Father dashed excitedly up the path.
3.   Dyane flounced out of the car, slamming the door.   **4.**   A forlorn cow blinked
at us with eyes that spoke of tragedy.

CHAPTER **8**   *Punctuation*
pages 147-170

Exercise 1   p. 150:   (The number of sentences should be estimated at either
9 or 11; the semicolons indicated on lines 15 and 20 could also signal a sentence

break. Internal punctuation is not given here, because not everyone will read with the same intonation.)   **Line 3**—below. This   **Line 4**—day. It   **Lines 6-7**—it. It   **Line 8**—vine. Horses   **Line 12**—San Luis Rey. St.   **Line 14**—side. The   **Line 15**—forever; it   **Line 16**—break. The   **Line 19**—again. People **Line 20**—muttering; they   **Line 21**—gulf.

Exercise 2   pp. 152-153:   (There is no single-bar juncture in sentences 2, 4, 6, 7, 9, 10, 11, 13, and 14.)   1. White | gritty dust lay on the top of the table. White, gritty dust   3. Mr. Jones is an honest | respectable citizen. an honest, respectable citizen   5. Careless | irresponsible campers have caused raging forest fires. Careless, irresponsible campers   8. The Browns just bought a comfortable | inexpensive home. a comfortable, inexpensive home   12. It was an unavoidable | regrettable error. an unavoidable, regrettable error   15. We will give the matter our careful | undivided attention. our careful, undivided attention

Exercise 3   pp. 154-155:   (In sentences 1, 5, 6, 8, 9, 10, 11, 13, 14, and 15, the clause is restrictive.)   2. Jim is a salesman for the Union Gas Company || which has its main office on First Street. Company, which   3. Michelangelo | who worshiped beauty | regarded himself as ugly. Michelangelo, who worshiped beauty,   4. Dr. Ambrose | who graduated from Johns Hopkins University in 1949 | will lecture at the seminar. Dr. Ambrose, who graduated from Johns Hopkins University in 1949,   7. Annie said that she would have to consult her husband || who is in the real estate business. husband, who   12. The new *Bounty* | which was launched in the summer of 1960 | is thirty feet longer than the original. The new *Bounty*, which was launched in the summer of 1960,

Exercise 4   pp. 158-159:   1. The brave company fought bitterly, but . . . troops.   2. Why . . . there, Paula?   3. The mayor of the village, a dignified . . . beard, conducted . . . castle.   4. On May 12, 1883, a . . . Akron, Ohio. 5. The . . . benediction; the . . . leave.   6. Dad's . . . Robert Frost's "Mending Wall."   7. On the other hand, we . . . again.   8. The . . . squeaks, squawks, and . . . blowhole.   9. If Dad's . . . materialize, we . . . summer.   10. "I'll defend you," said the lawyer, "but we'll . . . carefully."   11. Waddling in Indian file, the . . . barn.   12. Frank is a good student; nevertheless, he'll . . . Stanford. 13. "Why doesn't . . . time?" asked Florence.   14. A . . . Fourth of July, when . . . fireworks.   15. Two giraffes, legs . . . angle, were . . . pool.   16. It . . . late, and . . . soon.   17. Ladies and gentlemen, may . . . attention?   18. An article called "The Great Antagonism" appeared in the <u>Atlantic Monthly</u> of November, 1958. (*or* November 1958.)   19. You . . . <u>and</u>'s and <u>but</u>'s in your writing.   20. Mrs. Malaprop asked, "What business have you, Miss, with the words <u>preference</u> and <u>aversion</u>?"   21. When . . . away, Grandfather . . . swim. 22. There are three <u>8</u>'s in our new license number.

Exercise 5   p. 162:   1. In . . . burned; a . . . mountain.   2. There is, to be sure, more . . . eye.   3. On December 5, 1955, Walter Reuther . . . Organizations (AFL-CIO).   4. Shippers, for example, could . . . rates.   5.

In the 1850's clipper ships (two of the most famous were the Sea Witch and the Flying Cloud) challenged . . . seas.   **6.** They had, however, other . . . commendable.   **7.** Mayor Thomas Walsh, who . . . years, will retire in November.   **8.** He's . . . nails, yet . . . corniness.   **9.** Simple machinery, such as . . . gates, is . . . China.   **10.** Young . . . pinafore—sometimes white, sometimes black— over . . . dresses.

Exercise 6   *pp. 165-166:*   (Most appositives may be set off by dashes or commas.)   **1.** The minister . . . Psalms LXXXIV:8, "Show us, O Lord, thy mercy and grant us thy salvation."   **2.** We . . . Nassau Harbor, where . . . boats.   **3.** They . . . desperado, an ex-convict . . . record, in one of the canyons north of Globe City.   **4.** Joy sat on every countenance, and there was a glad . . . intensity in every eye. (Here, the ellipsis marks are part of the inserted punctuation.)   **5.** The . . . orders: Company K . . . Camp Wadsworth.   **6.** Enjoying . . . Everest: much . . . approach.   **7.** The . . . Act II; then . . . began.   **8.** A sail. . . Albany—a distance of about 150 miles—provides . . . history.   **9.** She . . . change: three shillings, a half-crown, and five pennies.   **10.** Two . . . Smith— William and Andrew—are . . . throat.   **11.** In . . . question, "Why so pale and wan, fond lover?"   **12.** There's good news tonight!   **13.** The . . . Brother Orchid . . . at 2:45.   **14.** "Oats," said Mrs. MacGregor, "are best for feeding young stock: calves, puppies, colts, and boys."   **15.** We enjoyed John Keats' sonnet "On the Grasshopper and Cricket"; it . . . Leigh Hunt.   **16.** Miss Watts asked, "Have you read Byron's 'Darkness,' a poem of speculation on the end of the world?"   **17.** My, what a fright you gave me!   **18.** The farmer exclaimed, "Look out for that horse!"   **19.** I've . . . Josephine Tey's Miss Pym Disposes, a . . . favorite.   **20.** The . . . success—a never-to-be-forgotten . . . memories.   **21.** The . . . kilometers (a kilometer is about five-eighths of a mile), and . . . way.   **22.** Johnny . . . said, "Yes, I'm ready"; however, the . . . stomach.   **23.** Joel . . . inn—an exceedingly poor one as it later turned out—he . . . meal.   **24.** The . . . July 14, 1846; in it . . . greeting.   **25.** Emerson urged Americans to think independently: "We have listened too long to the courtly muses of Europe . . . ." (The ellipsis is part of the inserted punctuation.)   **26.** To . . . you, I really don't . . . energy.   **27.** "You may go," said Mother, "but you'll . . . eleven."

Chapter Test, Form A   *pp. 167-168:*   **1.** On November 10, 1951, Lieutenant Ted Gunn of the sheriff's police was cruising near Oxford, Michigan, when . . . Route 4.   **2.** The . . . yesterday.   **3.** Freedom . . . Africa; nevertheless, rapid . . . way.   **4.** Harry's convinced that he's . . . afternoon: a visit to the zoo, a leisurely stroll through the park, and a . . . milkshake.   **5.** Mother remarked fearfully, "I wouldn't drive so fast on this road, James; it's much too bumpy."   **6.** Did you know, for example, that . . . soapmaking—a thriving . . . West Indies?   **7.** "Help!" shouted Mr. Abernathy. "I've been robbed!"   **8.** Few towns . . . Paris, France, but . . . development.   **9.** "Who can identify the meter in William Blake's 'The Chimney Sweeper'?" asked Miss Pym.   **10.** The lake, which . . . hillside, shone . . . morning.   **11.** In Miss Kenway's English II class, the use of too many and's and but's is known as "overcoordinitis."   **12.** The . . . room, her . . . anger.

Chapter Test, Form B   *pp. 168-169:*   1. My . . . ambitions: to graduate from college with honors, to get a good job, to marry his high school sweetheart, and to own a home in Beacon Hill.   2. The . . . Port-au-Prince, Haiti, sold, of all things, chandeliers . . . cans.   3. The novel <u>Dr. Zhivago</u> has . . . century; some critics, however, believe . . . overrated.   4. There are four <u>s</u>'s in <u>stresses.</u>   5. Our luncheon, which cost seven shillings (about ninety-eight cents), consisted of four dishes: mutton steak, boiled potatoes, cabbage, and a tart for dessert.   6. The Irish uprising on April 24, 1916, marked the beginning of a long, bitter struggle for independence.   7. Was . . . said, "Diplomacy . . . cool"?   8. "Scat! Get out of there!" shouted George, flapping . . . tree.   9. The . . . yard, its . . . breathing.   10. "At every dinner party," said Kin Hubbard, "there's somebody who eats all the celery."   11. Be sure to read "Which Old Wives Tale Do You Believe?" on page 211 of the <u>Reader's Digest.</u>   12. Were you aware, for example, that frozen foods now include these delicacies: Chinese egg roll, frog's legs, and pressed pheasant?

The Structure of Your Language   *pp. 169-170:*   A. 1. Ì am gôing hóme.
2. Whên are yóu góing hòme?   3. Ì was going hóme, but it râined.   4. It was níce to mêet yòu.   5. Ì néver eat spînach.   6. Mary Jâne is mỳ síster.
7. Henry Jàmes wòn the príze.   8. Môther, you have my fàther much offénded.

B. 1. I know the answer # (stress marks: 2 3 1)   2. Have you a headache || (2 3)   3. Where are my sneakers # (3 1 2)   4. Are these your sister's books || (2 3)   5. His story is unbelievable # (2 4, 3 1)   6. Are you Harry Jones || (2)   7. You're really going to Paris || (3 2, 4)
8. Please keep off the grass # (2 3 1)   C. 1. Professor Henry Watts | the successful physicist | lectured to the science faculty #   2. How many were going to St. Ives #   3. Do you live in Brooklyn || 4. When the cat's away || the mice will play #   5. The little old lady who lived in a shoe had so many children she didn't know what to do #   6. The troops hiked eight kilometers | five miles | to the camp #   7. Did you watch the late movie last night || 8. Mrs. Lowe served apple pie || ice cream | and hot chocolate #

CHAPTER 9   *Phonemes and Graphemes in English*
pages 171-192

Exercise 1   *p. 174:*   1. ai, oo, ou   2. the, there, other   3. sh, ti
4. ph   5. tt   6. ch   7. 9   8. graphemes, are, there, figures

Exercise 2   *p. 175:*   1. nine, -ty, eight, Rose, Mary, six, leg, -ed   2. re-, examine, -ing   3. create, -ure, -s   4. insects, concluded, different

Exercise 4   *pp. 179-180:*
\ri-'fyüt\   \bō-'kāz, bü-'kāz\   \fərst-'rāt\
\'kraŋks\   \'hwēd-əl\   \plē-ziŋ-lē\
\'myülz\   \'laŋ-gwij\   \'bät-əl-ˌnek\
\'ātth\   \'plezh-ər, 'plāzh-ər\   \'thȯt-fəl\
\'chȯis\   \'liŋ-gwəsts\   \'fōt-ə-ˌgrafs\
\'maȯnt\   \ig-'zis-təns, ig-'zis-tənts\   \'līt-'fȯt-əd\
\'klōthd\   \ik-'spəl-shən\   \ˌen-ər-'jèt-i-klē, ˌen-ər-'jet-i-kə-lē\

Exercise 5   *pp. 182-183:*   1. island (isle)   2. psychology   3. gnarled
4. khaki   5. pneumonia   6. hymn   7. mnemonic   8. psychiatrist
(psychologist)   9. indict   10. solder   11. aisle   12. rhythm   13.
wholly   14. jamb   15. knickknacks   16. thigh   17. diaphragm
18. behalf   19. wrench   20. wrought

Exercise 6   *pp. 184-185:*   1. council   2. plane, descent   3. past (through)
4. dessert   5. deceased   6. thorough   7. fair (right)   8. bridal
9. stationery, write   10. counsels (advises), our   11. advice   12. berth
13. whole   14. whose   15. bridle   16. desert   17. coarse   18.
through (past), conscious   19. lightning   20. capital   21. complimented
22. personnel   23. conscience, right   24. allusions   25. dyeing

Exercise 7   *p. 187:*   1. cashier, received   2. wiener, neither   3. leisure
4. friend, heinous   5. hygiene   6. weird   7. weir   8. shrieking, fierce,
lie   9. seized, reins   10. believe, shield, pierced   11. siege, yielded
12. neigh, heifers, neighboring, field   13. Conceit, grievous   14. lien   15.
pier, priest, fierce, mien   16. eighth   17. friend, piece, beige   18. financier, deceived, frieze

Exercise 8   *pp. 188-189:*   1. description   2. experience   3. criticize
4. fascinated   5. amateur   6. hindrance   7. professor   8. nuisance
9. temperament   10. ingenious   11. committee, eliminate   12. supersede   13. consistent   14. indispensable   15. sophomore, twelfth   16.
medieval, Renaissance (Note that *Renaissance* is usually capitalized in this context.)
17. disappear   18. analyze   19. religious   20. legitimate, accommodate
21. characteristics, appearance   22. heroes, villains   23. connoisseur

The Structure of Your Language   *pp. 191-192:*   1. chiropractor   2. khedive
3. psaltery   4. bazooka   5. chalice   6. dilemma, Scylla, Charybdis   7.
Eurydice   8. physiotherapy   9. rhynchocephalian   10. Phoenicians
11. chloroform, anesthesia   12. euphonium   13. excessive, gibberish   14.
lymph   15. saccharine   16. soporiferous   17. melee   18. occult

19. knowledgeable 20. psittacosis 21. recalcitrance 22. xerophthalmia 23. psychrometer 24. chautauqua 25. Hephaestus

CHAPTER **10** *Effective Sentence Structure pages 193-212*

Exercise 1 **pp. 196-197:** ¶ My English classroom is in the main building of South High School. To get to the room, I use the doorway on the west side of the building. I then proceed up the stairway to the second floor and down the hall to Room 205. ¶ Room 205 is about thirty feet wide and forty-eight feet long. It is exactly twelve feet high. About three feet from the floor on the front wall is a chalkboard with a small bulletin board at either end. The chalkboard-bulletin board arrangement extends nearly the whole width of the front wall. On the left portion of the chalkboard, a king-size calendar and a school information chart of equal size are propped in the chalk tray. There is usually a handwritten assignment on the right portion of the chalkboard. Only the center of the chalkboard is used while class is in session. Against the front wall on the left side is a green file cabinet made of wood. Between the side wall and the cabinet, two pipes run out of the wall and back down into the floor. Above the chalkboard are three black-framed prints representing three episodes in the life of Oliver Twist. To the right of the chalkboard just below the bulletin board is a pencil sharpener. The section of the wall above the chalkboard is painted creamy beige. The section below the chalkboard is deep brown. The side walls and the back wall continue this beige-brown combination. ¶ The left side of the room is solid wall broken only by six framed pictures. These pictures depict the life of another character from Dickens, David Copperfield. ¶ A large bulletin board is centered on the back wall at eye level. This board usually displays outstanding themes. ¶ The right wall is broken by two white-framed windows with brown cotton shades. Between the two windows is another bulletin board featuring book jackets. ¶ The ceiling is white with six modern fluorescent fixtures spaced in two rows of three. ¶ [Omission of the final paragraph improves the theme.]

Exercise 2 **p. 199:** ¶ Because they do not realize the responsibility of marriage, many young people rush into it without stopping to think of the consequences. Indeed, they seem to think that marriage is all love and kisses. On the contrary, it is an important step that should be planned carefully. ¶ Statistics about teen-age marriages—most of which end up in the divorce court—are grim. To begin with, young adults or teen-agers who have no sense of responsibility find it hard to settle down. If they marry while still in high school, the boy usually has to leave school to support his wife and, in time, his children. The boy has not finished high school, however, and cannot get a decent job. ¶ In effect, the young marrieds have deprived themselves of the right to grow up and enjoy life. It seems a shame to waste the teens—the most wonderful years of life—on marriage. ¶ When the stress and responsibility of marriage eventually kill it, the great love soon fades and married couples start quarreling while they are still young. ¶ People who marry should be mentally as well as physically mature. Although some young marrieds have made the necessary adjustments, they are in the minority. In my opinion, early marriages are a mistake. To make their marriages successful, teen-agers should wait until they are older and more mature with jobs and the money to buy what they need.

Exercise 3   pp. 200-201:   (One suggested solution is given for each item.)
1. Work on the new General Hospital to be built on Hill Street will start next Monday. The hospital will have two hundred beds and will be staffed by forty nurses and five resident physicians.   **2.** Dad's uncle, a well-known novelist who has written several best sellers, will publish his latest work, *Dead Leaves*, in October.
3. Mother knows that Charley wrecked Father's car; however, she told Charley that she would have it repaired.   **4.** Carl Sandburg, one of the great American poets, was born in Galesburg, Illinois, in 1878 and gained critical and public acclaim when his second poetic work, *Chicago Poems*, was published in 1916.   **5.** Jenny Couch will go to college in September. Since she wants to become a teacher, she plans to major in English and specialize in rhetoric.   **6.** Alfred, Lord Tennyson attended Cambridge University, but he was obliged to leave when his father died in 1831. He fell in love with Emily Sellwood, and although he had many family responsibilities, he was finally able to marry her in 1850.   **7.** Mr. Selby Swift was injured seriously when his car overturned on Route 66 near Williams, Arizona. Mr. Swift was driving seventy miles an hour at the time of the accident.   **8.** Willie Fitz, a shortstop with the Yuma Giants, hit two home runs in the game last night with the Bisbee Eagles, which Yuma won, 13 to 6.   **9.** A search is being made by a sheriff's posse for Jim Scott, an experienced prospector, who has been reported lost in the desert. He was last seen on Thursday in the Estrella Hills.
10. George B. McClelland—born in Philadelphia of wealthy parents, a top scholar at West Point, a railroad president at 32—commanded the Union Army in the War Between the States.

Exercise 4   pp. 201-202:   (One revision of each sentence is given here.)
1. This year Jim looked forward to making some money on the hay crop which was good in spite of the dry weather.   **2.** When World War II ended, the army was demobilized, and the soldiers were returned to their homes.   **3.** When the Reds lost to Milwaukee, the Dodgers moved into first place; but since there are more than two months of play remaining, victory for either team is only a possibility.
4. When the *Great Bear* sank in 1916 during an expedition to the Bering Sea, John Borden, the noted explorer who was first mate aboard the schooner, helped rescue other survivors.   **5.** Alessandro Volta, born in Como, Italy, in 1745, was able to obtain a continuous flow of electrical energy from an electrical battery which he invented.   **6.** Installment buying, called "hire purchase" in Britain, has almost doubled there since 1958, and now there is a car to every ten persons and a TV set to almost every family.   **7.** Mr. Watkins was so proud of his new car that he drove it around the block four times, but his wife became angry when he attempted the fifth circle.   **8.** Henry Hanks, working his way through college, had to work overtime to pay his food bills since his appetite was so enormous.   **9.** Thomas Hardy, born in Dorchester, England, in 1840 and educated as an architect,

became one of England's greatest novelists, but his real love was poetry.   **10.**
Although the detective knew who had committed the robbery, he was unable to find
a witness who would supply the evidence which was necessary to convict the suspect.

Exercise 5   *p. 204:*   1.   At sixteen a boy usually gains more freedom because
he is old enough to drive a car.   2.   After the sentimental songs which left the
audience practically in tears, some of the girls presented a clever fashion show as
their contribution to the church program.   3.   A boy who is deprived of a car
by his parents may well be pushed into idolizing money.   4.   I mow, weed, and
trim the lawn each week; then I water it to make it grow; and the following week
I start the same process all over again.   5.   When a girl hasn't been invited to
a dance—either by any boy or by the right boy—she sometimes goes alone to meet
someone new, to have a good time, or—as is more often the case—just for spite.

Exercise 6   *pp. 204-205:*   ¶ On May 18, 1960, Herbert Filbrick—an American counterspy who was known and trusted by some of the top Communist agents
in the country—strolled into a Chicago variety store with two American agents and
received a small wrapped package. ¶ After leaving the store and walking a couple
of blocks, Filbrick and the agents thought it would be wise to split up. Filbrick
caught a taxi and arrived home at five o'clock, where he waited impatiently for his
nine o'clock meeting with several Communist agents. While waiting, he unwrapped
the package which contained a cigarette lighter—actually a miniature tape recorder
with which he planned to tape the conversation at the meeting. When nine o'clock
arrived, Filbrick sped to a vacant warehouse in the industrial part of the city. Ten
or fifteen minutes after he arrived, everyone went in and sat at a long table. Present
at the meeting were the six top Communist spy ring leaders, a top Soviet agent
who had entered the country illegally, two strong arms, and two secretaries—one
of them Filbrick, who had been chosen because he could be trusted. ¶ Feeling more
and more at ease, Filbrick taped all the important conversation at the meeting,
whose purpose was to advance plans for stealing all the top secret information on the
rocket and missile programs in Washington, D.C. ¶ The meeting was nearing its
end when one of the Communist agents asked Filbrick for a light for his cigar. He
fumbled around and finally told the agent that his lighter didn't work. When the
agent insisted upon checking for himself, Filbrick was afraid not to let him have
the lighter. After looking at it, the agent gave it back, thinking it was out of fluid.
¶ After the meeting, Filbrick went home where he waited for the two American
agents to pick up the tape. When they arrived, they congratulated him on his
fine job.

Exercise 7   *p. 207:*   1.   Looking through my binoculars, I saw the enemy
troops coming over the crest of the hill.   2.   Father lost his upper denture while
he was swimming in Lake Tahoe.   3.   Having spent all his money at the circus,
Harold had nothing to do but return to school.   4.   To make a light, digestible
cake, add sour milk to the baking powder.   5.   While I was sitting on the park
bench, a beautiful red bird flew over the palm trees.   6.   We saw fifty beautiful
white swans flying gracefully across the lake.   7.   Helpers will record all of the

grades in a computer.   8.   Many times I have visited the spot where the Battle of Gettysburg was fought.   9.   Because Tin Roof was a very fast horse, Uncle Ben picked him to win by six lengths.

Exercise 8   *pp. 209-210:*   1.   The horse stumbled when he threw a shoe while jumping over the fence.   2.   When the band began to play, the young people started to dance.   3.   C   4.   He was the boy whom Martha used to date when she was a cheerleader.   5.   She always begins her concert with an aria from *Carmen;* then she continues with popular numbers that she has sung many times before.   6.   The boys in their hurry to get away had neglected to thank their hostess for a pleasant evening.   7.   The child clung to her mother in terror when she saw the roaring lions in the cage.   8.   C   9.   The entire class rose when Johnny raised the flag.   10.   Yesterday Sam gave us all the facts about the Battle of Bull Run.   11.   A great many books have been written on the battles of World War II.   12.   Before the use of modern drugs, many people became ill and died.   13.   Our teacher said she would let us do whatever we cared to during the last period.   14.   He said that he would try to improve his grades. 15.   Before his rescuers arrived, the trapper learned that his feet had frozen.

Chapter Test, Form A   *pp. 211-212:*   1.   The view from the mountain was very clear that afternoon; however, we . . . (comma fault)   2.   To raise good potatoes, one must have sandy soil enriched with . . . (dangling modifier)   3. The TV program I enjoyed last evening centered around an English teacher who had a great many problems. (run-together sentence)   4.   At the class picnic on Saturday, we swam in a beautiful lake and ate our lunch under some trees. (excessive coord)   5.   Father has just bought a new four-door Buick sedan with a blue body and a white top and foam-cushion seats equipped with seat belts. (lack of coord)   6.   Although my grades aren't as high as I had hoped they would be, I plan to go to college. (illogical sub)   7.   Walking down Main Street, we saw the get-away car turning the corner. (dangling mod)   8.   Today farmers are experimenting with better methods of producing grain; they are so . . . (comma fault)   9.   Reformers with fire in their eyes are always fighting for law improvements. (misplaced mod)   10.   In our commencement play, Bob, who is the class president, will have the leading role. (misplaced mod)

Chapter Test, Form B   *p. 212:*   1.   The army was halted temporarily by the river; therefore, the enemy troops . . . (comma fault)   2.   When the rain had stopped and while the campers were drying themselves out, many of us merely sat by patiently enjoying some good hot coffee. (parallel structure)   3.   Sitting in the stadium, the crowd enjoyed a fine game of football. (misplaced mod)   4. We were driving fast down Central Avenue when suddenly we heard the scream of a siren. (incorrect verb form)   5.   As the procession moved slowly along the street, we were suddenly aware of . . . (tense shift)   6.   My sweater has shrunk to about . . . (incorrect verb form)   7.   To keep well, one must eat the right foods. (dangling mod)   8.   My brother, who is much younger than I, moved to California. (misplaced mod)   9.   When he heard the bad news, he flew into a rage. (inconsistency of tenses)   10.   At the party last evening we toasted marshmallows and sang one song after another. (tense shift)

Key

PART II

CHAPTER **1** *Using the Dictionary pages 221-252*

NOTE: See Guide page 26 for an explanation of why many of the exercises in this chapter have not been keyed.

Exercise 5B　　*pp. 230-231:*　　**1.** (c)　**2.** (c)　**3.** (b)　**4.** (d)　**5.** (b)　**6.** (d)　**7.** (c)　**8.** (d)　**9.** (a)　**10.** (e)　**11.** (c)　**12.** (b)　**13.** (a)　**14.** (d)　**15.** (b)

Exercise 13　　*p. 240:*　　(The spellings that follow are from the G. & C. Merriam dictionaries.) understudy, war zone, tiger lily, stagecoach, snow tire, self-help, sad sack, photo finish, pasteboard, dreamworld, court-martial, coach dog, betweentimes, Bermuda shorts, able-bodied seaman, battle line, battlefield, birthmark

Exercise 14C　　*pp. 242-243:*

aborigines	B	codicil	B	genteel	B	prophesy	B
adjourn	A	coerce	B	germane	B	risqué	B
balustrade	B	debut	A	grimace	A	sachet	A
bivouac	B	deign	B	inveigh	A	silhouette	B
blaspheme	B	demesne	B	morale	B	skein	B
caviar	A	demur	B	negligee	B	slough	B
champagne	B	dissuade	B	paradigm	B	snood	A
chastise	B	eccentric	B	persiflage	A	trousseau	A
chyle	B	faille	B	prevalent	B	yacht	B

Exercise 17　　*p. 245:*　　amateurishness—*-ish:* of, relating to, or being; *-ness:* state, condition, quality, degree　　anthropologically—*anthropo-:* human being; *-log* (logy): the science of, the study of; *-ic:* having the character or form of, of or pertaining to; *-al:* relating to, characterized by; *-ly:* in the manner of, from the point of view of　　anticipation— *-ion:* act or process, result of act or process, state or condition　　disintegration— *dis-:* do the opposite of; *-ion:* act or process, result of act or process, state or condition　　dissimilar—*dis-:* absence of, not　　pneumonoultramicroscopicsilicovolcanoconiosis—pneumo-: pneumonia; ultra-: beyond the range or limits of; micro-: enlarging; -scopic: viewing or observing; silico-: silicosis (a disease of the lungs); coni-: dust; -osis: an abnormal or diseased condition. (The unexplained *no* after the combining form *pneumo-* can probably be traced to *pneumonoconiosis,* a variant spelling of *pneumoconiasis,* a disease of the lungs.)

Exercise 18　　*pp. 245-246:*　　(The words that follow are capitalized according to the G. & C. Merriam dictionaries.) Milky Way galaxy, democratic (*often cap*), Cronus, brussels sprout (*often cap* B), Mafia, Egyptology, sweet William, Gypsy,

Sunday school, republican *(cap)*, federal *(often cap)*, Kodak, southwest *(cap)*, jayhawker *(often cap)*, Horatian, German measles, Dunker, Levi's, Low Church, X ray, Hereford, brown Betty, Welsh rarebit, Wall Street, riviera *(often cap)*, continental *(often cap)*, Underground Railroad, Vaseline, Neolithic, Frigidaire, King's English, Freudian

Exercise 19   p. 246:

A and M: agricultural and mechanical
AAR: against all risks
ACTH: adrenocorticotropic hormone
AM: amplitude modulation (air medal, Albert medal, master of arts)
cent: centigrade (century, centum, central)
EB: eastbound
AS: Anglo-Saxon (airspeed, after sight, antisubmarine)
astron: astronomer (astronomy)
BMR: basal metabolic rate
obs: obsolete (obstetrical, obstetrics, observatory, observation)
COD: collect on delivery (cash on delivery)
OAS: Organization of American States
pseud: pseudonym (pseudonymous)
DAR: Daughters of the American Revolution
vt: verb transitive
Vt: Vermont
distinguished flying cross: DFC
DVM: doctor of veterinary medicine
mademoiselle: Mlle
for your information: FYI
Her Majesty's Ship: HMS

doctor of philosophy: PhD
vertical takeoff and landing: VTOL
zoological: zool
q.t.: quiet
pfc: private first class
neurol: neurological (neurology)
mpg: miles per gallon
mph: miles per hour
MST: mountain standard time
mag: magazine (magneto, magnitude, magnetism)
southeast: SE
kwh: kilowatt hour
juv: juvenile
IPA: International Phonetic Alphabet
hp: horsepower
ft lb: foot pound
frwy: freeway
exec: executive
deriv: derivative (derivation)
chg: charge
kilowatt: kw
apt: apartment
adm: administration (administrative, admiral)
ADC: aide de-camp
APO: army post office
C of C: Chamber of Commerce
HC: House of Commons (Holy Communion)

Exercise 21   pp. 251-252:   1. The experiment involved a container of water vapor wherein the ionization process could be observed.   2. Named after Gerhardus Mercator, a Flemish geographer who died in 1594, this principle permitted a representation of the *spherical* surface of the earth to be projected in a particularly useful way onto *flat* maps.   3. Cervantes' fictional hero, Don Quixote, attacked windmills; the person spoken of in this statement apparently combines similar qualities of self-deception and superabundant idealism.   4. The term *buncombe* (or *bunkum*) refers to an irrelevant statement and derives from a remark made by a Congressman (1820) who explained the irrelevancy of a speech he was making by stating that it was addressed not to Congress but to his constituents back home in Buncombe County.   5. This batter was not credited with a hit because in the judgment of the official scorer, he could have been put out at first base, if the fielder handling the ball had chosen to make a play at that base. Since the fielder elected to throw the ball to some other base to retire another baserunner, however, the batter is safe at first.   6. The men in question are probably rival football coaches whose teams oppose each other on the gridiron where the front rank of each opposing force is known as the "line of scrimmage"; here, however, the two coaches meet as personal rivals in a debate where the only line separating them is that formed by the table between them.   7. Literally, one who "burns his bridges" cannot go back the way he came; he cuts off his means of retreat. By being frank with his boss, this person has apparently destroyed his chances for staying on his present job in the event he should fail to find the one he is seeking.   8. This statement alludes to Napoleon's defeat at Waterloo, Belgium, in 1815; the battle marked the point of Napoleon's eventual undoing, just as the ninth hamburger and the eleventh bottle of pop might mark the point of the undoing of one with an overactive appetite.   9. The comparison here is with Richard E. Byrd, 1888-1957, who, as an officer in the United States Navy, made several exploratory and scientific expeditions to the polar regions, particularly Antarctica.   10. This may be an allusion to the days when logs were moved (usually downhill) on rails of other logs called "skids"; thus to "hit the skids" would mean to begin one's downfall or one's decline. (Since these skid roads or rails were often coated with grease to speed up the movement of the logs, we sometimes speak of expediting any process as "greasing the skids.")   11. The expression comes from a very functional part of carriages and semitrailer trucks, but it also refers to a *spare* wheel; thus, in a four-wheeled world, a fifth wheel is often superfluous or simply out of place.

CHAPTER 2   *Looking at Sentence Structure pages 253-270*

Exercise 1   *pp. 257-258:*   1. Casey struck out when the bases were loaded, and the crowd groaned.   2. When the senator made a speech, the audience applauded, and the band struck up "The Happy Warrior."   3. When the driver tried to avoid hitting a dog, the car struck the bridge, and the driver was injured. 4. Mr. Stryker was angry when the boys damaged his hedge, and he called the police.   5. Rangers came to fight the fire in Tonto Basin, but the wind caused it to spread rapidly, and they were able to bring it under control only when a shower brought heavy rain.   6. When Charley Jones ran the 100-yard dash in ten seconds, he almost broke the record, and he finished two yards in front of his nearest competitor.   7. The hunter missed the deer because he was nervous,

and although he sat and waited all day, he didn't see any more animals.   8. The
fire started in the garage when the gasoline exploded, and although the house burned
down quickly, no one was seriously injured.   9. The Ancient Mariner shot the
albatross, and the dead bird hung from his neck since he had destroyed one of
God's living creatures.   10. If the weather is clear, we will go to Lake Pleasant
on Sunday; however, we can stay only one day since Father has to work on Monday.

Exercise 4   pp. 263-264:   1. In the city of Plaguesburg are many congested
tenement districts.   2. Here come my sister and my little brother.   3. Although
George Brokaw earns a good salary, he never has any money to spend.   4. Here
is the answer to your problem.   5. To the last man, the courageous company
defended its position.   6. What the final outcome will be, I am sure I know.
7. All the children will return to school when the summer is over.   8. The
Bronx Zoo in New York is one of the largest zoos in the country.   9. The Turf
Club will show fireworks on Independence Day.   10. There is a large picture
of Horace on the dresser in my room.   11. Where you have put my umbrella
is what I want to know.   12. On a windy day in the Mohave Desert, the sand
blows so hard that visibility is poor.

Exercise 5   pp. 264-265:   (Except for sentence A-7, the passive voice is generally ineffective. In B, the transformation improves the sentence structure.)   A. 1.
Willie Jones was followed by the dog all the way to school.   2. His new barn
is being painted by Mr. Smith.   3. The race was run over the new 500-mile
course.   4. A new music center will be constructed on the campus of State
College by the City of Milltown.   5. This girl has been taught ballet dancing
by the best instructors in the country.   6. The fight will be shown on television
on Friday night by the Regional Broadcasting System.   7. The ball game had
to be canceled on account of the rain.   8. A beautiful mural was painted on
the wall of the library by Henry Hernandez.   9. The fight was won by Joe
Lamb in the ninth round.   10. An interesting book about the ancient gladiators
of Rome is being read by Hester.   B. 1. Archeologists dug up gold ornaments
in the old ruins.   2. Willie Speed hit a home run in the fifth inning.   3.
The Symphonic Band will play a concert in the high school auditorium Friday night.
4. The sheriff's posse has captured nearly all the alligators which escaped last
Thursday.   5. Last night a fire which started in the laundry burned the Atlantic
Hotel to the ground.   6. A careless hunter in the neighboring forest shot
Richard Deere in the back.   7. The Egyptians built the pyramids as tombs
of the Pharaohs.   8. The former occupants of the cabin had painted the walls
a bright blue.   9. The fierce winds of the hurricane uprooted the trees.   10.
The great clouds of the approaching storm blotted out the stars and darkened the
whole world.

Exercise 6   pp. 266-267:   1. The solution is not to quit your job, but to
have an understanding with your employer.   2. When the war had ended and the
armistice period had followed, the armies of allied troops were idle in their cantonments.   3. Having warned his children to be quiet and having readied himself

for almost any annoying situation, the nervous Mr. Widget lay down for a refreshing nap.   **4.** The director wanted to know where I had been and why I had made so many mistakes.   **5.** There are too many restrictions on this property; there are many reasons for refusing to consider it.   **6.** That the subject is difficult, I know, but that you are indifferent, I am also aware.   **7.** Singing in the rain and stretching out on a sunny beach are two of Henry's favorite forms of recreation.   **8.** It was a hill difficult to climb, and steep cliffs bordered the sides of the road.   **9.** What the children want and what they actually need are two entirely different things.   **10.** He defeated his first opponent; he overwhelmed his second; but he lost to his third.

Exercise 7   *p. 267:*   **1.** What the city needs and what the city gets are two different things.   **2.** I know how much the car costs and how little it is worth. **3.** Uncle Ferd bought a car that has twelve cylinders and that cost twelve thousand dollars.   **4.** The men would work when food was scarce and when money was short.   **5.** Jim wants to buy a cheap house and to find a thrifty wife.   **6.** The man running down the road and shouting at us must want us to stop.   **7.** Driving too much and sleeping too little are poor habits for the tourist.   **8.** Ann enjoys reading good books and hearing classical music.   **9.** Joe was playing a harmonica and singing folk songs all evening.   **10.** Jim has money in the bank, a car in his garage, and food in his deep freeze.

CHAPTER 3   *Organization and Outlines*
pages 271-288

Exercise 1   *pp. 276-277:*   **Leaf**—cabbage, lettuce, mustard greens, spinach **Stem**—asparagus, celery, potato   **Root**—beet, carrot, radish, sweet potato, turnip **Seeds**—corn, rice, beans (lima)   **Fruit**—beans (green), cucumber, peppers, squash **Bulb**—onion   **Flower**—cauliflower

Exercise 2   *pp. 277-278:*

AIR FORCE	ARMY	COAST GUARD	MARINE CORPS	NAVY
General	General	Admiral	General	Admiral
Lieutenant General	Lieutenant General	Vice Admiral	Lieutenant General	Vice Admiral
Major General	Major General		Major General	
		Rear		Rear
Brigadier	Brigadier	Admiral	Brigadier	Admiral

Colonel	Colonel	Captain	Colonel	Captain
Lieutenant Colonel	Lieutenant Colonel	Commander	Lieutenant Colonel	Commander
Major	Major	Lieutenant Commander	Major	Lieutenant Commander
Captain	Captain	Lieutenant	Captain	Lieutenant
First Lieutenant	First Lieutenant	Lieutenant Junior Grade	First Lieutenant	Lieutenant Junior Grade
Second Lieutenant	Second Lieutenant	Ensign	Second Lieutenant	Ensign

Exercise 3   *pp. 278-279:*

My Freshman Activity in Music

Thesis Statement: Music took up all of my time, outside of classes, in my freshman year.

I. I found instrumental music more demanding than vocal music.

   A. When the band tryouts came, I was grateful that my parents had encouraged me to study clarinet, rather than violin.

      1. On a crisp autumn night there is something grand and satisfying about participating with the marching band at half time.

      2. Nothing matches the tense excitement of playing for basketball games as a member of the pep band.

   B. When the spring concerts came around, I felt lucky to get into the orchestra as the last draft choice.

II. Vocal music offered me the enjoyment of succeeding in an undertaking in which I had no previous experience.

   A. *Mixed* chorus is never dull because it is *mixed*—boys and girls.

   B. I'll never forget the evening at Christmastime, when we went caroling with the glee club.

   C. No one was ever more scared than I to face the Fine Arts Festival judges to sing a solo.

CHAPTER 4   *Description and Narration*
pages 289-310

Exercise 3   *p. 298:*   A.   Spatial—2, 4   Dominant impression—1, 3

CHAPTER 5   *Exposition and Argumentation*
 pages 311-326

Exercise 1   *pp. 312-314:*   Example A—A; Example B—E; Example C—N; Example D—E; Example E—D; Example F—N

CHAPTER 6   *Newspaper Writing*
 pages 327-354

Exercise 3   *pp. 340-341:*   Fact—1, 2, 3, 5, 6, 9, 10   Opinion—4, 7, 8, 11, 12, 13

Supplementary Tests
 pages 361-364

PART I

1. (The labels also identify the basic sentence elements.)   (a) The president of the company / addressed the stockholders.   (b) The beagle that won the blue ribbon / belongs to Mr. Stockman.   (c) The sycamore / is a shade tree.   (d) The man talking to Father / offered him a job in Alaska.   (e) The Republican Party / elected Lincoln president.

2. inflection, auxiliary verbs, position (*Bud* has wax*ed* the floors.)

3. inflection, determiners, position (*The* planes are flying low.)

4. (a) The boy has *written* his theme.   (b) The boy *brought* his books to school. (c) The children *wash* every day. Brother *should wash* every day. Henry forgot *to wash* this morning.

5. hurt, set, hit, cut, cost—Jim's knee *hurts* where he fell and *hurt* himself, and he hopes that it will not be *hurting* long. *Set* the books on that table where Miss Small

sets hers and where Jack is *setting* his. See if Joe can *hit* the mark as well as Hank consistently *hits* it, and then you try *hitting* it. Dad *cuts* wood better than Tom can *cut* it without *cutting* himself. If your books *cost* more than my dictionary *costs,* try to find some *costing* less.

6. Jim knows *what he wants.* This is the book *that he wants.* We will all rise *when the parson walks in.*

7.

Headword	volcano
Modifiers	ancient
	which . . . dormant

Headword	been
Modifier	long

Headword	clouds
Modifiers	of black smoke
	which . . . sky

Headword	smoke
Modifier	black

Headword	sky
Modifier	morning

8. The young lady in the blue dress looked extremely attractive as she walked down the aisle.

9. (a) Jim belongs to a *fraternity.* Jim is a *fraternity* man. (b) The player hurt his *shoulder.* The player will *shoulder* his way through the line. (c) Miss Kelso always uses *correct* English. Miss Kelso will *correct* our themes this morning. (d) The halfback was thrown *down* by a tackler. The halfback ran on the third *down.*

10. Jim lost *his* book. This is *Freddy's* hat. The coach has a *winning* team. I lost my *Latin* book. Lulu took a step *forward.*

11. Subject noun—*To study* requires concentration. Complement—Tom wants *to improve* his grades. Linking-verb complement—He appears *to work* hard. Noun-modifier—It is time *to leave* now. Adjective-modifier—We will be happy *to go.*

12. (a) subj (b) mod (Walt Disney) (c) mod (peaches) (d) mod (huddled) (e) mod (revolver)

13. (a) Jim, *the lad from Greenpoint,* has done it again. (b) *To tell the truth,* I am not going. (c) The fact *that you are old* shouldn't prevent your going on the stage. (d) *He* is my brother. This is *his* book. We spoke about *him.* (e) Joe Black told me that *he* likes Clara White.

14. (a) who worry (b) in a new sport jacket (c) up to Mother and me (d) My sister . . . has gone (e) standard (f) asked Tom and me (g) Bill Jones is working this summer. The experience should be very helpful to him. (h) standard (i) anyone . . . his car (j) car that costs

PART II

1. (a) The riot spread through the village; army troops finally had to be called out. (b) "George," Mother exclaimed, "we've run out of gas!" (*Or* "George!" Mother exclaimed. "We've run out of gas!") (c) The obscure poet MacIntosh wrote a ballad which he called "Skating in the Highlands." (d) This report, according to a reliable source, tells of a secret attempt to overthrow the current dictator. (e) If the weather is clear tomorrow, we'll go to the Blue Water Inn for a lobster dinner. (f) Mother gave a party for Mrs. Smith, who is leaving for Denmark tomorrow. (g) "Who's afraid of the big bad wolf?" joked Uncle Joe, as he moved hesitantly toward the shed.

2. (a) Martha's husband knows how to repair the plumbing, how to cook the Sunday dinner, and how to save his money. (b) The search party found the old prospector dead, twenty miles out in the desert where he had fallen in the thick brush. (c) Twenty miles out in the desert where he had fallen in the thick brush, the search party found the old prospector dead. (d) His material success had no limit; his spiritual failure had no parallel. (e) The woman carried a baby that was crying, and the man walked along a few steps behind.

3. See Chapter 4.

4. (a) The city will erect a new park on the south side of town. (b) effective (c) Mr. Downs found a twenty-dollar bill in his overcoat pocket.

5. Some possible areas for discussion—(a) guide to definitions (b) guide to knowledge about the things that words are made to stand for (c) guide to different "senses" or "contexts" in which one word may be used in many ways (d) guide to changes in meaning, through passing of time, specialization, generalization of use (e) guide to synonyms (f) guide to antonyms (g) guide to etymology (h) guide to special use of general words (i) guide to spelling (j) guide to pronunciation (k) guide to grammatical function (l) guide to inflections (form changes) (m) guide to prefixes, suffixes, and combining forms (n) guide to capitalization (o) guide to abbreviations (p) guide to usage—appropriateness of words to time, place, and degree of formality (q) guide to interpretation and general knowledge in the things we read

7. Through random association (pp. 282-283); through logical divisions (pp. 283-284); from a central idea (pp. 284-285); by anticipating questions (pp. 285-287)

9. As discussed in Chapter 4, point of view describes the relationship between the narrator and the events he relates. If the narrator participated in the events, as either a major or minor figure, he may discuss the events in the first person, using the "I" ("we") point of view. On the other hand, when a narrator writes about what happened to others without his participation, he usually writes from the "third person" ("he," "she," "they") point of view.

10. Through definition (pp. 315-316); through partition (pp. 316-317); through comparison or contrast (pp. 317-318); through classification (pp. 318-319); by explaining a process (pp. 319-320); through cause and effect (pp. 320-321) and through patterns which combine the foregoing patterns.

11. (a) The writer or speaker should be well informed about the question being discussed. (b) He should state the question clearly. (c) He should follow a definite plan or outline. (d) He should follow a chain of reasoning, making a new point link into the one preceding it. (e) He should back up his statements, supporting them with facts or with opinions given by reliable authorities. (f) He may find it advisable to anticipate counterarguments that may be raised and deal with such questions in advance.

13. **News story**—characterized by an inverted lead which gives the most important information first, followed by other details in descending order of importance; tells *who, what, when, where* as precisely as possible and offers the information whereby the reader can determine *why* and *how;* based on verifiable data—facts without opinions of the reporter; deals with significant current happenings which touch upon the lives of or are important to many persons   **Feature story**—characterized by purpose to embellish the day's news, it entertains, offers general information, reports what is timely but not necessarily current; it often features an interesting person, place, or object; it is often developed in more traditional ways, such as the "central idea" approach, rather than with an "inverted lead"   **Editorial**—characterized by location, on the editorial page, unsigned, but reflecting the viewpoint of the editor or publisher; based on opinion, rather than on the news; varied in purpose—provides extra background for news, analyzes a situation, influences or persuades readers, expresses an opinion on a current topic; sometimes developed by a pattern which includes: (1) a title, (2) an introduction presenting the main point, (3) logically developed discussion of that point, and (4) a concluding punch line   **Column**—characterized by daily or otherwise regular appearance under a columnist's name; dealing with one of a very wide range of topics, one on which the writer has a special interest or special background; it may entertain or offer serious discussion; its style is often brisk, forceful, and easily understood

NOTES

2

MODERN GRAMMAR
AND
COMPOSITION

David A. Conlin
George R. Herman

AMERICAN BOOK COMPANY

David A. Conlin

Professor of English Education, Arizona State University, and Coordinator of Teacher Training in English. Dr. Conlin is active in in-service training for teachers of high school English. He is the author of a college text in modern grammar for teacher-training classes and has written articles for the *English Journal* and other publications.

George R. Herman

Assistant Professor of English, Arizona State University, and a former coordinator of teacher training; previously a teacher of junior high school and high school English. Mr. Herman has had numerous short stories, poems, and articles published in a variety of literary and professional magazines.

Copyright © 1965 by American Book Company
New York   Cincinnati   Atlanta   Dallas   Millbrae

Philippines Copyright 1965 by American Book Company

Conlin-Herman: *Modern Grammar and Composition 2*. Manufactured in the United States of America. All rights reserved. No part of this book protected by the copyrights hereon may be reprinted in any form without written permission of the publisher.

1   3   5   7   9   11   13   15   EP   16   14   12   10   8   6   4   2

Contents

Contents   5

6 Agreement   111

7 Substitution   127

8 Punctuation   147

9   *Phonemes and Graphemes in English*   171

10   *Effective Sentence Structure*   193

Contents 7

3   *Organization and Outlines*   271

4   *Description and Narration*   289

5   *Exposition and Argumentation*   311

6   *Newspaper Writing*   327

Contents

Preface

Throughout your lifetime, the study of language has been a continuous process. There have been two periods in your life, however, during which language learning has been greatly accelerated. The first of these periods came very early—in the years from babyhood to school age. During those years, you became fairly skilled in the use of spoken English. By the time you entered school, you were able to use complicated patterns of sound to convey meaning effectively to your family and friends. You were able to respond adequately to the language which they in turn directed to you.

The second period of accelerated language learning began in the first grade when you started your formal study of printed and written symbols. You are now in the latter part of this second period, which will continue to the end of your school years. You have made a serious beginning in the study of grammar and composition. Most of you will have completed the first book in this series. Building on your previous experience in language, *Modern Grammar and Composition 2* will help you take still another step forward in your study of grammar and composition. The text is referred to as a "modern grammar" because in it we have tried to incorporate the best that is available in language study today. The nomenclature is largely traditional, but the method and the emphasis are structural.

The first two chapters of *Modern Grammar and Composition 2* have been planned to refresh and reinforce your knowledge of the sentence and its parts. In the third chapter, you will move on to a detailed study of form and function and of the relation of the two in English. After studying function and functional shift, you will go on to the study of verbals and of the appositive and absolute structures—devices of syntax that give flexibility and power to English and make its expression more concise. Next, you will proceed to the study of the grammatical principles of agreement and substitution, followed by more practice with punctuation and spelling.

In the last chapter in Part I ("Effective Sentence Structure"), you will put grammar to work. Here you will apply your knowledge of the subject by practice in eliminating the structural errors to which high school students are most susceptible.

You will begin Part II with a detailed study of the dictionary and of the uses that you can make of this wordbook in your study of language, particularly in your study of written composition. After a consideration of the importance and means of gaining variety in sentence structure, you will proceed to the process of outlining and to the special problems of organization.

The major emphasis in Part II is on the study and practice of writing for a variety of purposes: narration, description, exposition, and argumentation. These writing experiences will prepare you for advanced work in written composition in the final years of high school. The last chapter in Part II deals with newspaper writing and provides practice in this medium.

Modern Grammar and Composition 2 has been planned to provide you with new and more involved experiences in grammar and composition. Your intelligent application to the work assigned will help you to develop skills that will be of service to you not only today but in the school and work years that lie ahead of you.

PART I

GRAMMAR

Chapter 1

The Structure of the Sentence

A Look Back and A Look Forward

In your previous experience in the study of grammar and composition, you have in all probability found two skills to be of major importance. One of these is a command of the English language; the other is the ability to write clear sentences.

A mastery of sentence structure is the foundation upon which you must build in order to develop power in written composition. In Chapter 1, you will therefore return once again to the study of the English sentence — its physical characteristics, its basic patterns, its potential for expansion.

WHAT IS A SENTENCE?

If you expect a pat definition, you will not find the answer to this question in this book. Instead of a definition, you will find six characteristics that signal whether a structure is or is not a sentence.

The Signals

SIGNAL 1: CAPITALIZATION AND END PUNCTUATION

Suppose you were asked to count the sentences in the following excerpt from an encyclopedia article:

> All meteors belong to the solar system of which the earth is a part. They travel in a variety of orbits and velocities about the sun. The faster ones move at about 18 miles a second. When meteors meet the earth's atmosphere head-on, the combined velocity reaches about 44 miles a second. Those traveling in the same direction as the earth hit the atmosphere at much slower speeds.*

Chances are that you read just enough of the above excerpt to know that it is from an article on meteors. No doubt you counted the sentences by giving your attention to the capital letters and the marks of end punctuation. In standard written English, a sentence begins with a capital letter and ends with a period, a question mark, or an exclamation point. These signals help the reader to sort language into normal patterns of syntax.

Some structures that are marked with a capital letter at the beginning and with suitable punctuation at the end are not, of course, sentences. It is obvious, then, that this first signal must be accompanied by other signals.

SIGNAL 2: SUBJECT-PREDICATE STRUCTURE

English is a bipolar language. Its grammar reflects on one hand a world of persons, places, and things. Its grammar reflects on the other hand a world of movement and change, of being and becoming. In communication the first world is represented by words called NOUNS; the second by words called VERBS.

A noun or a noun substitute combines with a verb to form the basic subject-predicate structure of the English sentence. The SUBJECT is the noun or a noun substitute with all its modifiers; the PREDICATE is the verb with all its modifiers and, frequently, with one or more complements.

What is the subject of each of the following sentences? What is the predicate?

The World Book Encyclopedia, copyright 1963 by Field Enterprises Educational Corporation.

Montpelier, the family estate of James Madison, / is in Orange County, Virginia.

Some packers / cure meat in a pickle bath.

These tribal masks / represent ghosts of the dead.

John Marshall / became Chief Justice of the United States in 1801.

In these sentences, everything to the left of the slash mark is part of the subject; everything to the right is part of the predicate.

SIGNAL 3: FINITE VERB

The headword in the predicate is the verb. In a sentence, the verb must be a FINITE VERB—a verb that is neither an infinitive nor a participle without an auxiliary.

In this illustration, which structure is a sentence? Which is not?

Father hired two new employees. A man to sell real estate and a girl to do the filing.

The first structure is a sentence with a finite verb. The second structure is not a sentence, because the verb is an infinitive — in this case the plain form of the verb used with the function word *to*.

Now look at this illustration:

The Jones family decided to drive to Big Horn Springs. The day being cool and clear.

Here again, the first structure is a sentence with a finite verb. The second structure is not a sentence, because the verb is the present participle form without an auxiliary. When the present participle form is used with an auxiliary, it is a finite verb:

A beautiful mare was running across the pasture.

Exercise 1   *The following structures are not sentences because the headword in the predicate is not a finite verb. As shown in the examples, provide a finite verb for each structure.*

EXAMPLE: Henry to go to camp next summer.
Henry will go to camp next summer.

EXAMPLE: Josephine helping the teacher every afternoon.
Josephine is helping the teacher every afternoon.

1. The shoes to have been ready today.

2. The gifts being sent overseas to the boys for Christmas.

3. The packages to be mailed early.

4. The troops to go by plane to Germany.

5. Nancy to return before Sunday.

SIGNAL 4: SUBORDINATION

Words like *after, when, who, where, because, since, if, although, that, unless, until, while,* and so forth, are called subordinators and ordinarily signal a subordinate clause, not a sentence.

> The chuck wagon pulled into camp after the sun had set.

The subject-predicate word group *after the sun had set* cannot stand as a sentence. It modifies the verb *pulled* and is part of a N-V PATTERN (see page 17).

In this illustration, which structure is a sentence? Which is not?

> The seniors are going to Washington. Where they will meet the President in the White House rose garden.

The first structure is a sentence. The second is not a sentence. The subordinator *where* is a signal of subordination. It tells us that the subject-predicate word group which it introduces should be included as part of a basic sentence pattern:

> The seniors are going to Washington, where they will meet the President in the White House rose garden.

The subject-predicate word group introduced by *where* modifies *Washington* and is part of a N-V PATTERN.

SIGNAL 5: WORD ORDER

The normal word order in a sentence is SUBJECT-VERB-COMPLEMENT. If the order of the subject and the verb is inverted, the structure that results usually begins with *who, why, where, when, what,* or *how.* This structure is, of course, a question and is recognized as one of the seven basic sentence patterns:

> Where is my copy of *Seven Days in May?*
> What have you there?
> Why did you come here?
> When are you leaving for El Paso?

In the last two examples, where does the subject come? Remember that *did* is an auxiliary and that *come* is the verb.

SIGNAL 6: INTONATION

When it is spoken aloud, the written sentence follows the characteristic intonation patterns of English. These patterns— which include pitch, stress, and juncture—are described in detail in Chapter 8.

Linguists recognize four degrees of pitch: low, normal, high, and very high. There are also four degrees of stress, or loudness: zero, tertiary, secondary, and primary, as the voice moves from a soft tone to a loud tone.

Juncture describes the joinings or pauses between the sounds, words, and word groups that separate speech into meaningful patterns.

The patterns of intonation serve as signals in the recognition of sentences. The juncture between sentences is a longer break in sound than that between the syllables, words, or word groups within a sentence. The ear is especially sensitive to terminal juncture. When this juncture is accompanied by a fall in pitch, we can be almost certain that we have come to what should be the end of a sentence. When the same terminal juncture is accompanied by a rising pitch, it is quite likely that the structure is a question.

Basic Sentence Patterns

Some linguists count seven basic sentence patterns in English:

1. N-V (NOUN-VERB)

    $\quad\quad$ N $\quad\quad\quad\quad$ V

    Charles Beebe was born in Brooklyn.

2. N-V-N (NOUN-VERB-NOUN)

    $\quad\quad$ N $\quad\quad$ V $\quad\quad$ N

    Beetles have four wings.

3. N-V-N-N (NOUN-VERB-NOUN-NOUN)

    $\quad\quad$ N $\quad\quad$ V $\quad\quad$ N $\quad\quad$ N

    Miss Pratt dropped Willie a hint.

    $\quad\quad$ N $\quad\quad$ V $\quad\quad$ N $\quad\quad$ N

    Doctors call the condition hypertension.

4. N-LV-N (NOUN-LINKING VERB-NOUN)

    $\quad\quad$ N $\quad$ LV $\quad\quad$ N

    Asia is a continent of extremes.

5. N-LV-ADJ (NOUN-LINKING VERB-ADJECTIVE)

    $\quad\quad$ N $\quad$ LV $\quad\quad$ ADJ

    Asia is the largest of the continents.

6. THE INVERTED SENTENCE

    $\quad\quad$ V $\quad\quad$ N

    Here is the home of the giraffe and the rhino.

    $\quad\quad$ V $\quad\quad\quad\quad$ N

    There are numerous methods of treating arthritis.

7. THE QUESTION

    Have you a coat?

    Do you have a coat?

    Where is your coat?

    Where have you left your coat?

Exercise 2   Label the pattern in each of the following sentences, as shown on page 17 in the sentences illustrating the first five basic patterns. Then change each statement into a question. Do not mark this book.

EXAMPLE:
N   LV ADJ
Vegetation is sparse in the Holy Land.
Is vegetation sparse in the Holy Land?

1. The Dutch settled in the Hudson River Valley.

2. Oxygen is a life-giving gas.

3. The saguaro cactus is found in the great deserts of the Southwest.

4. Mother has gone to Chicago to visit Aunt Belle.

5. Sarah will attend the State University.

6. The soccer game has been postponed.

7. The hurricane caused great loss of life in the West Indies.

8. Helen has the chicken pox.

9. Dad parked the car behind the grocery store.

10. Mrs. Kelly has fourteen boarders.

BASIC SENTENCE ELEMENTS

The two main parts, or constituents, of a sentence are the subject and the predicate. The headword in the subject is a noun or a noun substitute. The headword in the predicate is the verb. The predicate usually contains one or more complements. The complement may function as a direct object, an indirect object, an objective complement, or a linking-verb complement.

N   V
The third-quarter moon / rises about midnight. (The headword in the subject is sometimes called the subject noun. The headword in the predicate is sometimes called the predicate verb.)

N   V   N
The moon / produces no light by itself. (The subject noun is *moon*; the predicate verb is *produces*. The complement *light* is the direct object.)

N   V   N   N
Mr. Ames / showed Les the first photograph of the far side of the moon. (In this sentence there are two complements, *Les* and *photograph*. The outer complement—*photograph*—is the direct object. When the outer

complement is the direct object, the inner complement — *Les* — is called the indirect object.)

        N   V   N N

Early astronomers / called the shaded areas seas. (Here, the inner complement — *areas* — is the direct object. When the inner complement is the direct object, the outer complement — *seas* — is called the objective complement.)

      N   LV   N

The earth / is not the only planet with a moon. (Here, the complement — *planet* — is a linking-verb complement and is sometimes called the predicate noun.)

     N   LV   ADJ

The moon / is actually dark brown. (Here, the linking-verb complement — *brown* — is an adjective and is sometimes called the predicate adjective.)

What happens when the positions of the subject noun and the complement are reversed?

             N   V   N

The Ancient Mariner / killed the albatross.

     N   V   N

The albatross / killed the Ancient Mariner.

As you can see, when the positions of the subject noun and the complement are reversed, the meaning becomes something quite different from that of the original sentence. In English, the SUBJECT-VERB-COMPLEMENT order is fixed and is a significant determiner of meaning.

Exercise 3

Are the following structures sentences or non-sentences? Indicate the basic pattern of each structure you identify as a sentence. Explain how you decided that a structure is a non-sentence.

1. Henry being the best pinch hitter on the bench.

2. Mountain streams carry rich soil. From the highlands to the flood plains.

3. Where is my umbrella?

4. Whenever you are ready.

5. After the rain had stopped and the sun was shining once more.

6. Then the band began to play some cheerful music. Which we all enjoyed.

7. A good book, a warm fire, and the smell of steak broiling over the coals.

8. Wherever you go, you will meet friendly people.

9. Nothing to look back on with pride and nothing to look forward to with hope.

10. The coach plans to give the boys a day off.

11. There will be no school the Friday after Thanksgiving.

12. The car overturned, injuring all of the occupants.

13. Because you had gone to the trouble of painting the porch furniture white.

14. Because Germany is not rich in natural resources, the Germans must rely on hard work and technical skill to produce wealth from their raw materials.

15. Granting, of course, that what the witness said is true.

16. Serving as a short cut between two oceans, the Big Ditch weaves across the Isthmus of Panama.

17. Hoping but not expecting to win the free trip to Texas.

18. Thus Captain Hornblower was able to rout the enemy without any casualties.

19. That you will graduate with honors must be a source of pride to your parents. (If you are puzzled by this structure, turn to page 34.)

20. Peeking into the dimly lighted room, but not seeing anyone there.

21. When you are on your way to the theater and thinking about the wonderful evening ahead of you.

22. The wind having let up, we decided to start for home.

23. The night shall be turned into music.

24. Tecumseh served in the War of 1812 as a brigadier general.

25. Whenever I hear that song, I think of that summer at Camp Twintrees.

26. In 1961, Roger Maris hit 61 home runs in 164 games.

27. Not realizing what dangers were ahead of us.

28. The kind of cake that Mother used to bake.

29. A rolling stone gathers no moss.

30. Very little to be seen from the portholes.

When a word group that is not a sentence is unintentionally written as a sentence, the error is called a sentence fragment. A sentence fragment is best corrected either by connecting it to the sentence that precedes it or by rewriting it to meet the basic sentence requirements.

of h
Homer always ordered a man's breakfast Ham and eggs
∧
with lots of ham, pancakes, and good strong coffee.
This usually included   h
Homer always ordered a man's breakfast. Ham and eggs
∧
with lots of ham, pancakes, and good strong coffee.

Exercise 4

Correct each sentence fragment in Exercise 3 either by making it part of a preceding sentence or by rewriting the fragment so that it is a sentence. If necessary, refer to the above examples.

Exercise 5

Divide each of the following sentences into its subject and predicate. Identify (1) the headword in the subject; (2) the headword in the predicate; and (3) each complement. Indicate the basic pattern of each sentence.

1. Pitcairn Island belongs to Great Britain.

2. The bill of the pelican can hold several quarts of water.

3. Prince barked fiercely at the intruder.

4. Thomas Edison was a productive inventor.

5. The family across the street left for Europe this morning.

6. Anne looks beautiful in her new coat.

7. The neighbor's cat has eaten our canary.

8. Kathy seemed nervous during the first act.

9. The taxes on our home have been raised again this year.

10. The horses raced wildly through the mountain pass.

11. The girl who lives next door won a scholarship to Vassar.

12. The boys elected Henry captain of the soccer team.

13. Mother told the children the legend of Pecos Bill.

14. This is your last opportunity to see the circus.

15. The painting was sold to Mrs. Rumkin who lives on Pine Street.

16. The crowd became angry because the referee stopped the fight.

17. The Pecos River is a branch of the Rio Grande.

18. We'll be very happy when this day is over.

19. When the fire started, the children were not at home. (Rearrange the sentence to make the separation of subject and predicate more convenient: The children were not at home when the fire started.)

20. After the game was over, we ate a buffet supper in the club house.

21. In 1934, Jean Riccard made a stratospheric ascent of almost 58,000 feet.

22. Because there was very little food in the freezer, Mrs. Smathers had to dash out to the grocery store.

23. Although it was very late, the butcher sold her a side of beef.

24. In the morning we went down to the harbor to survey the storm damage.

25. The Shawnee Chief refused the offer of General Harrison.

26. Maybelle likes the heavyset boy who plays left end for the Rams.

27. Here is your library card.

28. There are the two reference books that you were looking for.

29. The construction boss handed Cassidy a shiny new shovel.

30. Why did you bring your little brother to the party?

31. Where is the paint brush?

32. The girl in the white dress slipped into the seat which the usher found for her.

33. There is no more gas in the tank.

34. When Mother hears about the accident, there will be trouble with a capital T.

35. Charley didn't wait for the bad news.

IDENTIFYING NOUNS AND VERBS

> Better show results.
> Bill shops early.

What do these structures mean? Is the first intended as a threat (You better show results!) or is it a complimentary statement of fact (A better show results)? As for the second, is Bill doing his shopping early, or is someone advising someone else to bill certain shops early?

Both structures are ambiguous because in neither do you have any way of identifying the noun and the verb. English is essentially a noun-verb language. In order to communicate, it is therefore necessary that you be able to recognize these word classes.

> A better show results.
> Better show some results.
>
> Bill the shops early.
> Bill always shops early.

All four structures now provide grammatical signals that help in the identification of nouns and verbs. There is therefore no longer any uncertainty of meaning.

In the first structure *show* is clearly a noun because it is preceded by two words that usually mark nouns: the determiner *a* followed by the inflected adjective *better*.

In the second structure, the determiner *some* identifies *results* as a noun and also aids in the identification of *show* as a verb by virtue of its position before a complement.

The determiner *the* in the third structure identifies *shops* as a noun. By virtue of its position before the complement, *bill* is identifiable as a verb.

In the fourth structure, the adverb *always* identifies *shops* as a verb by virtue of a habitual response to the adverb-verb relationship as determined by position.

Position of Nouns

Nouns are identified in communication by position and by form. The seven simple sentence patterns on page 17 show almost all the normal noun positions. There are others.

In the following sentence the underscored noun follows a word in color. To what word class does the word in color belong?

I'm going home to <u>Mother</u>.

The preposition *to* is a function word. Most prepositions are followed by nouns.

Now look at this sentence:

This house belongs to a man who lives in the city.

The function words *this, a,* and *the* are determiners. Determiners signal nouns.

Like other function words, determiners have little meaning out of context, but they are grammatically important in communication patterns. Here is a partial list of determiners:

a	many	the
all	most	their
an	one	these
both	several	this
each	some	those
few	that	two

. Several members expressed their opinions.

Many people attended both meetings.

He works in an attic with only one window.

Sometimes a noun follows another noun in a side-by-side relationship. Nouns that take this position are called APPOSITIVES and occur in different sentence patterns.

The *Venus de Milo*, a magnificent Greek statue, was probably made during the first or second century B.C.

Inflection of Nouns To Show Number

Nouns are identified by form as well as by position. Nouns are inflected, or undergo a change in form, to show plural number and to form the possessive.

NUMBER expresses the idea of singular or plural, of one or of more than one. Nouns are inflected to show plural number in different ways. The more common ways are summarized below. For the last word on the correct plural form, refer to the dictionary.

1. butcher	butchers	stone	stones	bus	buses	peach	peaches
radio	radios	hero	heroes	alto	altos	belief	beliefs

How do these nouns form their plurals? Most nouns form the plural by adding *s* or *es* to the singular form.

2. city	cities	copy	copies	butterfly	butterflies

How do nouns ending in *y* preceded by a consonant form their plurals? Such nouns usually change the *y* to *i* and add *-es.*

3. calf   calves   knife   knives   thief   thieves   wife   wives

Certain nouns ending in *f* or *fe* form the plural by changing *f* to *v* and adding *s* or *es*.

4. foot   feet   goose   geese   mouse   mice

How is the plural of each of the above nouns formed? Some nouns form the plural with an internal change.

5. child   children   ox   oxen   brother   brethren

Some nouns form their plurals with *en*.

6. alumna   alumnae   analysis   analyses   datum   data

Many nouns that have come into English from other languages still keep their foreign plural forms.

7. deer   moose   salmon   species   Japanese

Some nouns have the same form in both the singular and the plural.

8. anger   peace

Some nouns have no plural.

9. daughter-in-law   daughters-in-law   passer-by   passers-by

The plural of a compound noun is usually formed by inflecting the headword in the compound. Note, however, that a few compounds have double plurals: *manservant, menservants*

Exercise 6	*Change the headword in the subject of each of the following sentences from the singular form to the plural form:*

1. The analysis of the report showed that business had fallen off.

2. The editor-in-chief went to the convention in Maine.

3. The wolf attacked the men.

4. The child ate and went straight to bed.

5. The alumnus returned to the campus for a reunion.

6. The deer quickly ran to cover.

7. The mouse quivered when the cat walked by.

8. The princess returned to the castle at midnight.

9. The torpedo exploded in mid-air.

10. The quiz will be given on Friday.

Inflection of Nouns To Show the Possessive

The possessive shows a close relationship between nouns.

the boy's book   a man's ambition
Hemingway's novel   men's overcoats
Brooklyn's finest   my heart's content
a week's pay   Kajinski's blocking

Nouns are inflected to show the possessive by the addition of an apostrophe and *s* or, in some cases, by the addition of an apostrophe.

1. Singular and plural nouns that do not end in the letter *s* form the possessive by adding an apostrophe and *s*:

   brother's   Elizabeth's   oxen's   women's

2. Singular nouns that end in the letter *s* form the possessive by adding an apostrophe and *s*:

   Thomas's   boss's   Columbus's

   Some writers, however, omit the *s*:

   Thomas'   boss'   Columbus'

3. Plural nouns that end in the letter *s* form the possessive by adding an apostrophe:

   brothers'   helpers'   officers'

Exercise 7

A. *Write the possessive form of each of the following nouns. Then write a meaningful sentence using each possessive formed.*

Navajo	church
children	hero
horses	Socrates
Cortez	boss
Doris	lady
month	river
brother-in-law	ship
alumnus	duchess
money	patient
ally	crowd

B. *Write sentences in which each of the following words is part of an of phrase that communicates the same meaning communicated by the possessive inflection.*

EXAMPLE mother   She is a friend *of my mother.*

father	Jones
dog	Florence
apple tree	high school
table	fraternity
sister-in-law	Robert Frost
book	Japanese
gentleman	America

C. *Write all the inflected forms of the following nouns:*

man	fox	wife
ally	mouse	boss
child	tomato	information

D. *Write a sentence containing the plural form of each of the following nouns:*

ox	bus	deer
goose	alley	knife
curriculum	alumna	woman

Noun Suffixes

Many nouns have characteristic suffixes that, unlike the plural and the possessive endings, are not inflectional. Here is a partial listing of the suffixes that terminate nouns and help in their identification:

-acy	-ee	-ing	-let
-ade	-eer	-ion	-ment
-age	-er	-ior	-ness
-al	-ery, -ary, -ry	-ism	-ship
-ance, -ence	-ess	-ist	-th
-ant, -ent	-ful	-ity	-ure
-dom	-hood	-le	-y

Exercise 8

Identify all the nouns in the passage below. Be prepared to tell how you identified each noun.

No story of human survival can be complete without considering the sea, an environment which occupies more than two-thirds of the Earth's surface and extends in depth further that the highest mountains—a volume in all of 324 million cubic miles.

This vast and virtually unexplored region is on man's very doorstep, yet its exploitation has been very largely neglected. One cause has been cumbersome diving equipment which has restricted a diver's movement and has needed a skilled support team on the surface. But hydrographers, oceanographers and marine biologists have revealed something of the great wealth hidden beneath the waves — oil, coal, and other minerals, as well as a teeming animal life which could provide an almost unlimited source of food.

Compared with the achievements of man in other directions — to the tops of the highest mountains and more recently into outer space — man has made little progress in the conquest of the sea. However, the development of a self-contained breathing apparatus, the aqua lung, is revolutionizing his attitude to it. Diving is no longer a career in marine salvage. Instead it is providing valuable information for marine scientists and engineers. The equipment is cheap and allows the diver free movement for a first-hand exploration of the sea's secrets.

While the free movement of the diver is important, the remarkable achievements of the submarine, the diving bell, and the bathyscaphe cannot be discounted. With these craft the deepest valleys of the oceans have been probed. Nevertheless, they are limited by the physical shield which prevents any intimate link between man and the surrounding sea. But, as diving advances, these vehicles will find new use as diving headquarters. Fitted with pressure locks, they will allow divers to pass in and out just as astronauts will leave and re-enter their space ships.

The analogy with space is a very real one and scientists in both fields find common problems with pressure, respiration, endurance and human adaptation. Yet in recent years money and technical effort have been poured into space research with little hope of immediate returns, whereas underwater, where the fruits of exploration are rich and obvious, the effort has been minimal.*

Position of Verbs

Verbs can be identified in a sentence both by their form and by their position. The normal position of the verb is illustrated on page 17 in the basic sentence patterns. The verb ordinarily follows the subject noun and comes before the complement if there is one. Subject-verb-complement is the usual word order in English, and we are extremely sensitive to this order as a signal of meaning.

* From "Man Against the Sea" by Stanley Miles. Reprinted by permission of *Discovery*, London.

Inflection of Regular Verbs

Form is also an important signal in the identification of verbs. Verbs are not inflected uniformly. The most common type of verb inflection is that of the regular verb:

PLAIN FORM	SINGULAR	PAST FORM	PRESENT PARTICIPLE
move	moves	moved	moving
work	works	worked	working
jump	jumps	jumped	jumping
worry	worries	worried	worrying

The PLAIN FORM is used in the present tense with a plural subject; it functions as the main verb with auxiliaries such as *can, will, must,* etc.; and it is used with the function word *to* as an infinitive.

> Sand dunes form shifting hills along Lake Michigan.
> An iceberg can carry away huge boulders from its glaciers.
> Mother and Dad want to move to Flatbush.

The SINGULAR FORM is used in the present tense with a singular subject.

> Jim Brown works in a cheese factory.
> The Snake River drains most of Idaho.

The PAST FORM is used in the past tense with singular and plural subjects. It is also used as a past participle with certain auxiliaries and groups of auxiliaries.

> The man worked all day.
> The men worked all day.
> The men should have worked all day.

The PRESENT PARTICIPLE FORM is used with forms of the verb *to be* as an auxiliary or with combinations of auxiliaries in which some form of *to be* is next to the main verb.

> The man is working today.
> The men are working tomorrow.
> The men will be working all day.
> The men should have been working all day.

Inflection of Irregular Verbs

Irregular verbs are inflected with an internal vowel change to form the past form or the past participle form. Many irregular verbs have a special form for the past participle, contrasting with regular verbs which form the past by adding *-ed* to the plain form, and which do not have a special form for the past participle.

The most irregular of the irregular verbs is the verb *to be* which has eight different forms: *be, am, is, are, was, were, being,* and *been.*

> Mary will be sixteen tomorrow.
> I am happy about your success.
> New York is a very large city.
> The boys are away for a week.
> The verdict was against the plaintiff.
> The cows were in the corn.
> Henrietta is being difficult about her role in the play.
> The carpenters have been here all morning.

Some irregular verbs have five different forms, some four, and some three. Here are some examples of FIVE-PART IRREGULAR VERBS:

PLAIN	SINGULAR	PAST	PRESENT PARTICIPLE	PAST PARTICIPLE
swim	swims	swam	swimming	swum
eat	eats	ate	eating	eaten
grow	grows	grew	growing	grown
begin	begins	began	beginning	begun
lie	lies	lay	lying	lain

The PAST PARTICIPLE FORM is a specialized form which is used with auxiliaries such as forms of *have* or of the verb *to be*. This function is usually filled by the past form of regular verbs and of four-part irregular verbs.

> Great-grandmother has lain down for a nap.
> Cotton has been grown in Arizona for many years.
> The program was begun with a prayer.

The following table provides examples of FOUR-PART IRREGULAR VERBS:

PLAIN	SINGULAR	PAST	PRESENT PARTICIPLE
fight	fights	fought	fighting
hold	holds	held	holding
find	finds	found	finding
sit	sits	sat	sitting
shoot	shoots	shot	shooting

The PAST FORM of four-part irregular verbs fills two main functions. It is used for the past tense with both singular and plural subjects and also as a past participle with appropriate auxiliaries:

> The Indians fought off the invaders.
> The children have fought all morning.
> The war was fought to preserve our freedom.

The following table provides examples of THREE-PART IRREGULAR VERBS:

		PRESENT
PLAIN	SINGULAR	PARTICIPLE
bet	bets	betting
set	sets	setting
hurt	hurts	hurting
put	puts	putting
burst	bursts	bursting

The PLAIN FORM of a three-part irregular verb functions not only as the plain form but also as the past form and the past participle form.

Plain Form	Paris and London set the fashions for women.
	Harold was told to set the chairs on the patio.
	You may set the books on the desk.
Past Form	Mother set the table long before the guests arrived.
Past Participle Form	The date has been set for Priscilla's wedding.

Auxiliaries as Verb Signals

Most auxiliaries are not really verbs since they do not perform the function of a verb. AUXILIARIES are function words in that they help make communication coherent while taking their meaning from context.

Here is a list of the verb forms most commonly used as auxiliaries:

am	is	are	was	were		keep	keeps	kept
can	could					may	might	
do	does	did				must		
get	gets	got				ought to		
going to						shall	should	
have	has	had				used to		
			will	would				

Some of the verbs listed as auxiliaries can also function as main verbs and are inflected as verbs. These include *to be, have, get, do,* and *keep.*

The combination of one or more auxiliaries with a verb is called a VERB PHRASE. The auxiliary serves to identify the verb.

Bright blues and deep reds are being featured in this month's issue of *House Beautiful.*

Verb Prefixes and Suffixes

Characteristic prefixes and suffixes serve to signal certain verbs. Some of the more common of these affixes are listed below:

be-	befriend, bewitch
de-	degrade, derail
em-	empower, embody
en-	endear, enable
re-	refill, recall
with-	withstand, withdraw
-ate	dominate, officiate
-en	frighten, moisten
-fy	classify, purify
-ize	sterilize, oxidize

Exercise 9   *Complete each of the following sentences with the appropriate inflected form of the verb in parentheses:*

1. The old gentleman has ____ on that bench every morning for the past five years. (sit)

2. The boys have ____ into trouble again. (get)

3. The knight ____ the dragon and rescued the beautiful princess. (slay)

4. Mother has been ____ there for an hour. (lie)

5. The rookie catcher ____ the ball into the dugout. (throw)

6. The dam ____ and thousands were left homeless. (burst)

7. The trap had ____ and still we did not catch the fox. (spring)

8. The robbers had ____ and gagged the bank clerk. (bind)

9. I've ____ across the lake twice this summer. (swim)

10. The girls have ____ a beautiful scarf for Miss Lee's birthday. (weave)

11. The witness ____ to tell the truth. (swear)

12. Mother has ____ a piece of plastic over the tablecloth. (lay)

13. The principal ____ the students to leave the school grounds during lunch period. (forbid)

14. The first night out we were ____ at four in the morning for a lifeboat drill. (wake)

15. The news has ____ the whole nation. (shake)

16. The cougar ____ away quietly into the night. (slink)

1. Make up a list of ten five-part irregular verbs not given in this chapter. Write all the inflected forms of each verb in your list.
2. Make up a list of ten four-part irregular verbs not given in this chapter, and write out all the inflected forms of each verb listed.
3. Make up a list of ten three-part irregular verbs and write out all the inflected forms of each verb listed.
4. Make up a list of ten regular verbs. Write meaningful sentences illustrating the use of all the inflected forms of five of these verbs.
5. Write sentences illustrating the use of each of the forms of the verb *to be*.
6. Write five sentences illustrating the use of a verb with one auxiliary. Use different verbs in each case and as many auxiliaries as you can.
7. Write five sentences illustrating the use of a verb with two auxiliaries. Use different verbs and as many combinations of auxiliaries as you can.
8. Write five sentences illustrating the use of a verb with three auxiliaries. Use different verbs and as many combinations of auxiliaries as you can.
9. Write sentences using verbs with the prefixes *en-, em-, re-, de-,* and *with-*.
10. Write sentences using verbs with the suffixes *-ize, -ate, -fy,* and *-en*.

COORDINATION

The basic sentence patterns can be added to by means of the grammatical device called COORDINATION. In coordination one or more basic patterns are added on to an existing pattern either with or without connectives. The connective may be a COORDINATOR (*and, but, or, not, so, yet,* etc.) or it may be a CONJUNCTIVE ADVERB (*therefore, however, nevertheless, then, consequently, hence,* etc.). Note the punctuation in the following coordinated sentences:

Every sweet has its sour, every evil has its good. RALPH WALDO EMERSON

My forefathers didn't come over on the *Mayflower*, but they met the boat. WILL ROGERS

There are too many words in prose, and they take up altogether too much room. EDWIN ARLINGTON ROBINSON

Tomorrow is rodeo day in Phoenix; consequently, schools will not be in session.

When two or more basic sentence patterns are joined by coordination, the sentence that results is a COMPOUND SENTENCE. If no connective is used, the word groups are usually separated by a semicolon. When the connective is a coordinator, a comma usually precedes the coordinator. A conjunctive adverb is usually preceded by a semicolon and followed by a comma.

SUBORDINATION

The basic sentence patterns may also be expanded by means of subordination. SUBORDINATION is the grammatical process of including subject-predicate word groups within a basic sentence pattern. The connectives used to include subject-predicate word groups in this way are called SUBORDINATORS. The subject-predicate word group thus included is called a SUBORDINATE CLAUSE. Subordinators include words such as *when, where, who, whom, that, which, unless, although, because, if,* etc. In Chapter 7, you will learn more about relative pronouns, a special kind of subordinator.

Noun Clauses

When a subordinate clause is substituted for a noun in any of its functions it is called a NOUN CLAUSE. A noun clause may function as a subject noun, a direct object, a linking-verb complement, the object of a preposition, an appositive, and so forth.

Subject Noun	What I gave you is of little value.
Direct Object	I only regret that I have but one life to lose for my country. NATHAN HALE
Linking-Verb Complement	One of my chief regrets is that I couldn't sit in the audience and watch me. JOHN BARRYMORE
Object of Preposition	You can always judge a man by what he eats. ARTHUR BAER
Appositive	It is a fact that the only graceful way to accept an insult is to ignore it.

Adjective Clauses

A subject-predicate word group that is included within a basic sentence pattern and substitutes for an adjective is called an ADJECTIVE CLAUSE. Adjective clauses modify nouns or noun substitutes. The subordinators *who, whose, whom, that, which,* and sometimes *where, when,* and *why* introduce adjective clauses.

Victoria Land, which lies on the shore of the Ross Sea, is part of the Antarctic subcontinent.

The violin has four strings that run from the tailpiece to the head.

A weed is a plant whose virtues have not yet been discovered. RALPH WALDO EMERSON

Adverb Clauses

A subject-predicate word group that is included within a basic sentence pattern and substitutes for an adverb is called an ADVERB CLAUSE. Adverb clauses usually modify verbs or the linking-verb complement in the N-LV-ADJ PATTERN. Adverb clauses sometimes modify adverbs.

Lizzie ran because she was frightened.
Mother is anxious that we arrive on time.
He ran so fast that he was out of breath.

SENTENCE COMBINATIONS

Some sentences combine subordination and coordination, and many sentences include more than one subordinate clause.

The apple trees were old, and it seemed a miracle that their misshapen limbs could support so many apples.

Here we have a sentence in which a second basic sentence pattern (*and it seemed a miracle that their misshapen limbs could support so many apples*) is added on by the coordinator *and*. A noun clause that functions as an appositive (*that their misshapen limbs could support so many apples*) is included in the basic N-LV-N PATTERN of the second subject-predicate word group. This sentence combines coordination and subordination and is called a COMPOUND-COMPLEX SENTENCE.

Now study these examples of sentences with more than one subordinate clause:

People who were critical of Peter Cooper's locomotive said that it was a teakettle on wheels. (In this complex sentence, the adjective clause *who were critical of Peter Cooper's locomotive* modifies the subject noun *People*. The noun clause *that it was a teakettle on wheels* is the direct object of the predicate verb *said*.)

Nothing in the upper reaches of the Thames, whose source is a stony spring in an English meadow, suggests that this is one of the most renowned rivers in the world. (In this complex sentence, an adjective clause modifies the object of a preposition, and a second subordinate clause functions as a complement. Identify both clauses.)

Exercise 11   *Identify each of the following sentences as a compound sentence, a complex sentence, or a compound-complex sentence. Circle the connective and identify each subordinate clause as a noun clause, an adjective clause, or an adverb clause and explain its function in the sentence. Do not write in this book.*

1. The Eskimo eats mainly meat, and his diet consists of very little carbohydrate.

2. The government is taking emergency measures since so many people are out of work.

3. The successful man is one who is willing to work.

4. The magazine published an article about the four men who reached the top of Everest on the same day.

5. We shall go when you are ready.

6. The car ran into a bus, but no one was injured.

7. Whoever robbed the store must have known where the the money was kept.

8. Automobile tires must be inflated properly, or they will not wear well.

9. Kate Conroy caught a fish that weighed all of six ounces.

10. I don't know what you mean.

11. The team lost four games, yet the coach claims that the season was successful.

12. Rainsford tried to wrench his foot back, but the muck of Death Swamp sucked viciously at his ankle.

13. If the rain stops before noon, we will leave for the fairgrounds at two.

14. The driver who takes desperate chances often discovers that excessive speed does not pay.

15. The boys had been hunting since sunup, and when they returned to the camp they were exhausted.

16. The natives were curious about our dress; they had never seen Americans before.

17. After the fire went out, the trapper beat his mittened hands violently against his side, but no sensation was aroused in his fingers.

18. Jake is a pitcher whose future looks very bright.

19. The guide showed us the place where the treaty had been signed.

20. The farmer said he knew the road to Circleville.

21. Mother guessed where I had been.

22. The house that Uncle Al just bought is on the road that runs past Wallowa Lake.

23. Whatever you say will be used as testimony in the trial.

24. The fact that you were ill yesterday does not relieve you of the responsibility of completing the assignment.

25. Whenever we drive through Regina, we stop at the police barracks where the famous Mounties are trained.

Exercise 12

1. Write a complex sentence containing an adjective clause modifying the subject noun.

2. Write a complex sentence containing a noun clause as a direct object.

3. Write a complex sentence containing an adverb clause modifying the verb.

4. Write compound sentences using the connectives *and, but, or, nor, yet, so.*

5. Write five compound sentences using five different conjunctive adverbs as connectives.

6. Write a complex sentence containing an adjective clause modifying the direct object.

7. Write a complex sentence containing a noun clause as the subject noun.

8. Write a complex sentence containing an adverb clause modifying a predicate adjective.

9. Write a complex sentence containing a noun clause that functions as the object of a preposition.

10. Write a complex sentence containing an adjective clause that modifies a predicate noun.

11. Write a complex sentence containing a noun clause that functions as a linking-verb complement.

12. Write a complex sentence containing a noun clause in apposition with the subject of the sentence.

13. Write a compound-complex sentence that contains an adjective clause.

14. Write a compound-complex sentence that contains an adverb clause.

15. Write a compound-complex sentence that contains a noun clause.

16. Write a compound-complex sentence that contains two subordinate clauses.

17. Write a compound sentence that contains three basic sentence patterns.

18. Write a complex sentence with a noun clause.

Summary

This chapter examines six useful characteristics that signal whether a structure is or is not a sentence:

Signal 1 Capitalization and End Punctuation
Signal 2 Subject-Predicate Structure
Signal 3 Finite Verb
Signal 4 Subordination
Signal 5 Word Order
Signal 6 Intonation

This chapter next recalls the seven basic sentence patterns:

Pattern 1 N-V
Pattern 2 N-V-N
Pattern 3 N-V-N-N
Pattern 4 N-LV-N
Pattern 5 N-LV-ADJ
Pattern 6 The Inverted Sentence
Pattern 7 The Question

and then goes on to describe the basic sentence elements (SUBJECT-VERB-COMPLEMENT) and the underlying noun-verb structure of the English language. The chapter next reviews the signals of form and of function that aid in the identification of nouns and of verbs.

The chapter concludes with a review of coordination and subordination—two grammatical devices for expanding the basic sentence patterns.

A NOTE ON THE CHAPTER TESTS: There are two chapter tests: Form A and Form B. Form A is a preliminary test. If you have difficulty completing the exercises into which Form A is divided, turn to the page indicated in parentheses. Then—to be sure that you've mastered the chapter—do the exercises in Form B without help.

Chapter Test, Form A

1. Which of the following expressions are sentences according to the requirements of standard written English? (Pages 14-17)
   (a) To kill a mockingbird
   (b) Being the oldest of seven children, Carol had to take care of her younger brothers and sisters.
   (c) It was an ugly little shack, 14 by 20 feet in size.
   (d) No one could come into Camp Lazear but its immune members.
   (e) The troops were to advance at sunrise.
   (f) Gaining the position on the high ground and holding off the enemy.
   (g) What they did there will never be forgotten.
   (h) In order that they might find religious freedom.

2. Write the plural forms of each of the following nouns: (Pages 24-25)

wolf	datum	potato
church	moose	ox
alumnus	pliers	woman

3. Write the possessive of each of the following nouns: (Page 26)

Agnes	uncle	mother-in-law
children	wives	friend

4. Write sentences illustrating two different ways in which the past form of the verb *fight* is used. (Page 30)

5. In the following sentences, fill in the blank with the appropriate form of the verb in parentheses. (Pages 29-31)
   (a) I've never ____ the full length of the pool. (swim)
   (b) The witnesses have ____ to tell the truth. (swear)
   (c) The city has ____ this unnecessary expense for years. (bear)
   (d) The woolen skirt ____ when it was washed in the hot water. (shrink)
   (e) The cowboy had ____ Old Paint for the last time. (ride)

6. Classify and describe the function of each of the underlined subject-predicate word groups in the following sentences. (Page 34)
   (a) <u>What troubled me</u> was the red-and-black dinner jacket worn by Mr. Trumper.
   (b) The porpoise seemed livelier <u>after it had been force-fed 25 pounds of squid.</u>

(c) The doctor suggested <u>that we drink plenty</u> of water.

(d) Henry finally mailed the letters <u>he had been carrying</u> with him since Tuesday.

(e) Mother told me to take in the clothes <u>if it rained</u>.

Chapter Test, Form B

1. Which of the following expressions are sentences according to the requirements of standard written English?
   (a) Being seventy and just over a bout of pneumonia, Mr. Schmidt did not want to get his feet wet.
   (b) Because the sun was just going down.
   (c) To succeed in business was the goal of Henry James.
   (d) To tell the truth, there is little evidence to convict the suspect.
   (e) Going about the fairgrounds and enjoying all the side shows.
   (f) What bothers me most is the dreadful heat.
   (g) All the people assembled in the galleries and the king with his court.
   (h) There will be no more questions.

2. Write the plural form of each of the following nouns:

wife	child	tooth
curriculum	intelligence	trousers
mouse	tornado	box

3. Write the possessive form of each of the following nouns:

Morris	wolves	Mr. Alden
aunt	brother-in-law	brethren

4. Write sentences illustrating three different ways in which the past participle form of the verb *drink* is used.

5. In the following sentences, fill in the blank with the appropriate form of the verb in parentheses:
   (a) Grandfather has ____ on the couch all afternoon. (lie)
   (b) The shipwrecked man had ____ all the water from his canteen. (drink)
   (c) The old lady had ____ the yarn into a beautiful scarf. (weave)
   (d) The boat ____ a leak and began to submerge. (spring)
   (e) The distracted mother ____ her hands in despair. (wring)

6. Classify and describe the function of each of the underlined word groups in the following sentences:
   (a) Ocean rains lashed the coast and <u>gale warnings were broadcast from Seattle to San Francisco</u>.
   (b) Jim Baker was a simple-hearted miner <u>who had lived in the mountains of California for a good many years</u>.
   (c) Jasper's dainty feet and legs were black, and <u>his tail was magnificent</u>.
   (d) The outcome of the election was <u>just what Father had predicted</u>.
   (e) <u>When the rain finally stopped</u>, the pavements glistened like washed glass.

A NOTE ON "THE STRUCTURE OF YOUR LANGUAGE": The material in the section that follows is addressed to those of you who are ready to venture beyond the text in your study of the structure of your language.

The Structure of Your Language

The following sentences have been taken from the writings of men of literary distinction. Observe the way in which these authors have used coordination and subordination. Be prepared to discuss the force of the sentence structure in each case.

1. The play's the thing wherein I'll catch the conscience of a king. WILLIAM SHAKESPEARE

2. It is allowed on all hands that the primitive way of breaking eggs before we eat them was upon the larger end: but his present Majesty's grandfather, while he was a boy going to eat an egg and breaking it according to the ancient practice, happened to cut one of his fingers. Whereupon the Emperor his father published an edict commanding all his subjects, upon great penalties, to break the smaller end of their eggs. JONATHAN SWIFT

3. When I am in a serious humor, I very often walk by myself in Westminster Abbey, where the gloominess of the place, and the use to which it is applied, with the solemnity of the building and the condition of the people who lie in it are apt to fill the mind with a kind of melancholy, or rather thoughtfulness, that is not disagreeable. JOSEPH ADDISON

4. Those who are angry may be reconciled; those who have been injured may receive a recompense: but when the desire of pleasing and willingness to be pleased is slightly diminished, the renovation of friendship is hopeless; as, when the vital powers sink into languor, there is no longer any use of the physician. SAMUEL JOHNSON

5. For all good poetry is the spontaneous overflow of powerful feelings; and though this be true, poems to which any value can be attached were never produced on any variety of subjects but by a man who, being possessed of more than usual organic sensibility, had also thought long and deeply. WILLIAM WORDSWORTH

6. This is why great creative epochs in literature are so rare, this is why there is so much that is unsatisfactory in the productions of many men of real genius; because for the creation of a masterwork of literature two powers must concur, the power of the man and the power of the moment, and the man is not enough without the moment; the creative power has, for its happy exercise, appointed elements, and these elements are not in its own control. MATTHEW ARNOLD

7. The soil is strongly impregnated with sulphur, copperas, alum, and Glauber salts; its various earths impart a deep tinge to the streams which drain it, and these, with the crumbling of the banks along the Missouri, give to the waters of that river much of the coloring matter with which they are clouded.   WASHINGTON IRVING

8. The judge, who was a shrewd fellow, winked at the manifest iniquity of the decision; and when the court was dismissed, went privily and bought up all pigs that could be had for love or money.   CHARLES LAMB

9. If we wish to be free, if we mean to preserve inviolate those inestimable privileges which we have been so long contending, if we mean not basely to abandon the noble struggle in which we have been so long engaged and which we have pledged ourselves never to abandon until the glorious object of our contest shall be obtained — we must fight!   PATRICK HENRY

10. The boy, who was staggering under the weight of his [drum], had been expecting this command, and without waiting for the midshipman to communicate the order, he commenced that short rub-a-dub air that will at any time rouse a thousand men from the deepest sleep, and cause them to fly to their means of offence with a common soul.   JAMES FENIMORE COOPER

11. Some may think these trifling matters not worth minding or relating; but when they consider that though dust blown into the eyes of a single person, or into a single shop on a windy day, is but of small importance, yet the great number of the instances in a populous city and its frequent repetitions give it weight and consequence, perhaps they will not censure very severely those who bestow some attention to affairs of this seemingly low nature. BENJAMIN FRANKLIN

12. In that space, prosperity will polish some, vice and the law will drive off the rest, who uniting again with others like themselves will recede still farther, making room for more industrious people, who will finish their improvements, convert the loghouse into a convenient habitation, and rejoicing that the first heavy labors are finished, will change in a few years that hitherto barbarous country into a fine, fertile, well-regulated district. MICHEL GUILLAUME JEAN DE CREVECOEUR

Chapter 2

Headwords and Modifiers

A Look Back and A Look Forward

In Chapter 1, you reviewed the basic sentence patterns and the subject-predicate structure of the English sentence. You recalled that the basic patterns can be expanded in communication by means of coordination and subordination.

In Chapter 2, you will study the use of modifiers in the expansion of the basic sentence patterns. You will note how headwords form the nuclei around which clusters of modifiers (both single-word and word-group modifiers) are formed.

In Chapter 1, you reviewed the signals that aid in the identification of nouns and verbs. In this chapter, you will be asked to identify the headwords and modifiers in some typical sentences.

EXPANDING BASIC SENTENCE PATTERNS

> N   V
> The porpoises are fed.

In the sentences that follow, what is the HEADWORD — or nucleus — about which modifiers have been built to add more precise meaning to the above basic sentence pattern?

> The sick porpoises are fed.
> In the aquarium the sick porpoises are fed.
> In the aquarium, the sick porpoises who won't eat are fed.

The headword about which the modifiers have been built is, of course, the noun porpoises. The modifiers include the single word *sick* and the word groups *in the aquarium* and *who won't eat. The* is a function word called a determiner; *sick* is an adjective. The word group *in the aquarium* is a prepositional phrase, and the word group *who won't eat* is an adjective clause.

Go back once more to the basic sentence pattern that heads this section. Then note how the verb *fed* (with its auxiliary *are*) has been used as the headword in the following expanded sentences:

> The porpoises are fed forcibly.
> The porpoises are fed forcibly in the evening.
> The porpoises are fed forcibly in the evening until a natural feeding pattern is established.

Here, the modifiers include the single word *forcibly* and the word groups *in the evening* and *until a natural feeding pattern is established. Forcibly* is an adverb. The word group *in the evening* is a prepositional phrase, and the word group *until a natural feeding pattern is established* is an adverb clause.

By building modifiers about the subject noun and the predicate verb as headwords, the basic sentence pattern

> N   V
> The porpoises are fed.

has been expanded into

> N   V
> In the aquarium, the sick porpoises who won't eat are fed forcibly in the evening until a natural feeding pattern is established.

Although the sentence has been expanded, the pattern remains the same. Now study the four examples of sentence expansion that follow:

EXAMPLE 1

N   V   N
The children drink the milk.
The little children in our school drink the milk.

Headword	children
Modifiers	little
	in our school

The children, when they are thirsty, eagerly drink the milk.

Headword	drink
Modifiers	when they are thirsty
	eagerly

The children drink the pure rich milk which the teacher gives them.

Headword	milk
Modifiers	pure
	rich
	which the teacher gives them

N
The little children in our school, when they are thirsty, eagerly drink the

V

N
pure rich milk which the teacher gives them.

In the third part of the expansion in example 1, what is the function of the noun *milk*? (Here, the direct object of the verb serves as the headword for single-word modifiers and a word-group modifier.)

EXAMPLE 2

N   V   N   N
The teachers tell the children stories.
The teachers in our school tell the children stories.

Headword	teachers
Modifier	in our school

The teachers, when they have time, gladly tell the children stories.

Headword	tell
Modifiers	when they have time
	gladly

The teachers tell the little children who behave stories.

Headword	children
Modifiers	little
	who behave

The teachers tell the children the beautiful old stories which they listen to eagerly.

Headword	stories
Modifiers	beautiful
	old
	which they listen to eagerly

 N   V
The teachers in our school, when they have time, gladly tell the little
 N   N
children who behave the beautiful old stories which they listen to eagerly.

In the third part of the expansion in example 2, the headword is a direct object. What is the function of the headword in the fourth part of this expansion? (Here, an indirect object serves as the headword for single-word modifiers and a word-group modifier.)

EXAMPLE 3

 N   LV   N
The dogs are animals.
The old dogs in our neighborhood are animals.

Headword	dogs
Modifiers	old
	in our neighborhood

The dogs are, in my opinion, usually animals.

Headword	are
Modifiers	usually
	in my opinion

The dogs are the intelligent animals which their owners describe.

Headword	animals
Modifiers	intelligent
	which their owners describe

 N   LV
The old dogs in our neighborhood are, in my opinion, usually the intelligent
 N
animals which their owners describe.

What is the function of the headword in the third part of the expansion in example 3? (In this case, a predicate noun serves as the headword for a single-word modifier and a word-group modifier.)

EXAMPLE 4

 N   LV   ADJ
The sunsets are beautiful.
The lingering sunsets on the Hudson River are beautiful.

Headword	sunsets
Modifiers	lingering
	on the Hudson River

The sunsets are especially beautiful when the Palisades are blanketed with snow.

Headword	beautiful
Modifiers	especially
	when the Palisades are blanketed with snow

$$\overset{\text{N}}{} \qquad \overset{\text{LV}}{} \qquad \overset{\text{ADJ}}{}$$

The lingering sunsets on the Hudson River are especially beautiful when the Palisades are blanketed with snow.

What is the function of the headword in the second part of the expansion in example 4? (Here, a predicate adjective serves as the headword for a single-word and a word-group modifier.)

In the four preceding examples, you saw that sentence elements other than the subject noun and the predicate verb serve as headwords for modifiers. In example 1, you observed a direct object as a headword; in example 2, an indirect object; and in example 3, a direct object. Obviously, then, nouns in any of their functions may be modified.

OBJECT OF A PREPOSITION

He searched for a young man whom he had known in the service.

Headword	man
Modifiers	young
	whom he had known in the service

IN APPOSITION WITH ANOTHER NOUN

We called on Henry Samson, the noted author from Chicago who has written many popular novels.

Headword	author
Modifiers	noted
	from Chicago
	who has written many popular novels

Words other than nouns serve as headwords. What is the function of the word in color in the sentence below? Does *popular* have a modifier?

The locally popular reporter won the journalism award.

Here, the adjective *popular* functions as a noun-modifier (*popular reporter*) and is in turn modified by the adverb *locally*.

The man approached so quickly that he startled us.

Headword	quickly
Modifier	so . . . that he startled us

In the above example, the adverb *quickly* is modified by *so . . . that he startled us*. When an adverb serves as a headword, the modifiers are called ADVERB-HEADED. What word class functions as the headword in noun-headed modifiers? In verb-headed modifiers? In adjective-headed modifiers? Word classes and their modifiers are sometimes called NOUN CLUSTERS, VERB CLUSTERS, and so forth.

Noun Cluster	The jeweler examined the rare, deep-blue stone of the Hope diamond.
Verb Cluster	The stone is traditionally associated with death.

Exercise 1   *Identify the basic pattern of each sentence. Then pick out the headwords and modifiers in the elements that make up the basic pattern. Arrange the headwords and modifiers as shown in the four numbered examples on pages 45-46.*

1. Lines of chestnut trees had been planted along the strip of lawn that divided the avenue down the center.

2. The white yacht that was anchored in the harbor yesterday has sailed for a cruise to Delaport Point.

3. The little girl in the blue dress scraped her elbow when she fell from the swing.

4. His father is the noted architect who designed the shopping center for the city-planning group.

5. The elderly woman standing in the bus stop gave the mischievous boys a penetrating look that instantly subdued them.

6. The bowerbirds of Australia and New Guinea are skilled architects who build nests of arched twigs and colorful decorations.

SINGLE-WORD MODIFIERS

The sick porpoises are fed forcibly.

What word does the adjective *sick* modify in the above sentence? What word does the adverb *forcibly* modify? Most of the single-word modifiers you've been working with in this chapter fall into these two word classes: ADJECTIVES and ADVERBS.

Verbs, in their function as verbals, also serve as single-word modifiers, as do nouns. In this chapter, you will look at verbals as modifiers but will study them in detail in Chapter 4. In this chapter, you will also look closely at the signals that aid in the identification of adjectives and adverbs.

Adjectives

Both form and function aid in the identification of adjectives.
What are the word parts in color in the following sentence called?

The nervous salesgirl didn't seem capable of suggesting an inexpensive gift for a golden anniversary.

Like *nervous, capable, inexpensive,* and *golden,* many adjectives have characteristic suffix endings. Here are some of the suffixes that commonly terminate adjectives:

-able	-ary	-ful	-like
-al	-ate	-ing	-ly
-an	-ed	-ish	-ous
-ant	-en	-ive	-some
-ar	-ent	-less	-y

Many adjectives are inflected to show degree. This inflection is sometimes called the COMPARISON OF ADJECTIVES.

POSITIVE	COMPARATIVE	SUPERLATIVE
big	bigger	biggest
cold	colder	coldest
soft	softer	softest
sweet	sweeter	sweetest

Function words called INTENSIFIERS frequently precede adjectives and are helpful in their identification.

> Helen is the most intelligent girl in the class.
> This decision is the least dangerous.
> Henry Clump is a rather dull companion.
> Vyvyan always wears the very latest creations.
> Walkup is a really capable elevator man.
> The sergeant was quite satisfied with the inspection.

Adjectives have two functions within the sentence — ATTRIBUTIVE and PREDICATIVE. Note the position of the attributive adjective in the following sentence:

> The fertile valley lay behind towering cliffs.

Here, the adjective comes before the noun it modifies and after a determiner. This is the usual position of an attributive adjective.

In poetry, in advertising, and in ornate prose, the attributive adjective sometimes follows the noun it modifies: the house beautiful; the lover, pale and nervous.

In the following sentence, what is the position of the adjective? What is its function?

> Rice is nutritious.

Here, the adjective is predicative. It completes the sense of the linking verb *is*, and is called a PREDICATE ADJECTIVE.

Adverbs

Basically, adjectives are thought of as the modifiers of nouns, and adverbs as the modifiers of verbs. Although this is an oversimplification of English structure, it is essential in communication that the reader or listener know whether a word relates as a modifier to a noun or to a verb.

Like adjectives, adverbs are identified by both form and function. Which suffix is the most common adverb marker?

> a cheerful smile *but* smile cheerful _____
> heavy breathing *but* breathe heavi _____

Many adverbs are formed by adding the suffix *-ly* to a simple adjective form or to an adjective ending in a characteristic adjective suffix: timid, timidly; unfortunate, unfortunately.

Other suffixes that serve to identify the adverb to the reader or listener are:

-long	headlong
-side	inside
-time	sometime
-ward	backward
-way	anyway
-where	somewhere
-wise	likewise

Some adverbs are formed by adding the prefix *a-* to certain word classes: *away, aboard, apart, across, abroad, ahead, abreast, aground, anew.*

Like adjectives, some adverbs are inflected to show degrees of comparison:

> Pete can run faster than any of his friends.
> Catherine works hardest in the evening.

Not all adverbs may be identified by signals of form. There are many miscellaneous adverbs in common use. Among them are:

already	here	often	there
back	near	soon	today
east	never	south	tomorrow
far	north	still	west
forth	now	then	yesterday

Intensifiers sometimes precede adverbs:

> The men worked more carefully after the accident.
> Cora looked rather blankly at the picture.
> Harold spoke most politely to Mr. Eldridge.
> We always drive very slow past the school.

Adverbs ordinarily function as modifiers of verbs and usually come either immediately before or after the verb:

> John drove quickly to the village.
> John quickly drove to the village.

A verb-modifier, however, sometimes takes other positions in the sentence:

> Quickly, John drove to the village.
> John drove to the village quickly.

Adverbs also function as modifiers of adjectives, especially of predicate adjectives:

> Lillian is never sad.
> Feitelbaum is often nervous before a game.
> Miss Flynn is a delightfully pleasant person.

Adverbs sometimes function as noun-modifiers:

> The meeting tonight will be a long one.
> First you take a step forward.

Adverbs also function as adverb-modifiers:

> Mother arrived early today.
> The plane will leave late tonight.
> Johnson stepped quickly backward.

Adverbs even function as linking-verb complements:

> The opportunity is now.
> Your chance will be tomorrow.
> The library books are here.

Noun Adjuncts

As what word class do the words underlined in color in the following sentences usually function?

> A college education is an important asset.
> Morton Tone is a piccolo player.
> The class studied sentence structure.

Sometimes a word that usually functions as a noun functions as a noun-modifier in an adjective position. When a noun modifies another noun, the modifier is called a NOUN ADJUNCT or an attributive noun.

Possessive Nouns

Nouns that function as possessives modify other nouns:

> child's play
> a dog's life

Exercise 2   *Identify the single-word modifiers in each of the following sentences. Be prepared to explain your reasons for identification.*

1. The doctor looked grave when he left the patient's bedside.

2. The anxious parents waited patiently for the telephone to ring.

3. The Bruins played well in the game last Saturday.

4. The whole school is very unhappy about having to postpone the dance.

5. Jimmy's teeth are dazzlingly white.

6. Jerome can run faster than any other boy in the school.

7. We were barely on Route 30 when the snow began to thicken.

8. Dad left the office early yesterday.

9. The south meadow was lush with timothy and red-top.

10. A balmy breeze blew steadily along the creek.

11. I am certain that this is a suitable building for you.

12. We trudged farther and farther into the desert.

13. Mary rode hard for twenty minutes but could not escape the storm.

14. The news made me very happy.

15. The Winchesters have gone south for the winter.

16. Mr. French looked weary as he walked slowly home from the shop.

17. That chocolate cake looks temptingly delicious.

18. It was a very carefully arranged meeting.

19. You are requested to drive slow when you turn into the parking lot.

20. The stumpy bull moved sideways across the corral.

Exercise 3   1. Write sentences containing the following adjectives used predicatively: *young, old, poor, pretty, cruel, fine, kind, soft.* Use a variety of linking verbs.

2. Write sentences containing the adjective *beautiful* used with five different intensifiers. Repeat this using the adjectives *ugly* and *nervous*.

3. List fifteen different adjective suffixes. Make a separate list of all the adjectives that you can find for each suffix.

4. Write ten sentences using different adjectives selected from the lists in item 3. Use five adjectives in the attributive function and five in the predicative function.

5. Write eight sentences, each containing a different adverb ending in *-ly*.

6. List seven adverbial suffixes other than *-ly*. Find and list as many adverbs as you can which end in each of these suffixes.

7. Write fifteen sentences using the adverbs listed in item 6.

8. Rewrite each of four sentences used in item 7 shifting the position of the adverb in as many different conventional ways as possible.

9. Write ten sentences, each of which includes one of the miscellaneous adverbs listed on page 50.

10. Write two sentences in which adverbs modify an adjective in the predicate position.

11. Write two sentences in which adverbs serve as the modifiers of nouns.

12. Write five sentences illustrating the use of nouns as modifiers.

Exercise 4

Select the adjectives in the following passage. Explain the means by which you were able to identify the adjectives. Differentiate between the attributive function and the predicate function in each case.

As Jane Collins walked out onto the court behind her husband, she felt once more the private, strong thrill of pride that had moved her again and again in the time she had known him. Jane and Stewart had been married six years, but even so, as she watched him stride before her in that curious upright, individual, half-proud, half-comic walk, like a Prussian drill sergeant on his Sunday off, Jane felt the same mixture of amusement and delight in him that had touched her so strongly when they first met. Stewart was tall and broad and his face was moody and good-humored and original, and

Jane felt that even at a distance of five hundred yards and surrounded by a crowd of people, she could pick him out unerringly. Now, in well-cut white trousers and a long-sleeved Oxford shirt, he seemed elegant and a little old-fashioned among the other players, and he looked graceful and debonair as he hit the first few shots in the preliminary rallying.

Jane was sensibly dressed, in shorts and tennis shirt, and her hair was imprisoned in a bandanna, so that it wouldn't get into her eyes. She knew that the shorts made her look a little dumpy and that the handkerchief around her head gave her a rather skinned and severe appearance, and she had a slight twinge of female regret when she looked across the net and saw Eleanor Burns soft and attractive in a prettily cut tennis dress and with a red ribbon in her hair, but she fought it down and concentrated on keeping her eye on the ball as Mr. Croker, Eleanor's partner, sliced it back methodically at her.*

Exercise 5

1. Identify the adverbs in the selection in Exercise 4. Explain the clues to identification in each case.

2. Identify the nouns used as modifiers (noun adjuncts) in the selection in Exercise 4.

3. Pick out the noun-headed modifiers in the selection in Exercise 4. Identify the headword in each case and list both the single-word and word-group modifiers.

4. Pick out the verb-headed modifiers in the selection in Exercise 4. Identify the headword in each case and list both the single-word and word-group modifiers.

5. Pick out the adjective-headed modifiers in Exercise 4.

6. Pick out the adverb-headed modifiers in Exercise 4.

WORD-GROUP MODIFIERS

How many kinds of word-group modifiers are there?

The boy with the wheelbarrow is my brother.
The boy who is pushing the wheelbarrow is my brother.
The boy pushing the wheelbarrow is my brother.

* From "Mixed Doubles" by Irwin Shaw. Copyright 1947 by Irwin Shaw. Reprinted from *Mixed Company and Other Stories* by Irwin Shaw by permission of Random House, Inc. Originally appeared in *The New Yorker*. Reprinted by permission of Jonathan Cape Limited, publishers.

In each of the above sentences, the modifier is a word group. In the first sentence, the word group is a prepositional phrase; in the second sentence, a subordinate clause; and in the third sentence, a verbal phrase. You have been identifying these word groups as modifiers. Now you will look more closely at their structure.

Prepositional Phrases

PREPOSITIONAL PHRASES are word groups signaled by such words as *in, on, of, at, to, into, by, down, from, through, out, up, off, with, above, across, toward, under, beyond, over, beneath, beside, among, against, after, about,* and so forth. These words are prepositions. Prepositions, like determiners, belong to that large word class called function words.

Now let's determine the usual pattern of a prepositional phrase:

> in the city
> on the hill
> over the mountain
> into the house
> under the table
> after the game
> beyond that tree
> above our flagpole

In these phrases, the preposition is followed by a determiner which is in turn followed by a noun:

> PREP D   N
> after the show

In a prepositional phrase, an adjective sometimes precedes the noun:

> PREP D ADJ N
> after the last show

Subject-Predicate Word Groups

In Chapter 1, you examined the adjective clause as part of the process of subordination. In this process, a subject-predicate word group sometimes functions as a modifier when it is included within a basic sentence pattern. Subordinate clauses that function as modifiers are either ADJECTIVE CLAUSES or ADVERB CLAUSES.

Adjective Clause Thunderbird Park, which contains fine specimens of Indian totem poles, is a main tourist attraction in British Columbia. (Here, the subject-predicate word group in color modifies the subject noun *Thunderbird Park.*)

Adverb Clause Since we have two more vacation days, we plan to do some fishing at the Typee Club on the Campbell River. (Here, the subject-predicate word group in color modifies the predicate verb *plan.*)

Verbal Phrases

Verbal phrases used as modifiers are either participial phrases or infinitive phrases. Verbals are discussed in detail in Chapter 4. In this section, however, you will look briefly at verbals in their function as word-group modifiers.

A PARTICIPIAL PHRASE is a word group made up of a participle with its modifiers and completers. The participle in a participial phrase is the past participle or the present participle form of the verb (usually an *-ed*, an *-en*, or an *-ing* form). Participial phrases usually modify a noun or a noun substitute:

> I stood in the barn, enjoying the smell of the hay.

Here, the noun substitute *I* is modified by the word group *enjoying the smell of the hay*.

In these sentences, what noun does each participial phrase modify?

> The fighter, dazed by too many head punches, sagged against the ropes.
> This is a picture taken by an expert photographer.
> The man weeding the petunia bed is Miriam's husband.

In the first sentence, the participial phrase modifies the subject noun *fighter*; in the second sentence, the linking-verb complement *picture*; and in the third sentence, the subject noun *man*.

An INFINITIVE PHRASE is a word group made up of an infinitive with its modifiers and completers. An infinitive is a verb form ordinarily introduced by *to*. When used as a modifier, an infinitive may function as either an adjective or an adverb.

> Polo is an exciting game to watch.

In this sentence, the infinitive *to watch* modifies the linking-verb complement *game*.

In the sentences that follow, what noun does each infinitive modify?

> Samuel Soaper is the candidate to consider.
> The dishes to be washed are in the sink.
> An electric can opener is a useful gadget to have in the home.

In the first sentence, the infinitive modifies the linking-verb complement *candidate*. In the second sentence, the passive form of the infinitive *to wash* modifies the subject *dishes*. In the third sentence, the infinitive phrase modifies the linking-verb complement *gadget*. In all three sentences, the infinitive functions as an adjective.

In the following sentences, how does each infinitive phrase function?

> Sally has gone to find her little sister.
> The neighbors always come to watch our television.

The expedition left to explore the Antarctic regions.
Jimmy is sailing next week to visit his cousins in Ireland.

In each of the above sentences, the infinitive phrase functions as an adverb modifying the predicate verb.

Exercise 6   *The word-group modifiers in the following sentences are prepositional phrases and verbal phrases. The verbal phrases are either participial phrases or infinitive phrases. Identify each word-group modifier and indicate the headword which it modifies.*

1. There goes Bill Bunch running for a touchdown.

2. The teller at the first window will cash your check.

3. The gentleman sitting in the first row is the assemblyman from Canatruga County.

4. The huge waves breaking over the sand heralded the arrival of the hurricane.

5. The horse to watch in this race is Armageddon.

6. Lou had plenty of money to spend at the County Fair.

7. Aunt Agatha is ready to go to church.

8. The Parker Pioneers traveled all the way from Pittsburg to play the Prescott Pirates.

9. Walking along Main Street, Uncle Thatcher stopped often to greet his friends.

10. The excited kitten wound herself around my neck, licking my face with her little red tongue.

11. The submarine rose to the surface to point its deadly torpedoes at the carrier.

12. After the flash flood, we found a strange new river running through the ranch.

Exercise 7   1. Construct a N-V sentence that includes noun-headed modifiers made up of two single-word modifiers.

2. Construct a N-V sentence that includes verb-headed modifiers made up of two single-word modifiers.

3. Construct a N-V sentence that includes a noun-headed modifier made up of a prepositional phrase.

4. Construct a N-V sentence that includes verb-headed modifiers made up of a single-word modifier and a prepositional phrase.

5. Construct a N-V sentence that includes a noun-headed modifier made up of a subordinate clause.

6. Construct a N-V sentence that includes a verb-headed modifier made up of a subordinate clause.

7. Construct a N-V sentence in which both the subject noun and the predicate verb are headwords of several modifiers that have as much variety of structure as you can devise.

8. Construct a N-V-N sentence in which the subject is the headword of a noun cluster made up of single-word and word-group modifiers.

9. Construct a N-V-N sentence that includes verb-headed modifiers with as much variety of structure as you can devise.

10. Construct a N-V-N sentence in which the complement is the headword of a noun cluster made up of a variety of single-word and word-group modifiers.

11. Construct a N-V-N sentence in which each basic element is the headword of a group of modifiers. Use as much variety of structure as you can.

12. Construct a N-V-N-N sentence in which the subject is the headword of a noun cluster made up of a variety of modifiers.

13. Construct a N-V-N-N sentence in which the predicate is the headword of a verb cluster made up of a variety of modifiers.

14. Construct a N-V-N-N sentence in which the inner complement is the headword of a noun cluster made up of a variety of modifiers.

15. Construct a N-V-N-N sentence in which the outer complement is the headword of a noun cluster made up of a variety of modifiers.

16. Construct a N-V-N-N sentence in which each basic element is the headword of a group of modifiers. Use as much variety of structure as you can.

17. Construct a N-LV-N sentence in which each basic element of the sentence is the headword of a group of modifiers. Use as much variety of structure as you can.

18. Construct a N-LV-ADJ sentence in which each basic element of the sentence is the headword of a group of modifiers. Use as much variety of structure as you can.

19. Construct a sentence of the inverted pattern (There is . . ., There are . . ., Here is . . ., Here are . . ., etc.) in which the predicate verb and the subject noun are headwords of groups of modifiers.

20. Construct a sentence with a question pattern in which the subject noun and the predicate verb are headwords of groups of modifiers.

Exercise 8

1. In the following sentence, use *field* as the headword of a group of single-word and word-group modifiers:
   The farmer ploughed the field.

2. In the same sentence, use *ploughed* as the headword of two modifiers made up of an adverb and an adverb clause.

3. In the following sentence, use the indirect object as the headword of two modifiers made up of an adjective and a prepositional phrase:
   The cashier gave the lady her change.

4. In the same sentence, use the subject noun as the head-word of three modifiers made up of an adjective, a prepositional phrase, and an adjective clause.

5. In the following sentence, use the object of the preposition as the headword of two modifiers made up of an adjective and an adjective clause:
   Fire damaged the basement of the house.

6. In the following sentence, use the predicate adjective as the headword of two modifiers made up of an adverb and an adverb clause:
   Father became angry.

7. Expand the sentence you wrote for item 6 by adding noun-headed and verb-headed modifiers.

8. In the following sentence, use the subject noun as the headword of two modifiers made up of a prepositional phrase and an adjective clause:
   The fire spread rapidly.

9. Expand the following sentence with an adverb-headed modifier:
   The boy ran up the hill quickly.

Summary

Basic sentence patterns may be expanded by building single-word modifiers and/or word-group modifiers around any of the basic sentence elements. The nucleus around which modifiers are built is called the headword. Modifiers in turn serve as headwords. Noun-headed modifiers are sometimes called noun clusters; verb-headed modifiers, verb clusters; adjective-headed modifiers, adjective clusters; and adverb-headed modifiers, adverb clusters.

Single-word modifiers include adjectives, adverbs, noun adjuncts, and possessives. Function words called determiners frequently precede adjectives, as do intensifiers.

Both form and function aid in the identification of adjectives. Many adjectives have characteristic suffix endings. Most adjectives may be inflected to show degrees of comparison. Within the sentence, adjectives have two functions: attributive and predicative. The attributive adjective usually precedes the noun it modifies. The predicative adjective completes a linking verb and is called a predicate adjective.

Like adjectives, adverbs have characteristic affixes and are often identifiable by the suffix *-ly*. Some adverbs are inflected to show degrees of comparison. The adverb usually comes after the verb it modifies, but it may take other positions in the sentence. While the adverb is normally a verb-modifier, it may also modify adjectives, nouns, and other adverbs. Adverbs also function as linking-verb complements.

Word-group modifiers include prepositional phrases, subject-predicate word groups, and verbal phrases. Subject-predicate word groups include adjective and adverb clauses. Verbal phrases include participial phrases and infinitive phrases.

Chapter Test, Form A

(Since the items that follow represent a cumulative review of headwords and modifiers, no attempt has been made to provide specific page references.)

1. Expand each of the following sentences by using the underlined word as the headword of a cluster of single-word and word-group modifiers.

   (a) Mother became <u>anxious</u>.
   (b) The little boy was <u>running</u>.
   (c) The <u>house</u> burned down.
   (d) Our cat Missy caught the <u>gopher</u>.
   (e) Miss Sweet is the <u>teacher</u>.

2. Write sentences that illustrate the following:

   (a) The N-V-N PATTERN in which the complement is the headword of two single-word modifiers.
   (b) The N-V PATTERN with verb-headed modifiers made up of a single-word and a word-group modifier.
   (c) The N-V-N PATTERN in which the subject noun is the headword of a single-word and a word-group modifier.
   (d) The N-LV-ADJ PATTERN in which the complement is the headword of a word-group modifier.
   (e) The N-V PATTERN in which the subject noun is the headword of a single-word modifier, a prepositional phrase, and a participial phrase.

3. In each of the following sentences, identify (a) the basic sentence pattern, (b) each headword, and (c) the single-word and word-group modifiers. Where possible, classify the modifiers.

   (a) The rain came down in torrents.
   (b) Father remained in the city for the night.
   (c) The coach was greatly pleased when the team won its first game.
   (d) The young man who lives across the street is shoveling our driveway.
   (e) We drove quickly to the field where the game was to be played.
   (f) The first group to leave was the delegation from Oklahoma.
   (g) The man in the blue suit casually tipped his hat to Mother as he walked by.
   (h) This is the young lady who has just completed her first concert tour.

Chapter Test, Form B

1. Expand each of the following sentences by using the underlined word as the headword of a cluster of single-word and word-group modifiers.

   (a) Father seemed <u>nervous</u>.
   (b) The <u>car</u> was wrecked.

    (c) Mother baked a <u>cake</u>.

    (d) Mr. Jones is an <u>officer</u>.

    (e) The dog <u>was</u> <u>barking</u>.

2. Write sentences that illustrate the following:

    (a) The N-V-N PATTERN in which the verb is the headword of a single-word and a word-group modifier.

    (b) The N-V PATTERN in which two single-word modifiers are clustered about the subject noun.

    (c) The N-LV-N PATTERN in which the complement is the headword of one or more word-group modifiers.

    (d) The N-V-N PATTERN in which the complement is the headword of a single-word modifier, a prepositional phrase, and a verbal phrase modifier.

    (e) The N-V PATTERN with a verb-headed single-word and word-group modifier.

3. In each of the following sentences, identify (a) the basic sentence pattern, (b) each headword and (c) the single-word and word-group modifiers. Where possible, classify the modifiers.

    (a) The wind blowing from the northeast piled the snow in great drifts.

    (b) The corn will not grow well unless the ground is fertilized.

    (c) The new car in our driveway belongs to Mr. Scott.

    (d) The young lady who is sitting on the platform is the speaker who will tell us about the Peace Corps.

    (e) Father became angry when the waitress served him bluefish.

    (f) The car had stopped on the bridge because the tank was empty.

    (g) Mother bought a new dress which was made in Mexico.

    (h) The sailor in the neat white suit smiled gallantly at Hilda when she stumbled over the winch.

The Structure of Your Language

In the exercise on page 48, you analyzed the headwords and modifiers in the elements making up the basic sentence pattern. Now you will analyze all the headwords within certain sentences including those headwords and their modifiers that are part of word-group modifiers.

EXAMPLE Last June the Congress of the United States proposed to the sovereign states of the Union that the country's citizens who live in the District of Columbia be given the right to vote in national elections.
—The Phoenix *Gazette*

Headword	Congress
<u>Modifier</u>	<u>of the United States</u>

Headword	proposed
Modifiers	<u>Last June</u>
	to the sovereign states of the Union

Headword	June
Modifier	<u>Last</u>

Headword	states
Modifiers	sovereign
	<u>of the Union</u>

Headword	citizens
Modifiers	country's
	<u>who live in the District of Columbia</u>

Headword	right
Modifier	<u>to vote in national elections</u>

Headword	elections
Modifier	<u>national</u>

■ The following sentences have been developed by professional writers. As shown in the example, analyze them in terms of headwords. Treat a compound sentence as two separate sentences.

1. The third day came, and the sun, looking through the white-curtained valley, saw the outcasts dividing their slowly decreasing store of provisions for the morning meal.   BRET HARTE

2. Three gentlemen, on the grass, at a distance, sat under the great trees, while the fourth figure showed a crimson dress that told as a bit of color amid the fresh rich green.   HENRY JAMES

3. The wheel of the world swings through the same phases again and again.   RUDYARD KIPLING

4. Suddenly one of the soldiers who had accompanied him came stealthily round the corner.   STACY AUMONIER

5. Far below on the black river, spaced red and white stars suggested slow-moving tugs, and beyond, faint lights splintered in the rain hinted at the city.   HELEN R. HULL

6. She purchased from the newsdealer in the cubbyhole beneath them a next month's magazine and a tomorrow morning's paper and, with these tucked under one plump arm, she walked.   KATHERINE BRUSH

7. Easter Sunday dawned cold and clear across most of the nation and thousands of sunrise worshippers greeted Christianity's joyous feast with coat collars turned against stiff breezes and snow flurries. — The Arizona *Republic*

8. The town lay in the midst of a checkerboard of prosperous farms with fields of grain and hillsides of orchards where, in spring, white clouds of bloom drifted above the green fields.   RACHEL CARSON

9. Ernest turned sadly from the wrinkled shrewdness of that sordid visage and gazed up the valley, where, amid a gathering mist, gilded by the last sunbeams, he could still distinguish those glorious features which had impressed themselves into his soul.   NATHANIEL HAWTHORNE

10. When the hearse backed up to a wooden sidewalk before a naked, weather-beaten frame house, the same composite, ill-defined group that had stood upon the station siding was huddled about the gate.   WILLA CATHER

11. Resuming his horizontal attitude, Moby Dick swam swiftly round and round the wrecked crew, churning the water in his vengeful wake.

HERMAN MELVILLE

12. The concrete highway was edged with a mat of tangled, broken, dry grass; and the grass heads were heavy with oat beards to catch on a dog's coat.

JOHN STEINBECK

Chapter 3

Form and Function

As you rediscovered in Chapter 1, the basis of communication in English is the subject-predicate structure of the sentence. In Chapter 3, you will be reminded of something you have been habituated to since infancy: the almost automatic response to the word order of the subject and the predicate.

In this chapter, you will also look closely at the basic functions in the sentence. You will work with form and position as clues to meaning, and you will discover what happens when these clues point in different directions. You will also build sentences in which you use a given word in a variety of functions as well as a variety of words and of word groups in a given function.

WORD ORDER AND MEANING

> The whale / swallowed Jonah.

So he did. But note how the simple interchanging of the subject and of that part of the predicate called the complement results in a sentence with a completely different message:

> Jonah / swallowed the whale.

In English, the subject-predicate word order is fixed. When that word order is changed, some other message is transmitted.

THE SUBJECT NOUN AND PREDICATE VERB FUNCTIONS

The subject noun and predicate verb are functions. In the sentence in which the whale swallows Jonah, what is the subject noun? Here, we say that everything to the left of the slash mark is the subject and that the noun *whale* functions in the subject as the subject noun. You naturally do not think in terms of this explanation when you hear or read the sentence. However, you immediately recognize the subject noun because you know from the word order who did the swallowing.

In the same sentence, everything to the right of the slash mark is the predicate. The verb *swallowed* functions as a predicate verb with *Jonah* as its complement. The complement is another important function.

THE MODIFYING FUNCTION

The basic sentence patterns (page 17) include the subject and the predicate, with or without one or more complements. In Chapter 2, however, you saw how the basic patterns can be expanded by building single-word and word-group modifiers around a headword. The headword may be the subject noun or the predicate verb; it may be a noun in any of its other functions; or it may be one of the modifiers itself. Another important grammatical function, then, is that of modifier.

MODIFIERS are words or word groups that qualify or limit meaning; that is, they make meaning more explicit. Position, again, is of dominant importance in transmitting meaning by modifiers. In each of these sentences, for example, to which word does the modifier in color relate?

> The Senator stood firm against the opposition.
> The Senator stood against the firm opposition.

In the first sentence, *firm* relates to the verb and is an adverb. In the second, *firm* relates to the noun *opposition* and is an adjective. Position determines this relationship. Now note the difference in meaning in the following pairs of sentences:

> The house on the corner belongs to the policeman.
> The house belongs to the policeman on the corner.
>
> Walking down the street, I met Louis' brother.
> I met Louis' brother walking down the street.
>
> We found him in the desert where the mesquite grows.
> We found him where the mesquite grows in the desert.
>
> He drinks only water when he goes to town.
> He drinks water only when he goes to town.

As illustrated in the above sentences, the position of the modifier, whether it is a single-word or a word-group modifier, determines the meaning derived from the sentence by the reader or listener. In order to communicate the intended meaning, a modifier should ordinarily be as close as possible to the word to which it relates.

SIGNALS OF FUNCTION

Word order, or position, is often reinforced by other signals of function. In the following rhyme, for example, what signals help you distinguish between *work* as a verb and *work* as a noun?

> Man may work from sun to sun.
> But a woman's work is never done.

In the first line, the auxiliary *may* marks *work* as a verb. In the second line, the determiner *a* and the possessive modifier *woman's* mark *work* as a noun.

In the following sentence pair, what signal helps you distinguish between the adjective *furtive* and the adverb *furtively*?

> The boy looked furtive to the examiner.
> The boy looked furtively at the examiner.

In the first sentence, *furtive* is a predicate adjective that completes the linking verb *looked*. Since the adverb modifier of *looked* takes the same position, the characteristic *-ly* suffix helps to identify the adverb in the second sentence. Form, in this case, reinforces position as a signal of function and therefore of meaning.

Now look at this sentence pair:

> The swallow perched all day.
> The perch swallowed all day.

What verb ending helps to identify the verb in these two sentences? When a word functions as a verb it is inflected like a verb. Here, the inflectional verb-ending *-ed* marks *perched* in the first sentence and *swallowed* in the second sentence as verbs. In this case, an inflectional ending, reinforced by position, serves to identify the verb.

In the following examples, the inflectional verb-endings are in color.

> Mr. Wilson calendars all special events.
> The Elks' Hall functioned last evening as an auditorium.
> The registrar is processing all of her papers.
> Jack Benny debuted last night at Carnegie Hall.

To sum up, then, word order, or position, is often reinforced by other signals of function. These signals include inflectional endings, characteristic prefixes and suffixes, and certain function words — noun-marking determiners and verb-marking auxiliaries, for example.

Although form usually reinforces position in determining meaning, sometimes form and function do not point in the same direction.

> Only the very ambitious would sacrifice their friends.

The word *ambitious* has a characteristic adjective suffix. This signal is apparently supported by the use of the intensifier *very*, a function word that frequently precedes an adjective. The position of *ambitious* before the verb *would sacrifice*, however, strongly establishes its function as the subject noun. In this sentence, *ambitious* functions as a subject noun — a function normally filled by a noun or a noun substitute. But is *ambitious* a noun in this sentence? Some grammarians think it is. It would be more accurately descriptive, however, to say that in this sentence *ambitious*, a word with the formal characteristics of an adjective, functions as the subject of the sentence — a function normally filled by a noun.

Now study these sentences:

> Fighting is forbidden by the principal.
> The fighting continued for days.

In the first sentence, *fighting* has the formal characteristic of a verb, the *-ing* suffix. However, its position in the sentence establishes it as the subject. However, *fighting* cannot be called a noun since it does not have the formal characteristics of a noun. In this sentence, *fighting* — a word with the formal characteristics of a verb — functions as the subject, a function normally filled by a noun. Actually there is a word to describe this usage. *Fighting* is classified as a verbal — a verb form functioning in some way other than as a verb. Verbals that function as nouns are called GERUNDS. Verbals are discussed more fully in the next chapter.

In the second sentence, oddly enough, *fighting* is usually classified as a noun. The presence of the determiner *The* before *fighting*, together with its position as subject, lends support to this classification.

Remember that in English, words do not have an absolute identity or classification. What a word is depends on how it is used. Nouns, verbs, adjectives, and adverbs may be classified only in context.

FUNCTIONAL SHIFT

As you have just seen, English depends primarily on position and word order as the chief clues to function. English can therefore be described as an analytic language. Latin, on the other hand, is a synthetic language. It depends on inflection, or certain changes in form, to determine the syntax, or function, and therefore the meaning of a word. We have inherited parts of our language from Latin and other inflected languages. While many of the inflections have been lost, many still remain. However, the dominant factor in English is position, not inflection. We are therefore not bound by the inflectional requirements that limit the function of a particular word.

In English, a given word is often used in a number of functions. This is called functional shift. Functional shift adds great flexibility to the communicating power of the language but creates some problems for the grammarian.

What is the functional shift in each of the following sentence pairs?

Otto joined the army.
Otto hopes to become an army officer.

The dormitory is closed for the summer.
The dormitory rules are posted in the hall.

Herman has been initiated into a fraternity.
Bertha is engaged to a fraternity man.

Hyman Diggs is a criminal.
Casper Mahoney is a criminal lawyer.

In the preceding sentence pairs, each of the words in color has the formal characteristics of a noun and each can be inflected like a noun (*army, armies, army's*). In the second sentence of each pair, the function shifts from that of noun to that of noun-modifier.

Now note the functional shift in these sentence pairs:

Your good qualities should face inward.   SENECA
The good must be chosen for its own sake.   CICERO

No evil man is happy.   CERVANTES

The evil comes upon us all at once like blows to a dog.   CERVANTES

The distance one should keep from a wicked man cannot be measured.
UNKNOWN

The wicked flee when no man pursueth.   *Proverbs*

If there is food left over in the kitchen, there are poor people in the street.
CHINESE PROVERB

Remember the poor; it costs nothing.   MARK TWAIN

In the above sentence pairs, the function shifts from adjective in the first sentence to noun in the second sentence.

In each of the following sentence pairs, a word that may be inflected as a noun is first used in its normal noun function. How is this same word used in the second sentence. Does it undergo a change in form?

Mr. Carmen built a fence around his yard.
Mr. Carmen fenced his yard to keep out the cows.

The child fell on the rough floor.
The fighter floored his opponent in the second round.

The manager kept in contact with his salesman.
The manager contacted his salesman.

In the second sentence of each of the above pairs, the word used as a noun in the first sentence is inflected as a verb and used in a verb function.

Identify the functional shift in each of the following sentence pairs:

The smooth surface reflected the light.
He smoothed the surface with steel wool.

The clean shirts are in the drawer.
George cleans the cellar every Saturday.

The opponents played a rough game of basketball.
Joe roughed up the opposing center.

It was an even game until the last quarter.
Smithville evened the score in the last minute of play.

In each of the above sentence pairs, a word is used first in an adjective function and then in a verb function. Note the inflection in the second sentence of each pair.

In the illustrations given so far, words have been used in two different functions. The following sentences demonstrate the use of a word in three different functions.

Verb   We play dominoes every Friday night.
Noun   Henrietta saw the play in Las Vegas.
Adjective   Barbara bought new play clothes for the children.

Adverb	Father drove slow past the school.
Adjective	The slow train stopped at every station.
Verb	The bus should slow down at the crossing.

Adjective	Mr. Schumann takes a daily walk.
Adverb	Mr. Schumann walks daily in Prospect Park.
Noun	The *Irish Times* is a daily published in Dublin.

Now note the four different functions in these sentences:

Adjective	The troops were in a forward position when the bombardment began.
Adverb	The woman stepped forward and claimed the prize.
Noun	Jay Cooper is the new forward on our basketball team.
Verb	The postmaster will forward the mail to Naugatuck.

The sentences that follow demonstrate the use of a word in five different functions:

Adverb	Don't worry; the money will turn up.
Connective	The frightened cat scrambled up the flagpole.
Adjective	The sun is up.
Verb	The dealers have upped the price of gasoline again.
Noun	Life is filled with ups and downs.

Exercise 1

Write each of the words listed below on your paper. Next to each word, record the functional labels given in your dictionary. Then for each word, write sentences illustrating its different functions. (If you have forgotten what a functional label looks like, see page 243 of this book.)

move	ready	near
plane	far	below
brave	call	down
out	round	top

Exercise 2

A. *To what word class or word classes does each of the following words ordinarily belong? Indicate noun, verb, adjective, or adverb. Check your classification against that of the dictionary.*

desk	educate
book	breeze
climb	knuckle
prepare	furnish
carve	finish
foundation	carelessly

cement	often
consciousness	religious
intelligent	backward
careless	away
abbreviate	reform
abbreviation	style
nail	unhealthy
complex	water

B. *How do you account for the fact that many of the above words are classified in more than one way? Write sentences to illustrate the different functions of those words classified in more than one way.*

C. *Are there any words in the list which belong to only one word class? Write sentences to illustrate the function of each of these words.*

D. *Develop a general statement that describes what this exercise teaches us about English words.*

Exercise 3

1. Write a sentence in which the predicate verb is a word that sometimes functions as a noun and has a characteristic noun suffix.

2. Write a sentence in which a word that may be inflected as an adjective is used as the object of a preposition.

3. Write a sentence in which a word that is ordinarily used as a verb functions as the subject noun.

4. Write a sentence in which a word with a characteristic adjective suffix functions as a direct object.

5. Write a sentence in which one pronoun functions as a noun-modifier and another as the subject noun.

6. Write a sentence in which a word that is ordinarily used as a noun functions as a noun modifier.

7. Write a sentence in which a subject-predicate word group functions as the subject noun.

8. Write a sentence in which a subject-predicate word group functions as a noun modifier.

9. Write a sentence in which a subject-predicate word group functions as a verb modifier.

10. Write a sentence in which a verbal phrase functions as a noun modifier.

VARIETY OF FORMS IN A GIVEN FUNCTION

So far you have examined the use of a word in two or more different functions. Now let us look at each function within a sentence and observe the variety of word forms that may be used in this function.

SUBJECT NOUN

In each of the following sentences, the word in color functions as a subject noun. What does the word class in parentheses tell you about each of these words?

The children like to play games. (Noun)
Swimming is a healthful exercise. (Verb)
The old like to read in the evening. (Adjective)
Tomorrow will be a rainy day. (Adverb)
We like to hear music. (Function Word)
Nobody likes to go to bed. (Function Word)
Those are my gloves. (Function Word)

While we usually think of the subject as a noun function, it is evident from the above sentences that words ordinarily thought of as belonging to other word classes also function as subject nouns.

You have already noted that certain subject-predicate word groups function as the subject noun. Verbal phrases also serve in this function.

Noun Clause   What I have to tell you is very important.
Verbal Phrase   Lifting weights strengthens the arm muscles.
Infinitive Phrase   To write effectively takes much practice.

PREDICATE VERB

The farmer conditioned his soil with crop rotation.
Mother will dry the clothes on the line.
The angry voices were stilled.
The champion downed his opponent in the fifth round.

Here, and in the sections that follow, use your dictionary to help you find out the word class or word classes which describe the ordinary function of the words in color.

COMPLEMENT

In the sentences below, each of the words in color is a complement— a position ordinarily filled by a noun. With the help of your dictionary, find out the word class or word classes to which the words in color ordinarily belong.

Mother handed me a dollar.
I will give this to Henry.
The meeting will be tomorrow.
The trainees did not ask why.

A noun clause sometimes functions as a complement as does a verbal phrase.

Noun Clause	**The general knew** what the enemy was about to do.
Verbal Phrase	**The class enjoyed** writing a short story.
Verbal Phrase	**Alice wants** to go to the movies.

NOUN-MODIFIER

In the following sentences, each of the words in color functions as an adjective—the word class to which most noun modifiers belong. With the help of your dictionary, find out the word class or word classes to which the words in color ordinarily belong.

The Smiths drove away in the family car.
These books must be returned to the library.
The officer examined our passports.
The dying man was taken to the hospital.
The road back seemed much shorter.
The meeting tomorrow will be at eight.
The fight developed into a near riot.
The down payment will be ten dollars.

Certain subject-predicate word groups, prepositional phrases, and verbal phrases also function as noun-modifiers.

Adjective Clause	Here is a watch that runs by electricity.
Prepositional Phrase	**The lady** of the house **has gone out.**
Verbal Phrase	**The fishermen,** rowing parallel to shore, **carefully laid the net.**
	Blessed with ideal weather, **we sailed for days in a moderate easterly breeze.**
Verbal Phrase	**Football is the game** to watch on television.

VERB-MODIFIER

In the following sentences, each of the words in color functions as an adverb—the word class to which most verb-modifiers belong. Find out the word class or word classes to which the words ordinarily belong.

The sheriff looked hard at the stranger.
Our company will arrive Sunday.
The boys came running when the bell rang.
The men looked up when the boss shouted.

Subject-predicate word groups, prepositional phrases, and verbal phrases also function as verb-modifiers.

Adverb Clause	**The crowd let out a roar** when Casey came to bat.
Prepositional Phrase	**The lemmings plunged** into the sea.
Verbal Phrase	**Mrs. Pinch diets** to keep her weight down.

Exercise 4   *In the sentence, there are four main functions: subject noun, predicate verb, complement, and modifier. Classify each of the underlined words or word groups in the following sentences according to one of these functions.*

1. The archeologists found the buried <u>city</u>.

2. The express company should have <u>delivered</u> the parcel.

3. The wedding <u>bells</u> are ringing for that old gang of mine.

4. The <u>careless</u> maid emptied a bowl of soup on the flower bed.

5. Many ranchers believe <u>that the most dangerous animal in the United States is the dairy bull</u>.

6. The men in the accounting department are all <u>college</u> graduates.

7. Luella was disappointed when she placed second in the <u>cooking</u> contest.

8. The building <u>on the corner</u> will be torn down next week.

9. The horse ran <u>because he was frightened</u>.

10. The <u>courageous</u> succeed when others fail.

11. <u>Whatever develops in the referendum</u> will displease some voters.

12. Oliver <u>elbowed</u> his way through the milling crowd.

13. Little Lucy <u>rounded</u> the corner on her tricycle and ran smack into Mr. Crump.

14. The <u>championship</u> fight lasted four unexciting rounds.

15. The architect <u>who designed this house</u> has a keen sense of humor.

16. Hinkman can never see the <u>good</u> which frequently results from being generous.

17. Door prizes will be given to whoever comes in <u>before nine o'clock</u>.

18. <u>To call him at this hour</u> would be very thoughtless.

19. Henry wanted to know <u>where I had been</u>.

20. Most experts agree <u>that a lion can run 100 yards in four seconds flat</u>.

21. An age passed <u>before we reached the top of the ravine</u>.

Exercise 5

Fill in the blanks according to the lettered descriptions after each of the items below. Write a separate sentence for each substitution.

1. The lady gave ____ to the Salvation Army.
   (a) a function word
   (b) a noun
   (c) an adverb

2. ____ is a healthful exercise.
   (a) a verb form
   (b) a noun

3. Mrs. Simpson lost her ____ pocketbook.
   (a) an adjective
   (b) a noun adjunct

4. Joe Daly is a ____ student.
   (a) an adjective with a characteristic suffix
   (b) a noun adjunct

5. The livingroom will be painted ____.
   (a) an adverb
   (b) an adjective
   (c) a noun

6. The man looked ____ when we shouted.
   (a) an adverb
   (b) an adjective

7. Success is the reward of the ____.
   (a) a noun
   (b) a word ordinarily classified as an adjective

8. The class likes to read ____ stories.
   (a) a noun adjunct
   (b) a modifier with an -*ing* ending
   (c) a possessive noun
   (d) a pronoun
   (e) a function word

Exercise 6

1. Use each of the following forms as a subject noun:
   (a) a function word
   (b) a noun clause
   (c) a word ordinarily classified as a verb

2. Use each of the following forms as a complement:
   (a) a function word
   (b) a noun clause
   (c) a word ordinarily classified as a verb

Summary

The important functions in the English sentence are the subject noun, the predicate verb, the complement, and the modifying function. The most significant clue to function, and therefore to meaning, is position. Form, as indicated by inflectional changes or by characteristic prefixes and suffixes, often reinforces position as a clue to meaning. Function words also provide clues to function.

At times, however, form and position point in different directions. While in such cases definite classification is not entirely possible, it is position that actually determines the function of the word in question.

English is essentially an analytic language. In English, most words can therefore be used without regard to form. This procedure leads to functional shift, a grammatical device whereby a given word may be used in a variety of functions. A variety of words and of word groups may also be used in the basic sentence functions.

Chapter Test, Form A

(Since the chapter test is a cumulative review of word classes and of function, no attempt has been made to provide specific page references. Refer to the dictionary and to the index of this book for help with those items that may puzzle you.)

1. In the following sentences, select all the words that may be identified by characteristics of form. Classify them as nouns, verbs, adjectives, and adverbs.
   (a) The momentous occasion arrived at last.
   (b) His attention was directed immediately to the conductor.
   (c) The boy was playing games with his sister.
   (d) The farmer walked homeward across the fields.
   (e) All the guests sat at the captain's table.

2. In the following sentences, identify the function of each underlined word or word group.
   (a) The brakeman gave the <u>engineer</u> the signal.
   (b) The manager has <u>engineered</u> another big deal.
   (c) <u>To make the world safe for democracy</u> was the objective of World War I.
   (d) The coach likes <u>winning</u> teams.
   (e) The teacher knew <u>what the class wanted</u>.
   (f) Mr. Wilson is a <u>science</u> teacher.
   (g) The <u>good</u> sometimes die young.
   (h) When Lot's wife looked <u>back,</u> she turned into a pillar of salt.
   (i) Harold's beard is growing <u>thin</u>.

3. Write sentences using the word *walk* first as a verb and then as a noun.

4. Write sentences using the word *work* first as a noun, then as a verb, and then as a noun-modifier.

5. Write sentences using the word *dance* first as a noun, then as a verb, and then as a noun-modifier.

6. Write sentences using the word *up* first as a preposition, then as an adverb, and then as a noun.

7. Write sentences using the word *good* first as an adjective and then as a noun.

8. Write sentences using the word *ready* first as an adjective and then as a verb.

9. Use each of the following forms as the subject of a sentence:
   (a) a function word
   (b) a noun clause
   (c) an adjective
   (d) a word ordinarily classified as a verb

10. Use each of the following forms as a modifier:
    (a) an adverb
    (b) an adjective clause
    (c) a noun
    (d) a word ordinarily classified as a verb

Chapter Test, Form B

1. In the following sentences, select all the words that may be identified by characteristics of form. Classify them as nouns, verbs, adjectives, and adverbs.
   (a) The dreadful accident occurred last night.

    (b) His intentions were obvious.
    (c) The farmer's son was milking the cows.
    (d) The director walked slowly toward the stage.
    (e) The principal sometimes comes to our parties.

2. In the following sentences, identify the function of each underlined word or word group.
    (a) We were met by a <u>highly</u> excited young woman.
    (b) <u>What we believe</u> shapes our character.
    (c) The <u>meek</u> shall inherit the earth.
    (d) The chairman seems <u>nervous</u>.
    (e) Herbert Preston is a <u>child</u> actor.
    (f) <u>Sedgewick Holmes</u> was named athlete of the year.
    (g) Helen is the girl <u>who graduated from</u> Vassar.
    (h) The ballet star has chosen her <u>dancing</u> partner.
    (i) The tackle <u>shouldered</u> his way <u>through</u> the opposing line.

3. Write sentences using the word *climb* first as a verb and then as a noun.

4. Write sentences using the word *play* first as a noun, then as a verb, and then as a modifier.

5. Write sentences using the word *team* first as a noun, then as a verb, and then as a modifier.

6. Write sentences using the word *down* as a preposition, as an adverb, and as a verb.

7. Write sentences using the word *ambitious* first as an adjective and then as a noun.

8. Write sentences using the word *long* first as an adjective and then as a verb.

9. Use each of the following forms as a complement:
    (a) a function word
    (b) a noun clause
    (c) a word ordinarily classified as a verb
    (d) a phrase

10. Use each of the following forms as a predicate verb:
    (a) a word ordinarily classified as a noun
    (b) a word ordinarily classified as an adjective
    (c) a word ordinarily classified as an adverb
    (d) a word ordinarily classified as a function word

The Structure of Your Language

    The great vitality and flexibility of English is in no small degree due to the fact that it is an analytic language, that we do not depend on inflections for clues to syntax, that position or word order is the main clue to function or meaning. For this reason, a great variety of forms may be used in a given function.

■ Fill in the blanks in the following sentences with the form suggested in parentheses.

EXAMPLE The ＿＿ was printed in color.
           (A word with the characteristic noun suffix.)
           The *advertisement* was printed in color.

1. The ＿＿ will need assistance.
   (A word ordinarily used as an adjective and inflected as an adjective.)

2. A formal ＿＿ will be held on Friday evening.
   (A word that may be inflected as a verb or a noun.)

3. ＿＿ will be a holiday.
   (An adverb with no characteristic affix.)

4. ＿＿ is an education in itself.
   (An inflected verb form.)

5. ＿＿ to Yuma will be fun.
   (A verbal phrase.)

6. ＿＿ this bad news would be a mistake.
   (An infinitive phrase.)

7. ＿＿ has not been determined.
   (A noun clause.)

8. The hint escaped my ＿＿.
   (A word with a characteristic noun suffix.)

9. She gave me a nasty ＿＿.
   (A word that may be inflected like a verb.)

10. We promised ＿＿ a party.
   (A personal pronoun.)

11. The ministry is a ＿＿ which attracts unselfish men.
   (An inflected verb form.)

12. The state gives the ＿＿ a pension.
   (An inflected verb form.)

13. Life rewards the ＿＿ with success.
   (A word with a characteristic adjective suffix.)

14. He is coming, but I do not know ＿＿.
   (A function word often used as a connective.)

15. The ladies want ＿＿.
   (An infinitive phrase.)

Chapter 4

Verbals

A Look Back and A Look Forward

In Chapter 2 and in Chapter 3, you were introduced to certain words which have the formal characteristics of verbs but which sometimes function as nouns, adjectives, and adverbs. The use of verbals, as these words are called, is, of course, consistent with the grammatical device of functional shift, which you learned about in Chapter 3.

In this chapter, you will study in detail the function and form of verbals. You will note how this word class contributes to effective communication.

FORM OF VERBALS

Verbals are used in three forms. The plain form of a verb – or the past or past participle form with certain auxiliaries – is sometimes introduced by the function word *to.*

> I want to go home.
> This is the problem to be solved.
> I would like to have seen the play.

The *-ing,* or the present participle, form of the verb is the second verbal form. The *-ing* form has two classifications, as will be discussed later in this chapter.

> The police caught the man breaking into the store.
> Swimming provides healthful exercise.
> Helen's first love is acting.
> Alice is his favorite dancing partner.
> The men did not like hiking in the rain.

The past form or past participle form of the verb is the third type of verbal. This type is usually an *-ed* or *-en* form.

> The defeated candidate retired from politics.
> The fighter, beaten and bruised, was carried from the ring.

VERBAL PHRASES

Although a verbal takes on the function of a noun or a modifier, it still retains some of its prerogatives as a verb. Many verbals may take a complement, and all verbals may have modifiers. When a verbal takes a complement or has modifiers, the word group that results is called a VERBAL PHRASE. Note the structure of the verbal phrases in these sentences:

> Alice likes to play tennis with her sister. (The verbal *to play* has a complement, *tennis;* the word group *with her sister* modifies the verbal.)
> Walking past the cemetery, Hennesey heard a strange noise. (The word group *past the cemetery* modifies the verbal *Walking.*)
> The odor of roast pig, browned to a delicious crispness, assailed the nostrils of the puzzled Bo-bo. (The word group *to a delicious crispness* modifies the verbal *browned.)*
> Henry went out to the barn to milk the cows. (The verbal *to milk* has a complement, *cows.)*
> Eating corn on the cob can sometimes be a challenge. (The verbal *Eating* has a complement, *corn;* the word group *on the cob* modifies *corn.)*
> Driven to madness by his pursuers, the horse plunged over the cliff. (The word groups *to madness* and *by his pursuers* modify the verbal *Driven.)*

Exercise 1   *Identify the modifiers of the verbals in the following sentences. Indicate the complements, if any, of each verbal.*

1. Worn out by the day's work, Mr. Featherby trudged wearily home. (In this sentence, the verbal is a past form that does not end in *-ed* or *-ing*.)

2. The city wants to build the school on the east side.

3. Playing hopscotch on the pavement is the great delight of many city children.

4. Mrs. Washburn wanted desperately to be seen in her new mink coat.

5. Mother wants the boys to go to camp next summer.

6. The children's greatest delight was to eat homemade fudge just before bedtime.

7. The order was to move forward at daybreak.

8. Mother said she would ask Alice to make a cake for the party.

9. Rowing easily over the calm water of the lake, the boys soon reached the village on the other side.

10. Chilled by the wind, the men trudged slowly over the hard snow.

11. Charles earned a dollar by washing his father's car.

12. Cheering wildly, the crowd rose to its feet.

FUNCTIONS OF VERBALS

Verbals have a variety of functions. In the preceding section, you looked at the different verbal forms. Now you will study the three kinds of verbals — infinitives, gerunds, and participles — and how they function.

Infinitives

The INFINITIVE is used in a variety of functions in the sentence.

SUBJECT NOUN

> Success **was his goal.**

In this sentence, *Success* is a noun in the subject noun function. Now change the noun form to the infinitive form:

> To succeed **was his goal.**

Here, the infinitive fills a function normally filled by a noun. Note the form of the subject nouns in the following sentences:

To win the war was the aim of the nation.
To lose gracefully is the mark of a gentleman.
To fight on when all seems lost proves the courage of the soldier.

In all three sentences, the subject noun is an infinitive phrase.

COMPLEMENT

Georgie wants a job.

In this sentence, *job* is a noun that functions as a complement—the direct object of the verb. Let's change the noun form to an infinitive form:

Georgie wants to work.

Here, the infinitive fills a function normally filled by a noun. Now note the form of the complements in these sentences:

Uncle Fred loves to play checkers.
The captain wanted to attack the enemy immediately.
Hilda's boy friend asked to be introduced to her father.

In all three sentences, the direct object is an infinitive phrase.

LINKING-VERB COMPLEMENT

The horse seemed restless.
The horse seemed to sense danger.

In the second sentence, an infinitive phrase takes on the same function as the predicate adjective in the first sentence. Infinitives may also be used in the predicate noun function as illustrated in the two sentences below.

The command is to attack at daybreak.
The best plan is to have the car repaired by a competent mechanic.

NOUN-MODIFIER

This is the crucial game.
This is the game to win.

In the second sentence, an infinitive takes on the same function as the adjective in the first sentence: both *crucial* and *to win* modify the noun *game*. Now note the modifying function of the infinitives or the infinitive phrases in the following sentences, and identify the noun modified by each infinitive:

Look Homeward Angel is a book to be read with discernment.
The coach has a strong desire to place among the top ten teams.

VERB-MODIFIER

> Luther has gone abroad.
> Luther has gone to visit his relatives in England.

Here, the infinitive phrase in the second sentence has the same function as the adverb in the first sentence: both modify the verb *has gone*. Now identify the verb modified by each infinitive or infinitive phrase in these sentences:

The crowd came to jeer and stayed to cheer.
The hikers ducked into the barn to escape the rain.
Ollie climbed the mountain to see what was on the other side.

ADJECTIVE-MODIFIER

In each of these sentences, what is the function of the infinitive or the infinitive phrase?

> The guests were sorry to leave.
> Mushrooms are good to eat.
> Dad will be glad to meet your train.
> You were lucky to find your wallet.
> Huck was eager to run away from his pappy.

Here, the infinitive or the infinitive phrase modifies an adjective, used predicatively.

ADVERB-MODIFIER

In each of these sentences, what is the function of the infinitive phrase?

> George walked back to look for Molly.
> Harry promised never to do it again.

In the first sentence, the infinitive phrase modifies the adverb *back*. In the second sentence, the infinitive phrase modifies the adverb *never*. In both sentences, therefore, the infinitive phrase functions as an adverb.

APPOSITIVE

If you're not sure what an appositive is, turn back to page 28. Then note the function of the infinitive phrases in these sentences:

The mother was granted her last wish, to see her only son.
Nellie has one consuming interest, to dance the polka.
The President's plan, to wage war on poverty, is a commendable project.

In each of these sentences, the infinitive phrase functions as a noun in a side-by-side, or an appositive, relationship with a noun.

ABSOLUTE CONSTRUCTION

> To tell the truth, I don't know where I'll get the money.
> To say the least, you should be thankful for your good fortune.

The absolute construction and the appositive are discussed more fully in the next chapter. Note, however, that in the above sentences, the infinitive phrases have no direct relationship with any function in the rest of the sentence. In these sentences, the infinitive functions as an absolute and helps establish coherence.

SUBJECT NOUN-INFINITIVE STRUCTURE

The nine functions of the infinitive illustrated above demonstrate the versatility of the infinitive and the infinitive phrase in communication. There is, moreover, still another function served by the infinitive. In the following sentences what is the difference between the infinitive phrases they contain and those contained in the previous illustrative sentences?

> Professor Miles encouraged him to persevere.
> The captain ordered the men to shoot.
> His lawyer advised him to plead guilty.
> I asked the operator to call me at 6:30 A.M.

In each of the infinitive phrases illustrated above, the infinitive is preceded by a noun or a noun substitute that functions as the subject of the infinitive. The infinitive itself functions as a non-finite verb in a subject-predicate word group.

In this structure the *to* of the infinitive is sometimes omitted:

> Mother saw Henry take a third helping of ice cream.
> Billy helped me rake the leaves.
> The onlookers watched the crane lift the load of lumber.

The subject-noun infinitive structure sometimes functions as the object of a preposition:

> I think it's wise for you to go.
> Dad made an appointment for Mother to see the doctor.

Exercise 2   *Identify the infinitives and the infinitive phrases in the following sentences. Describe the function of each.*

1. Emil wants to be a sailor.

2. To fail the examination would be a disgrace.

3. This passage from *De bello Gallico* is difficult to translate.

4. Hilda waited for Charlie to open the door.

5. Brock is planning to leave tomorrow.

6. The boys are coming this weekend to play tennis.

7. The orders are to advance cautiously toward the woods.

8. To erect a custom-built house would be too costly.

9. The general succeeded in his mission, to drive the rebel forces from the city.

10. The officer cautioned us to drive slowly.

11. Alice bought red shoes to wear with her new dress.

12. We've decided to leave before sunup tomorrow.

13. To be sure, why not check the correct spelling in the dictionary?

14. The game to be played tonight will decide the conference championship.

15. The twins have gone to see their married sister in St. Louis.

16. Mr. Johnson was happy to see his mother-in-law.

17. Mr. Soakum promised to wash the car in time for the wedding.

18. The flood waters appear to be receding rapidly.

19. Mother asked Dad to buy her an electric broom.

20. We saw Jane hide Tom's ice skates.

21. To put the matter briefly, I'm broke.

22. The problem to be solved is a difficult one.

23. The prisoner had one request, to be allowed to see his wife.

24. I think the customer is ready to buy the car.

25. The principal seems to know all about what happened.

Exercise 3

1. Write a sentence with an infinitive phrase that functions as a subject noun.

2. Write a sentence with an infinitive phrase that functions as a direct object.

3. Write a sentence with an infinitive phrase that functions as a linking-verb complement.

4. Write a sentence with an infinitive phrase that functions as a noun-modifier.

5. Write a sentence with an infinitive phrase that functions as a verb-modifier.

6. Write a sentence with an infinitive phrase that functions as an adjective-modifier.

7. Write a sentence with an infinitive phrase that functions as an appositive.

8. Write a sentence with an infinitive phrase that functions as an absolute structure.

9. Write a sentence containing a structure in which a noun is the subject of an infinitive.

10. Write a sentence containing a structure in which a pronoun is the subject of an infinitive.

Gerunds

The *-ing* form of the verbal serves in two important functions — as a noun and as a modifier. When an *-ing* verbal is used in a noun function, it is called a GERUND.

As illustrated in the following sections, gerunds function in the sentence in all the different ways that a noun functions.

SUBJECT NOUN

In the following sentence, the gerund phrase functions as a subject noun. What single-word modifier makes the idea of *Rowing* more explicit? What word-group modifier further explains *Rowing*?

> Rowing easily over the calm waters of a mountain lake is a delightful way to spend a summer afternoon.

In this sentence, the adverb *easily* modifies the gerund as does the prepositional phrase *over the calm waters*. The object of the preposition is in turn modified: *waters of a mountain lake*.

What is the function of *apple pie* in the gerund phrase which functions as the subject noun in the following sentence?

> Eating apple pie just before bedtime may bring on an attack of indigestion.

Here, *apple pie* is the direct object of the gerund *Eating*. Like the infinitive, the gerund is a verb form. While it functions as a noun, it retains many of its prerogatives as a verb. For example, a gerund may have modifiers of its own, and it sometimes takes a direct object.

The four sections that follow illustrate other noun functions of the gerund.

DIRECT OBJECT

> Most children enjoy digging in the sand.
> The law forbids selling liquor to minors.
> This treatment prevents shrinking of woolen garments.

OBJECT OF A PREPOSITION

> Charles is thinking of joining the Navy.
> The woman was given a ticket for driving recklessly in a school zone.
> Laura amuses herself by creating a wonderful world of make-believe.

LINKING-VERB COMPLEMENT

> Uncle George's hobby is mounting butterflies.
> Chumley's sole occupation is watching the migratory patterns of birds.
> Alec's job will be feeding the rhinoceros.

APPOSITIVE

> The pilot's job, steering the ship safely into its berth, is an important one.
> Aunt Carrie has a new interest, reading science-fiction stories.
> Henry has only one fault, pitching too many home-run balls.
> Her ambition, dancing in a ballet, was never realized.

Exercise 4   *Identify the function of the gerund or of the gerund phrase in each of the following sentences. If a gerund has a complement, identify it also.*

1. Descending almost seven miles to the floor of the Pacific Ocean must have been an exciting experience.

2. We made the bicycle look better by giving it a coat of bright red paint.

3. Barry's job, baby-sitting for the Sibleys on Saturday night, is one that nobody envies.

4. His job at the soup factory was sorting the culls from the ripe fruit.

5. Now that he's retired, Uncle Jeb's chief interest is cultivating rare varieties of orchids.

6. The grizzly breaks his long winter fast by chewing on the new grass.

7. After catching our quota of trout, we packed our gear and headed back for Lonetree Camp.

8. Some people enjoy rising at five in the morning for a brisk hike before breakfast; *I* don't.

9. Raising sandworms can be a rewarding hobby.

10. My little brother makes a career of squeezing out of tight corners.

11. You can't blame me for being suspicious.

12. Feeding the animals is prohibited.

-ing *Participles*

When the *-ing* form of a verbal is used as an adjective — as the modifier of a noun or of a noun substitute — it is called a PARTICIPLE. As was pointed out in Chapter 2, if the participle has a modifier or a complement the word group so formed is called a PARTICIPIAL PHRASE. The participle sometimes comes immediately before the noun it modifies and sometimes immediately after. As you study the illustrative sentences in this section, take special note of how the participial phrases are punctuated.

The crowd, cheering wildly at the efforts of the home team to make a first down, rose to its feet.

Here, the word group in color is a participial phrase. The participle is *cheering.* The modifiers are *wildly* and *at the efforts of the home team to make a first down.* The participial phrase modifies the subject noun *crowd.*

NOUN-MODIFIER

A participle or a participial phrase may modify a noun or a noun substitute in any of its functions. What, for example, is the function of the noun modified by the participial phrase in each of the following sentences?

Feeling along the wall of Kloochman Rock, **Doug** found a groove he could use as a handhold. (Here, the modified noun, *Doug*, functions as a subject noun.)

They found the lost **child** playing in the sand. (The modified noun, *child*, functions as a direct object.)

We caught sight of the **climbers** edging their way along the cliff. (The modified noun, *climbers*, functions as the object of a preposition.)

My brother Jimmy's best friend is the little **boy** hanging by his heels from the bottom branch of that oak tree. (The modified noun, *boy*, functions as a linking-verb complement.)

LINKING-VERB COMPLEMENT

The *-ing* participle functions as a predicate adjective after a linking verb.

> The boy's manner was aggravating.
> Sigrid becomes more charming every week.
> The news seems alarming this morning.
> Mary looks striking in her new gown.

The *-ing* verbal in this function may have adverbial modifiers, but it does not take a complement:

> The boy's manner was extremely aggravating when he spoke sharply to his teacher.

OBJECTIVE COMPLEMENT

The *-ing* participle sometimes functions as an objective complement:

> The class found the story boring.
> Henry thought the play exciting.
> Hilda considers her boy friend interesting.

-ed *and* -en *Participles*

The third kind of verbal, from the standpoint of form, is the *-ed* or *-en* verbal. This form always functions as an adjective and is therefore a participle, never a gerund.

NOUN-MODIFIER

> The broiled lobster was delicious.
> Henry is a married man.
> The wounded soldier cried for help.
> The jury heard the surgeon's sworn statement.
> Broken vows can never be mended.

The *-ed* or *-en* participle may have adverbial modifiers, but it does not take a complement unless it is used with the auxiliary *having.* In the sentences that follow, take special note of how the participial phrases are punctuated.

> The lobster broiled over charcoal was delicious.
> The soldier, wounded seriously in the battle, cried out for help.
> The statement sworn to by the surgeon was heard by the jury.
> The squad, having captured two of the enemy scouts, proceeded to the rear.
> Father, having defeated Mother at Scrabble, proudly announced his score.
> Pat Conlon, having completed his required courses, graduated with his class.

In each of the last three sentences, the participle is used with the auxiliary verb *having.* In these same sentences, the participle takes a complement.

LINKING-VERB COMPLEMENT

The *-ed* and *-en* participle may be used as a predicate adjective after a linking verb.

Dorothy looked frightened as she walked onstage.
Carl appears excited at the prospect of a new job.
The manager was mistaken in his decision to hire the new stenographer.
Perry Mason seemed worried over the outcome of the trial.

OBJECTIVE COMPLEMENT

The *-ed* and *-en* participle sometimes functions as an objective complement.

Henry found his new car wrecked.
Miss Welles wants the report completed by Monday.
The boss ordered the men fired.

Since in each of the above sentences the participle relates to the direct object, it may be considered an objective complement.

Sharpening Your Language Skills

On page 90 and again on page 91, you were asked to note the punctuation of participial phrases. It will help you in your own writing if you remember the following pointers about punctuating participial phrases:

1. A comma is used after a participial phrase at the beginning of a sentence.

   Hurtling from a snowy ridge, the skiers appeared to take wing.

2. A comma sets off a nonrestrictive participial phrase. A nonrestrictive modifier identifies rather than defines. In speech, there is usually a pause before and after a nonrestrictive phrase.

   RESTRICTIVE   The boy steering the skiff is Jake Hardesty.
   NONRESTRICTIVE   Jake, steering the *Flamingo* with all the skill at his command, inched ahead of the other skiffs.

Exercise 5

Each of the following sentences contains a participial phrase. Write the sentences, punctuating the participial phrases where needed.

1. Plunging waist-deep into the cold water Abe caught the fish with his bare hand.

2. Youngsters scrambling over the slopes on makeshift skis develop the fearless agility that makes for expert skiing. (Careful: Do all youngsters develop agility?)

3. Dropping anchor we baited our hooks and began to fish.

4. We found Mr. Duvitch sitting alone on his front porch. (Read this sentence aloud.)

5. The Kasimars thrilled by their first barbecue kept breaking into wide smiles.

6. We could see the headlights cutting through the fog.

7. The dogs whimpering with some unnamed terror pulled desperately against their ropes.

8. Turning down the trail Doc headed back toward the trading post.

9. The truck swerving wildly around a corner jumped the curb and crashed through a storefront.

10. The man carrying the shabby umbrella will be the first witness for the prosecution.

Exercise 6

1. Write a sentence in which a gerund functions as a subject noun.

2. Write a sentence in which a participial phrase modifies a direct object.

3. Write a sentence in which an introductory participial phrase modifies a subject noun.

4. Write a sentence in which a gerund phrase functions as a direct object.

5. Write a sentence in which a gerund phrase functions as the object of a preposition.

6. Using an *-en* participle, write a sentence in which a participle functions as a linking-verb complement.

7. Write a sentence in which a gerund phrase functions as a linking-verb complement.

8. Write a sentence in which an *-ed* participle functions as an objective complement.

9. Write a sentence in which a gerund phrase functions as an appositive.

10. Write a sentence in which a participial phrase modifies a noun that is the object of a preposition.

RECOGNIZING VERBALS

In the following pair, what makes the difference in meaning obvious?

> Mary's favorite pastime is dancing.
> Mary's sister is dancing.

In the first sentence, the *-ing* verbal, a gerund, functions as a noun and tells us that Mary likes dancing. In the second sentence, the *-ing* verb form together with the auxiliary *is* tells us what Mary's sister is doing.

When an *-ing* verbal or verb form follows some form of the verb *to be*, it may be a gerund, it may be the predicate verb preceded by one or more auxiliaries, or it may be a participle functioning as a predicate adjective. In order to respond adequately to what is being said, the reader or listener must be able to identify the verb form as a verbal or as a predicate verb. Context is usually a clue to this distinction. Sometimes however, other clues are a necessary aid to recognition.

> Mary was entertaining last night.

What is the function of *entertaining* in this sentence? Because we can't tell whether the *-ing* form is functioning as a gerund or as a predicate verb, we don't really know whether Mary was entertaining guests last night or whether, for some reason, she was a delight to watch and to listen to. Now note the clues to meaning provided in the following sentence pair:

> Mary was entertaining her bridge club last night.
> Mary was very entertaining last night.

In the first sentence the complement, *her bridge club*, helps us recognize *entertaining* as a predicate verb preceded by the auxiliary *was*. In the second sentence, the intensifier *very* marks entertaining as a participle.

Exercise 7   *Identify the participles, the gerunds, the participial phrases, and the gerund phrases in the following sentences. Describe the function of each. In several sentences, the -ing form is a predicate verb.*

1. Walking with Agnes is sheer delight.

2. Strolling down the road, I saw William in his Sunday suit.

3. I saw William strolling down the road in his Sunday suit.

4. Miss Askew will be teaching English 2 next year.

5. Henry received a quarter for going to the supermarket.

6. Shaken and overcome by panic, Herman fled from the stage.

7. Julie sat on the sidelines, aching with misery.

8. Uncle Frank's hobby is photographing hummingbirds.

9. Mr. Wakefield will not tolerate talking in assembly.

10. Slurvian is coming into common use in the United States.

11. The woman sitting on the park bench is my Aunt Betsy.

12. Pushing and shoving, the boys crowded into the room.

13. The baby, amused by the twinkling lights, began to laugh.

14. I never blame a man for doing his job.

15. Mother gave William a job, putting out the cat.

16. Dad enjoys growing his own asparagus.

17. Aunt Caroline appeared excited at the good news.

18. Someone on skis was standing in the shadow of the hut.

19. Sleeping seems to be more enjoyable *after* the alarm clock rings.

20. The brief day was drawing to a close in a long, soft twilight.   JACK LONDON

21. Running down the stairs, the little boy stumbled and fell.

22. We visited a castle built in the twelfth century.

23. The priceless vase lay on the floor, shattered by a careless hand.

24. Having finished their work, the painters left for the day.

Exercise 8   *In the following sentences indicate which verb forms belong to the predicate verb and which are verbals. Be prepared to discuss the form of each verbal and the reason for calling it a verbal.*

1. Father is willing to buy a new car.

2. Strawberries served with whipped cream is my favorite dessert.

3. Harold refuses to play in the park.

4. Winking his left eye slyly, Mr. Reilly walked sedately across the room.

5. The contractor has promised to finish the job before next June.

6. Without once looking back, Philip boarded the train.

7. Mr. Winkelman has been asked to run for Congress.

8. Elwood walked about the city feeling lost and out of place.

9. The old folks seem contented in their new home.

10. Our old house needs painting.

11. The order was to demolish the bridge before sunup.

12. The two cars were flagged down by an officer standing at the intersection.

13. From where we're standing, we can see the ships approaching the harbor.

14. The animals were excited by the wind blowing in sudden gusts.

15. He granted her wish, to hold the priceless diamond in her hand.

16. Rowing a boat helps develop the arm muscles.

17. The letter written by the students was sent to the President.

18. Mr. and Mrs. Simpson go walking every evening.

19. The farmer's job is milking the cows.

20. The farmer's son is milking the cows.

21. Flora ordered vanilla ice cream covered with strawberries and buried in whipped cream.

22. Henry had to stay after school for shouting in the classroom.

23. They found the old man bruised and broken from the fall.

24. Mother's hobby is collecting old cookbooks.

25. Mother is collecting old cookbooks for our next-door neighbor.

Summary

Verbals are verb forms whose function has shifted. While retaining many of the prerogatives of a verb, a verbal functions as a noun, as an adjective, or as an adverb. In most cases, a verbal may take a complement and it may have modifiers. When a verbal takes a complement or has a modifier the word group formed is called a verbal phrase.

The recognition of verbals is sometimes essential to effective communication. According to form, there are three kinds of verbals: (1) the verbal introduced by *to*; (2) the *-ing* verbals; and (3) the *-ed* or *-en* verbals.

The *to* verbal is called an infinitive. An infinitive serves a variety of sentence functions. It may be used as a subject noun; as a direct object; as the modifier of a noun, a verb, an adverb, or an adjective; as a linking-verb complement; as an appositive; as part of an absolute construction; and, finally, as a non-finite verb with a subject.

When an *-ing* verbal functions as a noun, it is called a *gerund*. A gerund may function as a subject noun, as a direct object, as the object of a preposition, as a linking-verb complement, and as an appositive.

When an *-ing* verbal functions as an adjective, it is called a *participle*. The *-ing* participle may be used as a linking-verb complement and as an objective complement.

The *-ed* or *-en* verbal functions only as an adjective, never as a noun, and is therefore always a participle.

The *-ed* or *-en* participle does not take a complement unless it is preceded by the auxiliary *having*.

Verbal phrases are classified as infinitive phrases, gerund phrases, and participial phrases.

Chapter Test, Form A

1. Write a sentence that illustrates each of the following functions:
    / (a) A participial phrase that modifies a subject noun   (Page 90)
    2 (b) A gerund phrase used as a direct object.   (Page 89)
    3 (c) An infinitive phrase that modifies a noun.   (Pages 84-85)
    4 (d) A gerund phrase used as a linking-verb complement.   (Page 84)
    5 (e) A participial phrase used as a linking-verb complement.   (Page 91)
    6 (f) An infinitive phrase that modifies a linking-verb complement.   (Page 85)
    7 (g) A gerund phrase used as the object of a preposition.   (Page 89)
    8 (h) An infinitive phrase used as a subject noun.   (Pages 83-84)
    9 (i) A participial phrase that modifies the direct object of a preposition.
                                                                          (Page 90)
   10 (j) A subject noun—infinitive structure.   (Page 86)

2. Identify the function of each of the verbals or verbal phrases in the following
   sentences:
    (a) Diving and striking, hummingbirds have been known to rout hawks
        many times their size.   (Pages 90, 84)
    (b) Camping in the mountains is, in my opinion, the best way to spend a
        summer vacation.   (Pages 88-89, 84-85)
    (c) Jim wants to go to agricultural college when he graduates from high
        school.   (Page 84)
    (d) The man to beat in this election is the candidate from Chatauqua County.
                                                                       (Pages 84-85)
    (e) The family enjoys strawberries frozen in rich cream.   (Page 91)
    (f) Father is thinking of buying a new car.   (Page 89)
    (g) The sign painted on the east side of the barn is an advertisement for
        baking powder.   (Page 91)
    (h) We are ready to go.   (Page 85)
    (i) A group of men from a nearby village came to fight the forest fire.
                                                                          (Page 85)
    (j) The children seemed terribly frightened by the storm.   (Page 92)

Chapter Test, Form B

1. Write a sentence to illustrate each of the following functions:
    (a) A gerund phrase used as a subject noun.
    (b) An infinitive phrase that modifies a verb.
    (c) A gerund phrase used as an appositive.
    (d) An infinitive phrase that modifies an adverb.
    (e) A participial phrase that modifies a direct object.
    (f) A participial phrase used as an objective complement.
    (g) An infinitive phrase used as a direct object.
    (h) An infinitive phrase used as a linking-verb complement.

    (i) An introductory participial phrase.

    (j) A subject noun — infinitive structure. (Use a noun substitute as the subject noun.)

2. Identify the function of each of the verbals or verbal phrases in the following sentences:

    (a) From the deck of the *Cypress*, we watched the cattle grazing clover along the banks of the river.

    (b) During summer vacation, I enjoy hiking in the mountains.

    (c) Jim's one goal in life is to ski down the Wall of Death, a slope in Zermatt, Switzerland.

    (d) In the United States, it is illegal to own a bald eagle.

    (e) The corn, roasted over the coals for an hour, was tender and tasty.

    (f) Midge's greatest interest is playing the clarinet in the school band.

    (g) Father was relieved when the orchestra stopped playing at midnight.

    (h) The captain ordered the men to advance cautiously along the highway.

    (i) Seizing the screaming child by the hand, the embarrassed woman rushed from the store.

    (j) When Kelsey gets into a game, he always plays to win.

The Structure of Your Language

The use of verbals and of verbal phrases gives the English language vitality and simplicity. For the inexperienced writer, however, verbals sometimes become a source of ambiguity in communication. Ambiguities arise partly because of position and partly because of the lack of structural signals. The careful placement of verbal phrases and the use of functional signals will help eliminate much of the ambiguity.

■ Discuss the ambiguity of each of the statements below and revise each sentence to make the meaning clear.

EXAMPLE   The dogs annoy our neighbors *barking in the front yard.*

The italicized participial phrase is misplaced. It should be close to the noun *dogs*, which it modifies.

     The dogs barking in the front yard annoy our neighbors.

Sometimes it is better to change the structure of the sentence:

     The dogs annoy our neighbors by barking in the front yard.

1. Little Mike was lonesome for his mother playing in the sandbox in kindergarten.

2. Seated on our front porch, the moon could be seen rising over the distant hills. (Hint: In your revision, use a noun substitute as the subject noun and make the predicate verb active.)

3. While barking, I dislike dogs. (Hint: In your revision, modify *dogs* with a subject-predicate word group.)

4. Herman was flagged down by an officer driving recklessly on the thruway.

5. He wore a scarf around his neck tied with two intricate knots. (Hint: Begin your revised sentence with a prepositional phrase.)

6. The books on the desk bound in leather belong to Helen. (Hint: In your revision, modify the subject noun with a compound adjective.)

7. Mrs. Prince hung a picture on the wall painted by Rembrandt.

8. Topped with ice cream, the minister ate a piece of Mother's delicious apple pie.

Chapter 5

*Appositives
and
Absolutes*

*A Look
Back
and
A Look
Forward*

In Chapter 4, you saw how verbals contribute to exactness and variety in communication. In this chapter, you will study in detail two devices—apposition and the absolute structure—that also help gain exactness and variety. You've already worked with appositives in Chapters 1 and 3. In Chapter 4, you dealt briefly with the absolute structure.

THE APPOSITIVE STRUCTURE

Structurally, what is the relationship between an appositive and the word or the word group to which it is apposed? In the following sentences, the APPOSITIVES are in color.

Henry Morgan, the manager, is going to resign.
Hemingway's novel *The Old Man and the Sea* received the Pulitzer prize for fiction in 1953.
The General, an old man of seventy, came to the gate to meet us.
The Jones boys, both of them, have joined the army.
The fact that you have failed your geometry indicates that you need tutoring.
Mother told Joe to clean up the yard, to rake the leaves and pick up the papers.

Appose means "to place next to." In the above sentences, each appositive has a side-by-side relationship with the apposing word or word group.

In the first sentence, what is the function of *Henry Morgan?* Can the appositive substitute for *Henry Morgan* as the subject noun?

The manager is going to resign.

In the second sentence, can the apposing name of *Hemingway's novel* substitute for the subject noun?

The Old Man and the Sea won the Pulitzer prize for fiction in 1953.

Now note the substitution of the word-group appositive in the last of the illustrative sentences:

Mother told Joe to rake the leaves and pick up the papers.

As just illustrated, the appositive has the same function in the sentence as the word or the word group with which it is in apposition.

Exercise 1   *Identify each appositive in the following sentences and discuss the function of the noun it apposes.*

1. Herbert, the gorilla, is kept in a steel cage.

2. The poet Robert Frost read a poem at the inauguration.

3. I'd like you to meet my old friend Bob Hornblower.

4. This is the cell, the identical cell, in which Billy the Kid was imprisoned.

5. Scottsbluff, Nebraska, was named for Hiram Scott, a fur trader.

6. Suzanne won a scholarship to William and Mary, the oldest college in the United States.

7. St. Louis, one of the largest cities in the United States, is located on the Mississippi, the largest river in the United States.

8. Robinson Crusoe and his man Friday are the principal characters in Defoe's novel *Robinson Crusoe.*

9. Seven species of the barracuda, a subtropical marine fish, live in American waters.

10. Helen won first prize in the bake-off, a trip to Bermuda.

Restrictive, or Identifying, Appositives

What does the appositive do in the second sentence of the following sentence pair? Does it identify the violinist, or does it add a descriptive detail?

> The violinist played at Carnegie Hall.
> The violinist Jack Benny played at Carnegie Hall.

In the second sentence, the two nouns in apposition have a close, or restrictive, relationship. The second noun helps to identify the first.

In the following sentences, note how the restrictive appositive identifies the noun it apposes:

> My cousin Harold has just graduated from college.
> The poet Byron was one of the great Romantic writers of the last century.
> The metal tungsten is added to steel to make it hard.
> The movie *The Friendly Persuasion* is being shown for the third time.

Nonrestrictive, or Descriptive, Appositives

Two nouns in apposition sometimes have a loose, or nonrestrictive, relationship. The second noun describes rather than identifies the first. Note the punctuation in each of the sentences that follow:

> Mistra, a deserted town near Sparta, has many imposing ruins.
> The officer, a captain of the guards, was given a citation for bravery.
> William Butler Yeats, the Irish poet, was awarded the Nobel prize.
> Polly's boyfriend, a pale youth of sixteen, plays an oboe in the school orchestra.

In each of the above sentences, commas set off the nonrestrictive appositive from the rest of the sentence.

Two nouns in apposition may sometimes be separated by a transitional word or phrase:

I suggest that you read a Victorian novel; <u>for example,</u> David Copperfield.
The general manager plans to take a long vacation, <u>probably</u> three months.
Agatha Amsdale is a very distant relative, <u>quite possibly</u> a third cousin twice removed.

Variety of Forms Used as Appositives

While nouns are most commonly used as appositives, other word classes and word groups sometimes function this way. What, for example, is the ordinary function of the appositives in these sentences?

We would all like to go to the circus.
Jimmy Calhoun himself will lead the St. Patrick's Day parade.
The Lennon sisters, all four of them, will sing on the radio tonight.
Whom did you call, Ellie or me?

Here the function words *all, himself, all,* and *me* are used as appositives (sentences 1 and 2) or as part of an appositive (sentences 3 and 4).

Sometimes prepositional phrases and verbal phrases function as appositives:

The Smiths will spend a week in St. Augustine, in the oldest city in the United States.
Father is anxious to get out of debt, to methodically pay all the money that he owes.

A noun clause is often used in apposition with a noun or a noun substitute.

The fact that you are so young may handicap you in finding a position.
The coach accurately predicted the result, that we would lose both games to Central High.
The statement, that Clancy is implicated in the robbery, is entirely false.
It has been said that the ancient gods of Ireland came from the sky.

In the last sentence, the noun clause is in apposition with the function word *it*:

That the ancient gods of Ireland came from the sky has been said.

A similar construction results from the use of an infinitive phrase instead of a noun clause.

It is wrong to tell a lie.	To tell a lie is wrong.
It is fun to drive a bobsled.	To drive a bobsled is fun.
It is difficult to write a story.	To write a story is difficult.

Sometimes a word or a word group apposes a complete sentence:

The countess could keep her jewels and starve or sell them and sacrifice her pride —a difficult choice.

Exercise 2

A. *Classify each appositive in Exercise 1 as an identifying appositive or a descriptive appositive.*

B. *Identify the appositives in the following sentences and discuss the function of each:*

1. The girls, all of them, wanted to go to the hop with Brudkin.

2. Alice looked forward to frosting the cake, to mixing the butter and sugar and spreading it evenly over the golden layers.

3. I am asking the members of this group, each one of you, to take part in the discussion.

4. To hear Aunt Phyllis sing, to listen to her clear tones, is always a pleasure.

5. Teaching children, instructing them in the useful skills and attitudes of society, is a rewarding occupation.

6. Willie finally told us the truth, that he had been releasing the animals from their traps.

7. Mrs. Winder is sailing to Europe next week, to France and Italy.

8. Two of us — Jenny Mae and I — are going to New York during Easter week.

9. The destruction of our great cities, of our centers of culture and industry, is what we fear in the war of tomorrow.

10. It has been said that fish reflect sound waves.

11. It is no longer possible to dismiss travel to the moon as a Jules Verne fantasy.

12. The fact that rats and mice serve humanity cannot be disputed.

Exercise 3

1. Write a sentence that includes a noun in apposition with a subject noun.

2. Write a sentence that includes a noun in apposition with a direct object.

3. Write a sentence that includes a noun in apposition with the object of a preposition.

4. Using four different structures, write four sentences that include restrictive appositives.

5. Using four different structures, write four sentences that include nonrestrictive appositives.

6. Write a sentence that includes two apposing prepositional phrases.

7. Write a sentence that includes two apposing gerund phrases.

8. Write a sentence that includes two apposing infinitive phrases.

9. Write a sentence that includes a noun clause in apposition with a subject noun.

10. Write a sentence that includes a noun clause in apposition with a direct object.

11. Write a sentence that includes a noun clause in apposition with the function word *it*.

12. Write a sentence that includes a verbal phrase in apposition with the function word *it*.

Exercise 4

Revise the selection that follows, using as many appositives as you can without destroying the sense or creating awkward constructions. What do you think this revision does to the style of the selection?

Henry James was a subway conductor. He worked every night from four until midnight. The subway in which he worked was in New York City. New York City is probably the busiest city in the world.

One night during the winter, while the train was heading south from 183 Street which is a station on the East Side in the Bronx, Henry saw a little girl who was all alone and in tears. He asked her what was wrong.

"I've lost my mother," she sobbed. "She got off at one of the stations back there and left me."

Henry looked at the child. She was a thin little waif who seemed half-starved. She was dressed in a skimpy coat that just about buttoned across her chest. She was very poor. It was evident. Henry James was an old man who had seen difficult times. He thought he was hardened to life. But now the plight of the little girl filled him with pity. Her tears and her poverty filled him with pity. "We'll find your mother," he said. "You just leave it to old Henry."

THE ABSOLUTE STRUCTURE

The absolute structure is a sentence element that apparently does not have a specific function within the sentence. It is an independent structure. From the standpoint of meaning, however, it has a coherent relationship to the idea expressed by the sentence and, in some instances, functions as a sentence-modifier.

> <u>Dinner being over</u>, the family scattered to their various haunts.
> <u>Weather permitting</u>, we shall land at O'Hare Field before noon.
> <u>Church over</u>, the hungry congregation hurried home to Sunday dinner.
> Hilda marched stiffly from the room, <u>her face blazing with anger</u>.

The absolute structure is usually made up of a noun-headed modifier. The modifier is usually an *-ing* or *-ed* participle with or without an auxiliary.

> <u>The guests having departed</u>, Father kicked off his shoes and stretched out on the couch.
> <u>His geometry homework finished</u>, Kelsey decided to celebrate.

Prepositional and verbal phrases are often used as absolutes:

> <u>To tell the truth</u>, we've already sold the house.
> <u>Considering the matter objectively</u>, the case was fairly tried.

Exercise 5

Identify the absolute constructions in the following selection and discuss their structure.

The weather being mild, Father decided to take the family for a ride in the country. The car had been cleaned and newly greased. As a matter of fact, Father had had the motor tuned the week before.

Breakfast over, we started off. The car ran smoothly, the engine purring like a healthy kitten. His eyes glowing with satisfaction, Father began to enjoy himself thoroughly. He prided himself on his expert care of the family car.

Suddenly, disaster struck. A herd of cows moved across the road about a hundred yards ahead. Careful driver that he is, Father saw them in time and pressed the brake pedal down. To be sure, the car *should* have stopped but it didn't. To conclude the story quickly, Father had to veer off the road and roll up a grassy hillside.

In my opinion, we were lucky to have escaped an accident. His face red with embarrassment, Father admitted that he had not checked the brakes.

Summary

Apposition is a grammatical device that helps make communication more explicit and varied. Structurally, apposition is a side-by-side relationship.

Nouns are most frequently used as appositives. Apposing nouns have the same function in the sentence. Nouns in apposition are called restrictive appositives when they have a close or identifying relationship. Nonrestrictive appositives have a loose relationship; the second noun is merely descriptive of the first. Nonrestrictive appositives are set off from the rest of the sentence, usually with commas.

Word classes other than nouns—function words, for example—are sometimes used as appositives. Word groups (verbal phrases, prepositional phrases) and subject-predicate word groups (noun clauses) also function as appositives. Frequently, a noun clause or a verbal phrase apposes the function word *it*, used as a subject noun. Sometimes a word or a word group apposes a complete sentence.

The absolute structure also contributes variety to communication. This structure usually consists of a noun-headed *-ing* or *-ed* participial modifier.

Chapter Test, Form A

1. Write sentences to illustrate the following:
    (a) A noun in close apposition with the subject noun.   (Page 103)
    (b) A noun in loose apposition with a direct object.   (Page 103)
    (c) A noun clause in apposition with the function word *it* used as a subject noun.   (Page 104)
    (d) An infinitive phrase in apposition with the function word *it* used as a subject noun.   (Page 104)
    (e) An absolute structure made up of a noun-headed modifier. (Page 107)
    (f) A subject noun with a nonrestrictive appositive.   (Page 103)
    (g) An object of a preposition with a nonrestrictive appositive. (Page 103)

2. Identify the appositives and the absolute structures in each of the following sentences. If two nouns are in apposition, indicate whether the appositives are restrictive or nonrestrictive. (Page 103)

(a) Albany, the capital of New York, is located on the Hudson River.
(Page 102)

(b) The class is reading Hardy's novel *The Return of the Native.* (Page 102)

(c) The services over, the congregation straggled down the aisle. (Page 107)

(d) Arthur won the top award in the essay contest, a scholarship to Roanoke College. (Page 102)

(e) The Little Leaguers all want to be pitchers. (Page 104)

(f) The voters elected the popular Mr. Askins, a sensible choice for water commissioner. (Page 102)

(g) The idea that you cannot be a good speaker is not a valid one. (Page 104)

(h) Martha climbed into the car first, her face wreathed in smiles. (Page 107)

Chapter Test, Form B

1. Write sentences to illustrate the following:

(a) A noun in close apposition with a direct object.
(b) A noun in loose apposition with the subject noun.
(c) A noun clause in apposition with a noun used as a direct object.
(d) An infinitive phrase in apposition with a noun used as a direct object.
(e) A direct object with a nonrestrictive appositive.
(f) A direct object with a restrictive appositive.

2. Identify the appositives and the absolute structures in each of the following sentences. If two nouns are in apposition, indicate whether they are restrictive or nonrestrictive appositives.

(a) George will never make the track team, his appetite being somewhat more developed than his speed.
(b) We visited Winchester, the apple capital of Virginia.
(c) The first prize in the cruller baking contest, a silver cup and a trip to Boston, was won by Abigail Adams, the popular young home economics student.
(d) The girls all like Mr. Swing, the new science teacher.
(e) The voters rejected the bond issue for new streets, a regrettable decision for the motorists.
(f) Mr. Simpson has made a formal announcement that he will be a candidate for governor.
(g) Helen's ambition, to become a graduate nurse, will be realized in a few weeks.
(h) Teeth chattering, the boys trotted home briskly.

The Structure of Your Language

Many writers rely on apposition to give greater simplicity to the structure of their sentences. In each of the following examples, note how the use of an appositive helps achieve greater economy in communication.

EXAMPLE   Mr. Klemson, who is the head cashier of the First National Bank, spoke to the seniors this morning about opportunities in banking.
Mr. Klemson, the head cashier of the First National Bank, spoke to the seniors this morning about opportunities in banking.

EXAMPLE   Most jazz has its roots in the music of Africa. African music is a kind of music in which complicated rhythms are prominent.
Most jazz has its roots in the music of Africa, a music in which complicated rhythms are prominent.

■ As shown in the two examples above, use an appositive to achieve greater economy of communication in each of the following sentences:

1. Father hired a new accountant who is a recent graduate of the University of California.

2. Margaret Mitchell was a native of the South of Irish parentage. She is famous for having written *Gone with the Wind* which became a singularly popular novel. (Use two appositives.)

3. The common law of England is a mighty instrument of freedom's growth. It also forms the basis of American law and justice.

4. Mr. Wilson is a chemical engineer. He is the man who lives next door to us.

5. During the night, a heavy rain washed out the roads. A total of four inches fell in three hours.

6. Nathaniel Hawthorne wrote *The Scarlet Letter*. It is the story of Hester Prynne.

7. The voters rejected the bond issue for a new sewer system. This is an unfortunate choice for a rapidly growing city.

8. Valparaiso is one of Chile's most progressive cities. It is also an important manufacturing center.

9. Valentine's Day was once a pagan feast. It is celebrated today as a festival of romance and affection.

10. Temperature affects viscosity. Viscosity is that property of a fluid that causes it to resist flowing.

Chapter 6

Agreement

We're all aware of the fact that in the English language there is a grammatical relationship between the subject and the verb — that under certain conditions when the form of the subject noun changes, the form of the predicate verb changes. In order to follow the conventions of standard English, you must know when and under what conditions these changes occur.

In Chapter 1, you examined the basic subject-predicate structure of the English sentence. The purpose of Chapter 6 is to explain the bound relationship of the subject noun to the predicate verb, to discuss certain limitations of this relationship, and to illustrate those situations that present particular difficulty to the writer.

SUBJECT-PREDICATE RELATIONSHIP

There is a grammatical generalization which says that a subject and a verb must agree in number. In other words, a singular subject takes one form of the verb and a plural subject takes another form of the verb. This generalization is true in certain structures, but it is not universally true.

Structures That Involve Agreement

In the present tense when the subject is a noun, a bound relationship exists between the subject and the verb:

> This boy likes to study English.
> These boys like to study German.

In the first sentence, the subject noun *boy* is singular, and the verb form *likes* is the singular form of the verb *like*. In the second sentence the subject noun *boys* is plural, and the verb form *like* is the plain form of the verb, the form which is used in the present tense with a plural subject.

Note the change in form in the second sentence of each of the following sentence pairs:

> This man earns fifty dollars a week.
> These men earn a much larger salary.
>
> Mary helps her mother with the dishes.
> The girls help their mother with the mending.
>
> The horse feeds every day in the new pasture.
> The cows always feed in the barn.
>
> Mr. Grinch reads his paper on the bus.
> Many people read the newspaper at home.

In each of the above sentence pairs, to what word class do the subject nouns belong? Now study the following sentences, in which the subject-noun function is filled by a pronoun in the third person instead of by a noun.

> He prefers the ocean.
> They prefer a pool.
>
> She eats salami for lunch.
> They eat onions.
>
> It feels ripe to me.
> They feel soft and overripe.
>
> He is a good tennis player.
> They are the best players on the court.

When the subject is a pronoun in the third person, there is agreement between the subject and between a verb in the present tense.

In the following sentence pair, the pronouns are in what person? (If you don't know, turn to page 128.)

> I am very proud of Joe.
> We are glad that the team won.

In the above sentence pair, the pronoun is in the first person and the verb is a form of the verb *to be*. In this situation, there is agreement between the subject and the predicate.

Now study the tense and the form of the verb in each of the following sentences as well as the structure of the subject noun:

> The captain was glad to reach port.
> The men were deliriously happy.
>
> Henry was always first in line at the cafeteria.
> The other boys were usually willing to wait.
>
> I was late for the recital.
> We were there in plenty of time.
>
> He was the captain of the team.
> They were the ringleaders of the gang.
>
> She was the prettiest girl in the class.
> They were all good spellers.
>
> It was a sunny day in Dublin.
> They were all pleasant days.

When the predicate verb is a form of the verb *to be* and the subject is a noun or a first-person or third-person pronoun, there is agreement between the subject and the verb in the past tense as well as in the present tense.

The generalizations illustrated so far in this section also apply when one or more auxiliaries are part of the predicate verb. Here, the agreement is between the subject and the first auxiliary:

> The baby has gone to sleep.
> The children have gone to bed.
>
> Grandpa does like to play checkers.
> The boys do plan to go camping.
>
> This boy keeps asking questions all day long.
> These people keep coming back year after year.
>
> This young man is going to college.
> These girls are staying home.

The bell has been ringing all afternoon.
The boys have been playing ball.

The ham is being baked in the oven.
The vegetables are being boiled in the kettle.

He has been taking too much of my time.
They have been taking too much for granted.

I am going to the bullfight.
We are going to the museum.

He is being initiated into the fraternity.
They are being married on Saturday.

The assignment was given to the class.
The assignments were given out last Friday.

I was reading an Agatha Christie mystery.
We were watching *Suspense Theater*.

She was dancing the polka.
They were dancing a quadrille.

Exercise 1

Fill in the blanks in the following sentences with an appropriate present tense form or past tense form of the verb in parentheses that involves subject-predicate agreement. Be prepared to indicate the nature of the subject-predicate agreement: (1) agreement between a noun in the subject noun function and a verb in the present tense; (2) agreement between a third-person pronoun in the subject noun function and a verb in the present tense; (3) agreement between a first-person pronoun in the subject noun function and the present tense form of to be; *(4) agreement between the subject and a past tense form of* to be; *(5) agreement between the subject and the first auxiliary.*

1. The Hinkson boy ____ fishing every Saturday morning. (go)

2. The children ____ dominoes on rainy afternoons. (play)

3. My cousin ____ exactly like my Uncle Fred. (look)

4. His brothers ____ more like Aunt Ada. (look)

5. I ____ a collector of rare prints. (to be)

6. We ____ not especially interested in modern art. (to be)

7. He ____ this year's star tackle. (to be)

8. He ____ the high scorer in last night's game. (to be)

9. They ____ the friendliest people I know. (to be)

10. He ____ short stories for *Argosy*. (write)

11. They ____ up sports events for the local paper. (write)

12. This man ____ to the Lions Club. (belong)

13. These men ____ to the Printers' Union. (belong)

14. The widow ____ borrowed more money than she can hope to repay. (Use an appropriate auxiliary.)

15. The partners ____ borrowed a thousand dollars. (Use an appropriate auxiliary.)

Exercise 2   Fill the blank in the second sentence of each sentence pair with the same verb or auxiliary in the same tense as in the first sentence. Be prepared to explain your choice of verb forms.

1. My oldest brother goes to North High School.
   My sisters ____ to Marjorie Webster Junior College.

2. These ladies live in Walla Walla.
   This man ____ in Tuscaloosa.

3. He is the oldest boy in the graduating class.
   They ____ the best debaters on the debating team.

4. The Smiths leave for Europe tomorrow.
   Mr. Smith ____ the house before sunup.

5. We were appointed to the executive committee.
   I ____ the chairman of the committee in charge of decorations.

6. Little children do like to run and shout.
   That boy certainly ____ enjoy riding the waves.

7. Dad is giving John a watch for Christmas.
   The students ____ giving Miss Straton a pair of bronze bookends.

8. The piano was lifted through the third-story window.
   The pulleys ____ manipulated by two young men.

9. She hates to go to bed at night.
   They ____ to get up in the morning.

10. The cows have broken out of the north pasture.
    The horse ____ been in the barn all week.

Structures That Do Not Involve Agreement

The foregoing discussion suggests that the bound relationship between subject and verb is not shown by a change in form in every structure. In the following sentence pair, for example, does the form of the verb change when the subject noun changes from singular to plural?

> This boy wanted to study English.
> These boys wanted to study French.

Although the subject in the first sentence is singular and the subject in the second sentence is plural, there is no change in the form of the verb. In a situation involving past tense, therefore, we cannot say that there is agreement of subject and predicate.

That man in the green cap caught a hundred-pound marlin.
The men caught a boatful of flounder.

The calf ran to its mother.
The horses ran neck and neck down the homestretch.

I bought a fur hat.
We bought matching red skirts.

You fought a good fight. (A particular soldier.)
You fought a good battle. (An entire company of soldiers.)

He sat in the orchestra.
They sat in the balcony.

She found my pocketbook.
They found the missing five dollars.

If a pronoun in the first or second person functions as the subject noun of a verb in the present tense, subject-verb agreement is not involved:

I go to the movies every Saturday.
We go to the opera whenever we're in Chicago.

I study French at college.
We study earth science in high school.

You remain here until I return. (A particular student.)
You remain in your seats until the bell rings. (The entire class.)

You have a 1-A classification. (A particular draftee.)
You have the opportunity to serve your country. (Several recruits.)

If a pronoun in the second person functions as the subject of the verb *to be*, subject-verb agreement is not involved in either the present or the past tense.

You are my best friend.
You are the nicest neighbors.

You were the best speaker on the platform.
You were the best dancers in the chorus.

When one or more auxiliaries are part of the predicate verb, there is no agreement involved between the subject and the first auxiliary when this auxiliary cannot be inflected to show number.

Your dog will fight the leash at first.
Barking dogs will sometimes bite.

A machine can do the work of many men.
These machines can operate for years with a minimum of repairs.

The manager must supervise the billing.
The accountants must follow his directions.

When one or more auxiliaries are part of the predicate verb, there is no agreement involved between the subject and the first auxiliary when this auxiliary is in the past tense and not a form of *to be.*

This book had been damaged by water.
The books had been placed on the wrong shelves.

The student did want to pass.
The students did decide to go on the picnic.

He kept humming the same tune over and over.
They kept losing one game after another.

When one or more auxiliaries are part of the predicate verb and the first auxiliary is a form of *to be,* there is no agreement between subject and verb if the subject is a pronoun in the second person. This is true in both present and past tense.

You are being nominated for chairman of the Valentine Dance.
You are all going to the dance, aren't you?

You were obliged to make restitution.
You were told to return the key before noon.

When one or more auxiliaries are part of the predicate verb and the first auxiliary is in the present tense and not a form of *to be,* there is no subject-verb agreement involved if the subject is a pronoun in the first or second person.

I have decided to fly to Boston.
We have decided to go by train.

You have been convicted by the jury.
You have been given a light sentence.

Exercise 3   *Identify the subject noun and the predicate verb in each of the following sentences and tell whether the structure is one that involves subject-verb agreement. If agreement is involved, indicate the nature of the agreement as outlined in the directions to Exercise 1.*

1. The cows were driven to the pasture for the night.

2. The children attend gym class every Friday.

3. He always leaves the chores to his son Amos.

4. I plan to study psychology in college.

5. The men are coming to thresh the wheat tomorrow.

6. The club will not meet again this summer.

7. She sweeps her front path three times a day.

8. Miss Garve likes chopped liver.

9. We can see the George Washington Bridge from our kitchen window.

10. You were the only league member to bowl 200.

11. We are planning to visit Aunt Phyllis in Bar Harbor.

12. This information must not fall into enemy hands.

13. He gave all of his money to the poor.

14. Most cameras are designed for use with flashbulbs.

15. Pistachio trees grow well in dry regions.

16. She is an exceptionally good tennis player.

17. The telephone has been ringing all afternoon.

18. This orange tastes sour.

19. You are a compelling speaker.

20. The elderly man was rushed to the hospital.

21. Jim keeps trying to do better in math but without much success.

22. The boys kept nagging their mother.

23. I am planning a Come-As-You-Are-Party for Friday night.

24. The foundation is being poured by a contractor from Albuquerque.

25. These people are government employees.

COMPLICATIONS OF AGREEMENT

What is the correct verb form in these sentences?

> The apple tree **are is** in bloom.
> The apple trees **are is** in bloom.
> One of the apple trees **are is** in bloom.

You probably had no difficulty choosing the correct form in the first two sentences. Many people, however, are led into the wrong choice in the third sentence by the word group that comes between the subject and the verb. Let us consider this complication of structure as well as several other complications that sometimes lead to errors in subject-verb agreement.

Intervening Word Group

An intervening word group sometimes obscures the number of the subject noun. In the following sentences, what causes the obscurity?

One of the older boys has promised to coach the eighth-grade basketball team.

Jim Olsen, not his parents, owns the Thunderbird.

Terry, along with her friends, goes skating every Saturday.

Attending on-campus concerts, in addition to other activities, is part of the pleasure of college life.

Mr. Henry, together with his wife and four children, plans to visit Crater Lake National Park next spring.

In each of the above sentences, the subject is singular but the intervening word group contains a plural noun. The verb form, however, must be singular to agree with the singular subject.

Inverted Sentence Pattern

In sentences that are inverted, the principles of agreement still hold. In an inverted pattern, find the subject and make the verb agree with it.

> There are two clean shirts in your bottom drawer.
> Here are three letters for you.
> Here come the Johnsons.
> Where were these books bought?
> Weren't the last two scenes exciting?

In each of the above sentences, the subject follows the verb or an auxiliary. In each sentence, the subject is plural and the appropriate verb form shows subject-verb agreement.

Compound Subject

When the compound subject is connected by *and* and is plural in sense, the plural form of the verb is used:

Mary and Martha are going to the party.
Thanksgiving and Christmas are two holidays rich in tradition.
Reading Ibsen and solving a quadratic equation are difficult assignments.
There go the Hatfields and the McCoys.

When the compound subject is connected by *and* and is singular in sense, the singular form of the verb is used:

Bacon and eggs is a favorite American dish.
Weeping and wailing does nothing toward solving the problem.
Bread and butter is a healthful between-meals snack.
A hi-fi set and a case of soap was the first prize in the beauty contest.

When the compound subject is made up of two singular nouns or noun substitutes connected by *or, nor, either . . . or, neither . . . nor,* the singular form of the verb is used:

An older man or a mature woman is needed for this job.
One or the other is always missing.
Either her father or her mother calls for her every afternoon.
Neither sleet nor snow stops Gustav from driving his new Mercedes-Benz.

In the above situation, the compound subject is sometimes made up of two nouns or noun substitutes that are different in number or in person. In this structure, the subject nearer the verb determines the verb form.

Neither the players nor the manager was satisfied with the umpire's decision.
(Here, the verb form is determined by the singular noun *manager.*)
Neither Helen nor I am planning to attend the conference. (Here, the verb form is determined by the pronoun *I.* Sometimes it is better to reword this type structure: Helen is not planning to attend the conference, and neither am I.)

If both members of the compound subject are plural, the plural form of the verb is used:

Neither the students nor the teachers were represented at the convention.

Function Words as Subject Nouns

Function words that serve as noun substitutes sometimes complicate subject-verb agreement. In standard written English, *anybody, everybody, somebody, anyone, everyone, someone, nobody, each, either, neither,* and *no one* are considered singular in sense and take the singular form of the verb.

> Each of the answers is correct.
> Neither is a sturdy enough pair of shoes for hiking.

The function words *both, few, several,* and *many* are considered plural. They require the plural form of the verb.

> Both of my parents are coming to Commencement.
> Few are expected to remain all season.

The function words *all, some,* and *none* may be singular or plural according to the sense of the sentence:

> All of the work has been finished.
> All of the men have been paid.
>
> Some of the money has been stolen.
> Some of the books were lost.
>
> None of the hay has been cut.
> None of the children walk to school.

Subject Nouns That End in s

Some words that end in *s* are especially troublesome because their number cannot always be determined. Some nouns ending in *s*, a plural inflection, are singular in meaning and take a singular verb form:

> Fifty-six dollars was stolen from the cash register.
> Two thirds of the swampland has been reclaimed as a recreation area.

Other nouns ending in *s* are singular in meaning but take a plural verb form:

> The scissors were not in the drawer.
> Joe's new trousers are black and white.
> Fireworks are banned in most states.
> High wages make most workers happy.
> His thanks were most profuse.

Still other nouns ending in *s* are plural in meaning but ordinarily take a singular verb form:

> The news is very bad this morning.
> Measles is a dangerous childhood disease.
> The United States is a country of people with varied origins.

Most nouns ending in the suffix *-ics* are singular and take a singular verb form:

Physics is an important subject these days.
Economics is a controversial discipline.

Some *-ics* words may be used in either a singular sense or a plural sense:

Acoustics is the science of sound.
The acoustics in the new concert hall are faultless.

Tactics is an important study for the soldier.
The tactics employed in his campaign were above reproach.

Athletics is an important part of our curriculum.
Athletics have been banned at the Institute.

Agreement in a Subordinate Clause

When a subordinator (*who, which, that*) functions as the subject of an adjective clause, the verb in the adjective clause agrees with the noun or noun substitute to which the subordinator refers.

The boys who were promoted have already reported to their new classroom.

The subordinator *who* refers to *boys*. Since *boys* is plural, the verb in the adjective clause must be a plural form.

He is one of those boys who are always willing to take on another assignment.

Two Important Usage Notes

Don't (a contraction of *do not*) is a plural verb form. It always takes a plural subject: They don't **but** He doesn't.

As illustrated on page 116, *you* is used with a plural verb form whether *you* refers to one person or to a group of people: You were, *not* "You was."

Exercise 4   *In the following sentences, select the appropriate verb form. Be prepared to describe the complication of agreement.*

1. Here **come comes** Uncle Joe and Aunt Ellen in their new Impala.

2. Here **are is** the deck of word cards for our game of Build-a-Word.

3. The pliers **are is** missing from the tool rack.

4. Statistics **are is** used to prove almost anything.

5. Neither the coach nor the players **want wants** to make the overnight trip.

6. Either Jim or you **are is** expected to take Lillian home tonight.

7. Ham and eggs **make makes** a hearty breakfast for a growing boy.

8. Milking the cows, in addition to several other chores, **was were** Jim's responsibility every morning before school.

9. There **go goes** Sally and her current beau.

10. Prudence is one of those girls who **object objects** to going steady.

11. Neither she nor I **am are is** going to the circus tomorrow.

12. Success and marriage **are is** the goal of most young people today

13. Ethics **deal deals** with what is good or bad.

14. He reached for the scissors which **was were** on the sewing table.

15. Fifty dollars **are is** too much to pay for a ski jacket.

16. **Was Were** you at the concert last Friday night?

17. Neither **are is** an appropriate answer.

18. He **doesn't don't** know the difference between squash and eggplant.

19. Ice cream and cake **are is** my favorite dessert.

20. Television, not the movies, **take takes** up most of Joe's spare time.

Exercise 5   Make the indicated changes in the following sentences, *revising for subject-verb agreement if necessary:*

1. Rewrite with a compound subject and change *flower* to *flowers:*
   The petunia is Mother's favorite flower.

2. Rewrite with a compound subject:
   Mr. Thew is leaving for Siberia next week.

3. Change *woman* to *women* and *mainstay* to *mainstays:*
   There is the woman who is the mainstay of our organization.

4. Change *meat* to *chops:*
   None of the meat is fit to eat.

5. Change *boys* to *boy:*
   Where are the boys who are looking for a summer job at Camp Walden?

6. Insert the phrase *along with his seven motherless children* after *Mr. Tewksbury:*
   Mr. Tewksbury is moving to Rainbow Springs.

7. Change *a girl* to *one of those girls:*
   Helen is a girl who always wants something to eat after a movie date.

8. Change the second member of the compound subject to the plural form:
   Neither the history test nor the French exam was especially difficult.

9. Substitute the pronoun *I* for *his friend:*
   Neither James nor his friend has been invited to Rosemarie's party.

10. Change *One or the other* to *Both.*
    One or the other is usually ravenously hungry.

Summary

The first part of this chapter outlines those structures of language that involve subject-verb agreement: (1) a noun in the subject noun function and a verb in the present tense; (2) a third-person pronoun in the subject noun function and a verb in the present tense; (3) a first-person pronoun in the subject noun function and the present tense form of the verb *to be*; (4) a noun or a pronoun in the subject noun function and a past tense form of *to be*. These generalizations are then applied to subject-auxiliary agreement.

The second part of the chapter considers several complications of structure to which the writer must be alert in order to avoid errors in subject-verb agreement.

Chapter Test, Form A

1. Write sentences to illustrate the structures that follow. Unless otherwise indicated, use a noun — not a pronoun — in the subject-noun function.

   (a) A singular subject noun with a verb other than *to be* in the simple present tense. (Page 112)

   (b) A plural subject noun with a verb other than *to be* in the past form. (Page 116)

   (c) The pronoun *I* with the simple present form of some verb other than *to be*. (Page 116)

   (d) The pronoun *he* with the simple present form of some verb other than *to be*. (Page 112)

   (e) A plural subject noun with the past form of *to be*. (Page 113)

   (f) The pronoun *he* with the present tense of *to be*. (Page 112)

   (g) A singular subject noun with a predicate verb in which an auxiliary must be inflected to show agreement. (Pages 113-114)

   (h) A plural subject noun in the same structure described in item 1g. (Pages 113-114)

   (i) A singular subject noun followed by a word group that complicates subject-verb agreement. (Page 119)

   (j) An inverted sentence pattern involving subject-verb agreement. (Page 119)

2. In the following sentences select the appropriate verb form: (Pages 119-122)

   (a) The faculty, together with the parents, **has have** adjourned to the auditorium for refreshments.

   (b) Here **are is** a carton of books to be unpacked.

   (c) Acoustics **are is** a scientific control of sound.

   (d) The scissors **has have** disappeared again.

   (e) Pancakes and syrup **are is** a tasty breakfast.

   (f) There **go goes** my father and mother for their evening stroll.

   (g) Cranston is one of those men who **refuse refuses** to wear a hat.

   (h) Neither Kelsy nor I **am are is** going to the fireman's ball.

   (i) This is my aunt and uncle who **come comes** from New Jersey.

   (j) Mathematics **are is** a study of patterns.

   (k) Among the conquerors of space **are is** Gagarin and Glenn.

   (l) One of the sharks **was were** within fifty feet of our skiff.

   (m) Either burned lime or wood ash **are is** a simple fertilizer.

   (n) Dave **doesn't don't** like pop art.

   (o) **Wasn't Weren't** you surprised to see us?

Chapter Test, Form B

1. Write sentences to illustrate the structures that follow. Unless otherwise indicated, use a noun — not a pronoun — in the subject noun function.

(a) A plural subject noun with a verb other than *to be* in the simple present tense.
(b) A singular subject noun with a verb other than *to be* in the past form.
(c) The pronoun *I* with the past form of some verb other than *to be.*
(d) The pronoun *he* with the simple present form of some verb other than *to be.*
(e) A singular subject noun with the past form of *to be.*
(f) The pronoun *he* with the present tense of *to be.*
(g) The plural subject noun with a predicate verb which an auxiliary must be inflected to show agreement.
(h) A singular subject noun in the same structure described in lg.
(i) A singular subject noun followed by a word group that complicates subject-verb agreement.
(j) An inverted sentence pattern involving subject-verb agreement.

2. In the following sentences select the appropriate verb form:
   (a) Here **come comes** Helen and Jim, our star debaters.
   (b) Physics **deal deals** with matter and energy.
   (c) Neither the captain nor his men **was were** ever heard from again.
   (d) Making the beds, together with other light jobs, **keep keeps** Grandma busy until noon.
   (e) Helen is one of those girls who **participate participates** in a variety of activities.
   (f) Cold cereal and milk **are is** Dad's favorite pick-me-up.
   (g) Each of the scouts **are is** to bring his own camping equipment.
   (h) My uncle and aunt, who **come comes** from Rhode Island, are visiting us this winter.
   (i) The acoustics in this hall **are is** very poor.
   (j) **Was Were** you the astronaut at the masquerade party?
   (k) Why **doesn't don't** Jeb want to join the expedition to Kalamalka Lake?
   (l) Neither the candidate nor the reporters **was were** prepared for the crowd at the airport.
   (m) Each of the boys **take takes** a turn doing the marketing.
   (n) Alice's intonation and diction **are is** excellent.

Chapter 7

Substitution

A Look Back and A Look Forward

In Chapter 3, you saw how a variety of forms can be used in a given function. This sort of substitution — words in place of other words; words in place of word groups; word groups in place of words and of other word groups — is a useful grammatical device. It is a device that gives great flexibility to our language and permits an economy of statement that contributes to the effectiveness of communication.

Throughout this book, you have worked with pronouns as noun substitutes. In this chapter you will work with these function words in greater detail.

PERSONAL PRONOUNS AS SUBSTITUTE WORDS

	A	B	C	D	E	F	G
I	I	you	he	she	it	we	they
II	my	your	his	her	its	our	their
	mine	yours		hers		ours	theirs
III	me	you	him	her	it	us	them

Although the function words charted above do not always refer to persons, they are commonly called PERSONAL PRONOUNS.

A review of four grammatical terms — *person, number, gender, case* — will help you understand the function of the twenty-three different forms appearing on the chart.

Person

If, in general, the first person is the person speaking, the second person the person spoken to, and the third person the person spoken about, how should the lettered columns be grouped according to PERSON?

First Person	Columns A and F
Second Person	Column B
Third Person	Columns C, D, E, and G

Number

NUMBER, of course, refers to singular and plural. Look at the chart. Do the pronoun forms to the right of the rule in color refer to one person or to more than one person? How are the forms in column F classified according to person? The forms in column G? If you study the chart in terms of these questions, you should discover that the forms listed in column F are the plural forms of the singular, first-person forms in column A and that the forms listed in column G are the plural forms of the singular, third-person forms in columns C, D, and E. The second-person pronoun (column B) keeps the same form for both singular and plural.

Gender

GENDER refers to masculine, feminine, and neuter. Which three columns on the chart show this distinction? Does this distinction apply to both singular and plural number? Does it apply to all three persons?

Masculine	Column C
Feminine	Column D
Neuter	Column E

Only the third-person, singular pronouns are distinguished according to gender.

Case

Classify the pronouns in color in the following sentences according to person and number:

Subject Form	I own the walkie-talkie.
Possessive Form	This is my walkie-talkie.
	The walkie-talkie is mine.
Object Form	Uncle Ed gave me the walkie-talkie.

CASE refers to the function of a pronoun in a sentence and the inflection of the pronoun according to that function. The above illustration shows the four case forms of the first-person singular pronoun. How should the numbered rows on the chart be broken down according to case forms?

Row I	Subject Form
Row II	Possessive Form
Row III	Object Form

If you study the chart carefully, you will note that the subject form and the object form of *you* and *it* are the same and that *her* is both a possessive form and an object form.

SUBJECT CASE FORM

The subject case form of a personal pronoun is most commonly used when the pronoun substitutes as the subject of a sentence or of a subject-predicate word group.

Jim is going to college next fall. He plans to study journalism.

In the second sentence, the third-person, singular, masculine pronoun *He* substitutes for *Jim*. The subject case form is used, because *He* functions in its sentence as a subject.

Make the necessary pronoun substitution in the following:

The MacPhersons are going to Scotland, where _____ will spend several weeks at Mr. MacPherson's ancestral home.

The third-person, plural pronoun *they* substitutes for *The MacPhersons*. The subject case form is used, because *they* functions in the subject-predicate word group as a subject.

Jane and I may move to Oklahoma. _____ hear that the climate there is healthful.

The first-person, plural pronoun substitutes for *Jane and I*. The subject case form is used, because *We* functions in its sentence as a subject.

The word or words for which a personal pronoun is substituted are called ANTECEDENTS. A pronoun agrees with its antecedent in person and number. It also agrees in gender when a third-person, singular pronoun is involved. The case of the pronoun, however, depends on its function in its own sentence or in a subject-predicate word group.

POSSESSIVE CASE FORM

The possessive case form of a pronoun is used when the pronoun modifies a noun or when it substitutes for a structure consisting of a pronoun used as a modifier and a noun.

> This is my letter.
> This letter is mine.

In the first sentence, *my* is a first-person, singular pronoun. The possessive case form is used, because *my* modifies *letter*. In the second sentence, the possessive case form *mine* substitutes for *my letter*.

Note (1) the modifying function of the pronoun and (2) the substitution in the following sentence pairs:

> Her dress is white.
> Hers is bright red.

> Our home is faced with brick.
> Ours is faced with asbestos shingling.

> My hobby is photographing birds.
> Is this slide of a white-winged dove mine?

> Have you heard about their trip to Canada?
> This brochure is theirs.

OBJECT CASE FORM

The object case form of a pronoun is used when the pronoun substitutes as a direct object, an indirect object, the object of a preposition, or the subject of an infinitive. In the following examples, note – in addition to the case form – the agreement between each third-person pronoun and its antecedent.

Direct Object	Joe is a varsity tackle. Sally asked him to the Spring Dance.
Indirect Object	Sally bought the decorations for the dance at the five-and-ten. The checkout clerk gave her a king-size shopping bag.
Object of a Preposition	Sally handed the bulky package to me.
Subject of an Infinitive	She wanted me to carry it.

Exercise 1   *Identify the personal pronouns in the following sentences. Indicate person, number, gender, and case and—where possible—the antecedent.*

1. Doris and Mae hunted everywhere for their Pekingese but without success.

2. I shall never submit to your outrageous demands.

3. Mrs. Leman has sold her fruit farm to my uncle.

4. After the phone call from his mother, Henry could not get her out of his mind.

5. Our new car loses its speed climbing even the mildest grade.

6. When Paul met Martha, he asked her to go to a concert with him.

7. We regret that you cannot attend our grand opening.

8. I am sure that this is your book, not mine.

9. Father always buys us candy on payday.

10. Mary Jane told me that her mother won't give her permission to wear eye makeup.

11. Mrs. Smith says that she will be glad to baby-sit.

12. The mongrel wagged its tail enthusiastically when it heard the dinner bell.

13. When the boys tramped into the house, Mother told them to change their clothes.

14. "It's my book," said Bobby. "That's his."

Exercise 2   *Use the appropriate personal pronoun as a substitute in each of the following items. Be prepared to identify person, number, gender, case, and antecedent.*

1. Mrs. Sullivan has gone to Philadelphia. ____ will remain there for a week.

2. Here comes the mailman. I must give ____ the letter I wrote to Harriet.

3. Jack is planning to study abroad. ____ hopes to attend the Sorbonne.

4. The Andersons have a new station wagon. ____ have driven past our house four times.

5. Do not be discouraged. Success will come if ____ keep on trying.

6. ____ will never know what I can do until I try.

7. The boys worked out for an extra hour this morning. The coach expects ____ to be in shape.

8. Mr. Brown picked up ____ hat and coat and stalked out of the meeting.

9. I give you ____ word that I will not sell the property.

10. Jimmy pumped so much air into the tire that ____ burst.

11. Jack and I live on State Street. ____ moved there four years ago.

12. When I looked over at Harvey, he nodded and gave ____ a friendly smile.

13. We don't own the house, but the furniture is ____.

14. I was eating ____ dinner when the phone rang.

15. The ship sailed triumphantly into the harbor with all ____ flags flapping in the breeze.

Exercise 3   *Write meaningful sentences according to the directions that follow. When you use a pronoun in the third person, construct the sentence so that it includes an antecedent. (See Exercise 1.)*

1. Use the first-person, plural pronoun as the subject.

2. Use the first-person, plural pronoun as the object of a preposition.

3. Use a third-person, feminine, singular pronoun as an indirect object.

4. Use a third-person, plural pronoun as a possessive modifier.

5. Use the first-person, singular pronoun as the subject of an infinitive after the predicate verb *want*.

6. Use a third-person, singular, masculine pronoun as the object of a preposition.

7. Use a third-person, plural pronoun as a direct object.

8. Use the possessive case form of the third-person, singular, neuter pronoun.

9. Use the third-person, singular, masculine pronoun in the possessive case, but not as a modifier.

10. Use all the third-person, singular, feminine pronouns in the same sentence.

11. Use two different case forms of a first-person, singular pronoun in the same sentence.

12. Use the same form of the second-person pronoun in two different functions in the same sentence.

SUBORDINATORS AS SUBSTITUTE WORDS

The SUBORDINATORS *who, whose, whom, which,* and *that* are used as connectives to include an adjective clause within a basic sentence pattern. Subordinators also function in the adjective clause as a subject (*who, which, that*); as a complement (*whom*); and as a possessive modifier (*whose*).

Who, Whom, Whose

The form *who* is a subject case form, *whose* is a possessive case form, and *whom* is an object case form.

In the following sentence, what is the function of *who* in the adjective clause?

Ellen is a girl who loves to read.

The subordinator *who* substitutes for the noun *girl* in the subject-predicate word group *who loves to read,* an adjective clause modifying the noun *girl.* The subordinator *who* also serves as a connective and makes the adjective clause part of the basic N-LV-N PATTERN. The subordinator *who* functions in the adjective clause as the subject.

In the following sentence, what is the function of *whose* in the adjective clause?

This is the man whose car was stolen.

The subordinator *whose* substitutes for *man* (*the man's car was stolen*). The subject-predicate word group *whose car was stolen* is an adjective clause modifying the noun *man.* The subordinator *whose* serves as a connective and makes the adjective clause part of the basic NS-LV-N PATTERN. In the adjective clause, *whose* functions as a possessive modifier of the noun *car.*

In the following sentence, what is the function of *whom* in the adjective clause?

Miss Ryan is a teacher for whom the students have considerable affection.

The subordinator *whom* substitutes for *teacher* in the subject-predicate word group *for whom the students have considerable affection.* This subject-predicate word group is an adjective clause modifying *teacher.* The subordinator *whom* is a connective that makes the adjective clause part of the basic N-LV-N PATTERN. In the adjective clause, *whom* functions as the object of the preposition *for.*

In the following sentence, what is the function of *whom* in the adjective clause?

The girl whom you admire so much sits next to me in math.

The subordinator *whom* substitutes for the noun *girl* in the subject-predicate word group *whom you admire so much,* an adjective clause modifying *girl.* The subordinator *whom* serves as a connective that makes the word group part of the basic N-V PATTERN. The subordinator *whom* functions in the adjective clause as the direct object of the verb *admire.*

Which, Whose

The subordinators *who, whose,* and *whom* refer chiefly to people. The subordinator *which* refers chiefly to things, and to lower animals, but it may also refer to a body of persons. The subordinator *whose* is considered the possessive case form of *which* as well as of *who.*

Everest is a mountain which has been conquered by very few men.
Everest is a mountain whose snowy crown is the earth's highest point.

In the first sentence, the subordinator *which* substitutes for the noun *mountain.* Serving as a connective, the subordinator makes the adjective clause *which has been conquered by very few men* part of the basic N-LV-N PATTERN. The subordinator functions in the adjective clause as the subject.

In the second sentence, the subordinator *whose* substitutes for *mountain* (*mountain's crown*). Serving as a connective, the subordinator makes the adjective clause part of the basic N-LV-N PATTERN. The subordinator functions in the adjective clause as a possessive modifier of *crown.*

This is the party which conquered Everest.
This is the party whose historic climb made headlines all over the world.

In the above sentences *which* and *whose* substitute for the noun *party*, which refers to a group of persons. An analysis similar to that made in the preceding paragraphs can be made for these subordinators.

That

The subordinator *that* may substitute for almost any noun. This subordinator has only one form.

> The book that I like best is *Ivanhoe.*
> The contractor that built this house is an expert.
> He bought the horse that won the Derby.
> It is my back that I'm worried about.
> It was his conscience that made him uneasy.

Does the subordinator in each of the following have an antecedent?

> I wonder who told you the story.
> "Whose woods these are, I think I know." ROBERT FROST
> "Seek not to know for whom the bell tolls." JOHN DONNE
> I do not know which I will take.

In each of the above examples, the subordinator makes the clause part of the basic sentence pattern and functions in the clause as a subject, a possessive modifier, or an object. However, the subordinators do not have antecedents and are therefore not substitute words. In each example the subordinate clause is a noun clause.

REFLEXIVE PRONOUNS AS SUBSTITUTE WORDS

The *-self* pronouns are commonly called REFLEXIVE PRONOUNS. The reflexive pronouns listed below are arranged according to number. Which case forms of the personal pronouns combine with the suffix *-self* to form the reflexive pronouns?

SINGULAR	PLURAL
myself	ourselves
yourself	yourselves
himself	
herself	themselves
itself	

The personal pronoun forms used mostly in the formation of the reflexive pronouns are the possessive case forms. However, *himself* and *themselves* are formed from the objective case forms.

Reflexive Pronouns as Objects

What is the function of each reflexive pronoun in the following sentences?

> Father shaves himself every morning.
> The family enjoyed themselves at Disneyland.
> The wicked queen spent hours looking at herself in the mirror.
> Rags can open the door by himself now.

In the first sentence, *himself* substitutes for *Father* and functions as the object of the verb *shaves.* In the second sentence, *themselves* substitutes for *family* and functions as the direct object of the verb *enjoyed.* In the third sentence, *herself* substitutes for *queen* and is the object of the preposition *at.* In the fourth sentence, *himself* substitutes for *Rags* and is the object of the preposition *by.*

Reflexive Pronouns as Intensifiers

The *-self* pronouns are often used as intensifiers.

> You will have to read the book yourself in order to understand it fully.
> If I want things done right, I have to do them myself.
> Mary solved the puzzle herself.

In the above sentences, each reflexive pronoun functions as an appositive from the standpoint of syntax, but not from the standpoint of position. The appositive function becomes clearer when the sentences are rewritten:

> You yourself will have to read the book in order to understand it fully.
> If I want things done right, I myself have to do them.
> Mary herself solved the puzzle.

DETERMINERS AS SUBSTITUTE WORDS

The function words *this, that,* and *those,* ordinarily used as DETERMINERS, are sometimes used as substitute words.

> Determiner   This boy is my brother.
> Substitute Word This is my brother.
>
> Determiner   These books are mine.
> Substitute Word These are mine.

In the second sentence of the first pair, *This* substitutes for *This boy.* In the second sentence of the second pair, *These* substitutes for *These books.* The word *this* is a singular form; the word *these* is a plural form.

Identify the singular and plural forms in these sentences:

Determiner   That bird is a hawk.
Substitute Word   That is a hawk.

Determiner   Those birds are sheep-killing parrots.
Substitute Word   Those are sheep-killing parrots.

The word *that* substitutes for *that bird; those* substitutes for *those birds.* Again, *that* and *those* are singular and plural forms respectively.

Exercise 4   *Identify each of the substitute words in the following sentences as a personal pronoun, a subordinator, a reflexive pronoun, or a determiner used as a substitute word.*

1. The waters that surge from the Madison River sometimes flip campers from their beds.

2. My brother and I bought ourselves skis with safety bindings.

3. All the nurses autographed my cast before I left the hospital.

4. This is my ballpoint; where is yours?

5. According to my uncle, pahoehoe is a lava that cools with a porridgelike appearance.

6. We who have worked with Mr. Deaver are fully aware of his many talents.

7. You must ask your father to sign the application.

8. Henry had a walk-on part in *Julius Caesar,* but he came right out and took his curtain calls with the rest of us.

9. Mary gave herself a home permanent without reading the directions; we now call her Frizzletop.

10. This is my mother; that is my aunt.

COMPLICATIONS OF USAGE

Errors in case form and in reference to an antecedent sometimes complicate pronoun usage. The four sections that follow describe those situations in which most pronoun errors occur.

Errors in Case Form of Personal Pronouns

Be especially wary of pronouns answering the following descriptions:

PRONOUNS BEFORE AND AFTER A CONNECTIVE

Virginia and I ~~Virginia and me~~ ordered a sirloin steak for two. SUBJECT
FORM: Subject of the verb *ordered.*

The best speakers on the panel were Bill Ames and he ~~Bill Ames and him.~~
SUBJECT FORM: linking-verb complement.

Mr. Voorhees gave ~~Dick and I~~ Dick and me two passes to the motorboat
show. OBJECT FORM: indirect object.

PRONOUNS FOLLOWED BY A NOUN

~~Us boys~~ We boys plan to launch our sailplane next Saturday. SUBJECT FORM:
Subject of the verb *going.*

Mr. Sylvester will help us boys ~~we boys~~ launch the *Condor* next Saturday.
OBJECT FORM: complement of the verb *will help.*

PRONOUNS AFTER LET'S

Let's you and me ~~you and I~~ drive out to the wildlife sanctuary. OBJECT FORM:
same case form as *us* — let's = let us.

PRONOUNS IN AN INCOMPLETE WORD GROUP

No boy in the room was happier than he ~~him.~~ (Complete the word group:
than he was.)

Are they as well prepared as ~~us~~ we? (Complete the word group: as we are.)

Exercise 5   *In each sentence, choose the correct form in parentheses:*

1. Let's you and (I, me) write a note of appreciation to the
   producers.

2. When the current proved too strong for Dave and (I,
   me), we swam back to shore.

3. (Us, We) boys are petitioning for a 50 percent reduction
   in club dues.

4. Is that really (he, him) in that picture on the front page
   of today's paper?

5. No one sits a horse better than (her, she).

6. My sister and (I, me) are painting our bedroom furniture
   antique white.

7. The only contestants left in the round were Chris and
   (he, him).

8. The dishwashing chores are divided evenly between
   my brother and (I, me).

9. Joe excels at English, but Peggy is a better mathematician than (he, him).

10. During the second half, Barry sat with Joan and (I, me).

11. Esther gave the books to Eddie and (I, me).

12. (He, Him) and his father are expert skindivers.

Errors in the Use of Reflexive Pronouns

Use the correct form of a reflexive pronoun—*himself* and *themselves*, not "hisself" and "theirselves"—and do not use a reflexive pronoun when a personal pronoun is needed:

themselves
The boys helped ~~theirselves~~ to a whole platter of fried chicken.
I
Paula and ~~myself~~ decorated the front hall with garlands of holly.

Errors in the Use of Subordinators

Here are some errors to be avoided in the use of subordinators as substitute words.

WHO OR WHOM?

On what does the choice of *who* or *whom* depend?

The new center, **who** ~~whom~~ everyone thought would be a low scorer, racked up thirty points in his first game. (Here, the subordinator functions in the adjective clause as the subject. The subject case form *who* is the correct choice.)

Read the above sentence without the word group *everyone thought*. In choosing between *who* and *whom*, don't let word groups like *I believe, I know,* and *he thinks* distract you.

WHO, WHICH, OR THAT?

The subordinator *who* refers chiefly to persons, real or imagined. The subordinator *which* refers chiefly to things, to lower animals, and, occasionally, to nouns referring to a body of persons.

who
Here is the boy ~~which~~ won the tri-state oratorical contest.
that
The cock-of-the-rock is a bird ~~who~~ inhabits the highlands of Venezuela.

The subordinator *that* refers to persons, animals, or things but is never used when the adjective clause is set off by commas.

Belva Lockwood was one of the few women that were nominated for President of the United States.

The limpet is a small mollusk that lives on the rocky coasts of North and South America and Europe.

The limpet clings to rocks with its foot, which it uses as a sucker.

Do not use the subordinator *what* with an adjective clause.

that

The limpet has a tongue ~~what~~ is covered with rows of teeth.

Exercise 6   *Read the following sentences and supply an appropriate subordinator for each blank. Be prepared to justify the usage in each case.*

1. This is the weapon ____ was found on the prisoner.

2. Have you met the family ____ just moved into the vacant house on Sycamore Street?

3. Mr. Throggle is a candidate ____ we can count on to give us a balanced budget.

4. Lillian is a girl ____ ability is unquestioned.

5. The player ____ we think should get the MVP award isn't even mentioned as a contender.

6. Here are the books ____ covers need reinforcement.

7. November 22, 1963, is a day ____ will not soon be forgotten.

8. I will give you the name of the person to ____ you must apply for admission.

9. The police found the infant ____ they believe was abducted early yesterday.

10. *Zion* is a word ____ has many different meanings.

Errors in Reference

Since the personal pronoun is a substitute, the reader or listener must know exactly which word or word group it is referring to. If he doesn't know, communication ceases to be effective. In your writing, you must remember to provide the needed clues to reference.

AMBIGUOUS REFERENCE

Note the ambiguous pronoun reference in these sentences:

Father saw Bill driving his car down Main Street. (Whose car? Father's or Bill's?)

Mary wanted to see her aunt before she left for Brazil. (Who is bound for Brazil? Mary or her aunt?)

When I went to put the money in my wallet, I found that it was gone. (What was gone? The money or the wallet?)

Jim said that he didn't think that Fred should see his brother because he was sick in bed. (Who is sick in bed? Fred or Jim's brother?)

I finally threw out my dirty tennis shoes, which pleased Mother tremendously. (What pleased Mother? The tennis shoes or the fact that they were thrown out?)

Now note how each of the above sentences has been rewritten to make the meaning clear:

Bill was driving his car down Main Street when his father saw him.
Before Mary left for Brazil, she wanted to see her aunt.
I found the money gone when I went to put it in my wallet.
Jim said that since his brother was sick in bed Fred shouldn't see him.
When I finally threw out my dirty tennis shoes, Mother was tremendously pleased.

PRONOUN WITHOUT A NEEDED ANTECEDENT

A pronoun that has no antecedent or that refers vaguely to a general idea is confusing to the person with whom you are communicating. In the following sentences, for example, to what does each pronoun in color refer?

Silas ploughed the field north of the house this morning. He completed it in three hours.

Bill likes the way his mother cooks the meat. He likes them broiled with a little salt.

Joe went fishing at Lake Owyhee and caught four of them.

It says in the paper that you will have to pay higher taxes on property. They certainly make it hard for you.

In the first illustration, the pronoun *it* has no specific reference. Structurally, the antecedent of *it* could be either *field* or *house*. But does the writer really intend to imply that Silas has *completed* either the field or the house? We can only guess that he wished to communicate that Silas has completed the ploughing.

Similarly, *them* in the second illustration and *them* in the third illustration do not have specific antecedents.

The fourth illustration demonstrates the misuse of indefinite *it, they,* and *you.*

Note how each of the above illustrations has been rewritten to make the meaning clear:

Silas completed ploughing the field north of the house in three hours this morning.

Bill likes the way his mother cooks chops. She broils them with a little salt.

Jim went fishing at Lake Owyhee and caught four suckers.

According to the paper, the tax on property is going up. This increase is certainly hard on the homeowner.

FUNCTION WORDS AS ANTECEDENTS

Sometimes personal pronouns substitute for such function words as *each, either, neither, one, anyone, everyone, anybody, everybody, somebody,* and *nobody.* These words are considered singular, and a personal pronoun substituting for any one of them should be singular in number.

Anybody can attend the meeting if he is interested.

Everybody should bring his textbook to class tomorrow.

This crime was committed by somebody with a twisted mind. I wonder if the police will find him.

One must remember to remain very still when he attends a concert.

Each should learn to adjust his own lifebelt.

POSITION OF SUBORDINATOR

For clearer communication, place a subordinator as close to its antecedent as possible:

What is the girl's name who sang *America* at Friday's assembly?	What is the name of the girl who sang *America* at Friday's assembly?
The natives wore shoes on their feet that were made of fur.	On their feet, the natives wore shoes that were made of fur.

Exercise 7   *The pronoun reference in each of the following sentences is faulty. Rewrite to make the meaning clear or to make the pronoun agree with its antecedent.*

1. When Bud Ellis met Jody Baker at the Recreation Center, he challenged him to a game of chess.

2. The roof sprung a bad leak; it ruined all the clothes stored in the attic.

3. In this morning's paper it says that you can't use Route 4 until they repair the flood damage.

4. Patricia told Ellen that her essay on fire prevention won first prize in the Kiwanis contest.

5. Dad pointed out the ragged seat covers and the rusty tire rims, but they insisted on asking a thousand dollars for it.

6. Mother had lunch with Mrs. Ames when she drove into Tillamook last week.

7. Whitey asked Yogi where his baseball gear was.

8. The center outmaneuvered his guard and crammed it through the basket for two points.

9. We visited Buckingham Palace where we watched them change the guard.

10. Mike told Kevin that it was his turn to ask Dad for the car keys.

Summary

This chapter examines several kinds of substitute words: personal pronouns, subordinators, reflexive pronouns, and determiners.

Personal pronouns, which refer chiefly to persons, are inflected for person, number, gender, and case. Within this inflection, however, there is some duplication of form.

The word or word group for which a personal pronoun substitutes is an antecedent. A pronoun agrees with its antecedent in person, number, and gender. Only the third person singular pronouns indicate gender.

The case form of the personal pronoun depends on the function of the pronoun in the sentence or in a subject-predicate word group. A pronoun that functions as a subject or as a linking-verb complement is in the subject case form. A pronoun that modifies a noun or substitutes for a modifying pronoun and its noun (*mine* for *my book*, for example) is in the possessive case form. A pronoun that functions as a complement, as the object of a preposition, or as the subject of an infinitive is in the object case form.

The subordinators *who, whom, whose, which,* and *that* also serve as substitute words. The form *who* is a subject case form, *whose* is a possessive case form, and *whom* is an object case form. The subordinator substitutes for an antecedent in the basic sentence pattern and it also makes an adjective clause part of the basic sentence pattern. The case form of the subordinator depends on its function in the adjective clause.

Reflexive pronouns are the *-self* pronouns; the determiners *this, that, these,* and *those* are used frequently as substitute words.

It is naturally important that the reader know exactly what a substitute word is substituting for. In order to meet the standards of written and spoken English, it is also important to use the correct case form. The latter part of this chapter describes those situations that most commonly lead to errors in substitution.

Chapter Test, Form A

1. List all of the first-person personal pronouns. Then write sentences illustrating their use. (Page 128)

2. Identify each personal pronoun in the following sentences. Indicate the person, number, gender (if any), and case of each pronoun. (Pages 128-130)
   (a) The farmer lost his wheat crop in the windstorm.
   (b) Mrs. Lauren gave us a pleasant smile.
   (c) Your request will be forwarded to the proper authorities.
   (d) My mother plans to visit her sister in Jamestown this summer.
   (e) It may not be much of a car, but it's ours.

3. Write sentences to illustrate the following: (Pages 129-130)
   (a) The first-person personal pronoun used as the object of a preposition.
   (b) The plural third-person pronoun as a possessive modifier.
   (c) The singular first-person pronoun as the subject of an infinitive.
   (d) The plural third-person pronoun as an indirect object.
   (e) The singular third-person, masculine pronoun in the possessive case, but not as a noun-modifier.

4. Fill in each blank in the following sentences with an appropriate substitute word: (Pages 137-140)
   (a) Henry looked at ____ in the mirror; then he adjusted his tie.
   (b) The officer told Dad and ____ to turn left at the first traffic light.

    (c) One must be careful of the company _____ keeps.

    (d) He mailed the letter to the main office, _____ is located in Boston.

    (e) This is the boy _____ my father says will someday pitch for the Dodgers.

    (f) Mr. Canby is a person _____ you can trust.

    (g) Let's you and _____ bake some cookies for the Sophomore Open House.

    (h) Everyone likes to receive some recognition for _____ work.

    (i) _____ girls plan to visit Strawberry Mansion next Saturday.

    (j) Pauline is a better skier than _____, but I take fewer falls.

5. Improve the reference in each of the following: (Pages 140-142)

    (a) Henry saw Bill at the Snack Shop with his girl.

    (b) Mr. Grodsky mows the lawn by hand. He claims it keeps him physically fit.

    (c) What is the boy's name who ran the ball for a gain of twelve yards?

Chapter Test, Form B

1. List all of the third-person personal pronouns. Then write sentences illustrating their use.

2. Identify each personal pronoun in the following sentences. Indicate the person, number, gender (if any), and case of each pronoun.

    (a) Mary always puts on her gloves before she leaves the house.

    (b) The principal asked the boys why they were late.

    (c) When the Smiths come to town, Mother always asks them to dinner.

    (d) Your new hat is very attractive.

    (e) When the car wouldn't start, the boys pushed it into the garage.

3. Write sentences to illustrate the following:

    (a) The plural first-person pronoun as the subject.

    (b) The singular, third-person, feminine pronoun as an indirect object.

    (c) The second-person pronoun in a plural context as the subject.

    (d) The singular, third-person, neuter pronoun in the possessive case.

    (e) The singular, third-person, masculine pronoun as the object of a preposition.

4. Fill in each blank in the following sentences with an appropriate substitute word:

    (a) In her relationships with others, Martha thinks of _____ most of the time.

    (b) You understand, of course, that this matter is strictly between you and _____.

    (c) Everyone enjoys some recreation in _____ free time.

    (d) One must try to think of others, not of _____.

    (e) Clara went to the dance with a boy _____ she met last week. (Do not use *that*.)

    (f) Here is a letter _____ came for you this morning.

    (g) Give the package to _____ boys, and we'll deliver it for you.

(h) Fred is the boy ____ you sent for.

(i) Let's you and ____ drive Aunt Ellie to the airport.

(j) My brother is not as quick as ____, but his work is usually more perfect than mine.

5. Improve the reference in each of the following:

(a) There is a picket fence around our house which needs painting.

(b) Fred's father is a doctor; therefore, he wants to make it his profession.

(c) Joe's a fishing enthusiast; however, he never likes to clean them.

The Structure of Your Language

In Chapter 3, you worked with using a variety of forms in a given function. This, too, is a kind of substitution — one in which a word substitutes for a word group or a word group substitutes for a word. The wholesale substitution of word groups for words would, of course, lead to wordiness. Note, however, how selective substitution increases the effectiveness of each of the examples below. The choice of specific, lively words instead of vague, colorless words also adds to the overall effectiveness.

EXAMPLE I gave money to an unbelievably poor old beggar.
         I gave my last dollar to a beggar who was old and poor beyond belief.

EXAMPLE The boy was arrested for his crime.
         The young tough was arrested for holding up the Laundromat on Kissena Boulevard.

EXAMPLE Freddy came into the house then.
         Freddy scurried into the house when it began to rain.

■ In each of the sentences below, make the substitutions noted in the directions.

1. The walk home from church with Sally Jones was very pleasant.
   Substitute a verbal phrase for the subject noun and its modifiers. Replace the linking-verb complement and its modifier with a more colorful adjective.

2. Father walked very quickly up the path.
   Choose a more specific predicate verb and substitute a lively adverb for the intensifier-adverb structure.

3. Dyane got out of the car; then she slammed the door.
   Replace the verb in the first basic sentence pattern with a more colorful word expressing anger. Substitute a participial phrase for the second basic sentence pattern.

4. An old cow looked at us with sad eyes.
   Replace the modifier of the subject noun with a livelier adjective or series of adjectives and replace the predicate verb with a more specific word. Substitute an adjective clause for the modifier of the object of the preposition.

Chapter 8

Punctuation

A Look Back and A Look Forward

In Chapter 1, you worked briefly with intonation as one of the six signals that help in the identification of an English sentence. In Chapter 8, you will examine the vocal effects of intonation. You will note once again that effective punctuation relies not only on a sensitivity to intonation but also on a knowledge of grammar and on a working familiarity with certain conventions.

VOCAL EFFECTS OF INTONATION

The sound pattern of what you say may serve as a useful guide to the punctuation of what you write. In speech, we group our words by changes in pitch, by changes in degrees of loudness, and by minute separations into units of syntax—a noun with its modifiers, a verb with its modifiers, an absolute structure, for example. In writing, similar grouping is accomplished with the marks of punctuation: commas, periods, semicolons, and so on.

PITCH (high or low), STRESS (soft or loud), and JUNCTURE (the minute separations between patterns of sound) are the names given to those vocal effects that make up the intonation pattern of speech. Pitch, stress, and juncture are referred to by linguists as the SUPRASEGMENTAL PHO NEMES of our language. The segmental phonemes—the vowel and consonant sounds that make up spoken English—are treated in detail in Chapter 9.

Pitch

In speech the voice rises and falls. Most linguists recognize four levels of pitch in communication. These levels are designated as PITCH PHONEMES and are numbered 1, 2, 3, and 4 from low to high. In the following sentence the numbers indicating pitch are placed over the syllables where a certain pitch level begins.

2   3   1

Mary has a new handbag.

Pitch phonemes may also be expressed graphically. The horizontal lines indicate the changing pitch levels and the arrow at the end of the sentence indicates the fading out of the voice.

Mary has a new handbag ↘

The 2-3-1 pitch pattern illustrated above is typical of many statements. Now note the pitch pattern of the question below. On what level does the question begin? To what level does it rise?

Are you planning to visit Dublin

2   3

Are you planning to visit Dublin?

In questions where great surprise or amazement is expressed, the voice may rise to level 4.

You say you're going to Paris
2   4
You say you're going to Paris?

The rise in pitch from level 2 to level 4 is so rapid that the listener is not aware of the passage of the voice through level 3. This rapid change occurs also at the end of a statement when the voice drops quickly from level 3 to level 1. In designating the pitch pattern with numbers, therefore, the intermediate number in a rapid change is omitted.

Stress

While stress has little relation to the problem of punctuation, it is reviewed here because it is a part of the intonation pattern of speech. The four degrees of stress recognized by most linguists are primary stress, indicated by an acute accent ⟋′⟋; secondary stress indicated by a circumflex ⟋ˆ⟋; tertiary stress indicated by a grave accent ⟋ˋ⟋; and zero stress indicated by a breve ⟋˘⟋.

The following illustration shows all four degrees of stress.

The cáptain díed.

Juncture

As we speak, we separate our words and word groups with minute pauses that differ slightly in length. These junctures, as they are called, are important clues to meaning since they separate not only the words (sound patterns) but also the grammatical units of syntax — the word groups and the subject-predicate word groups you've been working with in this book.

The juncture between words is the plus juncture and is indicated by the symbol ⟋+⟋. There are three terminal junctures: the single-bar juncture (⟋ | ⟋) which occurs between word groups and is accompanied by no change in pitch; the double-bar juncture (⟋ ‖ ⟋) which occurs between word groups and is accompanied by a rising pitch; and the double-cross juncture (⟋#⟋) which occurs between word groups and is accompanied by a falling pitch.

The following sentences illustrate the four types of juncture. The illustration with arrows indicates the accompanying pitch.

Have + you + any + wool ‖

Have you any wool
Have you any wool?

I + have + three + bags + full #

I have three bags full
I have three bags full.

Baa + baa | black + sheep | have + you + any + wool ‖

Baa baa black sheep have you any wool
Baa, baa, black sheep, have you any wool?

Double-bar juncture frequently occurs at the end of a question, and double-cross juncture at the end of a statement.

Exercise 1   *Read the following passage aloud several times. Using in-tonation as a guide, try to estimate the number of sentences in the passage.*

On Friday noon July the twentieth 1714 the finest bridge in all Peru broke and precipitated five travellers into the gulf below this bridge was on the high-road between Lima and Cuzco and hundreds of persons passed over it every day it had been woven of osier by the Incas more than a century before and visitors to the city were always led out to see it it was a mere ladder of thin slats swung out over the gorge with handrails of dried vine horses and coaches and chairs had to go down hundreds of feet below and pass over the narrow torrent on rafts but no one not even the Viceroy not even the Archbishop of Lima had descended with the baggage rather than cross by the famous bridge of San Luis Rey St Louis of France himself protected it by his name and by the little mud church on the further side the bridge seemed to be among the things that last forever it was unthinkable that it should break the moment a Peruvian heard of the accident he signed himself and made a mental calculation as to how recently he had crossed by it and how soon he had intended crossing by it again people wandered about in a trance-like state muttering they had the hallucination of seeing themselves falling into a gulf[1]

[1]Adapted from the opening paragraph of *The Bridge of San Luis Rey* by Thornton Wilder. Copyright 1955 by Thornton Wilder.

RELATION BETWEEN INTONATION AND PUNCTUATION

The correlation between punctuation and intonation is not an exact one. The same mark of punctuation can represent a variety of patterns of pitch and juncture. A given pattern of intonation may be represented by a variety of punctuation marks or by no punctuation at all.

Intonation serves primarily as a guide in determining sentence structure. Sentences end with a double-cross juncture and a falling pitch or with a double-bar juncture and a rising pitch. Once you develop a sensitivity to these patterns of sound you will be able to avoid such errors as run-together sentences (page 194) and sentence fragments (page 21).

Sensitivity to juncture and pitch also helps in alerting the writer to the *need* for punctuation. In the following examples, read the sentence marked for juncture aloud before noting the actual punctuation:

Henry Adams │ that good-looking chap from Boston │ will serve on the Rules Committee #
Henry Adams, that good-looking chap from Boston, will serve on the Rules Committee.

The grasshoppers spread over the fields ‖ onto the highways ‖ and into the farmers' very living rooms #
The grasshoppers spread over the fields, onto the highways, and into the farmers' very living rooms.

When the cat's away ‖ the mice will play #
When the cat's away, the mice will play.

The aggressive North High Tigers made one touchdown after another ‖ while big Pete Shocker sat on the bench biting his fingernails #
The aggressive North High Tigers made one touchdown after another, while big Pete Shocker sat on the bench biting his fingernails.

The solar eclipse over ‖ Horace Wheetle carefully removed his dark glasses #
The solar eclipse over, Horace Wheetle carefully removed his dark glasses.

Marie ‖ are you going to the Senior Prom ‖
Marie, are you going to the Senior Prom?

The circus parade moved slowly down the wide street ‖ and the roars of the lions and the cries of the monkeys blended with the calliope into an exciting cacophony #
The circus parade moved slowly down the wide street, and the roars of the lions and the cries of the monkeys blended with the calliope into an exciting cacophony.

Coordinate Adjectives

The problem of whether to separate two or more adjectives with a comma may be resolved by listening carefully to the intonation pattern.

> a nice | old lady
> a kind | friendly | lady

In the first phrase there is a single-bar juncture between the coordinate adjectives *nice* and *old* but not between *old* and *lady*. The words *old* and *lady* are uttered as a single word; therefore, no punctuation is required between *nice* and *old lady*.

> the nice old lady

In the second phrase, a single-bar juncture separates *friendly* and *lady* as well as *kind* and *friendly*. The second single-bar juncture is the signal the coordinate adjectives should be separated by a comma.

> a kind, friendly lady

Now read the following illustrations aloud and write the phrases, properly punctuated, on your paper.

the sweet little boy	the big ugly man
the white summer suit	the old spavined horse
the wild racing mare	the beautiful modern fixture

Exercise 2   *Examine the coordinate adjectives in the following sentences. Read each sentence aloud. Then rewrite the sentence inserting the symbol for single-bar juncture where this juncture occurs. Rewrite the sentence a second time, inserting the necessary punctuation.*

1. White gritty dust lay on top of the table.

2. That nice young man with the tennis racket is my cousin.

3. Mr. Jones is an honest respectable citizen.

4. Uncle Hiram went to school in an old-fashioned red schoolhouse.

5. Careless irresponsible campers have caused raging forest fires.

6. My brother married a pretty Irish girl.

7. Her bright green hat enhances the beauty of her luxuriant red hair.

8. The Browns just bought a comfortable inexpensive home.

9. The drive was lined with tall black cypresses.

10. Alice wore a light blue coat.

11. We shuffled through the dry old leaves.

12. It was an unavoidable regrettable error.

13. Jackie is a quiet little boy.

14. The ancient brass cannon on the village green was last fired during the War of 1812.

15. We will give the matter our careful undivided attention.

Restrictive and Nonrestrictive Adjective Clauses

Which sentence requires commas?

The man who succeeds is the man who works #
Easter Island | which is noted for its mysterious monuments | is located 2400 miles off the coast of Chile #

The intonation pattern of the first sentence does not indicate any need for separating the adjective clauses from the nouns they modify. In the second sentence, however, the single-bar juncture after *Island* and the single-bar juncture after *monuments* signal that the adjective clause should be set off by commas.

In the first sentence, both adjective clauses are restrictive. A restrictive clause has a close relationship to the word it modifies. It helps to identify or explain the word.

In the second sentence the adjective clause is nonrestrictive. Its relationship to *Easter Island* is loose; it describes rather than identifies the island. A nonrestrictive clause is set off by commas to help the reader determine its function and therefore its meaningful relationship to the sentence.

Again, the pattern of intonation—reinforced by your grammatical insight—should help you to become more sensitive to the need for punctuation.

Now read aloud the following examples of restrictive and non-restrictive clauses. The intonation patterns should help you determine whether or not the clause should be set off with commas.

People who live in glass houses shouldn't throw stones#
This is the house that Jacquelon built#
The boy who lives next door sent these flowers#

The statue of Oliver Cromwell| which had stood on the square for many years| was taken down and destroyed#

This storm | which came up unexpectedly from the north | has caused great
  damage #
The letter is from Alice Applegate ‖ whom you admire so much #

The adjective clauses in the first three sentences are restrictive — or
identifying — and need not be set off with commas. The adjective clauses
in the last three sentences, however, are nonrestrictive — or descriptive — and should therefore be set off with commas.

The statue of Oliver Cromwell, which had stood on the square for many
  years, was taken down and destroyed.
This storm, which came up unexpectedly from the north. has caused great
  damage.
The letter is from Alice Applegate, whom you admire so much.

Exercise 3   *Although single-bar juncture is not an exact guide to the
determination of nonrestrictive adjective clauses, it often
helps in the identification of such clauses for purposes of
punctuation. Read the following sentences aloud several
times. Then rewrite the sentences, inserting the symbol for
single-bar juncture where this juncture occurs. Write the sentences a second time, letting the intonation pattern guide
you in punctuating the clauses.*

1. Father works for the man who lives across the street.

2. Jim is a salesman for the Union Gas Company which
   has its main office on First Street.

3. Michelangelo who worshiped beauty regarded himself
   as ugly.

4. Dr. Ambrose who graduated from Johns Hopkins University in 1949 will lecture at the seminar.

5. At the dance I met an officer who graduated from West
   Point in 1960.

6. On Frontier Day, the women of Cheyenne ransack their
   attics to find costumes which belonged to their grand-
   mothers or great-grandmothers.

7. Annie said that she would have to consult her husband
   who is in the real estate business.

8. Part of the coral reef which parallels the curve of the
   Florida Keys has been dedicated as America's first under-
   seas park.

9. Father insists on having a lawyer who is a Harvard graduate.

10. Ask the policeman who is directing traffic at the intersection.

11. New Zealand is the remnant of a continent which sank into the sea millions of years ago.

12. The new *Bounty* which was launched in the summer of 1960 is thirty feet longer than the original.

13. The kea is a large parrot which feeds on sheep.

14. A photo which tends to cause justice to miscarry may be held in contempt of court.

15. We bumped into a character who earns his living by catching grasshoppers and selling them for bait.

PUNCTUATION REVIEW

In order to refresh your memory, let us summarize here some punctuation usage that should be familiar to you.

USES OF THE COMMA

1. In a series. Words and word groups in a series are usually separated by commas:

> Books, papers, clothing, and remnants of a past meal littered the tiny room.
> Where to go, what to do, and how to get enough money to do it always bothered the little man.

2. To set off appositives. Nonrestrictive appositives (see page 103) are set off by commas:

> Clancy, the handsome policeman, smiled diffidently at his admirer.
> The honey ant, a remarkable insect, stores eight times its weight in honeydew in its elastic abdomen.

3. After introductory sentence elements. Introductory elements that are followed by double-bar juncture are usually separated from the rest of the sentence with a comma:

> In the meantime, the rain came down in sheets and washed away the riverbank.
> Since the bridge has been washed away, we will have to take a detour to Payson.
> Peering through the tiny porthole, he caught a glimpse of an almond orchard in full flower.

4. *Before terminal word groups.* Terminal word groups that are preceded by double-bar juncture are usually separated from the rest of the sentence with a comma:

> He spent a whole week in Denver, where he was entertained by the junior members of the organization.

5. *To set off an absolute structure.* Absolute structures (see page 107) are set off from the rest of the sentence with commas:

> Her parents having gone to the movies, Nancy had to stay home and baby-sit.
> The new luxury liner steamed out of the harbor, flags flying and whistles blowing.
> Dad stood at the top of the basement stairs, broom in hand, trying to look dangerous.

6. *Yes and No.* A comma sets off *Yes* and *No* at the beginning of a sentence:

> Yes, that's the man we've been looking for.
> No, you cannot borrow my white sweater.

7. *Direct address.* Commas are used to set off words in direct address:

> Fellow citizens of Milltown, I am glad to be your guest this evening.
> Look, Virginia, there's the Big Dipper.

8. *In a compound sentence.* A comma usually precedes the coordinator in a compound sentence:

> The battery must have a five-year guarantee, or I will not buy it.
> This little pig went to market, but that little pig stayed home.

9. *In dates.* A comma is used between the date and the year:

> On June 12, 1815, Napoleon left Paris to take command of his troops.

Note that when a date does not fall at the end of a sentence, the year is separated from the rest of the sentence with a comma.
When just the month and the year are given, usage varies:

> By April 1814, Napoleon had decided that his cause was hopeless.
> By April, 1814, Napoleon had decided that his cause was hopeless.

10. *Between the city and state.* A comma separates the city or town from the state:

> The Norwich terrier was named for Norwich, England.
> The burning lignite beds near Amidon, North Dakota, can be seen several miles away.

In the second sentence, note the comma after the state.

11. After the salutation of a social letter. In a social letter, a comma follows the salutation.

> Dear Bud,
> Dear Mrs. James,

12. Before a direct quotation. A comma sets off a direct quotation from the rest of the sentence:

> Hal asked, "How long will lunch period be tomorrow?"

A comma is not needed when the quotation is built right into the structure of the sentence:

> Did you say "Yes"?
> Paul's voice quavered when he said "I do."

USES OF THE APOSTROPHE

1. To show possession. The apostrophe indicates the possessive case form of a noun and of certain function words used as noun substitutes:

> Ellen's father was once a powerful nobleman.
> Civil defense is everybody's business.

2. To form contractions. The apostrophe indicates the omission of one or more letters in a contraction:

> We've run out of gas again.
> It's a long way to Tipperary.

3. To form certain plurals. The apostrophe is used to form the plural of a figure, of a symbol, of a letter, and of a word used as a word:

> Your 9's look like 7's, and your *a*'s look like *o*'s.
> Change all the %'s in your report to *percent*.
> There are no *if*'s about it.

USES OF THE SEMICOLON

1. In a compound sentence without a connective. A semicolon separates basic sentence patterns that are not joined by a coordinator:

> The hot summer afternoon was over; only the hum of the locusts broke the quiet of the evening.

2. Before a conjunctive adverb used as a connective. A semicolon is used before a conjunctive adverb that connects two basic sentence patterns.

> The king had lost the first skirmish; however, he would be ready for a second battle the following day.

USE OF ITALICS

1. For titles of books, plays, motion pictures, works of art, magazines, and newspapers. The titles of books, magazines, and newspapers are underlined as a signal that the title is italicized:

> The novel <u>Lilacs on Main Street</u> was first published in the <u>Thursday Review</u> and is now being serialized in the Rochester <u>Telegraph</u>.

2. For words, letters, and figures. Words, letters, and figures used not for their meaning but as words are underlined:

> There are two <u>o</u>'s in <u>too</u>.
> There are three <u>9</u>'s in the number <u>999</u>.

3. For foreign words. Foreign words are underlined:

> The legislature adjourned <u>sine die</u> on Friday.

4. For names of ships and trains. The names of ships and trains are underlined:

> The <u>Queen Mary</u> steamed into the harbor.

USES OF QUOTATION MARKS

1. To enclose a direct quotation. Quotation marks set off the exact words of a speaker:

> "The next dance is an exhibition waltz," explained Anna.
> "I think," said Elma, "that those boys drink a gallon of milk a day."
> "Have you an overactive thyroid?" asked Mrs. Bergwin.

2. To enclose certain titles. Quotation marks are used for the titles of articles, essays, short stories, poems, book chapters, songs, and the like:

> "How Beautiful with Shoes" is one of Wilbur Daniel Steele's finest short stories.
> Stephen Foster's first published song was "Open Thy Lattice, Love."

Exercise 4   *Punctuate the following sentences. Be prepared to give a reason for each punctuation mark you insert.*

1. The brave company fought bitterly but they could not withstand the superior numbers of the enemy troops

2. Why are you standing there Paula

3. The mayor of the village a dignified old gentleman with a long white beard conducted us through the ancient castle

4. On May 12 1883 a significant incident occurred in the city of Akron Ohio

5. The minister gave the benediction the congregation rose to leave

6. Dads favorite poem is Robert Frosts Mending Wall

7. On the other hand we may never get a chance like this again

8. The beluga emits a series of squeaks squawks and whistles from its blowhole

9. If Dads vacation plans materialize we may spend a month in the Adirondacks this summer.

10. Ill defend you said the lawyer but well have to plan the case very carefully

11. Waddling in Indian file the ducks followed us into the barn

12. Frank is a good student nevertheless hell have to work very hard at Stanford

13. Why doesnt the pitcher throw the ball over the plate all the time asked Florence

14. A big celebration is planned for the Fourth of July when the Chamber of Commerce will stage a spectacular dis play of fireworks

15. Two giraffes legs propped at an impossible angle were drinking from a small pool

16. It was getting late and Jim would be home soon

17. Ladies and gentlemen may we ask for your undivided attention

18. An article called The Great Antagonism appeared in the Atlantic Monthly of November 1958

19. You have a habit of using too many ands and buts in your writing

20. Mrs. Malaprop asked What business have you Miss with the words preference and aversion

21. When dinner was over and the dishes had been cleared away Grandfather suggested we all drive out to Jones Beach for a swim

22. There are three 8s in our new license number

GRAMMAR AND PUNCTUATION

Although a sensitivity to intonation in speech may help you punctuate your written work, your effective use of this graphic device depends largely upon your knowledge of grammar, upon the structure of the English language. This is particularly true in the punctuation of coordinate sentence elements; of subordinate clauses—both introductory and terminal—of appositives; of absolute constructions; and of transitional adverbs.

Compound Sentences

Many young writers have difficulty with the semicolon. Your effective use of this mark will depend largely on your recognition of a compound sentence and your identification of the coordinated basic sentence patterns. As reviewed on page 157, the semicolon is used mainly when the connective is omitted. In a sense, a semicolon represents the missing connective.

> Some of the city's new buildings are marble, most are white stucco.
> The slopes became more gentle, the ravines were mantled with orange and yellow tamarack.

When a connective is omitted between two coordinated basic sentence patterns, an adverb is frequently used to secure transition between the two ideas. Such adverbs are called CONJUNCTIVE ADVERBS, and they include words like *however, therefore, nevertheless, moreover, consequently,* and *then.* In a compound sentence, a conjunctive adverb is preceded by a semicolon. Because it is part adverb, a conjunctive adverb may be moved about within the basic sentence pattern in which it occurs.

> The noise died to silence at the finish line, then a deafening shout burst from the crowd.
> Scientific research in the space program is proceeding vigorously, it will nevertheless be many years before a flight to the moon can be made.

Interrupting Elements

On pages 155-156, you reviewed the punctuation of introductory sentence elements and of terminal word groups. Now let's examine the punctuation of certain elements that interrupt the normal sentence pattern:

> South Malden High School, which was built only two years ago, is already overcrowded.

When the normal sequence of a sentence pattern is broken by an interrupting word group, the word group is set off from the rest of the sentence with paired commas, dashes, parentheses, or brackets. The interrupting element in the above sentence is familiar to you as a non-restrictive adjective clause. Transitional phrases and words frequently serve as interrupting elements:

Your proposal ,on the other hand ,might well lead to disaster.
The Giants ,in the meantime ,had managed to win four games in a row.
Your salary ,moreover ,will continue during your absence.
The results ,however ,are highly uncertain.

As a rule, an interrupting element set off by paired dashes is not as closely related to the thought of the sentence as an interrupting element set off by paired commas.

The rain dance of the Hopis— a ritual which had been practiced for genera-tions —was followed by heavy thunderstorms and flash floods.
The reporters were shown politely to buses —exceedingly slow buses as it developed —and left sitting while every car in Afghanistan raced away behind the president. —The New York *Times*
Mayor Stockland's apparent determination to see that Glendale taxpayers get their money's worth —even at his own expense—is commendable. —The Phoenix *Gazette*

Parentheses are used to enclose material which is explanatory but has only a slight bearing on the rest of the sentence.

The gold bars, each weighing fifty ounces (the fixed value of gold in the United States is $35 per ounce) were carefully packed in the case.
The American Medical Association (AMA) is cooperating with the Food and Drug Administration (FDA) in the study of recently developed drugs.
The side walls (running S.W. and N.E.), though exceedingly fractured, yet remained standing; but the vast buttresses (at right angles to them, and therefore parallel to the walls that fell) were in many cases cut off, as if by a chisel, and hurled to the ground.   CHARLES DARWIN

Brackets are used to enclose parenthetical material that has been in-serted into a quotation.

"At two in the morning we swept through the Straits of Messina [between Sicily and the mainland of Italy] and so bright was the moonlight that Italy on the one hand and Sicily on the other hand seemed almost as distinctly visible as though we looked at them from the middle of a street we were traversing."   MARK TWAIN
"Go there, and light a camp-fire at wood's rim;
But tell your name and lineage [only] to him
Whose blade compels . . . ."   WILLIAM BUTLER YEATS

Exercise 5   *Punctuate the following sentences correctly. Be prepared to give a reason for each mark you insert.*

1. In the dimming west a last cloud burned a deep russet tinged the mountain MARY RENAULT.

2. There is to be sure more to her story than meets the eye

3. On December 5 1955 Walter Reuther and George Meany announced the merger of the American Federation of Labor and the Congress of Industrial Organizations AFL-CIO

4. Shippers for example could be ruined by excessive freight rates

5. In the 1850s clipper ships two of the most famous were the Sea Witch and the Flying Cloud challenged British vessels for supremacy of the seas

6. They had however other traits which were less commendable

7. Mayor Thomas Walsh who has served the city well for sixteen years will retire in November

8. He's as tough as a hogshead of nails yet he can be sentimental to the point of corniness

9. Simple machinery such as hand looms and irrigation gates is imported from China

10. Young Mongolian girls almost always wear a pinafore sometimes white sometimes black over their simple brown dresses

CONVENTIONS OF PUNCTUATION

Both intonation and grammar can be useful guides to correct punctuation. There are, however, certain conventions of punctuation that are matters of custom rather than of form or of sound. These conventions, or rules, are part of written English.

The Colon

In general, the colon is a device for directing the reader's attention forward. This direction may be toward an itemized list of particulars. It may be toward a statement that follows directly from a previous statement. It may be toward the verse of a particular chapter of the Bible. It may be in the salutation of a letter pointing toward the body of the letter which is to follow.

> Fred bought a complete camping outfit: a tent, two cots, a camp stove, a large tarpaulin, a lantern, and two sleeping bags.
> The captain quietly read us the orders: we were to advance to the enemy lines at daybreak the next morning.
> Matthew IV: 15
> Dear Sir:

The use of the colon as part of the salutation is ordinarily restricted to business letters. Other conventional uses of the colon include:

1. Between the hour and the minutes, when time is expressed in figures:

> 11:30 P.M.   12:40 A.M.

2. Between the volume number and the page numbers of a magazine:

> *Architectural Record,* 133:167–186

The Dash

In general, the dash is a device that directs the reader's attention backward. What follows the dash may be an explanation of what has preceded the dash, or it may provide the reader with added insight into what has been said.

> The Pirates won the second game   the score was five to four.
> No game demands more teamwork, strength, courage and alertness or provides a more thrilling spectacle than football —king of autumn sports in the United States.   The Arizona *Journal*

Do not use the dash indiscriminately. Overuse detracts from its strength and effectiveness.

The Ellipsis

The ellipsis is a punctuation mark of three spaced dots. An ellipsis is used chiefly to show an omission:

> When Tolstoy started upon his novel ... the historical incidents were to serve merely as background.   W. SOMERSET MAUGHAM

When the ellipsis occurs at the end of a statement, a fourth dot represents end punctuation:

> It is easy to say that Rousseau was a misfit ....   CLIFTON FADIMAN

When the ellipsis is used to show that a statement is left unfinished, only three dots are needed:

>   You can go if you want, but

The Exclamation Point

On pages 148-150, you examined end punctuation in relation to the intonation patterns of speech. The period, of course, occurs conventionally at the end of a statement, the question mark at the end of a question. The exclamation point is also a mark of end punctuation which occurs after a word, a word group, or a sentence that the writer intends to be emphatic.

>   The ship is sinking!
>   What a day this has been!
>   Help!

Punctuation Within Punctuation

In standard written English, the comma and the period are always put inside the closing quotation marks:

>   The exact words are "way down South in Dixie."
>   I once had to memorize "Dover Beach," but I've forgotten most of it now.

The semicolon and the colon are always put outside the closing quotation marks:

>   Miss Ayers read Robert Bridges' "London Snow", then she asked us to
>   identify the prominent sounds in the poem.
>   Death in battle is reduced to two terms in "The Death of a Soldier": still-
>   ness and motion.

The question mark and the exclamation point are placed inside the closing quotation marks when the quotation itself is a question or an exclamation:

>   The lady inquired, "Where can I park the car?"
>   The man exclaimed, "I've been shot!"
>
>   BUT:
>   Have you read "The Eve of St. Agnes"?
>   Stop singing "Hearts and Flowers"!

Quotations within quotations are indicated by single quotation marks:

>   Alice remarked, "I've just finished reading Wordsworth's The Solitary
>   Reaper, and I enjoyed it very much."

When there is internal punctuation within the coordinated basic sentence patterns, many writers prefer to use the semicolon before the coordinator in a compound sentence:

> After the storm had subsided, road crews worked on the main highways to clear away the debris; but although scores of workers engaged in the effort, many of the roads remained closed for twenty-four hours.

Exercise 6

Punctuate each of the following sentences. Be prepared to give a reason for each mark you insert.

1. The minister took as his text the lines from Psalms LXXXIV 8 Show us O Lord thy mercy and grant us thy salvation

2. We visited Sea Gardens in Nassau Harbor where coral and marine life may be viewed through glass-bottomed boats

3. They captured the desperado an ex-convict with a long record in one of the canyons north of Globe City

4. Joy sat on every countenance and there was a glad intensity in every eye   MARK TWAIN (Several words have been omitted between *glad* and *intensity*.)

5. The major issued the orders Company K was to proceed immediately to Camp Wadsworth

6. Enjoying Shakespeare is a little like conquering Everest much depends on the approach   CLIFTON FADIMAN (Here, the author wishes to direct the reader's attention forward.)

7. The play went along well until the middle of Act II then the excitement began

8. A sail up the Hudson River from New York to Albany a distance of about 150 miles provides the tourist with the opportunity to watch an ever-changing panorama of history

9. She slowly counted out the change three shillings a half-crown and five pennies

10. Two bearded brothers named Smith William and Andrew are familiar to anyone who has ever had a tickle in his throat

11. In the first line of the poem the poet asks a question Why so pale and wan fond lover

12. There's good news tonight

13. The matinee performance of Brother Orchid will begin promptly at 2 45

14. Oats said Mrs. MacGregor are best for feeding young stock calves puppies colts and boys

15. We enjoyed John Keats sonnet On the Grasshopper and Cricket it was written in competition with the poet Leigh Hunt

16. Miss Watts asked Have you read Byrons Darkness a poem of speculation on the end of the world

17. My what a fright you gave me

18. The farmer exclaimed Look out for that horse

19. Ive just finished Josephine Teys Miss Pym Disposes a marvelous whodunit by an old favorite (The old favorite's name is Tey.)

20. The class reunion was a great success a never-to-be-forgotten evening of fun and happy memories

21. The distance between the two towns was six kilometers a kilometer is about five-eighths of a mile and we had to push our bicycles all the way

22. Johnny swallowed hard and said Yes Im ready however the hard knot of fear was still in his stomach

23. Joel was so cold that when he saw an inn an exceedingly poor one as it later turned out he interrupted his journey for one last warm meal

24. The letter was dated July 14 1846 in it Jane Carlyle told of an extreme emotional reaction to a delayed birthday greeting

25. Emerson urged Americans to think independently We have listened too long to the courtly muses of Europe (Only the first part of Emerson's sentence is quoted here.)

26. To be honest with you I really dont know the first thing about nuclear energy

27. You may go said Mother but youll have to be home by eleven

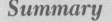

Summary

Punctuation is a graphic device that helps the reader of written English to understand what has been written. The purpose of punctuation is to help the reader divide written material into structural units of syntax. This division is accomplished in spoken English by means of pitch, stress, and juncture—the vocal effects of intonation.

A sensitivity to intonation—particularly to juncture and to changes of pitch—may be of considerable help in punctuating written material. This sensitivity aids in the identification of sentence structure. It also helps in the punctuation of nonrestrictive subordinate clauses and appositives, of coordinate adjectives, and of introductory word groups.

Sensitivity to intonation, however, is not enough. Effective punctuation is also based on grammar and convention. This chapter, then, presents three guidelines for approaching the problems of punctuation: (1) clues of intonation in the spoken language; (2) a knowledge of grammar; and (3) familiarity with certain conventions.

Chapter Test, Form A

Punctuate the following sentences and insert needed apostrophes. (*Since this test represents a cumulative review of punctuation, no attempt has been made to provide specific page references.*)

1. On November 10 1951 Lieutenant Ted Gunn of the sheriffs police was cruising near Oxford Michigan when he received a radio call to investigate an accident on Route 4

2. The little old lady who lives on Sycamore Street celebrated her one hundredth birthday yesterday

3. Freedom has not yet completely changed Africa nevertheless rapid changes are on the way

4. Harrys convinced that hes found the formula for the perfect Sunday after-
    noon a visit to the zoo a leisurely stroll through the park and a stop at the
    corner drugstore for a creamy double-thick milkshake

5. Mother remarked fearfully I wouldnt drive so fast on this road James its
    much too bumpy

6. Did you know for example that oil from coconut meat is used in soapmaking
    a thriving industry throughout the West Indies

7. Help shouted Mr. Abernathy Ive been robbed

8. Few towns can boast the architectural treasures of Paris France but almost
    every town has buildings or whole neighborhoods that provide a visual
    history of its architectural development   —The *Reader's Digest*

9. Who can identify the meter in William Blakes The Chimney Sweeper
    asked Miss Pym

10. The lake which curved for miles behind the wooded hillside shone like a
    mirror in the dim light of early morning

11. In Miss Kenways English II class the use of too many ands and buts is
    known as "overcoordinitis"

12. The queen swept into the room her eyes burning with anger

Chapter Test, Form B

Punctuate the following sentences and insert needed apostrophes:

1. My brother Paul has a series of ambitions to graduate from college with
    honors to get a good job to marry his high school sweetheart and to own a
    home in Beacon Hill

2. The bazaar which we visited in Port-au-Prince Haiti sold of all things
    chandeliers made of condensed-milk cans

3. The novel Dr. Zhivago has been acclaimed as one of the masterpieces of this
    century some critics however believe that it has been greatly overrated

4. There are four ____ in stresses (Complete the blank with the plural form of
    the appropriate letter.)

5. Our luncheon which cost seven shillings about ninety-eight cents consisted
    of four dishes mutton steak boiled potatoes cabbage and a tart for dessert

6. The Irish uprising on April 24 1916 marked the beginning of a long bitter
    struggle for independence

7. Was it William Jennings Bryan who said Diplomacy is the art of keeping
    cool

8. Scat Get out of there shouted George flapping his arms at the flock of crows in the oak tree

9. The train sat in the freight yard its engine chuffing like a giant breathing
   HELEN EUSTIS

10. At every dinner party said Kin Hubbard theres somebody who eats all the celery

11. Be sure to read Which Old Wives Tale Do You Believe on page 211 of the Reader's Digest

12. Were you aware for example that frozen foods now include these delicacies Chinese egg roll frog's legs and pressed pheasant

The Structure of Your Language

■ **A.** Read the following sentences aloud. Then rewrite them, using the phonemic symbols of stress. Limit your transcription to primary, secondary, and tertiary stress. Compare your stress patterns with those of a classmate. How does the use of different stress patterns affect the meaning of some sentences — sentence 6, for example? What does this effect on meaning suggest to you about the use in a theme of sentences that may have different stress patterns?

1. I am going home.

2. When are you going home?

3. I was going home, but it rained.

4. It was nice to meet you.

5. I never eat spinach.

6. Mary Jane is my sister.

7. Henry James won the prize.

8. Mother, you have my father much offended.

■ **B.** Read the following sentences aloud. Then rewrite them, using the phonemic symbols of pitch. Discuss your work with a classmate. How do you explain differences in transcription?

1. I know the answer.

2. Have you a headache?

3. Where are my sneakers?

4. Are these your sister's books?

5. His story is unbelievable.

6. Are you Harry Jones?

7. You're really going to Paris?

8. Please keep off the grass.

■ **C.** Read the following sentences aloud. Then rewrite them with the phonemic symbols of juncture. Discuss your work with a classmate. How do you explain the differences in transcription?

1. Professor Henry Watts, the successful physicist, lectured to the science faculty.

2. How many were going to St. Ives?

3. Do you live in Brooklyn?

4. When the cat's away, the mice will play.

5. The little old lady who lived in a shoe had so many children she didn't know what to do.

6. The troops hiked eight kilometers (five miles) to the camp.

7. Did you watch the late movie last night?

8. Mrs. Lowe served apple pie, ice cream, and hot chocolate.

Chapter 9

Phonemes
and
Graphemes
in English

A Look Back and A Look Forward

Throughout this book, you have been working with those forms of usage and punctuation that meet the standards of written English. In Chapter 9, you will examine certain problems of spelling that sometimes interfere with effective communication. You will also review in detail the relation between phonemes and graphemes in English.

In Part II, you will explore the dictionary as a wordbook and a world book. In the chapter you are about to study, you will concentrate on using the dictionary as an aid to accurate spelling.

THE RELATION BETWEEN
PHONEMES AND GRAPHEMES

Frequently during your school career, you have been reminded of the importance of accurate spelling. Since English is a highly standardized language, the spelling of words must be uniform. By now you realize that effective written communication depends on your spelling, as well as on your skill in expression. Besides, your reputation for competence or incompetence is often affected by your spelling. This is particularly true in applying for a job by letter or in filling out business forms. It is also true, as you know, in your classwork, whenever you write out a report or an examination.

Because English is basically alphabetic, a knowledge of the relationship between sounds and letters is indispensable to accurate spelling.

Sound and Spelling

Suppose you were being inaugurated as President of the United States and were taking this oath of office specified in Article 2 of the Constitution. Read the oath aloud, or think how you would pronounce the words if you were reading it aloud.

> "I do solemnly swear (or affirm) that I will faithfully execute the office of President of the United States, and will to the best of my ability preserve, protect, and defend the Constitution of the United States."

Notice how many *e*'s there are in the printed words of the oath. Try to identify four different sounds that the vowel letter *e* spells or helps to spell in the sentence. Which four different words contain silent *e*?

Now think about the words that are spelled with the vowel letter *i*, and identify five different sounds that *i* spells or helps to spell in the sentence. One of them is even a consonant sound.

There are many more sounds in the English language than there are letters in the alphabet. Consequently, the twenty-six graphic symbols, or GRAPHEMES, must represent more than one PHONEME, or sound, apiece. In fact, some of the graphemes represent several different phonemes in different words, as you have just observed.

Our alphabet is out of date. During the age of Chaucer, in the middle English period, English spelling was more nearly representative of its sounds. Many of the final *e*'s in *The Canterbury Tales* were pronounced, instead of being silent, as most final *e*'s are today. English pronunciation has changed a great deal since the fourteenth century, although the alphabet has not changed at all.

Just as many graphemes represent more than one phoneme, so are most vowel and consonant phonemes spelled in a variety of ways. Consider the phoneme \e\ in *ten*. How is it represented in the words below?

said	many	leopard
says	friend	weather
bury	heifer	aesthetic

English spelling is also complicated by the presence of silent consonants, many of which used to be pronounced. What four consonant letters are silent in the following words?

kneel	wrestle	psychiatry

Phonemes — Significant Units of Sound

A phoneme is a basic English sound, one that makes a difference in meaning. How do the words below differ in their pronunciation?

ton	bun	done
fun	run	shun
gun	won	none

It is the first sound in each word that makes it different in meaning from the other eight words. These nine initial sounds are a few of the phonemes, or significant units of sound, in our language. Linguists speak of all the vowel and consonant sounds as phonemes. (*Phon-* refers to "sound.")

Most of the phonemes in English are SIMPLE PHONEMES; but the DIPHTHONGS \au̇\ as in *out*, \ī\ as in *dine*, and \o͝i\ as in *joy* are referred to as COMPOUND PHONEMES. This is because, in each case, two simple phonemes are so completely blended within the same syllable that they seem to be a single vowel sound. Slowly pronounce the three words, *out*, *dine*, and *joy*, and try to determine what two simple phonemes are blended to form each of the compound phonemes, or diphthongs, in the words.

Graphemes — Significant Units of the Written Language

"The world is too much with us; late and soon,
Getting and spending, we lay waste our powers."
WILLIAM WORDSWORTH

The printed words in the above quotation are made up of graphemes, or letters of the alphabet.

Graphemes are the basic units of written language, representing the phonemes, or the basic units of spoken language. (*Graph-* refers to "writing.") What grapheme represents the phoneme \e\ in the words *getting* and *spending?* A single letter that represents a sound is referred to as a SIMPLE GRAPHEME.

What COMPOUND GRAPHEMES represent the diphthong \aú\ in the words *our* and *powers?* A compound grapheme is made up of two or more letters that stand for a single sound or a diphthong. See if you can find six different compound graphemes in the quotation besides the two just cited. Four of them stand for consonant phonemes and two of them for vowel phonemes. Be sure that each combination you find stands for a *single* phoneme, not two separate phonemes.

The main English graphemes are the twenty-six letters of the alphabet, but there are other graphemes, too, such as the figures 1-9 and 0, and the various punctuation marks.

Exercise 1   *Look once more at the sentence that concludes the above section on graphemes. Pronounce the words to yourself. Then answer these questions:*

1. What three compound graphemes represent three different vowel phonemes?

2. In what three different words does the compound grapheme th stand for the same consonant phoneme?

3. What two compound graphemes represent the consonant phoneme \sh\?

4. Which compound grapheme appearing in two different words stands for the consonant phoneme \f\?

5. What double letter is a compound grapheme?

6. Which compound grapheme represents the same sound as the first *t* in the word *punctuation?*

7. Which figure represents a word that contains a diphthong?

8. What four different words end in silent *e* or in *s* preceded by silent *e?*

Morphemes — Significant Units of Grammatical Form

Pronounce the word *eight* to yourself. What two phonemes are combined to form it? What compound grapheme represents the vowel phoneme \ā\? What simple grapheme represents the consonant phoneme \t\? Which two letters are silent?

A simple word like *eight* is referred to by linguists as a MORPHEME. A morpheme consists of one or more phonemes that form a simple word or of a prefix (like *un-*) or a suffix (like *-ly*). The *morph-* in *morpheme* refers to "form." A morpheme may therefore be defined as a significant unit of grammatical form.

In the expression *eight-letter word*, the morphemes *eight* and *letter* are combined to form a compound adjective. The morphemes *eight* and *-ty* may be combined to form the derivative *eighty*, and the morphemes *un-*, *letter*, and *-ed* may be combined to form the derivative *unlettered*. What does *unlettered* usually mean? What is its relation to the morpheme *letter*?

Exercise 2

Read the sentence below. Then answer the four questions that follow it.

After reexamining the ninety-eight different insects, Rosemary concluded that all insects are six-legged creatures.

1. What are the eight morphemes that are combined to form the two compound modifiers and the one compound noun?

2. What three morphemes make up the derivative *reexamining*?

3. What three morphemes form the derivative *creatures*?

4. What three other derivatives in the sentence contain the morphemes *-s*, *-ed*, and *-ent*?

The Different Graphemes That Represent the Same Phoneme

In the dictionary, as you know, PRONUNCIATION SYMBOLS are used to indicate the pronunciation of the words. Each symbol stands for only one phoneme, simple or compound, such as \sh\ and \ā\, \ī\ and \au̇\.

Consonant phonemes are produced in the throat and mouth with a certain amount of friction, whereas vowel phonemes are produced without any friction.

All the vowel phonemes are voiced, or produced with a noticeable vibration of the vocal cords. Nine of the consonant phonemes, including \h\, are voiceless, or unvoiced, but all the others are voiced. Each consonant phoneme in the right column below is the same as the matching phoneme in the left column except for this vibration. Try holding your finger over your vocal cords as you say each sound.

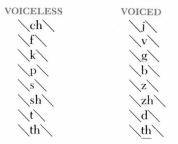

Only two of the phonemic symbols listed below are nonalphabetical —the SCHWA \ə\, which resembles an upside-down *e*, and the \ŋ\, which stands for the single sound of the compound grapheme *ng* in such words as *lung* and *ringing*. The schwa sound may be unstressed, as it is in the first syllable of *adjust* \ə-'jəst\, or stressed, as it is in the second syllable. (A superior schwa, as in \'sad-ᵊn\ or \'sad-ᵊl\, shows that there is no vowel sound in that syllable and that the \n\ or \l\ is a syllabic consonant.)

Following each symbol* are words that illustrate the different graphemes that represent the same phoneme. Each simple or compound grapheme is underlined.

Consonant Phonemes

\b\   ri<u>b</u>, ri<u>bb</u>on
\ch\   <u>ch</u>air, pa<u>tch</u>, sta<u>t</u>ure, pen<u>s</u>ion, ques<u>t</u>ion, cons<u>c</u>ious, cons<u>c</u>ientious,
        righ<u>te</u>ous (This sound is actually \t\ + \sh\.)
\d\   la<u>d</u>, la<u>dd</u>er, pull<u>ed</u>
\f\   <u>f</u>ire, o<u>ff</u>er, telegra<u>ph</u>, rou<u>gh</u>
\g\   be<u>g</u>, be<u>gg</u>ar, <u>gu</u>est (See also \gz\.)
\h\   <u>h</u>ome (See also \hw\.)
\j\   <u>j</u>am, <u>g</u>ym, exa<u>gg</u>eration, e<u>d</u>ucate, lo<u>dg</u>e, sol<u>di</u>er, a<u>dj</u>ourn (This sound is
        actually \d\ + \zh\.)
\k\   stea<u>k</u>, fa<u>c</u>t, sti<u>ck</u>, a<u>ch</u>e, a<u>cc</u>ount, <u>q</u>uit, anti<u>qu</u>e, a<u>cq</u>uire, ex<u>c</u>ept (See also
        \ks\.)
\l\   <u>l</u>ane, hi<u>ll</u>
\m\   ha<u>m</u>, ha<u>mm</u>er
\n\   ma<u>n</u>, ma<u>nn</u>er
\ŋ\   you<u>ng</u>, u<u>n</u>cle
\p\   wra<u>p</u>, wra<u>pp</u>er
\r\   <u>r</u>ise, me<u>rr</u>y
\s\   <u>y</u>es, le<u>ss</u>, <u>c</u>ivil, <u>sc</u>enery, quart<u>z</u>, (See also \ks\.)
\sh\   <u>sh</u>oe, ra<u>ti</u>on, para<u>ch</u>ute, spe<u>ci</u>al, o<u>ce</u>an, <u>s</u>ugar, omni<u>sc</u>ience, fi<u>ss</u>ion, pro-
        pul<u>s</u>ion, i<u>ss</u>ue, nau<u>se</u>ous, anx<u>i</u>ous, <u>sch</u>wa

* This system of pronunciation is used by permission of G. & C. Merriam Company, publishers of the Merriam-Webster dictionaries. For further information see *Webster's New Students Dictionary* © 1964 by G. & C. Merriam Company.

\t\ pat, pattern, wished
\th\ breath
\th\ breathing
\v\ alive, of, flivver
\w\ will, liquid, choir, (See also \hw\.)
\y\ yell, view (See also \yü\ and \yu̇\.)
\z\ zeal, drizzle, was, scissors, xylophone (See also \gz\.)
\zh\ decision, pleasure, azure, garage

Vowel Phonemes

\ə\ bun, about, fallen, capital, money, analysis, sergeant, surgeon, parlia-
ment, does, porpoise, blood, curious (See also \ər\.)
\a\ magic, plaid
\ā\ fade, pain, gauge, say, bouquet, great, vein, prey
\ä\ father, bother, sergeant, heart
\au̇\ loud, now, sauerkraut (This diphthong is \a\ + \u̇\.)
\e\ let, many bury, aesthetic, said, says, feather, heifer, jeopardy, friendly
\ē\ even, machine, any, clean, kneel, receive, people, monkey, believe,
Caesar, quay, phoebe
\i\ mill, here, year, queer, pier, rhythm, women, business, built
\ī\ side, cry, die, sleight, guy, dye, eye, aisle, kayak, coyote (This diphthong
is actually \ä\ + \i\.)
\ō\ cold, shoal, doe, outdoor, pour, snow, sewn, plateau, owe
\ȯ\ fall, taught, paw, awe, dog, broaden, bought
\ȯi\ boil, boy (This diphthong is \ȯ\ + \i\.)
\ü\ flu, pool, flew, rheumatism, lose, shoe, you, suit, blue, Sioux (See also
\yü\.)
\u̇\ push, wood, would, wolf (See also \yu̇\.)

Special Combinations of Phonemes

\ər\ germ, earn, third, worm, worry, courtesy, burn, surrender, myrrh
\gz\ example
\hw\ wheel
\ks\ relax
\yü\ union, pew, ewe, beautiful, euphony, queue, hue
\yu̇\ furious

Developing Graphemic Word Lists

The preceding chart listing most of the graphemes that are used to
spell the common English phonemes shows the relation between sounds
and spelling. One effective way of increasing your spelling power is to

compile your own lists of words having the same phoneme spelled the same way. Thus you will become more sensitive to the sounds of words, you will associate many words in which a given sound has a single spelling, and at the same time you will become familiar with the spelling of these words.

Consider, as an example, the phoneme \ch\. All words that begin with this sound have the *ch* spelling. You can find any number of such words in the dictionary. The words that have this spelling later on in the word, however, are more important to list. The *sci, sc,* and *te* spellings of this sound are uncommon, but the *tch, t, si,* and *ti* spellings are more common. Here are some starter lists:

ch	*tch*	*t*	*si*	*ti*
charge	batch	nature	pension	mention
charity	catch	picture	tension	attention
chimney	match	feature	dissension	detention
each	patch	creature	mansion	invention
beach	scratch	stature	transient	bastion
peach	snatch	fracture		suggestion
preach	dispatch	pasture		question
reach	etch	posture		conscientious
teach	fetch	adventure		
beech	sketch	fortune		
screech	stretch	mutual		
speech	wretch			
beseech	itch			
rich	ditch			
which	hitch			
niche	pitch			
bench	stitch			
drench	witch			
wrench	kitchen			
attach	notch			
detach	scotch			
bachelor	watch			

Exercise 3   *You can build useful graphemic lists by searching for appropriate words in your textbooks, in newspapers, in your general reading, and even in the dictionary. The more graphemes and words you include, the more you will benefit from this project. Try to include some unfamiliar words and be sure to check both pronunciation and spelling with your dictionary whenever you are not certain. You may wish to use 3 x 5 cards for easy handling.*

1. Begin with the consonant phonemes and the combinations \gz\, \hw\, and \ks\. Select at least two graphemes for each phoneme (unless there is only one) and list five or more words to illustrate each grapheme (if there *are* five).
2. Add the vowel phonemes and the combinations \ər\, \yü\, and \yu̇\.

Phonemic Representations of Words

Besides the vowel and consonant symbols which you have just been studying, the dictionary employs three other kinds of phonemic symbols to represent the pronunciation of words within the diagonals, or slant lines. The transcription, or respelling, for the word *coincidental* illustrates these three kinds of symbols:

co·in·ci·den·tal\(ˌ)kō-ˌin(t)-sə-'dent-ᵊl\

1. What marks indicate the number of spoken syllables? How many spoken syllables are there? How many written syllables are there?
2. Which syllable always receives the primary, or strongest, stress, as shown by the high vertical stress mark preceding it? Which syllable always receives the secondary, or medium, stress, as shown by the low mark? Which two syllables are always unstressed, or receive the weakest stress? How do you know?
3. What marks mean that the first syllable sometimes receives secondary stress and sometimes the weakest stress? What marks mean that the phoneme \t\ may or may not be pronounced in the second syllable?

If the four variant pronunciations were written in full, they would take up much more space, as follows:

\ˌkō-ˌin-sə-'dent-ᵊl, kō-ˌin-sə-'dent-ᵊl,
ˌkō-ˌint-sə-'dent-ᵊl, kō-ˌint-sə-'dent-ᵊl\

What superior symbol in the last syllable means that the consonant that follows it is a syllabic consonant, since there is no vowel sound in the syllable?

Exercise 4   *Copy the following words and correctly transcribe them into phonemic symbols, checking with your dictionary. Whenever there are variant pronunciations, write them out in full, as* coincidental *is written out above. Remember to include all the stress marks.*

refute	bouquets	first-rate
cranks	wheedle	pleasingly
mules	language	bottleneck
eighth	pleasure	thoughtful
choice	linguists	photographs
mount	existence	light-footed
clothed	expulsion	energetically

SPECIAL PROBLEMS IN SPELLING

When you compiled your graphemic word lists, you were concerned with the various ways in which the different phonemes are written. Naturally you were not considering the many silent letters which occur in English spelling. During the past four or five centuries the pronunciation of English words has changed more than the spelling has. This accounts for many of the silent *e*'s and other silent letters.

Words with Silent Letters

In the lists below, the words are grouped according to their silent letters. Such a grouping will help you to associate words with similar spellings, just as your graphemic lists did. Since these lists are not by any means exhaustive, you will be able to add many other words (and also derivatives and compounds of these words) from your reading or from the dictionary. Be sure to check the pronunciation of a word before you decide that it always has a silent letter. For instance, *calm, palm,* and *psalm* may be pronounced with or without the \l\. (The typical vowel-consonant-silent-*e* words, like *names* and *complete,* are so numerous that they are not listed here.)

Even though most of the words listed may be easy for you, there are probably a few that will be difficult for even the best spellers. Pick out the words that you are not sure of and study them in groups, according to their silent letters. Try to associate the harder words with the easier words in the same group. If you think you can spell them all, have someone test you on twenty-five of the less common words (not grouped) and see how well you do.

The following methods will be helpful in studying any of the words that appear in this section of the chapter, or other words you need to learn to spell:

1. Print each word on a 3 x 5 card and write a sentence using the word in a typical context. On the other side of the card transcribe the word into phonemic symbols. (In the case of homonyms or other words

that are easily confused, add a sentence containing a blank for the word.) Practice spelling each word from its phonemic transcription, checking yourself by turning the card over. Carry your cards with you and study your words whenever you have a spare moment.

2. Team up with someone else in your class. Study your cards or lists together, dictating the words to each other in context. Test each other until both of you have achieved mastery of your own words.

3. Use your words as a vocabulary list for your themes, being sure to spell them correctly every time you use them.

Silent b words

lamb	crumb	debt
jamb	dumb	debtor
climb	numb	indebted
limb	thumb	doubt
bomb	succumb	
aplomb	plumbing	
comb		
tomb		

Silent g words

gnarled	align
gnash	assign
gnat	assignment
gnaw	benign
gnome	consign
gnu	design
diaphragm	resign
phlegm	sign
	deign
	feign
	reign
	foreign

Silent gh words

high	blight	bough
nigh	bright	dough
sigh	delight	thorough
thigh	fight	though
straight	flight	through
eight	fright	bought
eighth	frighten	brought
freight	knight	fought
neigh	light	ought
neighbor	might	sought
weigh	night	thought
weight	playwright	wrought
height	plight	caught
sleight	right	distraught
	righteous	taught
	sight	
	slight	
	tight	

Silent h words

ghastly	rhapsody
ghost	rhetoric
ghoul	rhetorical
heir	rheumatic
honest	rheumatism
honor	rhinestone
honorable	rhinoceros
hour	Rhode Island
khaki	rhododendron
	rhubarb
	rhyme
	rhythm

Silent k *words*

knack	knob
knapsack	knock
knave	knoll
knavery	knot
knee	know
kneel	knowledge
knew	known
knickknack	knuckle
knife	
knight	
knit	
knives	

Silent l *words*

balk	behalf
calk	calf
chalk	calves
stalk	half
talk	halve
walk	halves
folk	salve
	could
	should
	would
	solder

Silent n *words*

autumn
column
condemn
hymn
solemn

Silent p *words*

pneumatic
pneumonia
psalm
pseudo
pseudonym
pshaw
psychiatrist
psychiatry
psychic
psychoanalysis
psychologist
psychology
receipt

Silent w *words*

who	wriggle
whom	wright
whose	playwright
whole	wring
wholesale	wrinkle
wholesome	wrist
wholly	write
wrack	writhe
wrangle	writing
wrap	written
wrath	wrong
wreak	wrote
wreath	wrought
wreck	wrung
wren	wry
wrench	
wrestle	
wretch	
wretched	

Other silent letters

Connecticut	aisle
indict	Arkansas
indictment	Illinois
handkerchief	island
handsome	isle
Wednesday	bouquet
every	croquet
several	listen
vegetable	mortgage
business	wrestle
mnemonic	tongue

Exercise 5

For each blank below write the word that best fits the context, choosing it from the list above that is specified in parentheses.

1. The Morgans have a cottage on an _____ in Great South Bay. (Other silent letters)

2. Mrs. Graves has taken several courses in child _____ so that she will be able to bring up her children properly. (Silent *p*)

3. The branches of the ancient oak are twisted and ____. (Silent *g*)

4. Soldiers in World War I were called the "boys in ____." (Silent *h*)

5. Mr. Hall is in the hospital with ____. (Silent *p*)

6. The congregation sang the opening ____ and then took their seats. (Silent *n*)

7. The association of words that have the same silent letters is a ____ device. (Other silent letters)

8. The ____ asked Aunt Harriet to tell him about her early childhood. (Silent *p*)

9. The grand jury is expected to ____ the two partners for conspiracy. (Other silent letters)

10. The two wires can be joined together with a little ____. (Silent *l*)

11. The wedding procession walked slowly down the ____ of the church. (Other silent letters)

12. Jazz sometimes lacks harmony, but it always has plenty of ____. (Silent *h*)

13. Joe was not ____ convinced that it was his duty to serve on the new committee. (Silent *w*)

14. As we were examining the model home, we saw a workman painting a door ____. (Silent *b*)

15. A well-decorated living room usually has a few interesting ____ arranged on the shelves, tables, and other furniture. (Silent *k*)

16. Walking and bicycling are especially good for developing the ____ muscles. (Silent *gh*)

17. Everyone should learn to use his ____ in breathing. (Silent *g*)

18. On ____ of the entire club, I wish to present this gift as a symbol of our appreciation for your untiring work as president. (Silent *l*)

19. A hammer, a screwdriver, and a ____ are handy tools to keep in the kitchen. (Silent *w*)

20. "More things are ____ by prayer than this world dreams of." (Silent *w* and *gh*)

Homonyms and Other Words Often Confused

The special word list that follows includes homonyms, or words that sound alike (such as *forth* and *fourth*), and words that are similar in sound or spelling (such as *loose* and *lose*). Determine which, if any, of these words are difficult for you when they are dictated in appropriate sentences. Then proceed to master them in whatever way you have found to be most effective. Be sure to associate the right meaning with the right word.

advice	coarse	died	passed
advise	course	dyed	past
allusion	complement	dual	personal
illusion	compliment	duel	personnel
altar	conscience	dying	plain
alter	conscious	dyeing	plane
angel	corps	fair	right
angle	corpse	fare	rite
berth	council	for	write
birth	counsel	fore	stationary
bare	consul	four	stationery
bear	dairy	hole	straight
bridal	diary	whole	strait
bridle	deceased	hour	thorough
canvas	diseased	our	though
canvass	decent	later	through
capital	descent	latter	who's
capitol	desert	lightning	whose
	dessert	lightening	

<table>
<tr><td colspan="2">*Exercise 6*</td></tr>
</table>

Write the word (or a form of it) from the preceding list which most appropriately fills each blank in the sentences below.

1. The city _____ passed an ordinance requiring all dogs to be kept on a leash.

2. The jet _____ made a graceful _____ from 39,000 feet, down to the jetport.

3. The Spanish dancer threw a shawl about her shoulders and walked proudly _____ the enthusiastic crowd.

4. Mother has apple pie and whipped cream for ____ tonight.

5. The newspaper states that the ____ will be buried in Rosemont Cemetery.

6. The officer made a ____ search of the premises to determine whether the fugitive might be hidden in one of the rooms.

7. There seemed to be no ____ solution to the problem of pleasing all the members of the club.

8. The ____ party is all ready to come out of the church.

9. If I had some ____, I would ____ a thank-you letter.

10. Miss James always ____ us before we decide on ____ courses for the next year.

11. It is said that ____ is often given but seldom taken.

12. Father had to sleep in an upper ____ on the train.

13. The ____ audience rose and cheered after the first number on the program.

14. The police never found out ____ fingerprints were on the safe.

15. Hank pulled on the ____ and brought the horse to a stop.

16. The sergeant persuaded the recruit not to ____ his comrades.

17. The food in the internment camp was ____ and unpalatable.

18. When Walter began to walk ____ the cemetery, he was suddenly ____ of an uncontrollable desire to start running.

19. Grandfather taught us not to be afraid of thunder and ____.

20. Honolulu is the ____ of Hawaii.

21. Mrs. Swanson ____ her neighbor on the appearance of her daughter.

22. Miss Gray is the ____ director of a large insurance company.

23. Your ____ tells you to do what you know is ____.

24. English and American literature is full of ____ to the Bible.

25. Ethel is ____ her old white dress blue.

Words with the ie *and* ei *Graphemes*

Below are two special lists, one of words containing the compound grapheme *ie* and the other of words containing the compound grapheme *ei*. Give these words the same sort of attention as you did the previous lists. One list should be mastered at a time, as confusion will result if you study the two lists together. Be sure you know the meaning of all the words before you start learning them. Testing, using mnemonic aids, drilling, practicing, and more testing will help you to master any words that you need to study.

Notice that in the *ie* list which follows no words are included which have *i* and *e* together as separate graphemes, such as *experience, medieval, convenient, ancient, efficient, proficient*, and *sufficient*. In the latter four words, what phoneme does the compound grapheme *ci* represent? In the word *convenient* what phoneme does the *i* stand for? Derivatives (such as *tries* and *tried*) which result from changing *y* to *i* are not included, either, because very few people misspell these words. The *ie* words below are grouped according to their phonemes as a spelling aid.

\ē\			\i\	\ī\
achieve	grieve	retrieve	bier	die
belief	hygiene	shield	cashier	lie
believe	lien	shriek	fierce	pie
brief	mien	siege	financier	tie
chief	niece	thief	pier	vie
field	piece	thieve	pierce	fiery
fiend	priest	wield	sieve	
frieze	relieve	wiener	tier	\e\
grief	reprieve	yield		friend

The following words all contain the compound grapheme *ei*. In most of them, as you can see, the *ei* grapheme represents either the phoneme \ā\, or the phoneme \ē\ preceded by the phoneme \s\, spelled *c*. These two types of words are always spelled with *ei*.

\ā\		\sē\	*Other Phonemes*
beige	reign	ceiling	foreign
deign	rein	conceit	forfeit
eight	seine	conceive	height
eighth	veil	deceit	heifer
feign	vein	deceive	heir
feint	weigh	perceive	leisure
freight	weight	receipt	neither
heinous		receive	seize
neigh			weir
neighbor			weird

Exercise 7   Write the correct spelling for each of the words containing a blank in the sentences below.

1. The cash____r told Mrs. Jones that she had rec____ved all the money that was due her.

2. Helen and Paul are giving a w____ner roast next Saturday night, but n____ther of us can go.

3. It is the hope of many people that automation will provide an abundance of l____sure time.

4. No one but a f____nd would have committed such a h____nous crime.

5. Courses in health and hyg____ne are required of all the students.

6. In Shakespeare's *Macbeth* the witches are called the "w____rd sisters."

7. The bodies of Eustacia and Wildeve were found in the icy water above the w____r.

8. The shr____king gale was so f____rce that we were obliged to l____ down behind a hedge for shelter.

9. The driver s____zed the r____ns and tried to stop the frightened horses.

10. I do not bel____ve that this heavy sh____ld can be p____rced by any projectile.

11. After a s____ge of four months the beleaguered city y____lded to the enemy.

12. The lonely horse was heard to n____gh as the young h____fers scampered joyfully across the n____ghboring f____ld.

13. Conc____t is a gr____vous fault.

14. The tax assessments are a l____n against the property.

15. When the ship docked at the p____r, the pr____st was accosted by a sailor with a f____rce-looking m____n.

16. Brutus and his fellow conspirators waited until the ____ghth hour to assassinate Caesar.

17. My fr____nd bought a four-yard p____ce of b____ge wool to make herself a new dress.

18. We found that the financ____r had dec____ved us about the cost of the fr____ze.

Other Words Frequently Misspelled

You have encountered lists of words with silent letters, words that are often confused, and words with the *ie* and *ei* graphemes. The list that follows does not repeat those words but includes 80 others that students misspell for various reasons. Some of these words, like *convenient, laboratory, library, probably, sophomore, temperament,* and *twelfth,* are easy to spell when pronounced syllable by syllable, without any silent letters except final *e.* Others can be learned by associating them with words pronounced and spelled in similar ways.

Look up the meanings of any words that are unfamiliar to you. Then find out which ones, if any, are difficult, and study them by the methods you have found to be most efficient. A final test in context will reveal whether you have mastered them all.

absence	continuously	incidentally	renaissance
accommodate	convenient	incredible	ridiculous
aggravate	criticism	indispensable	sacrifice
amateur	criticize	ingenious	separation
among	curriculum	laboratory	sergeant
analyze	description	legitimate	similar
apparent	disappear	library	sophomore
appearance	efficient	medieval	succeed
argument	eliminate	Negroes	successful
Britain	especially	noticeable	supersede
calendar	experience	nuisance	suppress
cemetery	familiar	obstacle	symbol
changeable	fascinate	paid	temperament
characteristic	finally	permissible	twelfth
clothes	frantically	probably	undoubtedly
collegiate	generally	proceeded	unnecessary
committee	guarantee	professor	until
congratulate	heroes	quarrel	valleys
connoisseur	hesitancy	relevant	vigorous
consistent	hindrance	religious	villain

Exercise 8   *For each blank in these sentences write the word from the preceding list (or a form of it) which best fits the context.*

1. The witness gave a good ____ of the accident.

2. An old adage states that ____ is the best teacher.

3. Too frequently we ____ others for faults which we ourselves possess.

4. All the girls are simply ＿＿ with Agatha's new ring.

5. A silver cup will be awarded to the winner of the ＿＿ golf tournament.

6. Early practice in the heat of September would be a ＿＿ to the proper conditioning of our football team.

7. Dr. Amos Ryan, who is a well-known ＿＿ of entomology, has a magnificent collection of native cockroaches.

8. The prevalence of smog over the city is both a ＿＿ to the citizens and a danger to their health.

9. Mr. Atkins must be a man of very even ＿＿, for he never seems to get angry.

10. This gadget is truly an ＿＿ device, but in my opinion it is impractical.

11. The members of the township ＿＿ met and decided to ＿＿ any possibility of a tax increase for the ensuing year.

12. The new set of rules will ＿＿ all previous regulations.

13. Our team this year has been very ＿＿ in winning all its home games but losing all the other games.

14. It is often said that no one is ＿＿ to an organization.

15. A ＿＿ is in the tenth grade, a junior is in the eleventh, and a senior is in the ＿＿.

16. In world history we studied both the ＿＿ and the ＿＿ periods in Europe.

17. The spectators watched the great rocket rise and then ＿＿ into the clouded sky.

18. We will not develop any conclusions until we have had time to ＿＿ all the statistical data.

19. Christmas and Easter are celebrated by Christians as ＿＿ holidays.

20. A ＿＿ theater does not usually ＿＿ as many people as a motion picture theater.

21. One of Ellen's most noticeable ＿＿ is her pride in her personal ＿＿.

22. Melodramas often have very noble ＿＿ and very fiendish ＿＿.

23. Mr. Lane is considered to be a ＿＿ of both classical and modern symphonic music.

Summary

Both effective communication and one's reputation for competence depend upon accurate spelling, which in turn hinges upon an understanding of the relation between phonemes and graphemes. English spelling is complicated by the fact that many graphemes, or letters, may represent different phonemes, or sounds, and that most of the phonemes have several possible spellings. The presence of silent letters creates another spelling problem.

A phoneme is a significant unit of speech-sound such as \g\ and \ȯ\, and a grapheme is a significant unit of written language. The vowel and consonant phonemes are represented by simple graphemes such as *t* and *i*, or by compound graphemes such as *ti* and *oy*. A compound phoneme is one of the diphthongs \au̇\, \ī\, or \ȯi\.

A morpheme is a significant unit of grammatical form. It is made up of one or more phonemes forming a simple word, a prefix, or a suffix. A compound word or a derivative results from combining two or more morphemes.

The dictionary uses phonemic symbols to represent the simple and compound phonemes used in pronouncing the words. The vowel phonemes and most of the consonant phonemes are voiced, but nine of the consonant phonemes are voiceless. Besides the vowel and consonant symbols, the dictionary uses primary and secondary stress marks, hyphens, and parentheses in its transcriptions, or respellings.

The words containing silent letters should be studied in groups, according to which letters are silent. The study methods suggested are equally applicable to other types of words that need to be studied. A knowledge of the pronuncia-

tion and meaning of each word is essential to spelling mastery.

Homonyms and other words that are frequently confused should be distinguished from each other in meaning and also in pronunciation whenever they are pronounced differently.

Words containing the *ie* and *ei* graphemes should be studied in separate lists to avoid confusion. All such words that are pronounced with \ā\ or \sē\ (in which \s\ is spelled *c*), plus a few others, have the *ei* spelling.

The list of 80 other frequently misspelled words, like the preceding lists, should be overlearned by all students who have not already mastered them.

A NOTE ON WHY THERE IS NO CHAPTER TEST. Instead of a regular chapter test, your teacher may wish to administer a test that will reveal which of the "Other Words Frequently Misspelled" you need to study. After you follow the method of study suggested on pages 180-181, your teacher may then want to administer another test that will measure your mastery of those words you find especially difficult.

The Structure of Your Language

If you needed to write the word pronounced \fə-'zish-ən\ and had no idea of how to spell it, how would you go about finding it in the dictionary? Here is a case in which your knowledge of the different graphemes that represent the same phoneme would be very useful.

You know four ways of spelling the phoneme \f\, but experience tells you that the *ff* and *gh* graphemes do not occur at the beginning of words. That leaves *f* and *ph*. You also know that the schwa may be represented by almost any vowel letter or combination of vowels. So you probably start by looking under *fa, fe, fi, fo, fu,* and *fy*. When you realize that the word does not begin with *f*, you turn to *ph* and look for *pha, phi,* and so forth. Finally you locate the word pronounced \fə-'zish-ən\ under *phys*, and you discover that the \sh\ phoneme has the *ci* spelling in *physician*.

A knowledge of silent letters is also important in locating words in the dictionary. Suppose you need to spell the geometric term \\'räm-ˌbȯid\\. After you fail to find it under *ram* or *rom*, you may think of the silent *h* in such words as *rhyme* and look under *rham* and *rhom*. You will find that the word spelled *rhomboid* is pronounced \\'räm-ˌbȯid\\.

■ By using your knowledge of the relation between phonemes and graphemes and your experience with silent letters, find the spelling of each of the transcribed words in the sentences below. Write the words you find.

1. When Mother had trouble with her back, she went to a \\'kī-rə-ˌprak-tər\\.
2. The \\kə-'dēv\\ of Egypt was a Turkish viceroy.
3. The \\'sȯl-tə-rē\\ was an Old Testament stringed instrument.
4. A soldier fired an explosive rocket from his \\bə-'zü-kə\\.
5. A golden \\'chal-əs\\ rested on the marble table.
6. Someone who is in a difficult \\də-'lem-ə\\ is said to be between \\'sil-ə\\ and \\kə-'rib-dəs\\.
7. The story of Orpheus and \\yu̇-'rid-ə-ˌsē\\ is a famous Greek myth.
8. The doctor prescribed \\ˌfiz-ē-ō-'ther-ə-pē\\ for the polio patient.
9. The lecturer told us about a three-eyed reptile of the South Pacific called the tuatara, or \\ˌriŋ-kō-sə-'fal-yən\\.
10. The ancient \\fi-'nish-ənz\\ were the first to use an alphabet.
11. Ether and \\'klōr-ə-fȯrm\\ have both been used to produce \\ˌan-əs-'thē-zhə\\.
12. Henry Baggs played a \\yu̇-'fō-nē-əm\\ in the city band.
13. The use of \\ik-'ses-iv\\ jargon is often termed \\'jib-rish\\.
14. The \\'limf\\ cells of the body secrete a fluid which is conveyed to the blood stream.
15. The receptionist gave us a \\'sak-ə-ran\\ smile as we entered the room.
16. Hot milk taken before bedtime has a \\ˌsäp-ə-'rif-ə-rəs\\ effect.
17. The fight resulted in a general \\'mā-ˌlā\\.
18. A medium claims to have \\ə-'kəlt\\ powers.
19. Dr. Lee is a very \\'näl-i-jə-bəl\\ person.
20. \\ˌsit-ə-'kō-səs\\ is a disease that may be transmitted to human beings by parrots and parrakeets.
21. The boy's \\ri-'kal-sə-trənts\\ resulted from the cruel treatment he had received.
22. A deficiency of vitamin A may cause \\ˌzir-ˌäf-'thal-mē-ə\\.
23. A \\sī-'kräm-ət-ər\\ is an instrument for measuring the water vapor in the air.
24. In the last century the \\shə-'tȯ-kwə\\ was a common form of adult education.
25. The Greek god of fire and metalworking was named \\hi-'fes-təs\\.

Chapter 10

Effective Sentence Structure

A Look Back and A Look Forward

So far in this book, you have—for the most part—been studying grammar. It seems reasonable to assume, therefore, that by now you have acquired considerable knowledge of the structure of your language. In Part II of this book, you will be given the opportunity to apply in your writing the knowledge you have absorbed in Part I. Before you go on, however, this chapter will direct your attention to certain problems of sentence structure which, once solved, will enable you to communicate more effectively.

A STUDY OF COMMON ERRORS

What are the most common errors in student writing? In an attempt to answer this question, many studies have been made at various high school and college levels. The results of one of these studies (reported by J. N. Hook and recorded on page 331 of *The Teaching of High School English*, New York: The Ronald Press) are given below. The study was based on the writing of one hundred University of Illinois freshmen; its purpose was to determine the kinds of errors made by high school graduates.

Error	Percentage of Students Making the Error
Sentence fragment	70
Comma fault	49
Excessive coordination	30
Pronounced incoherence or lack of logic	83
Dangling modifiers	37
Faulty word order	43
Faulty parallelism	52
Lack of agreement in number of verbs	70
Incorrect tense	83
Shift in point of view of verb or pronoun	68
Wrong case	8
Faulty reference of pronouns	91
Adjective-adverb confusion	31

In earlier chapters, you investigated sentence fragments, subject-verb agreement, and faulty pronoun reference. You will work with parallel structure in Part II. In the chapter sections that follow, you will examine examples of student writing in terms of the remaining errors listed above.

COMMA FAULT AND RUN-TOGETHER SENTENCES

The following illustrations are from themes written by high school students. Before reading the analysis below, try to detect the error in sentence structure in each illustration.

1.

On the front wall are three pictures the middle picture is a map of the world, the other two have people in them.

2.

My student teacher seems to be the quiet type this bothers me a little because I can rarely figure out what he's going to say or do next.

3.

Back to the interior of the classroom. The walls are a soft pink trimmed with green, however both colors are starting to fade.

4.

My English classroom has more than four faded pink walls, a white ceiling, and a wooden floor, it has an open window with a view of the river.

ILLUSTRATION 1

The four illustrations above show the common types of comma faults and run-together sentences that appear in student themes. Number 1 illustrates the comma fault as well as the run-together sentence.

In the first illustration, there are three basic sentence patterns. Identify them. Note that (1) the first two are run together without any separation between *pictures* and *the*. (2) The second and third are separated by a comma. The first error is called a RUN-TOGETHER SENTENCE; the second is called a COMMA FAULT.

On the front wall are three pictures. The middle picture is a map of the world, and the other two have people in them.

While the revision above is structurally correct, it can stand further improvement. The second sentence is a compound sentence, but the elements are not truly related.

On the front wall are three pictures. The middle picture is a map of the world, while the other two are of people of various countries.

ILLUSTRATION 2

In the second illustration, identify the two basic sentence patterns that have been run together. Then note the simple correction illustrated in the following revision:

T

My student teacher seems to be the quiet type⊙ ⁄this bothers me a little because I can rarely figure out what he's going to say or do next.

ILLUSTRATION 3

In the third illustration, the first structure is not a sentence. What is it? The second structure is a compound sentence in which a conjunctive adverb connects the two subject-predicate word groups. The misuse of the comma before *however* is not only unconventional but also structurally incorrect, since a comma does not signal coordination unless it is followed by a coordinator. In the following revision, note the correction of the sentence fragment and of the comma fault:

Let's look again at

~~Back to~~ $\wedge$ the interior of the classroom. The walls are a soft pink trimmed

with green$_{/}$ $\wedge$ however, both colors are starting to fade.

ILLUSTRATION 4

The comma fault in the fourth illustration is easy to overlook. The rising inflection of the voice after *floor* may prove deceptive. Here, a semicolon, a period, or even a dash should be inserted before the second basic sentence pattern.

My English classroom has more than four faded pink walls, a white ceiling,

and a wooden floor$_{/}$ $\wedge$ it has an open window with a view of the river.

Exercise 1   Rewrite the following theme, eliminating all sentence fragments, run-together sentences, and comma faults. If you have difficulty recognizing sentence fragments, review pages 14-22.

My English classroom is in the main building of South High School. To get to the room, I use the doorway on the west side of the building. Proceeding up the stairway to the second floor and down the hall to Room 205. Room 205 is about thirty feet wide and forty-eight feet long, it is exactly twelve feet high. About three feet from the floor on the front wall is a chalkboard with a small bulletin board at either end. Extending nearly the whole width of the front wall. On the left portion of the chalkboard, a king-size calendar is propped in the chalk tray. Also a school information chart of equal size. There is usually a handwritten assignment on the right portion of the chalkboard. Only the center portion is used. While class is in session. Against the front wall on the left side is a green file cabinet made of wood, between the side wall and the cabinet, two pipes run out of the wall and back down into the floor. Above the chalkboard are three black-framed prints. Representing three episodes in the life of Oliver Twist. To the right of the chalkboard, just below the bulletin board, is a pencil sharpener. The wall above the blackboard is painted creamy beige, the wall below the chalkboard is deep brown. Both side walls and the back wall continue this beige-brown combination.

The left side of the room is solid wall. Broken only by six framed pictures. These pictures depicting the life of another character from Dickens, David Copperfield.

A large bulletin board is centered on the back wall at eye level. Usually displaying outstanding themes.

The right wall is broken by two white-framed windows. With brown cotton shades. Between the two windows another bulletin board featuring book jackets.

The ceiling is white with six modern fluorescent fixtures. Spaced in two rows of three.

More about Room 205 in my next theme.

EXCESSIVE COORDINATION

The following paragraph is from a theme written by a third-year high school student.

I sit at the last desk, and it is in the second row from the windows, and the windows are to my left. There are two windows close together, and there is a heater, and the heater is just beneath the windows. There is a picture on the wall with the windows, and its of a horse.

Although communication is clear enough, the writer has failed to call on his grammatical resources to establish a more coherent relationship between his ideas. By using coordination alone—a series of basic sentence patterns strung together with coordinators—he has failed to communicate effectively. The reader is forced to slow down in order to relate the many separate ideas expressed through coordination.

I sit at the last desk in the second row from the windows, which are to my left. The two windows are close together, with a heater just beneath them. On the wall with the windows is a picture of a horse.

In the original selection there were three sentences with a total of fifty-nine words. In the revision there are three sentences with a total of forty-four words. Note that in the first and third sentences, one of the basic sentence patterns has been included as a subordinate adjective clause. In the second sentence, a prepositional phrase helps to reduce the number of coordinate elements.

Now examine the following example of ineffective writing:

My English classroom is a fairly large room. Its walls are painted a deep mint green on the lower part. The upper portion is soft pink. The ceiling is off-white. Across the front of the room stretch the chalkboards. They also extend partly along the right side. The left side of the room is covered with a series of long narrow windows. They extend almost the whole length of the wall. The back of the room is covered most of the way with a bulletin board. On one half we see pictures. On the other half there are some typewritten papers.

In the excerpt above, the writer avoids excessive coordination; however, he achieves much the same effect by stringing together a series of fairly short sentences. This kind of writing can be improved by employing techniques similar to those used in cutting down on coordinate elements.

> My English classroom is a fairly large room with walls painted a soft pink at the top and a deep mint green at the bottom. The ceiling is off-white. The chalkboards extend along the front wall and partly along the right side wall. On the left wall, a series of long narrow windows extends almost the whole length of the room. On the back wall is a bulletin board with pictures on one half and some typewritten papers on the other.

If you consistently fall into the structural error of excessive coordination, chances are that you have done very little reading and that your language environment is limited. This sort of error can best be avoided by mastering certain grammatical structures and by building sentences that include these structures.

Note the problem stated in the two illustrations that follow. Then note how the solutions call on the resources of sentence structure to express the ideas effectively.

ILLUSTRATION 1

> The Berlin crisis required immediate action by the government.
> The government decided to increase defense spending.
> The stock market made impressive gains today.

Problem: Combine the related items above into one or more coherent sentences.

Solution 1: Because the Berlin crisis required immediate action, the government moved to increase defense spending. The stock market made impressive gains following this decision.

Solution 2: The government's decision to increase defense spending because of the Berlin crisis prompted the stock market to make impressive gains today.

Solution 3: The stock market made impressive gains today after the government's decision to increase defense spending in response to the Berlin crisis.

ILLUSTRATION 2

> William Butler Yeats was born in Dublin in 1865.
> He became the great Irish poet.
> He called himself the last of the Romantics.
> Yeats died in 1939.
> He is buried in the little churchyard at Drumcliffe, Ireland.

Problem: Combine the related items above into one or more coherent sentences.

Solution 1: William Butler Yeats, the great Irish poet, was born in Dublin in 1865. He called himself the last of the Romantics. He died in 1939 and is buried in the little churchyard at Drumcliffe, Ireland.

Solution 2: William Butler Yeats, who became the great Irish poet, was born in Dublin in 1865. The last of the Romantics, Yeats died in 1939 and is buried in the little churchyard at Drumcliffe, Ireland.

Solution 3: William Butler Yeats, the great Irish poet, who called himself the last of the Romantics, was born in Dublin in 1865. He died in 1939 and is buried in the little churchyard at Drumcliffe, Ireland.

Exercise 2

Rewrite the following theme, eliminating excessive coordination and short, choppy, strung-together sentences. Use a variety of grammatical structures: verbal phrases (page 82), subordinate clauses (pages 34-35), appositives (pages 102-106), and prepositional phrases (page 55).

Many young people do not realize the responsibility of marriage and so they rush into it without stopping to think of the consequences and they seem to think marriage is all love and kisses but, on the contrary, it is an important step that should be planned carefully.

Statistics about teen-age marriages are grim. They eventually end up in the divorce court. Young adults or teen-agers find it hard to settle down. They have no sense of responsibility. A great many young people marry in high school. The boy has to leave school and support his wife. Soon there are children to be considered. The boy has not finished high school. He cannot get a decent job.

The young marrieds have deprived themselves of the right to grow up and enjoy life. The teens are the most wonderful years of life. It seems a shame to waste them on marriage. You can have this the rest of your life.

The great love soon fades. The stress and strain of responsibility eventually kills it. Couples usually start quarreling when they are too young.

When people marry, they have to be mature mentally as well as physically. Some young married people have made the necessary adjustments. They are in the minority, though. In my opinion, early marriages are a mistake. Teen-agers should wait a few years. Then they will be older and more mature. They will have jobs and money to buy what they need. This will help them to make their marriages successful.

Exercise 3   *Combine the following related statements into one or more coherent sentences. The object is to use the language resources of English to express related facts and ideas most effectively. Develop at least three solutions and indicate which is the most effective.*

1. The new General Hospital will be built on Hill Street.
   Work will start next Monday.
   The hospital will have two hundred beds.
   It will be staffed by forty nurses and five resident physicians.

2. Dad's uncle is a well-known novelist.
   He has written several best sellers.
   His latest work is called *Dead Leaves.*
   It will be published in October.

3. Charley wrecked Father's car.
   Mother knew this.
   Mother will have the car repaired.
   She told this to Charley.

4. Carl Sandburg is one of the great American poets.
   He was born in Galesburg, Illinois, in 1878.
   His second book of poems was *Chicago Poems.*
   This book was published in 1916.
   It brought him critical and public acclaim.

5. Jenny Couch will go to college in September.
   She wants to become a teacher.
   She plans to major in English.
   Jenny will make a special study of rhetoric.

6. Alfred, Lord Tennyson attended Cambridge University.
   His father died in 1831.
   Alfred was then obliged to leave the University.
   He had many family responsibilities.
   He fell in love with Emily Sellwood.
   He was finally able to marry her in 1850.

7. Mr. Selby Swift was injured seriously.
   His car overturned on Route 66.
   The accident occurred near Williams, Arizona.
   Mr. Swift was driving seventy miles an hour at the time.

8. Willie Fitz is a shortstop.
   He plays with the Yuma Giants.
   He hit two home runs in the game last night.
   The Yuma Giants were playing the Bisbee Eagles.
   Yuma won, 13 to 6.

9. Jim Scott has been reported lost in the desert.
   He is an experienced prospector.
   He was last seen on Thursday in the Estrella Hills.
   A search is being made by a sheriff's posse.

10. George B. McClellan commanded the Union Army in the War between the States.
    McClellan was born in Philadelphia.
    He was the son of wealthy parents.
    He was a top scholar at West Point.
    He was a railroad president at 32.

Exercise 4

Rewrite each of the following sentences in at least two different ways, using a variety of grammatical structures. Be sure that the revised sentences are clear as well as coherent.

1. The hay crop was good this year although the weather had been dry, and Jim looked forward to making some money from it.

2. World War II ended, and our army was demobilized, and the soldiers were returned to their homes.

3. The Dodgers moved into first place when the Reds lost to Milwaukee, but victory for either team is only a possibility since there are more than two months of play remaining.

4. John Borden, noted explorer, was first mate aboard the schooner *Great Bear* when it sank in 1916 during an expedition to the Bering Sea, and he helped rescue other survivors.

5. Alessandro Volta, who was born in Como, Italy, in 1745, built the first electrical battery, and by means of this invention he was able to obtain a continuous flow of electrical energy.

6. Installment buying has almost doubled since 1958 in Britain, where they call it "hire purchase," and now there is a car to every ten persons, and almost every family has a TV set.

7. Mr. Watkins drove his new car around the block four times because he was so proud of it, but his wife became angry when he started to make the fifth circle.

8. Henry Hanks worked his way through college, and his appetite was so enormous, and he had to work overtime to pay his food bills.

9. Thomas Hardy, who was born in Dorchester, England, in 1840 and was educated as an architect, became one of England's greatest novelists, but his real love was poetry.

10. The detective knew who had committed the robbery, but he was unable to find a witness who would supply the evidence which was necessary to convict the suspect.

ILLOGICAL SUBORDINATION AND INCOHERENCE

A subordinate clause must have a logical relationship to the rest of the sentence.

> The boy ate when he was hungry.
> He gave the ring to the girl whom he loved.
> She couldn't buy a new hat because she had no money.

The incoherent sentence is one in which the subordination has not been carefully considered. It frequently rambles and becomes involved. The following selections from themes written by high school students illustrate this error in sentence structure. Examine each example critically.

Example 1

The eighth grade Honor Roll picnic was an annual event. This picnic, as everyone knew, took place at the familiar Baker Park. Even so, all who had avidly worked to maintain their position on the Honor Roll during the school year anxiously awaited the occasion.

Knowing that we earned our own passage, it made it a delightful feeling which we rarely experience on doing the same thing with our own family. This knowledge makes it more special in itself. One would anxiously ask the parent's consent, and while one waited for the nod of approval from Mother, Dad would say proudly that he saw no reason for him to disapprove. One hurriedly made last-minute preparations for the coming event.

Incoherence in written composition is the result of several factors — careless subordination, dangling modifiers, inaccurate choice of words, shifts in person, ambiguous reference, lack of experience with the written dialect. It is impossible to isolate any one factor in a piece of writing and assign to it the dominant blame for confused communication.

In example 1, illogical subordination is only one factor of the resulting incoherence. The third sentence in the first paragraph does not logically follow the second. More careful coordination should relate the statements.

The first sentence in the second paragraph begins with a dangling participial phrase. The use of a subordinate clause would establish the logical relationship of the ideas expressed. The subordination in the third sentence is illogical and confusing.

Give special consideration to the effective use of coordination and subordination in the revision of example 1 that appears below.

The eighth grade Honor Roll picnic was an annual event. The picnic took place at the familiar Baker Park, and all who had worked to maintain their position on the Honor Roll during the school year eagerly awaited the occasion.

Since we had earned the right to go on the picnic, we all seemed to appreciate it more than just an ordinary picnic planned with the family. Mother and Dad's consent was anxiously requested and proudly given. Then came the pressure of last-minute preparations.

Additional examples of poor subordination appearing in student themes follow.

Example 2

The suit I wore, because I was a lawyer in the play, made me feel distinguished and proud.

Example 3

I went to the room behind the stage, where they made me up like a clown, which I don't think did anything for me.

Example 4

We all made it through the ordeal as if we were professional actors. We were glad it was over, but on the other hand sorry it was over, because now we would have to go back to our everyday school life, which was not the most fun in the world.

Example 5

There are many laws for the rights of man and whatever belongs to him. For example, if a house belongs to a person and some other person tries to take it away from him, the rightful owner has the right to fight for his house because there are laws to prohibit this and protect whatever belongs to the rightful owner.

Ambiguity results from failure to use correctly the grammatical device of subordination. In example 2, is the writer proud because he wore a suit or because the one he wore is the kind a lawyer might wear? In examples 3 and 4, to what do the terminal adjective clauses relate? In example 5, the second sentence almost runs away from the writer.

The revisions below are based on what the statements might mean; the precise meaning intended is impossible to determine.

I was a lawyer in the play, and the suit I wore made me feel distinguished and proud.

I was made up like a clown in the room behind the stage, but the makeup did nothing for me.

We survived the ordeal like professional actors. Although glad when the last performance was over, we were a bit sorry at the thought of returning to the routine of ordinary school life.

Laws protect the rights and property of all. For example, no one may deprive a man of his home unless he can establish a just claim in the courts.

Exercise 5

The following sentences from students' themes are mostly incoherent. They lack clarity because of the inability of the writer to make effective use of subordination and coordination. Read the sentences carefully and try to determine what the writer wants to communicate. Then revise the material trying to make the meaning clear.

1. When you turn sixteen, you figure on having more freedom because you are then old enough to drive a car.

2. With the audience practically in tears after all the sentimental songs, we moved on to the next item on the program which was a fashion show presented by some of the girls of the church which was quite cleverly done.

3. For instance, if a person wanted a car and his parents wouldn't let him have it, he might start idolizing money whereas if he had got the car he would have been all right.

4. Once a week I mow the lawn to make it look nice and then I must weed it because I want to make it look better and on top of it all I have to water it to make it grow so I can mow, weed, trim, and water it again next week.

5. A girl goes alone for other reasons only a little different, she has not been asked or the right boy didn't ask her and she goes to meet someone new, but she too goes alone to have a good time to spite the boys.

Exercise 6

Revise the following theme. The object is to achieve greater effectiveness by means of coordination and subordination.

On May 18, 1960, in Chicago, Herbert Filbrick and two other men strolled into a variety store and received a small wrapped package. Herbert Filbrick was an American counterspy and was known and trusted by some of the top Communist agents in the country. The other two men were also American agents.

After leaving the store and walking a couple of blocks, Filbrick suggested they split up. The two agents also thought it would be wise, so they turned and went back down the street.

Filbrick caught a taxi home. When he arrived home it was five o'clock. There he waited impatiently for nine o'clock to arrive. Nine o'clock was the time when he was to meet with several Communist agents. While waiting he unwrapped the package. Inside was a cigarette lighter, actually a miniature tape recorder. With this he was going to tape the conversation at the meeting.

When nine o'clock arrived, Filbrick sped to a vacant warehouse in the industrial part of the city. Ten or fifteen minutes after he arrived, everyone went in and sat at a long table. Present at the meeting were the six top Communist spy ring leaders, a top Soviet agent who had entered the country illegally, two strong arms, and two secretaries. Filbrick was one of these secretaries. The secretaries had been chosen because they could be trusted.

This meeting was to advance plans for stealing all the top secret information on the rocket and missile programs in Washington, D.C. Filbrick taped all the important conversation of the meeting and was feeling more at ease.

The meeting was nearing its end when one of the Communist agents asked him for a light for his cigar. Filbrick started fumbling around. He told the agent that his cigarette lighter wouldn't work. The agent then asked him to let him check it. Afraid not to, Filbrick let him have it. The agent looked at it and gave it back, thinking it was out of fluid.

After the meeting Filbrick went home and waited for the two American agents, the ones at the beginning, to pick up the tape. When the American agents arrived, he gave them the tape and he was congratulated on his fine job.

DANGLING MODIFIERS AND MISPLACED MODIFIERS

Modifiers and headwords are associated by position; the headword and the modifiers make up a cluster. If the modifiers are not close to the words to which they relate, there must be some other clue in the context of the sentence to establish the relationship.

Walking home from the graveyard, old memories haunted Aunt Agatha.

A participial phrase introducing a sentence should be followed immediately by the noun to which it relates. In this sentence, *memories* follows the participial phrase; the result is meaningless. A phrase without any relationship to the word it modifies is called a "dangling modifier." Here is the normal word order in a structure of this kind:

> Walking home from the graveyard, Aunt Agatha was haunted by old memories.

Before reading the revisions, determine the nature of each of the dangling constructions in the following examples from student themes:

1.

> Using America as an example, there are over 250 different denominations.

2.

> We made the trip to our new home quite safely, parakeets and all. After settling, as much as possible under the circumstances, the summer was almost over.

3.

> Of course, in the early days such a trip would have been dangerous, but the trail was too well marked to become lost.

4.

> I think that religion helps us in many ways, for one thing just by listening to your pastor or whoever it may be, that person usually can get some ideas through your head.

Dangling constructions take many forms. They all have something in common—they create ambiguity. In the first sentence, is America used as an example by the writer or by the denominations? In the second sentence, the modifier *after settling* lacks a headword. In the third sentence, to what does *to become lost* refer? And who is to listen to the pastor in the last sentence?

1.

> For example, there are over 250 different denominations in America.

2.

> We made the trip to our new home quite safely, parakeets and all. After we had settled, as much as we could under the circumstances, the summer was almost over.

3.

> Of course, in the early days such a trip would have been dangerous, but the trail was too well marked now for us to become lost.

4.

> I think that religion helps us in many ways. Listening to one's pastor is usually particularly helpful.

Since modifiers conventionally take a position close to the words to which they relate, you must be careful to avoid ambiguity in your placement of single-word and word-group modifiers. The following illustrations of misplaced modifiers are taken from student themes:

1.

I am now waiting to be executed for all my crimes <u>in Sing Sing</u>.

2.

Beany went over games they were to play <u>in his head</u>.

3.

This was my first blind date and it seemed to be a success. Then she turned around and my evening collapsed <u>with all those freckles and missing teeth</u>.

The effects of incorrect placement of modifiers are apparent in these illustrative sentences. Analyze the revisions:

1.

I am now waiting in Sing Sing to be executed for all my crimes.

2.

In his head, Beany went over the games they were to play.

3.

This was my first blind date, and it seemed to be a success. Then she turned around with all those freckles and missing teeth, and my evening collapsed.

Exercise 7   *Rewrite the following sentences to eliminate all dangling and misplaced modifiers:*

1. I saw the enemy troops coming over the crest of the hill looking through my binoculars.

2. Swimming in Lake Tahoe, Father's upper denture was lost.

3. Having spent all his money at the circus, there was nothing for Harold to do but return to school.

4. To make a light, digestible cake, sour milk should be added to the baking powder.

5. While sitting on the park bench, a beautiful red bird flew over the palm trees.

6. Flying gracefully across the lake, we saw fifty beautiful white swans.

7. All the grades will be recorded by helpers in a computer.

8. I have visited the spot where the Battle of Gettysburg was fought many times.

9. Being a very fast horse, Uncle Ben picked Tin Roof to win by six lengths.

INCORRECT VERB FORMS AND SHIFTS IN TENSE

Irregular verbs account for many errors made by student writers. If the student is unfamiliar with all the forms of the irregular verbs, or if the dialect of his community includes nonstandard English usage, he frequently uses incorrect forms in his writing. The following examples illustrate some common incorrect forms:

> I have drank all the water.
> The young mare throwed the rider over her head.
> The Giants win the ball game easily yesterday.
> George begun to study too late in the term.

If you show a weakness in correct verb forms, review thoroughly the principal parts of those irregular verbs that give you the most difficulty (see pages 29-31). The errors in the sentences that follow appear frequently in student themes. Try to identify each error before reading the discussion below.

1.
I have never rode a horse or even touched one, but I would like to learn how to ride.

2.
The wire come on down and wraps around two hooks behind the picture.

3.
Mary laid down for a short nap before dinner.

4.
When she step out of the car, she could feel the soft wet ground beneath her shoes.

5.
My father pretend not to notice when I fell off the diving board.

In the first sentence, the writer used the past form of *ride* instead of the past participle form. His unfamiliarity with the forms of irregular verbs and the uses of these forms is evident. The error in the second sentence is probably a carry-over into writing of a local dialect. The use of *laid* instead of *lay* in the third sentence results from a confusion between the verbs *lie* and *lay*. The past tense of *lie* is needed here. The errors in the fourth and fifth sentences illustrate the tendency of some students to drop the *ed* ending of past forms and past participles. Again, this error probably represents the carry-over of speech habits into writing.

1.
I have never ridden a horse or even touched one, but I would like to learn how to ride.

2.

The wire comes down and wraps around two hooks behind the picture.

3.

Mary lay down for a short nap before dinner.

4.

When she stepped out of the car, she could feel the soft, wet ground beneath her shoes.

5.

My father pretended not to notice when I fell off the diving board.

To change forms is confusing to the reader. Avoid shifting from the past form to the present, or from present to past, without any justification. The following illustrations from student themes are examples of this kind of writing:

1.

They were little and quite old. They look as if they were withered and ready to die.

2.

It was a warm spring day in San Bernardino. It was four o'clock, and Bob is coming home from his music lesson soon.

3.

A student leaves school because he didn't get along with his teacher, or maybe he neglected his homework and makes F's.

The first two illustrations may be easily revised to achieve consistency of form. The third illustration is more involved in the confusion of present and past.

1.

They were little and quite old. They looked as if they were withered and ready to die.

2.

It was a warm spring day in San Bernardino. It was four o'clock, and Bob would soon be coming home from his music lesson.

3.

A student may leave school because he doesn't get along with his teacher or because he neglects his homework and makes F's.

Exercise 8   *Decide which of the following sentences are correct and which need revision. Make any necessary corrections in verb forms and shifts in tense.*

1. The horse stumbled when he throwed a shoe while jumping over the fence.

2. When the band begun to play, the young people started to dance.

3. The little boy had drunk all the lemonade and left none for his sister.

4. He was the boy whom Martha use to date when she was a cheerleader.

5. She always begins her concert with an aria from *Carmen*, and then she continues with popular numbers that she had sung many times before.

6. The boys in their hurry to get away had neglect to thank their hostess for a pleasant evening.

7. The child clinged to her mother in terror when she saw the roaring lions in the cage.

8. The fighter sprang from his corner at the bell and rained a fury of blows on his weakened opponent.

9. The entire class rose when Johnny rose the flag.

10. Yesterday Sam give us all the facts about the Battle of Bull Run.

11. A great many books have been wrote on the battles of World War II.

12. Before the use of modern drugs, many people became ill and dies.

13. Our teacher said she would leave us do whatever we cared to during the last period.

14. He says that he would try to improve his grades.

15. The trapper learned that his feet had froze before his rescuers arrived.

Summary

Studies of student themes show that approximately 50 percent of high school students misuse commas. Only by recognizing sentence structure can the comma fault be avoided. A sentence forms its own basic pattern, and such patterns cannot be joined indiscriminately either with or without commas. The use of proper subordination of ideas eliminates any tendency to string sentences together with

commas in an incoherent manner. Only by relating ideas properly can coherence be achieved.

Try to avoid misplaced and dangling modifiers. Remember that the reader is guided by the position of modifiers. Meaning can be distorted by misplacement and by lack of relationship between a phrase and the headword it presumably modifies.

Above all, be careful of your verb usage. Familiarize yourself with the irregular verbs and never confuse the past form of a verb with a past participle. Try to be consistent in maintaining time sequences. Shifting from one tense to another only confuses the reader.

Chapter Test, Form A

Describe the structural error in each of the following sentences. Look for comma faults, run-together sentences, excessive coordination, lack of coordination, dangling modifiers, misplaced modifiers, and illogical subordination. Rewrite the sentences to correct the errors.

1. The view from the mountain was very clear that afternoon, however, we could not remain very long since we had to be home before dark.

2. To raise good potatoes, the soil must be sandy and enriched with fertilizer.

3. The TV Program I enjoyed last evening centered around an English teacher he had a great many problems.

4. On Saturday our class went on a picnic, and we swam in a beautiful lake, and then we ate our lunch under some trees.

5. Father has just bought a new car. It is a Buick sedan, It has four doors. It is blue with a white top. It has foam-cushion seats. It is equipped with seat belts.

6. My grades aren't as high as I had hoped they would be, although I plan to go to college.

7. Walking down Main Street, the get-away car was seen turning the corner.

8. Today farmers are experimenting with better methods of producing grain, they are so successful that they are raising excesses.

9. Reformers are always fighting for law improvement with fire in their eyes.

10. In our commencement play Bob will have the leading role who is the class president.

Chapter Test, Form B

Describe the structural errors in the following sentences. Rewrite each one correctly.

1. The army was halted temporarily by the river, therefore, the enemy troops were able to escape the encirclement.

2. When the rain had stopped and during the time when the campers were drying themselves out, many of us merely sat by patiently enjoying some good hot coffee.

3. The crowd enjoyed a fine game of football sitting in the stadium.

4. We were driving fast down Central Avenue when suddenly we hear the scream of a siren.

5. As the procession moved slowly along the street, we are suddenly aware of the awful silence that had settled on the crowd.

6. My sweater had shrank to about half its original size.

7. To keep well it is necessary to eat the right foods.

8. My brother moved to California who is much younger than I.

9. When he heard the bad news, he had flown into a rage.

10. At the party last evening we toasted marshmallows and sing one song after another.

Grammar Workshop

A NOTE ON THE WORKSHOP. The purpose of this workshop is to help you discover how much you have learned about modern grammar. Without referring to your text, see if you can answer these questions on the material in Part I. If you cannot answer a question, turn the page as indicated. For additional help, check the Index, which begins on page 405, and The Language of Grammar, which begins on page 365.

The Structure of the Sentence

1. What are three characteristics of a sentence? Which of the following structures is a sentence? (a) Jim to rewrite his theme. (b) Bob read his theme to the class. If you have not mastered the sentence, turn the page for help.

2. What are the seven basic sentence patterns? If you do not remember, turn the page.

3. How are nouns inflected? Give the plurals of these nouns: *leaf, beach, rodeo, fox, lady, tomato, woman, goose, sheep, ox, mother-in-law, news.* Now give the plural possessive form of each of these nouns: *friend, child, hero, baby, calf, coach, burro, salesman, dwarf, goose, witch.* If you do not remember, turn the page.

4. You know that verbs are not inflected uniformly. How are these verbs inflected: *burn, climb, break, throw, write, keep, lose, sleep, hit, spread, cut*? If you need help with the inflection of verbs, turn the page.

5. To prove that you know the difference between a coordinator and a subordinator, give four examples of each. If you need help, turn the page.

Headwords and Modifiers

1. What are the two main classes of modifiers? Point out and label the modifiers in this sentence: *Tall, dark, handsome young men danced slowly and dreamily with unusually pretty girls in beautifully decorated pavilions.* If you need help, turn the page.

2. Which of the adjectives in this sentence are attributive and which are predicative? *Bright, aspiring students are ambitious and eager to learn.* If you do not remember, turn the page.

3. What is a noun adjunct? Give an example. If you have forgotten, turn the page.

4. To prove that you can recognize prepositional phrases, participial phrases, and infinitive phrases, give five examples of each. If you need help, turn the page.

Helps with   *The Structure of the Sentence*

1. A sentence: (a) begins with a capital letter and ends with a period; (b) has a subject and a predicate; (c) has a finite verb. *Sentence:* Bob read his theme to the class.

2. Basic sentence patterns: NOUN-VERB, NOUN-VERB-NOUN, NOUN-VERB-NOUN-NOUN, NOUN-LINKING VERB-NOUN, NOUN-LINKING VERB-ADJECTIVE, the IN-VERTED SENTENCE, the QUESTION.

3. Nouns are inflected to show plural number and to form the possessive. *Plurals:* leaves, beaches, rodeos, foxes, ladies, tomatoes, women, geese, sheep, oxen, mothers-in-law, news. *Plural possessives:* friends', children's, heroes', babies', calves', coaches', burros', salesmen's, dwarfs', geese's, witches'.

4. *Inflection of verbs:* burn, burns, burned, burning; climb, climbs, climbed, climbing; break, breaks, broke, breaking, broken; throw, throws, threw, throwing, thrown; write, writes, wrote, writing, written; keep, keeps, kept, keeping; lose, loses, lost, losing; sleep, sleeps, slept, sleeping; hit, hits, hitting; spread, spreads, spreading; cut, cuts, cutting.

5. *Coordinators:* and, but, or, nor. *Subordinators:* when, where, which, that.

Helps with   *Headwords and Modifiers*

1. Main classes of modifiers: adjectives and adverbs. *Adjectives:* tall, dark, handsome, young, pretty, decorated. *Adverbs:* slowly, dreamily, unusually, beautifully.

2. *Attributive adjectives:* bright, aspiring. *Predicative adjectives:* ambitious, eager.

3. A noun adjunct is a noun that modifies another noun. Example: Our *science* teacher is absent today.

4. *Prepositional phrases:* across the street, under the desk, beyond the horizon, from the circus, to the garage. *Participial phrases:* The student studying in the library is Tom. The films taken by the tourists are in color. Standing at the corner, I saw the flames. Ann saw me crossing the street. The boy entering the store is my brother. *Infinitive phrases:* They plan to go to the Fair. Visitors hope to see many new inventions. Their plans to drive were changed. Arrange to visit us in June. We will be glad to call for you.

Form and Function

1. What is a modifier? What determines the relationship of a modifier to the word it modifies? Use the word *hard* in two sentences, first as an adjective and second as an adverb. If you need help, turn the page.

2. Many words can be used in different functions. In sentences, use the word *name* first as a noun, then as a verb, and finally as an adjective. If you need help, turn the page.

3. To prove that you recognize the functions of clauses, give an example of (a) a noun clause, (b) an adjective clause, and (c) an adverb clause. If you find that you are not sure which is which, turn the page.

Verbals

1. In sentences, use an infinitive as (a) a subject noun, (b) a complement, (c) a linking-verb complement, (d) a noun-modifier, (e) a verb-modifier, (f) an adjective-modifier, (g) an adverb-modifier, (h) an appositive. If you need help with the functions of the infinitive, turn the page.

2. In sentences, use a gerund as (a) a subject noun, (b) a direct object, (c) an object of a preposition, (d) a linking-verb complement, and (e) an appositive. If you need help with the functions of the gerund, turn the page.

3. In sentences, use a participle as (a) a noun-modifier, (b) a linking-verb complement, (c) an objective complement. If you need help with the function of the participle, turn the page.

Appositives and Absolutes

1. Exactly what is the function of an appositive? If you do not remember, turn the page.

2. What is the difference between a restrictive and a nonrestrictive appositive? Write a meaningful sentence as an example of each. If you are not certain of the distinction, turn the page.

3. What is an absolute structure? Use an absolute structure in a meaningful sentence. If you are not certain of the use of this structure, turn the page.

Helps with *Form and Function*

1. A modifier is a word or a word group that limits meaning. Relationship is determined by position. *Adjective:* The *hard* work caused his breakdown. *Adverb:* The students are working very *hard.*

2. *Noun:* Thompson is the *name* of the speaker. *Verb:* They will *name* the new baby for his father. *Adjective:* Do you have a *name* tag for your large suitcase?

3. *Noun clause:* Tom will announce what time the class picnic will start. *Adjective clause:* The committee that he has appointed will meet after school. *Adverb clause:* Everyone is happy because there will be no classes that afternoon.

Helps with *Verbals*

1. *Infinitives:* (a) To win his affection was not easy. (b) She tried to win the game. (c) She appeared to understand the lesson. (d) That is the movie to see. (e) Let's go to see it tomorrow. (f) I will be glad to go with you. (g) Was that sweater easy to knit? (h) Her wish, to visit the Fair, will be granted.

2. *Gerunds:* (a) Swimming in the calm waters of Miami Beach is not hard. (b) Who likes swimming in rough breakers? (c) We have thought of going to California on vacation. (d) We will be visiting relatives in the West. (e) There is only one problem, driving through the hot desert.

3. *Participles:* (a) I found Tray sleeping in Dad's favorite chair. (b) The reporter seemed agitated. (c) The class may consider this test somewhat boring.

Helps with *Appositives and Absolutes*

1. An appositive has the same function as the word or word group with which it is in apposition.

2. A restrictive appositive identifies the word with which it is in apposition, while a nonrestrictive appositive merely adds descriptive information not absolutely necessary. *Restrictive:* My brother *Tom* is younger than my only cousin. *Nonrestrictive:* The book I am reading, a *mystery* by Agatha Christie, is fascinating.

3. An absolute structure is a sentence element made up of a noun-headed modifier, usually an *ing* or *ed* participle. Example: The game being over, the crowd straggled out of the bleachers.

Agreement

Correct these sentences: 1. One of my books are missing. 2. Bob, in addition to his two cousins, are going abroad. 3. There goes my mother and father. 4. Neither Susy nor Kathy have agreed to go. 5. Economics are an interesting subject. 6. He insists he don't want to go camping. If you need help, turn the page.

Substitution

1. In connection with personal pronouns, to what do these grammatical terms refer: (a) person, (b) number, (c) gender, (d) case? Give an example of each. If you need help, turn the page.

2. What is the case form of these words: (a) who, (b) whose, (c) whom? Use these words in sentences. If you need help, turn the page.

3. Give an example of a reflexive pronoun functioning as (a) an object and (b) an intensifier. If you do not recall, turn the page.

4. Correct the errors in these sentences: 1. Sally gave some theater tickets to Ann and I. 2. She thought us girls would enjoy the new comedy. 3. At the news no one was more delighted than me. 4. Jean, who almost everyone considers beautiful, is my best friend. 5. He is the man which sold me my new car. 6. Everyone should bring their lunch tomorrow. If you need help, turn the page.

Punctuation

1. What are the three suprasegmental phonemes of our language? If you do not remember, turn the page.

2. Punctuate these phrases: (a) a plump little baby, (b) a beautiful gracious hostess, (c) a white racing car, (d) a dangerous unprincipled man. If you need help, turn the page.

3. Give an example of an adjective clause that is (a) restrictive, (b) non-restrictive. If you need help, turn the page.

4. State these rules: twelve for the use of the comma; three for the apostrophe; two for the semicolon; four for italics; two for quotation marks. If you do not remember, turn the page.

Phonemes and Graphemes in English

To prove that you understand the terminology of the text, give an example of each of the following: (1) a compound phoneme; (2) a simple phoneme; (3) a compound grapheme; (4) a simple grapheme; (5) a morpheme.

Helps with Agreement

Corrected sentences: 1. One of my books **is** missing. 2. Bob . . . **is** going abroad. 3. There **go** my mother and father. 4. . . . Kathy **has** . . . . 5. Economics **is** . . . . 6. . . . he **doesn't** want to go camping.

Helps with Substitution

1. *Personal pronouns:* (a) first person, or person speaking (I); second person, or person spoken to (you); third person, or person spoken about (he); (b) singular (her) and plural (they); (c) masculine (he), feminine (she), neuter (it); (d) subject case form (I), possessive case form (my), object case form (me).

2. *Case:* (a) subject case form: Mr. Stockton is the man *who* sold me the house. (b) possessive case form: It was my best friend *whose* arm was broken. (c) object case form: Sam is the student on *whom* we can depend for a good report.

3. *Reflexive pronouns:* (a) The blind man took the trip by *himself.* (b) I *myself* have seen that play three times.

4. *Corrected sentences:* 1. Sally . . . to Ann and **me.** 2. She thought **we** girls would . . . . 3. . . . more delighted than **I.** 4. Jean, **whom** almost everyone considers . . . . 5. He is the man **who** sold me my new car. 6. Everyone should bring **his** lunch tomorrow.

Helps with Punctuation

1. The three suprasegmental phonemes are pitch, stress, and juncture.

2. *Phrases:* commas are required in (b) and (d).

3. *Adjective clauses:* (a) The dress that I bought yesterday is lovely. (b) Alice, who is older than I, is now going to college.

4. *Comma rules:* (1) in a series, (2) to set off appositives, (3) after introductory sentence elements, (4) before terminal word groups, (5) to set off an absolute structure, (6) to set off *yes* and *no,* (7) in direct address, (8) in a compound sentence, (9) in dates, (10) between city and state, (11) after a social-letter greeting, (12) before a direct quotation. *Apostrophe:* (1) to show possession, (2) to form contractions, (3) to form certain plurals. *Semicolon:* (1) in a compound sentence without a connective, (2) before a conjunctive adverb used as a connective. *Italics:* (1) for titles of books, plays, motion pictures, works of art, magazines, newspapers, (2) for words, letters, figures used as words, (3) foreign words, (4) names of ships and trains. *Quotation marks:* (1) to enclose a direct quotation, (2) to enclose certain titles.

Helps with Phonemes and Graphemes in English

(1) the diphthong aù; (2) the \ā\ sound in *wave;* (3) the letters *pp* representing the \p\ sound in *flipper;* (4) the letter *p* representing the \p\ sound in *flip;* (5) the suffix *-ing.*

PART II

COMPOSITION

Chapter 1

*Using
the
Dictionary*

A Look
Back
and
A Look
Forward

What you have learned about grammar and sentence structure you can continue to use as long as you express your thoughts in speech or writing. As you now focus your attention on other skills involved in good writing, you frequently will find yourself groping for exactly the right word to convey your thought to your readers. It is important that you should struggle to find the right word, for if it is carelessly chosen and only partially expresses your meaning, your writing will be hazy.

One of the best ways to sharpen your facility with words is to learn how to use a certain valuable writer's guide known as the dictionary. In the chapter that follows, you will discover that a dictionary cannot be dull, unless you make it so by allowing a film of dust to accumulate on its cover.

EXPLORING THE WORLD WITH THE DICTIONARY

What is a dictionary? A dictionary may be a small book—pocket-size. It may be a large book—thick enough to use (with the telephone directory and the mail-order catalog) to raise little Jimmy up, so he can sit at the Christmas dinner table with the grownups.

Of course, a dictionary has other uses. You might call it a *word*book. Yet it is more. We use it to find how words are spelled and pronounced. In it we find the meanings of words. We learn how words function as nouns, verbs, adjectives. We can use the dictionary to find the appropriate word. The dictionary is many books in one volume.

We might call the dictionary a reference book about the world. Each word is a key to the person, place, thing, or idea for which the word stands. We can't study language without studying the world that language symbolizes. See what you can find out about the world by looking up *bandicoot, bansh, cohosh, glissade, glop, oozicks,* and *oolong* in an unabridged dictionary. Look these words up before going on to the next paragraph.

With a little hard work and some luck, you might have discovered or inferred from your dictionary that:

> There are large ratlike animals to be found in India, Ceylon, and Australia.
> Certain American herbs of the crowfoot family are sometimes used in making medicine.
> Mountain climbers sometimes deliberately "slide" slopes of ice or snow.
> The activity mentioned above is sometimes imitated in a dance step.
> The Algonquin Indians inhabited parts of Northern United States.
> One way tea is processed involves partial fermentation.
> This process is associated with China.
> The English language contains at least one word borrowed from the Chinese.

You could easily argue that such information is not particularly vital to your existence unless you happen to be studying zoology, botany, mountain climbing, or the tea industry. That is true, but still we can see a meaningful relationship between *words* on a page and the *world* around us. Contrast this direct tie-in between *word* and *world* with what you found (or didn't find) when you looked up: *bansh, glop,* and *oozicks.*

Not words, you say? Why? Because they are not to be found in the dictionary? There is a better reason. They are not words because there is no meaningful relationship between these particular combinations of letters and the world around us. At least, there was no such relationship in the author's mind. He made up these "words." The dictionary relates our words to our world.

If the dictionary is a record of the language which relates people to the world they live in, then it must change as our world changes. Otherwise, it will no longer serve its vital function. If your dictionary tells you no more about the word *silo* than that it is a "tall cylinder used for storing silage," your picture of the world is going to be somewhat distorted when you read in a newspaper that a missile was kept in a silo until ready for launching. Cattle feed and national defense will become strangely confused unless your dictionary is a reasonably up-to-date record of the language of a rapidly changing world.

A magazine article estimated that half of the college graduates of 1963 would go into types of work which did not exist when those students were born. If this estimate is correct and this trend continues, many of you will someday take a job which had no name, when your father went to school, because it didn't exist. The dictionary your father used in school would be useless or misleading if you looked in it for the word *computer* and the names of related processes, equipment, and jobs that have come into being with the development of the electronic computer. It may be that you will go to work at a silo as your grandfather did, but where his interest was in a cow, yours might be in a bird, which is what a missileman sometimes calls a rocket.

Meanwhile, let's go back to little Jimmy, elevated to the proper height by the dictionary, the phone book, and the mail-order catalog stacked under him. If all we wished to do with these three books was to sit on them, it would matter little if all three happened to be over twenty years old. But would you try to find in the twenty-year-old directory the telephone number of a friend who had moved into town last year? Would you try to order a color TV set from a 1944 mail-order catalog? Of course you wouldn't. The mail-order company sends you seasonal catalogs at regular intervals and smaller supplementary catalogs when the need arises. The telephone company not only gives its customers a new directory every year but makes information available about day-to-day changes. If catalogs and directories were not updated frequently, the words in their listings would not reflect the changing world. The same is true of a dictionary.

This is not to say that you must have a new dictionary every year. Revising dictionaries is expensive and time-consuming. Even the latest dictionary is likely to be a little behind the times, just as the telephone directory is behind the times as soon as the first customer is added or dropped from service. The best we can do is try to use the most recent reliable dictionary available, hoping it describes the language which describes the world of our daily lives. If it does, we can learn many things from it. Such a dictionary can be a whole shelf of books in one volume, as the rest of this chapter will prove.

THE DICTIONARY—A GUIDE TO MEANING

We probably use the dictionary most frequently to find out what a word *means*. How did the dictionary maker, called a "lexicographer," find out, in the first place, what a particular word means? Certainly, he did not just decide that a certain word should have a certain meaning.

What the lexicographer probably did was to study the language usage of a great many persons and record the way various expressions were used under widely ranging circumstances. From his collections of samples showing the variety of ways a particular word is used, the lexicographer compiled his dictionary. Today lexicographers of the most comprehensive dictionaries employ hundreds of specialists to collect and analyze samples of the language. In some cases, this process goes on all the time, with the collecting of samples for a future edition continuing as the current edition goes into print.

Exercise 1

It may help you to understand how a dictionary is compiled if you try writing some definitions from the context in which a word is used. Study each sample of usage as if it illustrated the use of a word or a special sense *of a word, as it has occurred over and over in your collection of samples. From these uses in* context, *construct your "dictionary definitions." In the word entries suggested, the functional class (noun, verb, and so on) is indicated by the abbreviation in italics, as it appears in a dictionary. Discuss your results with the class before you consult a dictionary to see how your conclusions compare with those of the professional lexicographer.*

dye *n*
dye *vb* **dyed; dyeing** *vt*
dye *vb* **dyed; dyeing** *vi*
dyed-in-the-wool *adj*
dyer *n*

Samples of Usage:

> Only her hairdresser knows she is *dyeing*.
> My uncle, a *dyer* at the garment factory, says those drapes will take magenta very well.
> Do not add the powdered *dye* until the water is boiling.
> Be sure the garment is completely submerged in the *dye*.
> Do you think this synthetic material will *dye*?

Dyeing is an industry which employs many persons in
the United States.

The clerk said it would take four hours to *dye* the blouse.

The garment kept its color well because its material
had been *dyed* professionally.

I have come to the conclusion that Harold is a *dyed-in-
the-wool* flatterer.

mastiff *n*

Sample of Usage:

Most of the club members were not pleased with my choice
of a *mastiff* for a mascot. When they saw how large he was—
two and a half feet high at the shoulder—they were even more
dissatisfied. If they had known, then, how powerful he was,
compared to collies or shepherds, I would have lost my club
membership immediately. However, Percy, as I named him,
put them at ease with his melancholy look; he had absurdly
hanging lips and the saddest, drooping ears you ever saw.
Furthermore, when he made no attempt to bite them, or even
growl, they began to pat his smooth coat, and soon admitted
him to full membership. Now Percy lies around the club-
house and sleeps. There is no hunting or guard duty for him,
as there used to be for his ancestors.

outpatient *n*

Samples of Usage:

Because I was an *outpatient*, the hospital should not
have billed me for a room.

I was fortunate enough to be treated as an *outpatient*;
otherwise, I might have been assigned to a ward, where
the children could not have visited me.

shot *n*

Samples of Usage:

The track coach is looking for athletes who can put the
shot.

Mel won the photographic competition sponsored by the
Daily News with his *shot* of the sparrows trapped in
last winter's ice storm.

Before modern rockets were developed, a moon *shot*
was out of the question.

Because the other candidates for carnival queen are
better known, Marilyn must be considered a long
shot.

My parents want me to go to Europe next summer, but I

am reluctant because I do not care for the immuniza-
tion *shots* that are required for the trip.

Charlie was turned down for the rifle team, despite the
fact that he is an excellent *shot*.

The principal asked for someone who would at least try
for the scholarship, so I said I would take a *shot* at it.

If you plan to hunt deer with a shotgun, your shells must
be loaded with a particular kind of *shot*.

In his record-breaking performance, Dave came off the
starting blocks like a *shot*.

Exercise 2

So far, you have had the dictionary to use in checking your
work. In addition, you have your own reading and speaking
associations with words like shot and dye. See what you can
do with the three "words" which were not words when you
encountered them earlier. Of course, after you have "defined"
them from the contexts given below, they will be words.
Or will they?

bansh *n*

Samples of Usage:

The first *bansh* was developed early in 1971 as a three-
wheeler, but that construction soon gave way to the
conventional four-wheel drive.

Banshes were soon popular in the South and Southwest,
where sunshine can be expected almost every day.

The economy of the solar-battery power unit in the
bansh was taken for granted, but no one wanted to be
stranded on the highway when the overcast moved in.

Since the *bansh* moved on to the race tracks, drivers of
conventionally powered vehicles can only hope for
cloudy weather.

Now a *bansh* holds the world's speed record for a
hundred miles, but its attempt at five hundred miles
was thwarted when an eclipse of the sun shut down its
power supply.

glop *n*

Samples of Usage:

Baby Sarah loves to make mud pies, but her mother
would prefer not to have to remove the muddy *glop*
from the child's playsuits.

Some modern painting seems to have been produced
by the artist's gathering up all his unused paint,

mixing it slightly, and tossing the resulting *glop* against a canvas.

When you permit the camp cooks to serve you potatoes, gravy, meat, green salad, gelatin salad, and dessert on one small plate, you should expect the *glop* to be nutritional but not particularly appealing to the eye.

oozicks *n sing*

Samples of Usage:

The zookeeper is afraid the spectators will try to feed the *oozicks*, destroying its delicately balanced diet.

Ours is one of the few remaining *oozicks* in captivity, and none has been observed in its native South American habitat for seven years.

Like the penguin and the ostrich, the *oozicks* cannot fly, but it can move rapidly on its two strong legs.

The plumage of the *oozicks* has been treasured by both primitive and civilized peoples. Some men have spent their lives hunting this strange creature.

The *oozicks* lays eggs as large as oranges, but its large clumsy feet usually crush the eggs before they can be hatched.

How the Dictionary Handles Definitions

You must remember that there are variations in the manner in which each dictionary publisher presents his information. As each use of the dictionary is discussed (defining, spelling, pronouncing), determine the order in which your particular dictionary handles the information in question.

A quick thumbing through a dictionary, especially an unabridged dictionary, will show you that only a small percentage of the words have or keep a single meaning. Look back at the word *shot* in Exercise 1, where by no means all of the different senses of the term were illustrated.

If more than one definition must be listed for a single word, in what order are these definitions to be given? In its instructions to readers, your dictionary will probably tell you what to expect. Some dictionaries give first place to the most commonly used sense. There is some logic in this placement, but it plays down whatever historical significance the sequence of definitions might have shown, since the most common might be the newest meaning. Another dictionary may give the newest meaning first. The most common practice is to stick closely to historical or chronological development. Check your dictionary. If it lists *silo* (for cow feed) ahead of *silo* (for missiles), it is probably giving traditional meanings ahead of current ones in its definitions. If, on the other hand, under the word *humor* your dictionary places the "quality of being funny" first and the "body's fluids" second, you may conclude that your dictionary is using some nonhistorical order of presenting its definitions.

Exercise 3   *Distinguish two or more senses in which each of the following words may be used. Indicate the pattern your dictionary seems to follow in presenting the various definitions, describing the pattern with an expression such as* traditional-to-modern, older-to-newer, most-common-to-less-common. *Write a sentence which illustrates at least two of the different senses in which the word may be used. Note that in some cases you can distinguish separate senses within the same functional class* (n, n), *but that in other cases the shift in meaning accompanies a shift in functional class* (n-to-v, v-to-n). *If the pronunciation changes with the meaning, indicate this by underlining the syllable to be stressed.*

accident	dialect	job
aim	dig	par
alert	escort	planet
caboose	exhaust	quarter
clodhopper	exotic	scrabble
conceit	gondola	sponsor
conscript	grill	tank
crown	ignition	vain

Exercise 4   *Look up the following words and try to summarize the life history of each word through its various senses. Include what seems to have been the earliest definition and follow it with the later senses in historical order. If there is clear evidence that, with the passing of time, the definition has narrowed as the word has come to stand for less and less, call this trend* specialization of meaning, *and point it out. If the contrary has occurred and the word has come to stand for more and more, call this* generalization of meaning. *If both these tendencies are evident in the background of a single word, as sometimes happens, point this out, too, but do not, for the time being, lose any sleep trying to comprehend why this complexity has developed.*

academic	handsome	sheriff
amateur	invocation	snorkel
bacillus	meteor	scruple

biceps	missile	smith
cash	orthodox	suite
domestic	picket	termagant
eavesdrop	pigboat	tinsel
filibuster	practice	underhanded
generous	ravel	vagrant
governor	revenue	warren

Synonyms and Antonyms

Before we go on to consider other uses of the dictionary, we should mention *synonyms* and *antonyms*. Explaining and pointing them out is another way your dictionary serves as a guide to definitions. The meaning of one word will often become clear to us if we can associate it with other words that mean *about* the same or *about* the opposite.

Synonyms. See how your dictionary defines *synonym*. Some dictionaries define the word strictly, stating that a synonym is a word which has the *same* meaning as another word. It is more realistic to say that two words are synonymous when their meanings are so similar that one word can be interchanged with the other in certain circumstances.

Look up the words, *son* and *boy*. Your dictionary probably suggests that one synonym for *boy* is SON. In at least one sense *boy* and *son* refer to the same *male child.*

> Jack Barrett is my *boy.* (my male child)
> Jack Barrett is my *son.* (my male child)

However, consider the following sentence.

> Harvey Williams is a *boy* I know, but Jack Barrett is my *son.*

In this context the two words are not synonymous. The kinship expressed in the word *son* is not always indicated by the word *boy.*

As you can see from this example, a synonym is not the same as a definition. Pretend, for example, that you do not know what the word *quick* means, and the dictionary gives you only one word: NIMBLE. Now, suppose that you do not know what *nimble* means, so you look it up, too, and again you get one word: QUICK. Your dictionary would be playing circle games with you, giving you a synonym in place of a definition. A nursery rhyme would have been more helpful:

> Jack be nimble,
> Jack be quick;
> Jack jump over
> The candlestick.

The rhyme gives you not only the synonyms but something besides words to go on. Candlestick-jumping may be a dying sport, but in this case it furnishes a living context for these two words, *quick* and *nimble*. The better dictionaries provide some reference to the world of candle-sticks and men. Furthermore, if they list synonyms at all, they offer several, so that familiarity with any one of them will throw light on the others. Some dictionaries explain differences in shades of meaning between the words they label *synonyms*. This treatment helps you recognize the fact that words should be used synonymously *only* when the finer distinctions that each word might otherwise convey can be overlooked.

Exercise 5

A. *What synonym(s), if any, does your dictionary list for the following words?*

amateur *n*	offer *v*
assurance *n*	origin *n*
circumference *n*	pacify *v*
critical *adj*	patience *n*
duty *n*	pity *n*
financial *adj*	poet *n*
gaunt *adj*	pungent *adj*
hesitate *v*	reach *v*
indifferent *adj*	recoil *v*
irregularly *adj*	related *adj*
liberty *n*	reward *n*
massacre *n*	sincere *adj*
melancholy *adj*	stick *v*
need *n*	trip *n*
noise *n*	voiceless *adj*

B. *Indicate, by letter, the word which is most generally synonymous with the* italicized *word on the left.*

1. a *cursory* reading
      a. unfair **b.** detailed **c.** superficial **d.** angry **e.** careful

2. *prosaic* language
      a. patched **b.** high-flown **c.** dull **d.** classic **e.** soft

3. a *brusque* manner
      a. businesslike **b.** blunt **c.** preoccupied **d.** hostile **e.** friendly

4. *simulate* an actual emergency
      a. cause **b.** precipitate **c.** stop **d.** imitate **e.** provoke

5. of *paramount* importance
   a. increasing
   b. supreme c. striking
   d. equal e. accepted

6. to *avert* a strike
   a. initiate b. end
   c. foment d. prevent
   e. arbitrate

7. a *lethargic* person
   a. witty b. forgetful
   c. inactive
   d. suffering
   e. gigantic

8. a jungle *safari*
   a. concoction b. camp
   c. chieftain
   d. expedition
   e. tribesman

9. an *opulent* person
   a. wealthy
   b. nearsighted
   c. stingy d. colorless
   e. hardworking

10. *myriad* uses of oil
    a. saintly b. undercover
    c. constructive d. new
    e. many

11. the *futility* of war
    a. inconsistency b. vigor
    c. uselessness
    d. awesomeness
    e. fruitfulness

12. to *deride* the plan
    a. improve b. ridicule
    c. support d. offer
    e. second

13. to come into *vogue*
    a. popularity b. sight
    c. being d. wealth
    e. use

14. a *saline* solution
    a. acceptable b. acid
    c. scientific d. salty
    e. watery

15. a *sinister* undertone
    a. widespread
    b. ominous c. right
    d. friendly
    e. cheerful

C. *Write a sentence in which each pair of words below could be interchanged without confusing the general meaning (although the precise meaning might change). Then write a second sentence using one of the terms in a way that would not permit the other to be substituted for it without either (a) confusing the meaning of the sentence or (b) violating a pattern of expression in standard use. Such a pattern of expression is known as an* idiom.

EXAMPLES
open   frank

Despite the personal nature of the subject, we were both very frank (*or* open) in our views. (*No confusion of meaning or idiom.*)

The mine shaft was left open and became a safety hazard. (*The use of* frank *would confuse the meaning.*)

admire   respect

I admire (*or* respect) his integrity. (*No confusion of meaning or idiom.*)

He did not respect authority. (*The use of* admire *would confuse the meaning.*)

shy   hesitant

hate   dislike

ability   skill

acute   critical

adjust   settle

advance   push

visit   frequent

light   illuminate

authority   power

bearing   appearance

toil   work

fertile   fruitful

wire   telegraph

astronaut   cosmonaut

abbreviate   shorten

fear   reluctance

give   donate

advertisement   commercial

aggravate   intensify

agriculture   farming

jargon   speech

kindly   benign

leisurely   slowly

make   construct

migrate   move

old   antiquated

pay   reimburse

person   individual

good   pleasant-tasting

politician   candidate

produce   vegetables

restrain   curb

sling   throw

sullen   glum

tired   fatigued

upright   honest

canine   dog

sick   ill

D. *Summarize briefly the information which all the words in the series below might convey. Then summarize the information which would not be conveyed unless a particular word in the series was chosen.*

EXAMPLE   amble   bounce   drag   inch   lurch
march   pace   plod   saunter   skip
stride   stroll   walk

a. Any one of the terms could be applied to a means of human locomotion.

b. The distinct motion, manner, and speed of a particular action might not be conveyed unless a particular term was selected: the child *skipped*; the old man *plodded.*

1. smile   grin   smirk   laugh

2. abode   home   residence   domicile   quarters   house
   shelter

3. speak   address   preach   lecture   talk   harangue
   sound off

4. co-worker   associate   colleague   employer   employee

5. car   vehicle   conveyance   transport   carrier

Antonyms. See how your dictionary defines an antonym. Does it suggest that a pair of words are antonyms only when they are precise opposites? Or does it suggest that antonym is a word which in some contexts is approximately the opposite or the negative of one or more of the meanings of another word?

As with synonyms, this pairing of words can be a useful way of remembering what words mean as long as we do not demand too much precision from the distinction we make. Synonyms are words which sometimes mean about the same; antonyms are words which sometimes mean about the opposite. That is fine, but we must always leave plenty of room for borderline cases. It might be reasonable to assume that the words *flammable* and *inflammable* are antonyms; therefore, one means "capable of burning" while the other means "not capable of burning." However, if you see a tank truck with any of these labels—*Flammable, Inflammable, Non-flammable, Non-inflammable*—please do not light a match and expect your dictionary to protect you from the explosion. The man who hauls the petroleum may not take his antonyms seriously. If he did, he might label his tank *combustible* or *explosive*, in the hope of reducing verbal confusion and the risk of fire.

Exercise 6   Ｌist as many words as you can for which antonyms may be formed by the addition of a prefix or by the substitution of one prefix or suffix for another, as shown in these examples:

ADDING PREFIXES

direct   indirect
grateful   ungrateful
conformist   nonconformist
symmetrical   asymmetrical
literate   illiterate
noble   ignoble
proper   improper
satisfied   dissatisfied
developed   undeveloped
curricular   extracurricular

SUBSTITUTING ONE PREFIX OR SUFFIX FOR ANOTHER

careful   careless
helpful   helpless
include   exclude
increase   decrease
underdone overdone
synonym   antonym
prefix suffix
prewar postwar
progress regress

A STORY BEHIND EVERY WORD

With the help of a good dictionary you can get an idea of how meanings of a word have changed from one period to another. Perhaps you will see how these changes resulted from changes in the thinking or the circumstances of the people who used the words. If you recognize these trends as you use your dictionary, you will be studying not just words but the world and its people. Once you learn the story behind a word, you are not apt to have trouble remembering the word you looked up.

Exercise 7

Here are two sentences so familiar to us that they could easily have appeared in this morning's newspaper. The first sentence probably did not appear in print before 1945, and the second, if written before 1958, must have appeared only in science-fiction fantasy. Write a one-paragraph story behind each of the three underlined words. Begin with the early use of the words. If you have access to The Oxford English Dictionary, *which gives the history of written English, you will find it helpful.*

Albania, a satellite of Russia, began to show signs of moving out of the Soviet sphere of influence.
Another satellite began to orbit the earth today.

Tracing the History of Words

The study of the origin and development of words is called "etymology." As you have learned, chronological arrangement of definitions helps to tell us the story behind a word. Information about the origin of the word is also part of that story. Consider the word *satellite* above. Did you trace it back to a time when it referred to the "follower or attendant of a prince"? Notice how we can add to the story if we learn that the word *satellite* probably comes to us through the French from

Latin *satelles*, which referred to "attendant" or "guard." What can you discover about the origin of the words *sphere* and *orbit*?

Etymology is an exhausting and sometimes highly speculative study. For careful research in word origins, it is better to consult the unabridged dictionaries, British and American, as well as other comprehensive etymological studies. However, you can learn a great deal about the history of words from your desk dictionary. The etymology of a word usually follows the pronunciation of the word under consideration. Keep in mind that the etymology is not part of the dictionary definition.

Exercise 8   *What information does your dictionary give you about the origin of each of the following words?*

adolescent	ferment	silhouette
adventure	grange	simulcast
affiliate	hawser	smidgen
ambiguous	helicopter	stalwart
antibiotics	induce	streptomycin
bailiwick	league	sycophant
beriberi	marquee	telemeter
braid	monarch	tennis
cannon	orient	trampoline
cybernetics	perforate	tutor
cyclotron	relapse	umpire
dumdum	scallop	veneer
dusk	shrapnel	watt

Labels That Indicate Outdated Words or Earlier Meanings

Sometimes a word or a definition, common in earlier writing, slips out of current use. The dictionary lists and explains many such words and meanings. Many dictionaries label such usages so we will not be misled into thinking they are widely used today.

Study the instructions in your own dictionary to see how such information is handled. This, too, is part of the story behind the word. Look for such signals, usually abbreviated, as *obsolete, onetime, archaic, rare, formerly*, or for some actual reference to a historical event. As you find these terms associated with a word or a definition, look up the terms themselves to see how they are defined. Note carefully that such labels may refer to one or more of the definitions. One dictionary uses "obsolete" or "archaic" to refer to the *word* in question, while an earlier *meaning* is labeled "formerly" or "onetime," or is given an actual historical reference.

Exercise 9   *Does your desk dictionary indicate in any way that the following words—in any of their meanings—are not now in standard use? If it does not, go to a college or an unabridged dictionary.*

anon	doff	inly
agone	don	list
ancient	doth	miscreancy
avaunt	dulcet	misdo
balefire	durst	monstrous
beck	fain	morrow
bedight	fast	naught
belike	flite	purse
boon	gentry	recognizance
chanceful	gossip	season
chaunt	guise	shire

Labels That Indicate a Special Use

It sometimes happens that writers and speakers in a certain subject area or field of interest, such as law, medicine, surveying, or baseball, begin to give a word special meaning—perhaps to refer to a new technique or a new idea. This is one kind of specialization of meaning, that you looked for in Exercise 4. The study of special meanings in various subjects or fields is an important part of the story behind the word. If a word is being used in a *special* sense, while you are thinking of it in the *general* sense, you are headed for confusion. Look at the following sentence:

On August 19, 1958, Walter X began to *water* the *stock*.

With nothing else to go on, you are not likely to know what activity Walter X started on August 19, 1958. If you know what subject or field Walter X specializes in, then you can at least make some logical guesses about what he actually did that day.

If Walter is . . .	*then he might have been . . .*
a chef,	watering (adding water to) the stock (base for soup or gravy)
a gunsmith,	watering (putting to soak in water) the stock (gunstock or wood for making gunstock)
a flower fancier,	watering (spraying, irrigating) the stock (common plant of the mustard family).
a farmer or cattleman,	watering (providing drinking water for) the stock (livestock: cows, horses).
a financier,	watering (inflating the value without justification) the stock (certificates of ownership).

If Walter X happens to be a financier by vocation and a cattleman, flower fancier, gunsmith, and chef by avocation, then your dictionary cannot solve the problem. You will need to know more of the context in which that statement appears.

Exercise 10   *The dictionary sometimes labels definitions that have strict applications in a certain subject or field of interest. Look up the words below to determine what application(s) they have in the subject or field indicated in parentheses. Again, if you cannot find the information in your desk dictionary, go to a college or an unabridged dictionary.*

attach (law)   paper (monetary usage)
bracket (military usage)   precipitate (meteorology)
chord (aeronautics)   range (surveying)
cover (journalism)   run (billiards)
direct (astronomy)   sheet (philately)
fan (baseball)   stress (phonetics)
guard (basketball)   trunk (shipbuilding)
line (military usage)   verge (watchmaking)

Exercise 11   **A.** *Reread the paragraph under the word* mastiff *in Exercise 1. Write a similar paragraph for each of the terms below. If the term has more than one definition, confine your illustration to one of the senses in which the term is defined. Pretend that your reader has not heard this word and has no previous association with it. Your purpose is to provide context for the word, showing how what it stands for fits into the lives of human beings.*

piggybank	livery	insulin
pad	jetstream	posh
Geiger counter	kinkajou	Sam Browne belt
futurity race	countdown	kiwi
riptide	kilt	handcar
hotfoot	cortisone	alpenstock
cold war	fallout	atoll
straphanger	Stradivarius	kangaroo court

B. *Look up the italicized word in each series below. For each sentence find a dictionary definition appropriate to the context in which the word appears. If necessary, consult a college or an unabridged dictionary.*

run *n*

A *run* in a nylon stocking can start the day wrong.

Tom scored the game-winning *run*.

The rumor of financial trouble caused a *run* on the bank.

The low-priced models performed best on the gasoline economy *run*.

The trapper plodded into town after completing his *run*.

The maker of the concrete blocks counted on one complete *run* in each day's operation.

Our aircraft was hit just as it started its bombing *run*.

rise *v*

Gentlemen, please *rise* when the foreign dignitaries approach.

If the stream should *rise* during the night, our marker will show it.

He could not *rise* to the chairmanship as long as his enemy was on the board.

The skyscraper will *rise* thirty-seven floors above this spot.

This bread dough will not *rise* without yeast.

The rescue attempt failed just as his spirits had begun to *rise*.

If prices *rise*, the supply will not be sufficient to meet the demand.

C. *By writing sentences which include the words below, illustrate by context the difference(s) in meaning of the terms in each group.*

allay	alley	alloy	ally	intellectual	intellect
a lot	allot	allotment		jeans	genes
alien	alienist			turbine	turban
affection	affectation			desert	dessert
ingenious	ingenuous			dining	dinning
candid	candied			gamble	gambol
alarm	alarmist			physic	physique
alchemist	chemist			Pisa	pizza

THE DICTIONARY—
A GUIDE TO OTHER LANGUAGE SKILLS

Without slighting the dictionary as a *word*book or as a book which gives us the life history of words and their meanings in our lives, let's admit that we use the dictionary also as a guidebook to everyday skills in writing and speaking.

Do you want to know how a word is spelled? Consult the dictionary. Do you wonder how a certain word may be pronounced? Look in the dictionary. What grammatical functions can this word have? How does the basic form of this word change as the function of the word changes? What do these prefixes and suffixes mean? Should this word be capitalized? Is this expression one word, or two words, or a hyphenated word? What does this abbreviation stand for? What is the meaning of this Latin phrase? Your dictionary can give you the answer to these questions—if it is a good dictionary, and if you are willing to learn how to use it.

Spelling

Since dictionary entries are alphabetically arranged, you must have some idea about how a word is spelled before you can hope to find it—unless you trust greatly to luck. This leaves many a poor speller in what he thinks is a hopeless trap. He cannot study the spelling of a word because he cannot find the word in his dictionary, and he cannot find the word because he cannot spell it.

Actually the situation is not nearly as hopeless as it appears. You have already heard the word, or you have seen it in print; otherwise, you would not know that such a word exists.

If your experience with the word was from reading it, perhaps you can go back and locate the passage. Otherwise, you may have to construct several approximations of the word as it appeared on the page. Then your dictionary can tell you which, if any, of your approximations was correct.

The same trial-and-error method can be applied to a word you know by sound but not by sight. You can write down all the ways you think the word might be spelled and then check them, one by one, in the dictionary. Let us say, for example, that you want to find the word which means "of or pertaining to the Middle Ages," and it is not listed under *Middle Ages.* Knowing roughly how the word sounds, you look for m-i-d-d-y-e-v-i-l, m-i-d-d-i-e-v-i-l, m-i-d-y-e-v-i-l, m-i-d-i-e-v-i-l,—all without any luck. By now you have glanced down the *mid* entries, just enough to satisfy yourself that the word must begin in another way. So you try: m-e-d-d-y, m-e-d-e. If you haven't given up before you get to *medi*, you will probably find it at last: *medieval.*

You will discover that *medieval* may be spelled in more than one way, but never in any of the ways you tried. Nevertheless, you found it. In the process, you might have noticed how much more you were sidetracked by a wrong guess about the beginning of the word (not *mid*, but *med*) than about the ending (not *evil*, but *eval*).

The very best of writers and spellers sometimes have to resort to this trial-and-error method of finding words, but there is a way to be somewhat systematic about it. You will have fewer guesses to check out if you study the ways the various *sounds* in our language may be spelled. Look for a review of such information in the explanatory notes given in your dictionary. In addition, a detailed discussion of the subject appears in Chapter 9, Part I.

Exercise 12   *When two or more spellings of a word are given, any one of the variants is acceptable in standard usage. The form in widest standard use is usually given first. Look up the words listed below. If your dictionary gives a variant, list it and try to determine whether that form or the form given here is the more common spelling.*

adviser	fondue	mollusc
adze	fulfill	mousy
analyze	fuse	organdy
bandanna	gaol	pickax
blueish	gladiolus	sabre
brunette	homy	savannah
catalog	honor	skillful
conjuror	idyl	sheikh
connecter	inquire	shoveler
cooky	installment	skulduggery
coquette	judgement	straightlaced
debris	jujutsu	synagogue
debonair	labeled	trampoline
dialog	license	tranquilize
disc	likeable	woollen
esthetic	lissome	yoghurt
fantasy	macintosh	zincy

Exercise 13   *Indicate which of the following terms are (a) not listed as vocabulary entries, (b) listed as a single word, (c) hyphenated (d) listed as separate words without a hyphen. All terms listed here are deliberately set as separate words.*

under study	dream world
war zone	court martial
tiger lily	coach dog
stage coach	between times
snow tire	Bermuda shorts
self help	able bodied seaman
sad sack	battle line
photo finish	battle field
paste board	birth mark

Pronunciation

Your dictionary can perform at least two important tasks as a guide to pronunciation: it can indicate how you are to sound the letters of a word; it can show you which syllable should be spoken with greater or lesser degrees of stress. Your dictionary will discuss this matter under either "Accent" or "Stress."

Sounding the Letters. Since dictionaries differ in their handling of pronunciation symbols, your first task must be to read the explanatory notes on pronunciation in your dictionary. (See also Chapter 9 of this text, and the International Phonetic Alphabet (IPA).) Your dictionary probably offers a key to the principal pronunciations on the inside front cover. This will be your handiest reference — after you have familiarized yourself with the general approach of your dictionary toward pronunciation.

Webster's New Students Dictionary* offers this shortened key at the bottom of facing pages:

ə abut; ᵊ kitten; ər further; a back; ā bake; ä cot, cart; au̇ out; ch chin; e less; ē easy; g gift; i trip; ī life; j joke; ŋ sing; ō flow; ȯ flaw; ȯi coin; th thin; <u>th</u> this; ü loot; u̇ foot; y yet; yü few; yu̇ furious; zh vision.

Stress or Accent. Dictionaries use varying kinds of marks (called stress marks or accent marks) to indicate the degree of intensity with which a sound should be uttered. There was a time when many wordbooks marked the syllable which was to be most heavily stressed and left the other syllables to take care of themselves. This left no further distinction between a syllable which was to receive some stress and a syllable which was to receive so little stress that we might refer to it as "unstressed."

Nowadays, we suspect that the matter of stress is much more complicated than can be indicated by one primary mark, so dictionaries often use a second mark to indicate somewhat less stress than the primary mark does, but more stress than unmarked syllables are to receive. Of course, even the practice of using both primary and secondary stress overlooks wide ranges of stress which all of us employ everyday in our speech. This fact should remind us that there are limits to what can be shown on the printed page about sounds we make and sounds we hear. To be sophisticated in this matter, we must train our minds and our hearing to record and appreciate the finer points of pronunciation. In the meantime, use your dictionary as a guide.

---

*These symbols are used by permission of G. & C. Merriam Company, publishers of the Merriam-Webster dictionaries. For further information, see *Webster's New Students Dictionary* © 1964 by G. & C. Merriam Company.

Variant Pronunciations. As with the spelling of certain words, the pronunciation of some words in our language varies among educated speakers. Your dictionary will probably list variant pronunciations for these words. Generally, if no other signal is given, the variants are equally acceptable in standard use. Although several pronunciations may be equally acceptable, one may enjoy much wider use than the others. If your dictionary has arranged its variant pronunciations to reflect this, its instructions will tell you what signal will indicate the more common variant.

Exercise 14 **A.** (Stress) *Consult your dictionary and indicate all of the stress marks it gives for the following words:*

fiduciary	preoccupation
inhabitant	macadamize
bathyscaphe	mineralogical
kilometer	mineralogist

B. (Variants) *By reproducing the marks your dictionary uses, indicate the various ways these words may be pronounced. If one variant is shown as enjoying wider use, indicate which it is.*

adult	fidelity	processes
advertisement	February	pumpkin
almond	gaseous	qualm
apricot	interesting	quarry
comfortable	literature	rationale
Caribbean	medieval	saga
catsup	modicum	somebody
cougar	naivety	sophomore
decadent	pommel	towards
economics	potato	trespass

C. (Rhyming Sounds) *Indicate which of the two common words comes nearest to rhyming with the entry word.*

Entry Word	*Choice A*	*Choice B*
aborigines	fines	knees
adjourn	turn	born
balustrade	façade	shade
bivouac	block	pack
blaspheme	diadem	dream
caviar	bar	air
champagne	bag knee	crane
chastise	ice	prize
chyle	flee	file
codicil	skull	pill
coerce	tree	purse

Entry Word	Choice A	Choice B
debut	do	cut
deign	dine	train
demesne	tense	train
demur	moor	purr
dissuade	façade	aid
eccentric	heck	hick
faille	scaly	pile
genteel	gull	feel
germane	man	main
grimace	pace	hiss
inveigh	lay	die
morale	floral	pal
negligee	see	say
paradigm	deem	dime
persiflage	garage	rage
prevalent	bent	bunt
prophesy	free	cry
risqué	key	may
sachet	day	let
silhouette	hate	bet
skein	teen	pain
slough	cough	snuff
snood	food	hood
trousseau	so	blue
yacht	cat	spot

D. (Pronunciation Varying with Function) *Which of the following show a pronunciation change when their function in the sentence changes? Describe the change, if any, indicated by your dictionary. Write a sentence illustrating each word in each functional class.*

address	convert	present
conduct	finance	produce
console	increase	program
construct	insert	progress
contest	minute	refuse
contract	object	research

Grammar

Notice what signal, if any, your dictionary gives to indicate the functional classification of the word being defined. In most dictionaries, the function of a word is labeled in terms of the eight traditional parts of speech. These labels can be easily translated into the word classes of modern grammar.

Exercise 15

Look up each of the words below, listing the different functions indicated in your dictionary. Then write sentences using each word in each of its functions.

EXAMPLE   **drive** *n, v, adj*

n   I could not find the skyline *drive.*
v   We will *drive* over to meet your train.
adj   The *drive* shaft snapped when the propeller of the boat struck a submerged log.

half	play	sleep	slow
habit	guide	buy	toy
haggard	master	shot	trail
flying	train	away	please
work	harness	man	worry
walk	high	yellow	start
run	advance	true	fire

Exercise 16

Look up the word inflection; *then find out how your dictionary labels inflected forms.*

Look up the following words. Record the changes in inflection to show (a) number in nouns, (b) time (tense) in verbs; and (c) comparative degree in adjectives. If one word is explained in different senses with different functions (as drive *n and* drive *v) indicate the various inflectional forms in each case. If inflected forms are not given, try to determine why.*

ghostwrite	loaf	rate	rap
leotards	index	orbit	veto
sari	dwell	blast-off	runoff
stolen	telemeter	blast off	probe
loaf	soup-up	blast	cite
piano	doctor	blather	unique
sky	snake	lift-off	bewilder
ski	criterion	monitor	laud
volley	tomato	trademark	photostat
imperil	unlucky	liquidate	minute

Prefixes, Suffixes, and Combining Forms

Although you are undoubtedly familiar with the words *prefix* and *suffix*, find out how your dictionary defines these terms. Also study the section in the explanatory notes of the dictionary which discusses *combining forms.*

Exercise 17   *Look up several frequently used prefixes, suffixes, and combining forms at random to make sure that your dictionary lists and defines them. Then isolate and define all the affixes you can identify in the following words.*

amateurishness
anthropologically
anticipation
disintegration
dissimilar
pneumonoultramicroscopicsilicovolcanoconiosis

Capitalization

The dictionary cannot be a complete guide to capitalization. It cannot, for instance, predict what words you are going to use at the beginnings of sentences or what words will require capitalization when used in a special sense. It is, however, a great help in deciding whether to capitalize many terms, such as adjectives derived from proper nouns or terms which were once proper nouns but have come to be used in a more general sense.

Exercise 18   *Look up the following terms (all deliberately printed without capitals) to see which ones your dictionary capitalizes. In the cases where your dictionary indicates that the word may sometimes appear capitalized, sometimes not, what guide is given you to help you decide which course to follow?*

president	southwest
milky way galaxy	jayhawker
democratic	horatian
cronus	german measles
brussels sprout	dunker
mafia	levi's
egyptology	low church
sweet william	x ray
gypsy	hereford
sunday school	brown betty
republican	welsh rarebit
federal	wall street
kodak	riviera

continental   diesel
underground railroad   frigidaire
vaseline   king's english
neolithic   freudian

Abbreviations

Most dictionaries include a comprehensive list of abbreviations as well as a list of those abbreviations used repeatedly in labeling the entry words. If abbreviations are not listed separately in your dictionary, look for them in alphabetical order among the entry words.

Exercise 19   *If an abbreviation is given below, supply the complete term. If a term is given, supply the abbreviation listed in your dictionary.*

A and M	distinguished flying cross	kwh
AAR	DVM	juv
ACTH	mademoiselle	IPA
AM	for your information	hp
cent	Her Majesty's Ship	ft lb
EB	doctor of philosophy	frwy
AS	vertical takeoff and landing	exec
astron	zoological	deriv
BMR	q.t.	chg
obs	pfc	kilowatt
COD	neurol	apt
OAS	mpg	adm
pseud	mph	ADC
DAR	MST	APO
vt	mag	C of C
Vt	southeast	HC

Expressions from Other Languages

See if the terms in Exercise 20 are listed in your dictionary. If so, are they in the regular vocabulary or in a special list? Are they labeled *foreign* if listed in the main vocabulary? Is there anything to indicate that they are given with foreign or anglicized pronunciations—or with both? A question for further thought: Why should any expression be labeled *foreign* after it has gained reasonably wide, though recent, acceptance in English? Are not all but Anglo-Saxon words "foreign" words, if we think back far enough?

Exercise 20 *Write the definitions given in your dictionary for each of the following expressions. Indicate whether you have ever seen the expression in print or heard it spoken. If you cannot find at least half of the expressions in your regular desk dictionary, turn to a college or an unabridged dictionary.*

cul-de-sac	con amore
sine qua non	jeune fille
sine die	luftmensch
aficionado	mot juste
joie de vivre	prima facie
doppelgänger	outrance
simpatico	reductio ad absurdum
mañana	sub rosa
magna cum laude	deus ex machina
weltschmerz	mutatis mutandis
dramatis personae	persona grata
ex cathedra	ad infinitum
ex post facto	a la carte

Usage

One of the most interesting and useful purposes a dictionary may serve is to help you choose words and expressions *appropriate* to the situations in which you wish to apply them.

Current fashion in an expression, like current fashion in an item of clothing, changes rapidly. A *dress* is still a *dress,* but a *sack* is neither a *sheath,* a *shift,* nor a *muumuu.* These styles in dresses, all nationally popular within the last few years, may be unfamiliar to you by the time this sentence is printed. Your dictionary, even a recent edition, is likely to be limited in its listing of the latest language fads, but it can be trusted to show you what has been traditionally acceptable. Wide experience with language—a keen eye and a keen ear for words—is the best guide to propriety in usage beyond the guidance your dictionary offers.

The usage labels in your dictionary will help you determine at least three measures of appropriateness. By means of some signal, the dictionary may indicate whether an expression is appropriate to (a) the *time,* (b) the *place,* or (c) the *degree of formality.*

Labels such as *archaic* or *obsolete* indicate that a word is inappropriate in point of time. A word is archaic if it is out of date, antiquated. Words such as *thy, hath, methinks* are archaic. They are no longer used in ordinary prose. The student of poetry and drama will find in the works of Shakespeare and Spenser many words now considered archaic.

A word is obsolete if it is so completely out of date that one no longer finds it used. Frequently it will be entirely strange to the reader. The words *enwheel, eft,* and *adownward* are obsolete expressions.

The label *dialect* indicates that a word is regional—commonly used only in certain geographical areas. In different parts of the country a certain object may have different names. A *doughnut* in Phoenix may be a *cruller* in Brooklyn. A paper *bag* in the North may be known as a *poke* in the South. Words indicated as dialect should be used cautiously.

The label *slang* indicates that a word is inappropriate from the standpoint of formality. Slang is colorful and may enrich the communication of those who make up certain groups with common interests, but it has little place in the writing of high school students.

THE DICTIONARY— A GUIDE TO GENERAL KNOWLEDGE

Most desk dictionaries provide such lists as names of famous persons, important places, colleges and universities, proofreader's marks, forms of address. Once you become aware of the extra information available in your dictionary, there will be no underestimating its value. Many a trip to the encyclopedia can be saved if you know how to use your dictionary.

Most vital to your general information are the vocabulary section and the lists dealing with well-known persons and places. You will discover the importance of this material repeatedly as it helps you understand and interpret what you read in other books.

Making Allusions Meaningful

Many shades of meaning, interesting associations, and points of comparison are locked up in the passing references a writer makes. We call such passing references *allusions,* or we may say the writer alludes to this or to that. The interesting interrelationships the writer is trying to give us are most certainly *locked up* if we lack the information required to understand the allusion.

It would be a fine thing to have read all that has been written. Then almost any allusion would be meaningful—if you remembered all you had read. As second-best, it would be ideal if you had the time and inclination to go to the encyclopedia to clarify a phrase. These are good and noble undertakings, but unless you have a reference book at your elbow, you are probably tempted simply to guess about the reference and go on. Fortunately, if you have a good desk dictionary, you have a reference book handy. If a writer speaks of his hero as "a regular Adonis," for example, your dictionary can help you discover that Adonis was famed for his good looks.

Even more essential to your understanding are the allusions to more recent persons, places, and things. Did you ever stop to think that thousands—yes, tens of thousands—of events which occurred between five and fifty years ago are part of the lives of your parents, teachers, and textbook writers? The very persons you hope to learn from lived through those thousands of events and refer to them frequently. What were current events to your parents are history book incidents for you. They may describe a man as a "Hitler"; a situation, as a "Dunkirk." They speak of a moment of crisis as "D day"; a moment of defeat or treachery as another "Pearl Harbor." They are describing today in terms of experience. That world is history, to you, but you can understand what your elders are saying about both yesterday and today by looking up unfamiliar allusions in your dictionary—or if you have the time and the inclination, in an encyclopedia or a history book.

Understanding Figures of Speech

Almost everything said in the previous section applies equally to figurative expressions or figures of speech. We speak of "making both ends meet," and "setting the world on fire," of "poking our noses in," and of "sticking to our guns," when, in the literal sense we are not talking about *circles, conflagrations, noses,* or *firearms.* These are figurative expressions.

Sometimes, as when we call an evil person a "Hitler," we combine a figure of speech with an allusion, putting still more of a burden of confusion upon the reader. Luckily your dictionary can come to your aid much of the time. Have you been accused of "fiddling away your time," of "playing second fiddle," of "fiddling while Rome burns"? Your dictionary should explain these charges to you.

Interpreting What You Read

Allusions, figures of speech, and many slants and shades of meaning appear in almost everything you read.

> Our baseball team was *shut out.*
> The jury was *locked up* for the night.
> A reporter's lips are *sealed* regarding informants.

The supreme test of your skill with allusions and figures of speech probably comes when you attempt to understand and interpret literature, particularly poetry. This poem by Alfred, Lord Tennyson was published in 1889. Pretend that you are seeing it for the first time. Use the dictionary to *discover* the poem. Look up the underscored words as they appear in the discussion that follows the poem.

Crossing the <u>Bar</u>

<u>Sunset</u> and <u>evening star</u>,
  And one clear <u>call</u> for me!
And may there be no <u>moaning of the bar</u>,
  When I <u>put out to sea</u>,

But such a <u>tide</u> as moving seems asleep,
  Too <u>full</u> for sound and foam,
When that which <u>drew</u> from out the <u>boundless</u> <u>deep</u>
  Turns again <u>home</u>.

<u>Twilight</u> and <u>evening bell</u>,
  And after that the <u>dark</u>!
And may there be no <u>sadness</u> of <u>farewell</u>,
  When I <u>embark</u>;

For tho' from out our <u>bourne</u> of <u>Time</u> and <u>Place</u>
  The <u>flood</u> may <u>bear</u> me far,
I hope to see my <u>Pilot</u> <u>face to face</u>
  When I have <u>crost</u> the bar.

Clearly the figure of speech most essential to understanding is the one in the title. Look up *bar* and study the different meanings of the word. If Joe's Bar & Diner comes to mind, all is lost. The word *crossing* rules against that kind of bar; furthermore, the words *tide* and *embark* will help lead you to the bar of deposited sand which stands at the mouth of a harbor and over which the tide sometimes makes a moaning sound (moaning of the bar). A traveler leaving the harbor must cross this bar.

It appears that the poet is preparing for a journey, a journey by sea, out of the quiet of the harbor, over the harbor bar. You have looked up one word, have fit it back into the context to get the right sense, and have fit the next word into all that has been brought together so far. After studying *full, drew,* and *boundless deep,* you can see that this journey represents a completing of something, a returning to the sea outside the harbor from which the writer originally came.

You are now ready to notice something else. This journey is in response to a *call.* A greeting? No, a summons. The trip is at the close of the day, at the time of *sunset, evening star, twilight,* and *evening bell.* The journey will be in the *dark.* Apparently such a trip might be an occasion for *sadness, farewells,* and *moaning,* but the poet hopes such will not be the case.

An unusual trip! Is it possible that you've been too literal about this journey? Well look again: sunset . . . evening star . . . twilight . . . evening bell . . . sadness . . . farewell . . . moaning . . . the close of day . . . the close of worldly light . . . darkness . . . Of course! This is no routine sea voyage.

Now look up more words. *Bourne* sounds like "born," or "borne," but it has a different meaning. It is a "boundary," the boundary of Time and Place. Well, the poet will have to leave the world of clocks and gravity for that.

The voyager needs the harbor *Pilot* to get him safely out of the harbor, as is often the case. This traveler hopes to see his Pilot (Leader? Guide? Leader whose designation is capitalized as a proper noun? He means God. Of course!)

Now you have it, the story of two journeys. First the journey a writer plans to take in the (literal) evening across a (literal) harbor out on to the (literal) dark sea. Then there is another story. In this story the writer looks forward to a different journey, leaving a different harbor (consciousness; life) crossing a different harbor bar (death) into a different *dark* (the unknown) from which he originally emerged as the wave recedes into the sea from which it came. Passing the boundary of Time and Place (worldly considerations), this poet hopes to meet his *Pilot* (God) face to face, when he has crossed to the boundless deep (the great unknown).

Exercise 21

A. *Consult your dictionary and explain the following allusions and figures of speech.*

1. The experiment was conducted in a *cloud chamber*.

2. The exploration of the new world was aided greatly by the *Mercator projection*.

3. The idealistic politician was described as a *quixotic tilter at windmills*.

4. The speeches in the recent campaign were right out of *Buncombe County*.

5. Johnson did not improve his batting average, but he got on base by a *fielder's choice* anyway.

6. The next time the two coaches joined battle, their *scrimmage line* was a debater's table.

7. He *burned his bridges* by telling the boss why he was looking for another job.

8. I met my *waterloo* on my ninth hamburger and my eleventh bottle of pop.

9. Bundled up for the sledding party, Calvin resembled a *junior version of Admiral Byrd.*

10. He *hit the skids* when misfortune began to pile up on him.

11. Not only was I the fifth person invited to the picnic, I felt like a *fifth wheel,* because I didn't have a date.

B. *Study this poem by John Keats in the same manner in which "Crossing the Bar" was discussed. In particular, check upon the allusions, figures of speech, and other expressions which have been underscored. (Chalk one up on Keats and look up Balboa instead of Cortez.)*

On First Looking into Chapman's Homer

Much have I traveled in the realms of gold,
    And many goodly states and kingdoms seen;
    Round many western islands have I been
Which bards in fealty to Apollo hold.
Oft of one wide expanse had I been told
    That deep-browed Homer ruled as his demesne;
    Yet did I never breathe its pure serene
Till I heard Chapman speak out loud and bold:
Then felt I like some watcher of the skies
    When a new planet swims into his ken;
Or like stout Cortez when with eagle eyes
    He star'd at the Pacific—and all his men
Looked at each other with a wild surmise—
    Silent, upon a peak in Darien.

SUMMING UP

In the course of this chapter you have considered the dictionary as a whole shelf of books, a library in one volume. It tells you what words mean. It helps you relate words to your world. It is your guide to a host of language skills: pronunciation, spelling, abbreviation, and many more. It is your guide to finding words *appropriate* to the occasion, although this is a complex matter—changing so rapidly that the dictionary can only guide you in the general direction. Finally you have considered the general information available to you in a good desk dictionary. By clarifying allusions and figures of speech, the dictionary can enrich your reading experience if you will let it. Clearly, the dictionary can be one of the most significant single volumes you can own. It can multiply beyond measure the value of every other book you will ever use.

Chapter 2

Looking
at
Sentence
Structure

A Look Back and A Look Forward

From exploring the wealth of information stored away in the dictionary and the many ways it can help you become more versatile with words, you now move ahead to another writing skill—variety in sentence structure. As in learning to drive a car or developing any other skill, you have to think carefully about each writing technique at first. With practice, many of the processes become almost second nature. However, as long as you drive or write, you will have to keep your mind on what you are doing. There is always the possibility of the unexpected situation.

The more skillfully you can handle the basic processes, such as stopping or starting, or writing a smooth-flowing paragraph with a pleasant variety of sentence structure, the more attention you can give to the major objective. That objective may be a good trip without accidents or writing so that others can understand what you wish to say.

LONG AND SHORT SENTENCES

English sentences are extremely flexible. Clusters of modifiers may be built about headwords. Subject-predicate word groups may be added. Clauses and phrases may be shifted about within the sentence. Word order may be changed. The good writer is able to use this flexibility wisely.

Variety in sentence structure is not an end in itself. It is a device you will find helpful as you try to make your writing flow smoothly. The more skillful you become in using the resources of the language system, the easier it will be to free your writing of monotony and to capture the rhythmic beauty of our language.

As with learning any skill, you have to make a conscious effort to vary your sentences until it becomes almost second nature to do so. The problem of handling complex language structures effectively is somewhat like that of the baseball pitcher who has varied techniques but has to decide which he will use. Remember that the pitcher doesn't just "mix it up," hoping for the best. He studies the batter, the situation, and makes his decision in the light of the needs of the moment. You, too, will have to make carefully considered decisions about the structure of your sentences.

Study one of your themes to see how skillful or how lazy you have become about using variety in sentence structure. How many short sentences begin with the subject? How many long sentences do you find? Are the long sentences well structured, or do they sometimes seem to run away from you? Could you improve the theme by rewriting it with variations in sentence structure? Do you think long and short sentences should be left to chance, or is this a matter for reasoned choice?

The following selection from a student theme is a succession of short simple sentences. The writing is ineffective because the student has not used the grammatical system to build coherence.

The Black Cat

Mother has a big black tomcat. His name is William. He is a beautiful cat. He sits and washes himself by the hour in the kitchen. Then his fur becomes sleek and glossy.

William has bad habits. He is fond of birds. He climbs up in our apple tree every day to wait for birds that roost there. Sometimes he catches two in one day.

Short sentences have their place, but they should be used for a purpose and in coherent development. With a few short sentences, Edgar Allan Poe closes his short story "The Cask of Amontillado" on a note of horror.

No answer still. I thrust a torch through the remaining aperture and let it fall within. There came forth in return only a jingling of the bells. My heart grew sick; it was the dampness of the catacombs that made it so. I hastened to make an end of my labor. I forced the last stone into its position; I plastered it up. Against the new masonry I re-erected the old rampart of bones. For the half of a century no mortal has disturbed them.

In expository prose, sentences usually vary in length. The longer sentences grow out of the need to communicate related ideas in compound or complex sentences, sometimes with appositives and modifiers; or a sentence may grow as a result of added details.

The following sentence is long because it includes several ideas or elements which belong together. It is followed by a short sentence which gives dramatic emphasis.

The woman sitting on the porch had the appearance of kindness and suffering—in her brown eyes with their soft shadows, in her mouth with the patient set of her lips, in the soft lines of her face that seemed to be lit by the lamp of sorrow. The woman was my mother.

You should remember that a longer sentence is more difficult to read than a shorter sentence and, therefore, must be carefully constructed. The reader has to focus his attention on a larger unit of language to get the meaning. Prose that was written more than a hundred years ago was often filled with long sentences awkwardly constructed.

The following selection is from James Greenwood's early grammar, *An Essay towards a Practical English Grammar, Describing the Genius and Nature of the English Tongue.* This was written in the early eighteenth century.

When William Duke of Normandy, called the Conqueror, brought over his Normans hither, having got Possession of England, he attempted an Alteration of the Language, endeavoring to introduce the French Tongue; that being the Language which he himself used in Normandy; for tho' Normans, or Northmans, while they were a people of Norway, as formerly they were, spoke the same Tongue with the Saxons who had been their Neighbours, namely, that which was then spoken by the Saxons in England; but after the Normans came into Neustria (which was long after called Normandy) they chang'd their Native Language for the French, which was made up of the Romans, or France Gallick; and this was the Language which the Conqueror had a Mind should be settled in England with himself, wherefore he took no small Care to have all Diplomas, Publick Edicts, and other judicial Matters, written and performed in the Neustrian, or French Tongue.

While this sentence is long, 154 words, it is still understandable. The writer did not lose himself nor does he let his reader overlook the manner in which the ideas are related. He could have conveyed his thoughts more clearly, however, if he had used four or five sentences, rather than one.

Most modern writers do not use extra long sentences, such as the one quoted above; but sentences of moderate length, thirty to forty words, are effective when required for coherent communication.

> Black clouds were rising quickly over the horizon; the air was hot and still, and the captain, listening for the approaching storm, thought he could hear the distant moaning of the winds.

You can learn much about the use of short and long sentences by studying good writing. Extensive reading is one of the best kinds of preparation for writing. Not only will it help you build vocabulary, but it will also help you master language structures and the framework which holds them together in coherent communication.

The following passage illustrates effective use of longer-than-average sentences. The reading is not difficult since the writer has used the language resources skillfully.

> The clairvoyant flight and voice of the swan, the world's largest and loveliest waterfowl, have been an inspiration for mankind throughout centuries. Closely linked with early man's spiritual sense, all primitive Eurasians as well as many North American Indians regarded the swan with superhuman and religious significance.
>
> Though mentioned in the Bible as well as inscribed in ancient Egyptian hieroglyphics, romantic accounts of the swan were particularly prevalent in the lives of Norsemen, epitomized in their sagas, sayings and deeds. The Scandinavian name of Swanson and derivatives are a common reminder of those days when the return of the swan to its northern nesting areas meant more than a passing of a flock of birds. In a way, it was a spiritual promise of renewing life. The great flight of graceful birds seemingly coming from nowhere heralded the end of another harsh, bleak and dreary winter.
>
> As these birds contributed to myth and legend, their purported supernatural prowess became part of many ceremonies conducted by priests and wizards. Even today, swans are revered by the more isolated Laplanders. *

Subordination and Coordination

In Chapter 1, Part I, you analyzed the grammatical devices of subordination and coordination. The construction of a compound sentence or a complex sentence fulfills a definite need in communication. It is important that you achieve a reasonable mastery of writing compound and complex sentences in order to develop coherent composition. The use of these sentences gives you access to considerable sentence variety, both in length and in structure.

°From "The Trumpeter Fights Back" by Willis Peterson. Reprinted from the Arizona *Republic.*

The occasional use of effective compound-complex sentences is particularly desirable. These sentences, which may be short or long, are important in communicating the relationship of ideas.

> When he caught the pass, Willie ran for a touchdown, and the crowd went wild.
>
> The boy dropped out of school because he wanted to earn money, but no one would give him a job.
>
> The car hit the bridge, and the driver was injured when his head struck the windshield.
>
> If the weather is clear, the game will be played tomorrow, and the winning team will move into the finals, which will be played on Saturday.

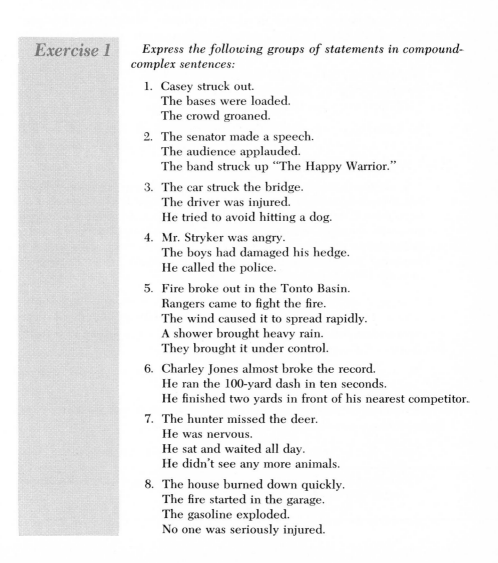

Exercise 1 *Express the following groups of statements in compound-complex sentences:*

1. Casey struck out.
   The bases were loaded.
   The crowd groaned.

2. The senator made a speech.
   The audience applauded.
   The band struck up "The Happy Warrior."

3. The car struck the bridge.
   The driver was injured.
   He tried to avoid hitting a dog.

4. Mr. Stryker was angry.
   The boys had damaged his hedge.
   He called the police.

5. Fire broke out in the Tonto Basin.
   Rangers came to fight the fire.
   The wind caused it to spread rapidly.
   A shower brought heavy rain.
   They brought it under control.

6. Charley Jones almost broke the record.
   He ran the 100-yard dash in ten seconds.
   He finished two yards in front of his nearest competitor.

7. The hunter missed the deer.
   He was nervous.
   He sat and waited all day.
   He didn't see any more animals.

8. The house burned down quickly.
   The fire started in the garage.
   The gasoline exploded.
   No one was seriously injured.

9. The Ancient Mariner shot the albatross.
   The dead bird hung from his neck.
   He had destroyed one of God's living creatures.

10. We will go to Lake Pleasant on Sunday.
    The weather must be clear.
    We can stay only one day.
    Father has to work on Monday.

Position of Subordinate Clause

The position of a subordinate clause in a sentence may determine emphasis; it may serve as a means of transition; it may develop coherence by pointing forward to what is to follow. Shifting a subordinate clause depends grammatically on the fact that an adverb clause may take a number of positions in the sentence.

When summer comes, I will have time for reading.
I will have time for reading when summer comes.
I will, when summer comes, have time for reading.

The following paragraph illustrates the use of initial subordinate clauses to secure transition. In each instance, the initial clause looks back at what has come before it in the passage.

Inside the Common Market there is a spread between high German and low French agricultural prices. *If the German formula is accepted as the basis for a Common Market agricultural policy*, it will tend to keep economically marginal acreage in production and shrink American imports. *If the prices stay nearer the French structure*, marginal acres would be forced out of production. This would leave an adequate margin for purchase from the U.S.A.*

When an adverb clause is placed at the end of a sentence, it may anticipate for the reader something that is to follow. This arrangement serves as preparation and may arouse reader interest, as is illustrated in the following sentence:

We were driving evenly down Central Avenue when suddenly we heard the scream of a police siren.

When an adverbial clause serves as an interrupting element in a sentence, it tends to emphasize what it communicates.

Father, after he had read the evening paper, would often doze in the Morris chair.
The audience would, whenever the speaker made a particularly appropriate remark, applaud encouragingly.

*Reprinted from the New York *Times* (Western Edition).

Although it is usual in writing to put the main idea within the basic sentence pattern and the subordinate idea in the subordinate clause, this arrangement should not prevent a writer from occasionally reversing this practice for good reasons. The following sentences illustrate the fact that the main idea can be adequately communicated by a subordinate clause:

> Uncle Joe retired when he had reached the age of seventy.
> Mother went to bed because she had a very bad cold.
> The information was that the enemy had surrendered.
> Then came the famine that almost depopulated Ireland.
> Father purchased the house which had formerly been the country home of
>   J. Rastor Goodrich.
> Although the child was crying bitterly, Mother did not seem to be disturbed.
> I won't go since I haven't a thing to wear.

A noun clause at the beginning of a sentence serves to give emphasis as well as to develop transition.

> So bold are the men in Peking that they have even dared include a devasting analysis of Khrushchev's program for building utopian Communism in the Soviet Union. *What emerges from this fascinating Chinese appraisal* is Peking's conviction that Khrushchev is an advocate of restoring capitalism in Russia, . . .
> *What the final impact of the doctrinal struggle will be on either group's attitude toward the West* is still unfathomable.*

Verbal Phrases

The use of a verbal phrase — infinitive, gerund, or participial — enables a writer to express himself succinctly. A verbal phrase may often be used instead of a subordinate clause.

> The boy who is wearing the blue sweater is Anne's cousin.
> The boy *wearing the blue sweater* is Anne's cousin.
>
> We came early because we wanted to get good seats.
> We came early *to get good seats.*
>
> The person who drives eighty miles an hour may cause an accident.
> *Driving eighty miles an hour* may cause an accident.
>
> After we had seen both pictures, we decided to leave the theater and go home.
> *Having seen both pictures,* we decided to leave the theater and go home.
>
> Since the storm was over, we decided to resume our journey.
> *The storm being over,* we decided to resume our journey.

*Reprinted from the New York *Times* (Western Edition).

The writer must be careful in shifting the position of a verbal phrase since there is always the possibility of developing a dangling or misplaced modifier. However, there are occasions when a participial phrase may be moved about in a sentence with an accompanying change of emphasis. This change is possible when there is a passive construction or when the predicate verb is an intransitive verb.

> Having served twelve years in the Air Force, Hank Smith was given an honorable discharge.
> Hank Smith was given an honorable discharge, having served twelve years in the Air Force.
> Hank Smith, having served twelve years in the Air Force, was given an honorable discharge.
>
> Screaming at the top of her voice, Aunt Mamie ran wildly out of the house.
> Aunt Mamie ran wildly out of the house, screaming at the top of her voice.
> Aunt Mamie, screaming at the top of her voice, ran wildly out of the house.

An infinitive phrase may be shifted in some sentences. Again, the writer must use caution.

> To succeed in life, a man must have a purpose.
> A man must have a purpose, to succeed in life.
> A man, to succeed in life, must have a purpose.
>
> There is no hope for this man, to tell the truth.
> To tell the truth, there is no hope for this man.

You can see that shifting verbal phrases in a sentence creates a change in emphasis. When a verbal phrase introduces a sentence, it may also serve as transition.

> The teacher instructed the class to read the passage as rapidly as possible. *Reading at top speed*, some students were able to complete it in four minutes.

Exercise 2   *Count the words in each sentence of the following selection. Discuss the structure of each sentence. Try to account for the length of the sentences. What is the average sentence length? Describe the variety in sentence length.*

A good book—what is it? This is a question that puzzles authors, publishers, readers, and salesmen alike. To each of these, identifying a good book is important; and to each of these a good book may be different.

To me a good book is a combination of various qualities. An all-around good book will contain all or most of these, but some good books contain only a great deal of one basic quality or of some lesser quality. Therefore good reading cannot be thoroughly defined, although the basic constituents may be outlined.

The most important basic quality in a good book is the theme. The theme must be of interest to me, or it is doubtful that the book will be good in my eyes. This theme can vary from the religious theme of *Exodus* by Leon Uris to the adventure theme of Jack London's *The Call of the Wild.* If I am stimulated by the theme of the book, I will probably enjoy its content.

Next comes the careful development of the theme. Literature with an excellent theme may be completely dull if the development is boring. For the most part, I find that a truly good book seldom becomes unexciting. Although the excitement may be of the nature of the psychological analysis of character in Thornton Wilder's *The Bridge of San Luis Rey,* it must exist throughout the book.

Another very important quality in a good book is application to life. As I grow older, I find more and more that the books which interest me the most are those which contain some ideas applicable to my own life. *The Scarlet Letter* by Nathaniel Hawthorne helped me to gain a better viewpoint on true justice. Harper Lee's *To Kill a Mockingbird* aided me in understanding the emotions and needs of others. In most books I have read, there are some qualities that can be so applied to my own life.

A fourth, though lesser, quality in a good book is escape. This is not necessary in all good literature, but this quality alone can often make a good book. Teamed with other of the basic qualities, it may form the essential being of a classic. I feel that this quality is so teamed in W. H. Hudson's *Green Mansions.* In Jack London's *White Fang* this quality stands out above all of the others in making this a good book.

The final and least important ingredient of good literature is uniqueness. Like escape, this quality is not necessary to every good book; but it alone can constitute good literature. When a book contains unique ideas or fosters such ideas in the minds of its readers, it can often thereby fit into the good book category. The utter strangeness of voluntarily living on only bare necessities made *Walden* by Henry David Thoreau a good book for me. This uniqueness joined with other qualities in Conrad Richter's *Light in the Forest.* And in the greatest of all books, the Bible, the many varied ideas fostered in my mind often keep me reading when I would put down another book.

Thus it can be seen that a great combination of qualities in many different proportions can compose a good book. No one or even all of these qualities insure that a book will be good; but few truly good books can be found that do not contain one or more of the basic ingredients.*

Exercise 3

1. Describe the position of each subordinate clause in the selection in Exercise 2. Does the clause introduce the sentence? Is it a terminal clause? Is it an interrupting element? What do you consider the effect of its position?

2. Does the writer secure transition by means of introductory subordinate clauses or verbal phrases? If so, identify the word groups involved.

3. Can you find any subordinate clauses in the passage which anticipate something to come?

4. Identify the verbal phrases in the passage. Has the writer used all three kinds—infinitive phrases, gerund phrases, and participial phrases? Does she use infinitive phrases in a variety of functions?

5. Has the writer used the noun clause, the adjective clause, the adverbial clause?

6. To what extent has the writer used modifiers effectively? List what you feel to be the limitations of the use of modifiers.

7. To what extent has the writer made use of the flexibility of the sentence—the change in position of certain word groups to secure changes in emphasis?

8. Are there any suggestions which you would like to make for the improvement of sentence structure in this selection?

CHANGING WORD ORDER

The normal order of sentence elements, as you have seen, is subject, verb, complement. Whenever this order is changed, communication is altered. The skillful writer uses this fact to his advantage. Pairs of sentences in which the normal order of basic elements is varied are given below:

My father and mother are coming.
There come my father and mother.

A meeting of all the former presidents will be held here on Saturday.
Here will be held, on Saturday, a meeting of all the former presidents.

*From "The Essence of Merit" by Linda Clements. Reprinted from the Arizona *English Bulletin.*

> The most important battle of the War Between the States was fought at Gettysburg on July 1, 1863.
>
> At Gettysburg on July 1, 1863, was fought the most important battle of the War Between the States.
>
> Many mansions are in my Father's house.
> "In my Father's house are many mansions."
>
> I think I know whose woods these are.
> "Whose woods these are, I think I know, . . ."

The use of the passive voice is, of course, a transformation of the sentence in which word order is manipulated. The word used as the complement in the active construction is used as the subject in the passive construction. This produces an important change of emphasis. Overuse of the passive construction tends to weaken a composition. The use of active voice tends to strengthen it.

Illustrations of sentences transformed to the passive construction are given here. The change in emphasis should be noted.

> Mr. Doane has donated one thousand dollars to the Library Fund.
> One thousand dollars has been donated to the Library Fund by Mr. Doane.
>
> The City of Phoenix will erect a new Municipal Building.
> A new Municipal Building will be erected by the City of Phoenix.
>
> Twenty cats followed the fish cart all the way down Market Street.
> The fish cart was followed by twenty cats, all the way down Market Street.
>
> Alfredo Murino is to paint the mural in the Memorial Building.
> The mural in the Memorial Building is to be painted by Alfredo Murino.

Exercise 4   *Change the word order in each of these sentences, either by changing the position of a modifier, by inverting subject and verb, or by changing the position of the complement:*

1. Many congested tenement districts are in the city of Plaguesburg.

2. My sister and my little brother are coming.

3. George Brokaw never has any money to spend, although he earns a good salary.

4. The answer to your problem is here.

5. The courageous company defended its position to the last man.

6. I am sure I know what the final outcome will be.

7. When the summer is over, all the children will return to the school.

8. One of the largest zoos in the country is the Bronx Zoo in New York.

9. There will be fireworks at the Turf Club on Independence Day.

10. In my room is a dresser and on the dresser is a large picture of Horace.

11. What I want to know is where you have put my umbrella.

12. The sand blows so hard that visibility is poor on a windy day in the Mohave Desert.

Exercise 5

A. *Change the following sentences from active to passive construction. What effect does this have on the statement? Does it improve it, weaken it, or make an awkward sentence?*

1. The dog followed Willie Jones all the way to school.

2. Mr. Smith is painting his new barn.

3. They ran the race over the new 500-mile course.

4. The City of Milltown will construct a new music center on the campus of State College.

5. The best instructors in the country have been teaching this girl ballet dancing.

6. The Regional Broadcasting System will show the fight on television on Friday night.

7. It was necessary to cancel the ball game on account of rain.

8. Henry Hernandez painted a beautiful mural on the wall of his library.

9. Joe Lamb won the fight in the ninth round.

10. Hester is reading an interesting book about the ancient gladiators of Rome.

B. *Change the following sentences from passive construction to active. What effect does this have on the statement?*

1. Gold ornaments were dug up by the archeologists in the old ruins.

2. A home run was hit by Willie Speed in the fifth inning.

3. A concert is to be played in the high school auditorium Friday night by the Symphonic Band.

4. Nearly all of the alligators which escaped last Thursday have been captured by the sheriff's posse.

5. The Atlantic Hotel was burned to the ground last night by a fire which started in the laundry.

6. Richard Deere was shot in the back by a careless hunter in the neighboring forest.

7. The pyramids were built by the Egyptians as tombs of the Pharaohs.

8. The walls had been painted a bright blue by the former occupants of the cabin.

9. The trees were uprooted by the fierce winds of the hurricane.

10. The stars were blotted out, and the whole world was darkened by the great clouds of the approaching storm.

PARALLEL STRUCTURE

The device called parallel structure consists of the use of the same grammatical structure to express a number of different ideas that are closely related.

"I came, I saw, I conquered."
"... of the people, by the people, for the people ...."
"... whither thou goest, I will go; and where thou lodgest, I will lodge ...."

The effective use of parallel structure in developing a sentence requires knowledge of all the sentence elements — nouns, verbs, modifiers, phrases of all kinds, subject-predicate word groups, as well as patterns of structure involving these elements. In other words, in order to use parallel structure you need to know the system of English communication. Many students who try to use parallel structure develop sentences with serious faults because they are unable to recognize the structural patterns.

The sentences which follow illustrate a variety of parallel-structure patterns.

1. The Pattersons have an apartment in the city, a cottage on the seashore, and money in the bank.
2. Where he goes every day, I do not know; what he does, I often wonder.
3. His heart is filled with hatred; his mind is filled with revenge.
4. The boy replied that he would go to college, that he would study hard, and that he would make his family proud of him.

5. Smiling at the audience, bowing to her admirers, the great Cassaza walked slowly to the center of the stage.
6. To build a great house in the country, to develop a park for hunting, and to live the life of a country gentleman was the ambition of plain Mr. Otto.
7. Henry likes working in the insurance business and competing with other salesmen.
8. It was the door that led into the attic, that opened a romantic world of imagined experience.
9. He arrived before they were ready for him, before they were prepared for the impact of his personality.
10. Hitler wanted to defeat France, to dominate Europe, but most of all to conquer England.

Each of the preceding sentences illustrates a different grammatical pattern of parallel structure, as indicated below.

1. Noun complements with prepositional phrase modifiers
2. Noun clauses used as direct objects with inverted order
3. Two independent subject-predicate groups of the noun, verb, adverbial-phrase pattern
4. Three noun clauses introduced by *that* used as direct objects following a single verb
5. Two participial phrases in which the verbal is modified by a preposi-tional phrase, both modifying the subject of the sentence
6. Three infinitive phrases used in a compound subject. In each there is a direct object of the verbal modified by a prepositional phrase.
7. Two gerund phrases used as the direct object of the main verb
8. Two adjective clauses introduced by *that* modifying a subjective complement
9. Two adverbial clauses introduced by *before* modifying the verb *ar-rived*
10. Three infinitive phrases used as a compound direct object. In each phrase there is a direct object of the verbal.

Exercise 6   *Criticize faulty parallelism in the following sentences and revise to perfect the parallelism where necessary:*

1. The solution is not to quit your job, but you should go and have an understanding with your employer.

2. When the war had ended and during the armistice period which followed, the armies of allied troops were idle in their cantonments.

3. Having warned his children to be quiet and being ready for almost any annoying situation, the nervous Mr. Widget lay down for a refreshing nap.

4. The director wanted to know where I had been and the reason for the many mistakes that I had made.

5. There are too many restrictions on this property; we have many reasons for refusing to consider it.

6. That the subject is difficult, I know; but I am also aware that you are indifferent.

7. Singing in the rain and being stretched out on a sunny beach are two of Henry's favorite forms of recreation.

8. It was a hill difficult to climb and where the steep cliffs bordered the sides of the road.

9. What the children want and their actual needs are two entirely different things.

10. He defeated his first opponent; he overwhelmed his second, but he was defeated by the third.

Exercise 7

1. Write a sentence with parallel structure, using two noun clauses in the subject position.

2. Write a sentence with parallel structure, using two noun clauses in the direct-object position.

3. Write a sentence with parallel structure, using two adjective clauses beginning with *that* and modifying a direct object.

4. Write a sentence with parallel structure, using two adverbial clauses that begin with *when* and modify the verb.

5. Write a sentence with parallel structure, using two infinitive phrases, each having a complement. Use the infinitive phrases as the direct object of the main verb.

6. Write a sentence with parallel structure, using two participial phrases modifying the subject of the sentence.

7. Write a sentence with parallel structure, using two gerund phrases as the subject of the sentence.

8. Write a sentence with parallel structure, using two gerund phrases as the direct object of the main verb.

9. Write a sentence with parallel structure, using a compound predicate with appropriate modifiers.

10. Write a sentence with parallel structure, using nouns in a compound direct object with similar modifying phrase structures.

BALANCED SENTENCES

A balanced sentence is a structure in which there are two or more coordinate clauses, similar in form and length. There is a close relationship between balanced structure and parallel structure. In a sense, the balanced sentence is a refinement of parallelism.

> His material success had no limit; his spiritual failure had no parallel.
> The boys left for a camp in the cool mountains; the girls remained for a summer in the hot city.
> Many of the men have been trained to be good soldiers; few of them have been trained to be good leaders.
> Children who behave will go home at three; children who misbehave will remain after school.
> The war has long been ended, but the peace has never been achieved.
> One of his duties was to give the prisoners aid and comfort; the other was to take from them their property and freedom.

The balanced sentence is frequently used to give emphasis to contrasts or comparisons. You should look for sentences of this kind in your reading and keep a notebook in which these sentences are recorded. Learning to use balanced sentences effectively comes only with considerable study and effort.

LOOSE AND PERIODIC SENTENCES

A loose sentence is one in which the ideas follow in normal sequence in the predicate. A periodic sentence is one that is constructed in such a way that the main idea is withheld until the very end of the sentence. It is written in this way in order to secure a high degree of emphasis. Most sentences are loose sentences. Occasionally a writer will use a periodic sentence. Which of these sentences are periodic?

> The search party found the old prospector dead, twenty miles out in the desert where he had fallen in the thick brush.
> Twenty miles out in the desert where he had fallen in the thick brush, the search party found the old prospector dead.
>
> The rushing torrents in the creek flooded the town of Globe and swept away many homes when flash floods dropped tons of water on the surrounding hills during the heavy thunderstorm yesterday.
> When flash floods dropped tons of water on the surrounding hills during the heavy thunderstorm yesterday, the rushing torrents in the creek flooded the town of Globe and swept away many homes.

One of the best examples of a periodic sentence may be found in Bret Harte's "The Outcasts of Poker Flat." It is the concluding sentence of the story.

"And pulseless and cold, with a Derringer by his side and a bullet in his heart, though still calm as in life, beneath the snow lay he who was at once the strongest and yet the weakest of the outcasts of Poker Flat."

Exercise 8   *Describe the sentence structure used by the authors of the following passages:*

It was market day, and over all the roads round Goderville the peasants and their wives were coming towards the town. The men walked easily, lurching the whole body forward at every step. Their long legs were twisted and deformed by the slow, painful labors of the country – by bending over to plow, which is also what makes their left shoulders too high and their figures crooked; and by reaping corn, which obliges them for steadiness' sake to spread their knees too wide. Their starched blue blouses, shining as though varnished, ornamented at collar and cuffs with little patterns of white stitchwork, and blown up big around their bony bodies, seemed exactly like balloons about to soar, but putting forth a head, two arms, and two feet.

Some of these fellows dragged a cow or a calf at the end of a rope. And just behind the animal, beating it over the back with a leaf-covered branch to hasten its pace, went their wives, carrying large baskets from which came forth the heads of chickens or the heads of ducks. These women walked with steps far shorter and quicker than the men; their figures, withered and upright, were adorned with scanty little shawls pinned over their flat bosoms; and they enveloped their heads each in a white cloth, close fastened round the hair and surmounted by a cap.

GUY DE MAUPASSANT, "The Piece of String"

In the bosom of one of these spacious coves which indent the eastern shore of the Hudson, at that broad expansion of the river denominated by the ancient Dutch navigators the Tappan Zee, and where they always prudently shortened sail, and implored the protection of St. Nicholas when they crossed, there lies a small market town or rural port, which by some is called Greensburgh, but which is more generally and properly known by the name of Tarry Town. This name was given, we are told, in former days, by the good housewives of the adjacent

country, from the inveterate propensity of their husbands
to linger about the village tavern on market days. Be
that as it may, I do not vouch for the fact, but merely
advert to it, for the sake of being precise and authentic.
Not far from the village, perhaps about two miles, there is
a little valley, or rather lap of land, among high hills,
which is one of the quietest places in the whole world.
A small brook glides through it, with just murmur enough
to lull one to repose; and the occasional whistle of a
quail or tapping of a woodpecker is almost the only sound
that ever breaks in upon the uniform tranquillity.

WASHINGTON IRVING, "The Legend of Sleepy Hollow"

The mountains were his masters. They rimmed in life.
They were the cup of reality, beyond growth, beyond
struggle and death. They were his absolute unity in the
midst of eternal change. Old haunt-eyed faces glimmered
in his memory. He thought of Swain's cow, St. Louis,
death, himself in the cradle. He was the haunter of himself, trying for a moment to recover what he had been
part of. He did not understand change, he did not understand growth. He stared at his framed baby picture in the
parlor, and turned away sick with fear and the effort to
touch, retain, grasp himself for only a moment.

THOMAS WOLFE, *Look Homeward Angel*

SUMMING UP

Variety of sentence structure is a desirable quality of written English.
It is the outcome of an effective use of the many resources of the language system. Long sentences are sometimes necessary when a number of ideas are communicated together, or when the use of coordination and subordination requires length to express the relationship of
ideas. Short sentences can be vivid and dramatic. Certain modifiers may
be moved about within a sentence to change emphasis or to secure
transition. Shifts in word order effect similar results. The use of parallel
structure, balanced sentences, and an occasional periodic sentence adds
effectiveness.

Chapter 3

Organization and Outlines

If you were to start building a house, you would not ask the contractor to begin work before the architect had made his drawings. Similarly with writing, you need a plan before you start constructing your theme.

You have been considering the basic materials of composition—words and sentences. To use these materials to the best advantage, you need to think about planning or outlining what you intend to say. Learning to think in an organized fashion will not only make you a better writer—it will help you in countless other ways. An immediate application, outside of your writing assignments, can be in organizing and outlining material as you study.

LEARNING TO SEPARATE MATERIAL INTO CATEGORIES

Consider the game called "Twenty Questions." First you select a *subject*. The subject may be anything within the realm of what you presume to be your common experience or knowledge. It might be from history, fiction, mythology, or current events. Your job is to ask questions which can be answered "Yes" or "No." Within twenty questions, the subject you had in mind is to be identified. To give a slight advantage, you may announce at the beginning whether the subject is "animal," "vegetable," or "mineral," but it isn't necessary.

Let us say that you choose as your subject *Mark Twain*. Your recent study of him in literature has brought him to mind. You announce that your subject is "animal." Begin the questions.

1. Is the subject real, rather than fictional or legendary?
   Yes.

2. Is the subject a human being, as distinguishable from other animals?
   Yes.

3. Is the subject male, rather than female?
   Yes.

4. Is the subject now living?
   No.

5. Was the subject a native of the Western Hemisphere?
   Yes.

6. Was the subject a citizen of the United States?
   Yes.

Recap: The class is now looking for the identity of a male American, now dead. The search could go in any one of several directions at this point. To name three directions: identification through (1) physical location of his birthplace, his fame, and so on; (2) narrowing the span of time in which he lived or worked, or (3) discovering his occupation. The latter is chosen. The questions from this point are designed to "close in" on the subject's principal fame-producing activity.

7. Was this man an official in either federal or state government?
   No.

8. Did he win his fame in business?
   No.

9. Did he win his fame in athletics?
   No.

10. Did he win his fame in science or technology?
    No.

11. Is he generally associated with the fine arts?
    Yes.

12. Painting or sculpture?
    No.

13. Music?
    No.

14. Literature?
    Yes.

15. Was he born in the twentieth century?
    No.

16. Was he born in the nineteenth century?
    Yes.

17. Was he a native of New England?
    No.

18. Is he chiefly famous for his poetry?
    No.

19. For his humor?
    Yes.

20. Mark Twain?
    Yes.

Well, your subject was discovered within the allowed twenty questions, but it took some wild guessing after Question 17, and you can probably see that the going would have been much tougher, if the subject had been more exacting. Famous living or historical figures usually make the easiest subjects in this game; that is why they are good subjects when one is explaining the game or just learning it. After school, try the game with some of your friends. You might choose names from this list—but of course you will think of others:

> Daniel Webster
> Stonewall Jackson
> Robert Fulton
> Henry Wadsworth Longfellow
> John Glenn

When you become a practiced player of the game, you can widen the range of choices and try to identify such subjects as:

> Victoria Falls
> The Great Pyramid
> King Henry VIII
> Captain Ahab (from *Moby Dick*)
> Tom Sawyer (from *The Adventures of Tom Sawyer*)
> Big Ben (London's famous timepiece)
> A two-dollar bill
> The New York Philharmonic Orchestra

Just when are you going to get down to the business of this chapter on *Organization and Outlines*? The answer is: "You have."

You are now practicing one of the basic steps in organizing and outlining. You are making a game of *dividing material! Logical division of material* is at the heart of organizing and outlining, as it is in playing "Twenty Questions."

In the game, it is necessary, as you think of each question, to make a single division of material, so that either a "yes" or a "no" answer will continue the process of narrowing the field. The divisions and the terms in which they are stated should be such that either response will convey an equal amount of information. In other kinds of organizing and outlining, however, you may subdivide as it suits your purpose. Yet, some of the same rules will apply.

What is to be counted under a subdivision must be reasonably understood between maker and user.

The subdivisions should be reasonably separate and distinct from one another. There should be no overlapping with earlier subdivisions.

The subdivisions should balance with one another on some logical basis. (*Soup* and *nuts* might serve equally well as subdivisions of *food*, but under *liquid nutrients* team *soup* with *gravy*.)

The relationship must be clear, not only between parallel subdivisions but between any one subdivision and (1) the larger entity from which it came, and (2) the further subdivisions which are drawn from it—as with *male*, below:

2. Human
   a. Female
   b. Male
      (1) Living
      (2) Deceased

A beginning outline of the "Twenty Questions" material might be developed by successively subdividing categories:

I. Animals
   A. Fictional and mythical animals
   B. Real animals
      1. Nonhuman
      2. Human, real animals
         a. Female, human, real animals
         b. Male, human, real animals
            (1) Living, male, human, real animals
            (2) Deceased, male, human, real animals
and so on.

On the other hand you might make a graphic division of the material.

Animal	
real	mythical, fictional
human	nonhuman
male	female
deceased	living
Western Hemisphere	Eastern Hemisphere
United States	not United States
government	not government
business	not business
athletics	not athletics
science	not science
fine arts	not fine arts
painting or sculpture	not painting or sculpture
music	not music
literature	not literature
twentieth century	not twentieth century
nineteenth century	not nineteenth century
New England	not New England
poetry	not poetry
humor	not humor
Twain	not Twain

WHAT IS AN OUTLINE?

In a general sense, anything—map, sketch, graph, table, or plan—which helps you visualize something you cannot observe directly might be called an *outline*. When you take notes of an address, it is because you do not have access to the actual text from which the speaker's remarks came. Moreover, when you plan, in outline form, something you are preparing to say or write, you make a rough sketch of the presentation because you do not, as yet, have access to the finished product. It has not yet been constructed. In class you may be asked to outline a passage which is given to you complete. This is a practice situation by which you may learn the outlining process. The outline you make will provide you with a skeletal summary of the whole passage.

The Mechanics of a Conventional Outline

The relationships between divisions and further subdivisions in outlines are commonly indicated by a pattern of numerals, letters, and indentations such as this:

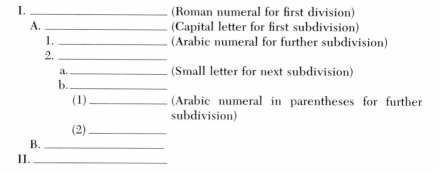

I. _____ (Roman numeral for first division)
  A. _____ (Capital letter for first subdivision)
    1. _____ (Arabic numeral for further subdivision)
    2. _____
      a. _____ (Small letter for next subdivision)
      b. _____
        (1) _____ (Arabic numeral in parentheses for further subdivision)
        (2) _____
  B. _____
II. _____

Entries on parallel levels of the outline structure, as with I and II, A and B, 1 and 2, a and b, and (1) and (2), should be parallel in grammatical structure as well. Single words or phrases or sentences may constitute the entries, but in any case, items at parallel levels of the outline should be parallel in level of generalization and parallel in construction.

Sentences:
  A. The Pimas are said never to have fought the white man.
  B. The Apaches engaged the United States Army on many occasions.

Topics (Nouns)
  1. Tigers
  2. Lions
  3. Leopards

Topic (Nouns and past participles)
  a. Movies attended
  b. Athletic events covered
  c. Dances suffered

Topics (Nouns and adjective clauses)
  (1) Jobs that I found on my own
  (2) Positions that were located through agencies
  (3) Opportunities that employers volunteered to me

Topic outlines are frequently used for material of uncomplicated structure. *Sentence outlines* usually provide more insight concerning the material. A sentence not only identifies a subject, but suggests an attitude or a direction.

The sample outline on page 274 has to be adjusted to handle the material the user has to work with, but in general this pattern may be considered a basic form. An adjustment that is often made is the addition of a statement of the main idea of the material being outlined, usually just before the first division of the subject matter.

Exercise 1   *Each vegetable listed on the right may be distinguished from or grouped with others, according to the part of the plant it comprises. As a simple exercise in dividing and classifying materials, enter logically appropriate labels in the blanks.*

The Edible Part of the Vegetable

Leaf
    endive _____
    brussels sprouts _____
    _____
    _____
    _____
    _____
    _____
    _____

Stem
    _____
    _____

Root
    parsnip _____
    _____
    _____
    _____
    _____
    _____
    _____

Seed
    peas _____
    _____
    _____

Fruit—the edible structure encasing or including the seeds
    eggplant _____
    _____
    _____
    _____
    _____

Bulb
    _____

Flower
    _____

asparagus
beans
beet
cabbage
carrot
cauliflower
celery
corn
cucumber
lettuce
mustard greens
onion
peppers
potato
radish
rice
spinach
squash
sweet potato
turnip

Exercise 2

By checking reference books, if necessary, and by looking for logical parallels, rearrange the lists at the top of page 278 in a highest-to-lowest order. Since the highest grade in the Army, the Air Force, and the Navy has no equivalent in the other services, this grade is not listed.

AIR FORCE	ARMY	COAST GUARD	MARINE CORPS	NAVY
Colonel	Second Lieutenant	Lieutenant	First Lieutenant	Lieutenant Commander
Lieutenant General	First Lieutenant	Captain	Major General	Vice Admiral
Second Lieutenant	Captain	Admiral	Second Lieutenant	Ensign
Major	General		Brigadier General	
Major General	Brigadier General	Ensign	Captain	Commander
Lieutenant Colonel	Major	Lieutenant Junior Grade	Colonel	Lieutenant
First Lieutenant	Lieutenant General	Lieutenant Commander	Lieutenant Colonel	Lieutenant Junior Grade
Captain	Lieutenant Colonel	Commander	Lieutenant General	Captain
General	Colonel	Rear Admiral	Major	Admiral
Brigadier General	Major General	Vice Admiral	General	Rear Admiral

Exercise 3 **A.** *From the list of sentences below, choose one to serve as a central idea for unifying the rest. Having listed that sentence under the title, rearrange the remaining sentences into outline form (see page 274). Add further statements only if the content or structure seems to require them.*

My Freshman Activity in Music

Vocal music offered me the enjoyment of succeeding in an undertaking in which I had no previous experience.

On a crisp autumn night there is something grand and satisfying about participating with the marching band at half time.

Music took up all of my time, outside of classes, in my freshman year.

When the Band tryouts came, I was grateful that my parents had encouraged me to study clarinet, rather than violin.

I found instrumental music more demanding than vocal music.

I'll never forget the evening at Christmastime, when we went caroling with the glee club.

No one was ever more scared than I to face the Fine Arts Festival judges to sing a solo.

When the spring concerts came around, I felt lucky to get into the orchestra as the last draft choice.

Mixed chorus is never dull because it is *mixed*—boys and girls.

Nothing matches the tense excitement of playing for basketball games as a member of the pep band.

B. *Expand the outline you made for Exercise 3A by adding statements based on imaginary experience. This should be done by adding two or more new statements to serve as subdivisions of the lowest-level entries you have made thus far.*

Exercise 4

A. *Add several items, on as many structural levels as you can, to make a more complete and balanced outline from the framework suggested below. If you prefer to do so, you may rework what is here, using a different order and new divisions and subdivisions.*

Helmets

I. In work
   A. Steelworkers
   B. Lumberjacks
II. In play
   A. Football
   B. Baseball
III. In war
   A. National difference in design
   B. Effectiveness for identification and protection

B. *After some preliminary reading in an encyclopedia or some other reference book, develop into a* sentence outline *the material suggested in Exercise 4A.*

Exercise 5

In the outline started below, add subdivisions to each of the main entries. Make additions appropriate to the statement of the central idea *and in accord with the trends al-*

ready established in content and structure. Subdivisions should suggest kinds of behavior or examples of behavior appropriate under the heading. You may add major entries if you wish. Should you happen to disagree with the central idea, which is your privilege, rework the statement until it makes a unifying generalization with which you can agree. Then support that central idea in the manner described above.

Effects of TV Viewing on Americans

Central Idea: The TV set in the American home has changed the behavior patterns of many of those who watch it regularly.

   I. To accommodate their TV viewing, many persons have changed their eating habits.
  II. Because TV viewing requires little or no muscular activity, the advent of TV has changed the patterns of physical activity of many of its viewers.
 III. For various reasons, TV viewing has come into conflict with certain social conventions — sometimes to the accompaniment of changes in traditional social customs.

TWO KINDS OF OUTLINES

With the conventional form of outlines clearly in mind, move on to consider the process of making outlines in greater detail. At this point it might be useful to speak of two kinds of outlines. Let us assume that a person who must take notes at a formal address and write an outline from his notes has a much different task than has the person who wrote the address in the first place. Continuing the presumption, let us look for a distinction between (a) an outline drawn from a magazine article, a speech, a lecture, a book, and (b) an outline for a theme, a report, or other presentation which is to come into being as the outline is expanded and filled in. In other words, one is *devised from* the finished product, while the other *develops into* the finished product. One outlines what someone else has already constructed. The other outlines what your mind is in the process of constructing.

Outlining What Someone Else Has Constructed

Your outline of another person's presentation can be only as complete, unified, and logical as the original author permits it to be. If you are working from written copy, you should have time to study the document until some conception of the author's intent becomes clear to you. Ask yourself some questions about the material:

Does it seem to have natural or logical parts?

Does it seem to have been written from a careful outline, or does it seem to come "off the top of the writer's head"?

Is there a single statement which seems to express a *central idea* which all the other statements seem to support?

Are there any noticeable parallels, either in divisions of subject matter, content, or language patterns?

How does the composition *form* suggest divisions? Why are the paragraphs separated as they are? Is the presentation formally divided in some other way, as with Sections I, II, . . . , or with asterisks or other marks of division?

What transitional words, phrases, sentences, or paragraphs can you find ("moreover, . . ." "on the other hand, . . .")? What aspects of the larger subject do they seek to interrelate?

With a document to study in detail, you should be able to construct a useful outline after answering the above questions and other questions of structure which the material suggests. From such an outline you can later summarize the material, report upon it, or even reconstruct it, in case the original document is no longer available.

The task of making an outline of another person's presentation is much more difficult when you do not have access to a printed document, but are required to get your information by listening to an address, a lecture, or some similar pronouncement.

If the presentation is carefully constructed to make a logical appeal to its hearers, the speaker may offer various *signals* which will suggest a structural pattern or outline which his minor points will support. Among other things, these signals might include:

A title which foreshadows what is to come in the talk

A title and an announced subject, wherein the title focuses attention on a portion of the broader subject so directly that the direction of development can easily be anticipated

A leading question addressed to you, the listener, dramatically posed (the anticipated answer to the question providing an unstated central idea)

Repetition or some other dramatic device which, through emphasis, may help distinguish major from minor points

A statement in the opening remarks which indicates the principal areas to be covered in the pronouncements to follow: "Our attention must go to the *four* main parts of this subject . . ." "Let us consider these *three* ways in which. . . ." "Only by asking ourselves the following questions can we . . . ."

With any of the structural signals above, or with similar previews of what is to come in the spoken presentation, you can then jot down noteworthy expressions as they are uttered, entering them where they will fit into the larger structure which the signals indicated.

When no structural pattern is signaled, it may be necessary to note, at random, as much detail as possible, later collecting and organizing the notes into a logical outline. With no indication of the direction the remarks will take, it will be difficult to know which details are important and which relatively unimportant. You can record only so much information and then (1) look for ways several bits of material may be grouped to make some larger unity – which, if found, may help you to make similar groupings of other random notes; (2) look for parallels in the content or structure of individual statements which would help set up points for division and interrelationship; (3) look for structural clues in the concluding statements which might help you arrange and relate the earlier notes to each other and to the whole.

Outlining as a Prelude to Writing a Theme

Since the emphasis of this text is on the craft of written composition, your main concern is with outlines through which you will commit your thoughts to the influence of logic in order to draw up an outline for the theme you will write.

Random Association. It is sometimes possible to develop an outline for a theme by beginning with the process known as random association. The principal usefulness of this approach may be found when you are to write on an assigned topic, to which you have given little previous thought. The procedure is simply to list whatever associations come to mind about the subject. After a number of these random entries have been made, you will probably discover some pattern, which you may then develop more consciously. For example, consider the subject "Coffee."

You may be reminded of:

> The smell of coffee as it is being ground
> Instant coffee
> Caffeine
> Coffee beans
> Percolators
> Things people put in coffee
> Iced drinks
> Price of a pound of coffee

From studying your list, you may find its entries might prompt these additions:

The smell of brewing coffee
Brewed (not instant) coffee
"Caffeine free" coffee
Coffee growing
Ways coffee can be served
Fluctuation of bulk price of coffee
Coffee as an imported commodity
Coffee prices in restaurants

By now you can clearly see far more aspects of the subject than you could possibly cover in a short theme, so you begin to look for promising *groups* of items, while you ignore less promising entries. You decide to concentrate on these:

The smell of coffee as it is being ground
The smell of brewing coffee
Ways coffee can be served

Thinking about these ideas leads to the beginning of an outline:

I. Ways coffee can be served
   A. Different brewing methods
      1. Percolator coffee (regular ground coffee)
      2. Boiled coffee
      3. Instant coffee
   B. Other variations in the serving of coffee
      1. Temperatures and strengths at which it is served
      2. What people like to put in their coffee
II. The pleasing aroma coffee has for some people
   A. The smell of coffee being ground in the store
   B. The smell of coffee as it is brewing

By this time, it may strike you as appropriate to direct your theme toward "The Usefulness of Coffee," or perhaps "What I Like about Coffee." Having chosen this line of attack, you will soon discover that at least one and perhaps two or more main entries are needed. From now on, it should be clear to you what items you may be able to salvage from your original lists, which items must be discarded, and what entries must be devised to accommodate essential information which your growing outline and the theme to follow clearly demand.

Exercise 6   *Develop the outline which you have just begun, adding entries at any level in the structure until you feel some completeness and unity have been achieved. At your teacher's discretion, develop your finished outline into a short theme.*

Outlining According to Logical Divisions. When your purpose is to convey factual information, you may be able to review several ways a subject might be broken down; then choose one of these patterns and develop an outline from it.

Suppose you are assigned a theme on our astronauts. You might:

Outline the qualifications and training required
Develop an outline based on the story of an astronaut
Consider what a high school student might do to fit himself for becoming an astronaut
Consider the value of an astronaut's work

Exercise 7   *Choose one of the subject breakdowns listed, making further logical subdivisions of the material as appropriate.*

Developing an Outline from a Central Idea. A third method of developing an outline for a theme involves directing the whole structural pattern toward one statement, the truth, validity, or significance of which seems to override all other considerations. This approach can be combined with the methods of outlining already discussed, as well as the one to follow.

When you are writing on a subject with which you have had actual experience, or have had time to read and reflect, it is likely that you already have formulated some general attitudes. If not, then you may be able to draw up some generalizations. From these generalizations, you may then choose one – the one you feel most strongly about, or the one you feel most needs to be promoted. This becomes your central idea. It will, by its nature, be *general,* and therefore not a matter of absolute fact, no matter how widely the idea is accepted. Your task will be to support the central idea, and your outline should be directed to that purpose. Consider the following generalizations:

Candy is good.   War is costly.   Babies are cute.   Home is happy.

Your first impulse might be to say these statements are *facts.* If you feel that way, ask yourself what you mean by *good, costly, cute,* and *happy.* Isn't it likely that these statements look like facts because you presume almost everyone would agree? What is the good of developing a statement which you have reason to suspect is overwhelmingly agreed upon to begin with? You might better choose as your significant generalization something readers will not agree with automatically.

Having hit upon a central idea which will direct the development of the outline, you may continue to develop the subject along the lines of the methods already discussed. As you go, you should consider carefully what to put in or leave out. In other words, "Does this new entry advance or support the central idea?"

Exercise 8

A. *Formulate a significant statement of attitude toward each of these subjects:*

> Accelerated classes in my high school
> Study halls in my high school
> Minor sports in my high school
> Cooperation between the upper and lower grades in my high school
> Scholastic achievement incentives in my high school

B. *Make an outline for developing one of your* central ideas.

Developing an Outline by Anticipating Questions. Another useful method of organizing one's thoughts on a subject involves posing questions which the finished theme will answer. You have no experience with a subject. You may have only hazy bits of knowledge — and your curiosity. Yet, by combining these two things, you may construct an exploration map by which you can come into knowledge of the subject at hand with a minimum of wasted effort.

Let us say that you overhear someone talking about a band of hardy people who formerly lived a strange, isolated life on a tiny, out-of-the-way island. Then a volcano began to erupt, and they were forced out into the more civilized world, against their will. Now, the volcano has stopped its rumbling, and islanders are going back to resume their lonely existence.

Suddenly, your imagination is caught by this overheard crumb of information. Where is this island? Who are these people? Do they really like to live that way? How big is the island? Can you go to live there if you wish? What will the people do if that volcano erupts again?

This is what can happen when curiosity is aroused. Handle it with care. You might learn something before you have stopped wondering. You might learn so painlessly you will actually enjoy the process.

The question approach works well as a guide to your own learning. It can be converted to acting as a guide to your readers, too. In your own case, the questions rise naturally out of your own curiosity. When you want to use the question method to develop an outline, you should forget, temporarily, what you know. Pretend you are standing in the dark looking for the light. What questions would be crossing your mind, if you were just embarking upon this subject? What would puzzle you about the subject? What would you most want to find out? From this point of view you should be able to formulate a meaningful list of questions.

Once a list of questions is before you, you may decide to cut out some of the less important questions, clarify questions that are vague or confusing, and combine two or more questions into one.

Finally, you should arrange the questions. Some may be appropriate as subheads under more significant entries. Others may have to be added, at this time, to complete the subdivisions. Deciding upon the order to be followed often presents a challenge. Two choices of pattern come immediately to mind. (1) *You may wish to arrange the questions in about the order they might arise in a person's mind.* This will vary from person to person, of course, but you might try to anticipate what would first capture the imagination. Would he want to know simple things first, or would he prefer to begin with general information? (2) *You may wish to arrange the questions in order of the significance of the information.* It will be your decision, then, whether to move from less significant to more significant information, or from more significant information to less significant.

Exercise 9

A. *To the lists of questions below, make any additions you feel are needed; then arrange the questions into outline form, showing subdivisions of the main divisions.*

1. Surfboard Riders
   What does a surfer do, anyway?
   Do surfers always wear regular swimming gear?
   Is surfing an expensive pastime?
   What is it like, standing up on that thing?
   Why can't they use words other people use?
   Do all surfers actually ride those boards?
   Did I see a surfer wearing cutoff blue jeans?
   Are there safe and easy ways to ride a surfboard?

2. Banquet Honoring the School Football Team
   What happens at a football banquet?
   Who is entitled to go, besides football players?
   What is a minister supposed to do there?
   What food is usually served?
   Are there speeches?
   What did last year's guest of honor mean when he re-
       ferred to the "rubber-chicken circuit"?
   Do the players have to say anything?
   Do they announce anything about next year's team?
   If there are speeches, do they come during the meal?
   Do you have to be self-conscious about table manners?
   Can you expect to get any dessert?
   Is there any choice about what you have to eat?
   Do they award the trophies at that time?
   What is the subject of conversation at the tables?
   Is the guest of honor always an athlete?
   What will he talk about?

B. *Develop a list of questions for the following subjects and arrange the questions in logical order. Translate the questions into either sentences or topics, so that your finished product is either a topic outline or a sentence outline.*

Square Dancing American Jazz Musicians
Summer Jobs Applying for Scholarships

Exercise 10   *Outline the brief essay which follows; then compare your results with those of your classmates. If several of you have made about the same divisions and subdivisions of the material, the logic of your approach will have had support. If the outlines differ widely in form, compare them to see which ones give an accurate summary of the sample material.*

The Deceptive Desert

Newspaper records will attest to the fact that motorists in the southwestern United States occasionally find themselves in danger on the desert. Sometimes the travelers are stranded through unavoidable circumstances, but more often their difficulty is caused by oversight or poor judgment. Each summer brings its tragedies.

Having your car stall on an unused desert road is a frightening prospect which anyone might wish to avoid. Unless certain precautions are taken, an automobile trip into the desert may end in just such a misfortune.

The dependability of his vehicle should be the desert explorer's most vital concern; it is one thing to *drive* the desert—and quite another to be forced to *walk* it. The mechanical condition of the equipment should be checked by a competent mechanic. Gas, water, and oil should be checked. Water for the radiator should be available to replace what might boil away in the high desert temperature—or in an engine laboring in sand.

Provisions for the travelers are also an important precaution. While some nonperishable food may be carried for emergencies, drinking water is the prime concern. The margin of safety lies in stocking much more water than is likely to be needed under normal conditions. For obvious reasons, it might be well to carry this water in a number of unbreakable containers.

Once provisions are secured, the desert motorist's safety may depend upon how he uses his head. Any good driver who keeps to main highways and uses reasonable judgment may enjoy the desert in reasonable safety. For the explorer, however, there is no substitute for knowledge of the country in general. He will need to be aware of the great daily range in temperature on the desert.

The experienced desert driver respects the midday heat of summer days. Knowing how rapidly the human system dehydrates under the extreme conditions of the desert, he adjusts his activities accordingly. He is not fooled into thinking distant mountains are "right out there," nor is he unaware that sudden storms make boiling, silt-laden torrents thunder down through "dry" desert washes. Even though he knows the country, generally, he will have a map of unfamiliar areas.

On main highways where service areas and other sources of assistance are usually available, one may overlook many of these tips for desert drivers. As one ventures farther from civilization, however, these precautions become more appropriate. Two final bits of advice may be especially offered: (1) Never leave a well-traveled road for a less-traveled road without knowing its condition or where it leads. Many such roads may look promising from the highway, but yet they may dwindle into a confusion of tire tracks or disappear entirely, somewhere in the desert. (2) Be sure that some competent person knows where you are going and when you expect to return, so that authorities may be alerted after a reasonable time beyond your anticipated return.

The desert offers great beauty, solitude, and the promise of adventure to those who come to it. These rewards need not be diminished by the steps one takes to insure his safety. On the contrary, the challenge of the desert can be faced most enthusiastically by the person who knows what he faces and is prepared for it.

SUMMING UP

Skillful outlining is a valuable aid, either in studying what someone else has constructed or in planning what you wish to construct. In this chapter you have considered the basic pattern of the conventional outline, noting that parallel entries should be parallel in structure.

You have considered the importance of outlining before starting to write a theme and have suggested techniques for developing the outline: from random association with a certain idea, outlining according to logical divisions, developing an outline from a central idea, developing an outline by anticipating questions.

As you continue working with outlines, you will discover that thinking in outline form increases your ability to think logically, to remember more of what you read or hear, and to write more clearly and effectively.

Chapter 4

Description
and
Narration

**A Look
Back
and
A Look
Forward**

In a sense, you might think of your work in the preceding chapters as the preparation an artist makes before he begins to paint a picture. He builds up his supply of materials, learns how to use his paints and brushes, and tries out his ideas in various ways as he makes preliminary sketches. When he has produced a sketch in which he sees definite possibilities, he refines it and begins to paint.

The type of writing you will have an opportunity to do as you study description and narration will bring into full use your command of words, your skill in handling sentences, and your ability to make an outline. The special quality that now is added is the power of your imagination. You must see, in your mind's eye, the scene you are describing; or live out, in your imagination, the story you wish to tell. It is at this point that writing becomes a creative experience.

WHY DO YOU WRITE?

In this chapter and the next, you will consider written composition as divided into four rather arbitrary categories: description, narration, exposition, and argumentation. Two of these categories have been treated together in this chapter, "Description and Narration," and the others in Chapter 5, "Exposition and Argumentation."

There is a logical reason for making these divisions; it will be obvious if you think about what people write and why they write it.

Here are some of the things that are probably being written at this moment:

> Grocery lists
> Laundry slips
> Parking tickets
> Notes for the milkman
> Friendly letters
> More friendly (love) letters
> Proposals of marriage
> Textbooks
> Magazine stories
> Bills for legislation
> Memorandums
> Applications for jobs
> Summonses to appear in court
> Word pictures of mountains
> Written records of surgery
> Reasons you should vote for one candidate
> Reasons you should not vote for another candidate
> Written records of trips to the San Diego Zoo
> Word pictures of mountains for gasoline ads
> Accounts of how electric lights work
> Explanations of the game of baseball

Suppose the authors of a composition text decided to devote a whole chapter to each of the things you, and others who study their book, may write. Do you think seven thousand chapters would be enough—give or take a few thousand?

Instead, let's bundle together some of these jobs of writing which are most alike. It will save having to repeat so much. You should, however, look for patterns to use in grouping the different pieces of writing. You might group them by *subject*: love, electricity, baseball, gasoline, mountains. Clearly, this is no great help because the number of possible subjects is almost endless.

Searching for other patterns, you might list a pair of these writings and try to point out their most noticeable differences. Two that seem widely dissimilar are: (a) explanations of the game of baseball and (b) magazine stories.

How do they differ? You might call (a) *factual* and (b) *fictional.* Some persons might call (a) *practical,* on the grounds that "you could learn something," and (b) *impractical,* on the grounds that "you will read a made-up story."

Suppose you said (a) was *useful* because it could do something for you — namely, teach you about baseball. Does it necessarily follow that (b) is *useless?* Suppose I care nothing for baseball, but like stories. Then, as far as I am concerned, (b) is useful because I enjoy the story, while (a) is useless because I am indifferent when it comes to playing baseball; (b) does something for me, while (a) does nothing for me.

I may *learn* little from my story, but I wouldn't be *entertained* by your explanation of baseball. We seem to be at odds because I want to be entertained by stories and you want to learn something.

Entertainment versus Information

Perhaps the different kinds of writing can be sorted out by using, as the distinguishing factor, "entertainment or information?" In one list will go writings which seem to be aimed more at enjoyment; in the other, writings aimed at telling you something you want to know — or something someone wants you to know.

Writing that entertains:

> Friendly letters (with little information)
> Love letters
> Word pictures of mountains
> Records of trips to the San Diego Zoo
> Magazine stories

Writing that informs:

> Grocery lists
> Laundry slips
> Parking tickets
> Notes for the milkman
> Textbooks
> Bills for legislation
> Memorandums
> Applications for jobs
> Summonses to appear in court
> Reasons you should vote for one candidate
> Reasons you should not vote for another candidate
> Accounts of how electric lights work
> Explanations of the game of baseball

The items fall rather easily into the two lists above, but what is to be done when it is necessary to classify a piece of writing which both entertains and enlightens?

If you think about the *story* of the hare and the tortoise, you recall that a few words of advice are tacked to the story. In which list does a fable belong?

Since you are separating items according to *purpose*, you might decide what the main, or primary, purpose of the hare-and-tortoise story is. Because an essential part of a fable is the tacked-on lesson, you could classify it with those writings aimed at informing.

In this light, consider the remaining items in the original list:

> Proposals of marriage
> Written records of surgery
> Word pictures of mountains for gasoline ads

There is no doubt that a written proposal of marriage might be an entertaining document, but the proposal it contains is its primary purpose. It gives the letter a functional quality that puts it into our second category. The word picture of mountains for a gasoline ad has assumed a primary purpose that also goes beyond the entertainment of the reader. While the records of surgery might resemble stories, their primary purpose is not to entertain medical students but to save lives.

You now have a major division of kinds of writing—if you recognize overlapping in borderline cases and classify such writing by primary purpose. For the sake of simplicity, assume that:

> The aim of one kind of writing is to enlighten—the other, to entertain.
> One type might change your mind—the other your sentiments.
> One type might appeal to your reason—the other to your emotions.
> The approach used in one type of writing might be largely intellectual,
> —the other imaginative.

On this basis let's proceed to the discussion of the ways one may write for each of these two purposes.

Exercise 1   *List twenty pieces of written composition you have encountered in the last few days or weeks. If necessary, confine yourself to a paragraph or some other fragment of a longer work and consider it an item in itself. Following the division just completed, write "Int." before items which clearly appeal most strongly to the* intellect *and "Imag." before items that appeal most strongly to the* imagination. *Where both appeals are present, as when an anecdote is used to illustrate an intellectual discussion, or when a word picture is used to influence your choice of products, mark the item "Border-line," and follow with "Int." or "Imag." depending upon whether you think the primary purpose was (a) to change your way of thinking or acting, or (b) to entertain you.*

Recreating Scenes and Events That Appeal to the Imagination

What stirs your imagination? The sound of a train in the distance at night? a view of the Grand Canyon? the aroma of good food cooking? an exciting experience?

The lonesome sound of the train from far away might make you wonder how locomotives work, or how sound travels, or what causes a lonely feeling. These are by-products of the initial experience. What caught your attention was the appeal to your feelings and to your imagination.

Consider for a moment ways to use words to recreate the scenes that capture your imagination, and to recreate the sequence of happenings that resulted in an unforgettable experience. When you use words to make pictures, you are using *description*. When you use words to relate stories, or sequences of events, you are using *narration*.

Perhaps this distinction will be clearer if you think of a reel of motion-picture film. If you look at one frame, you see a picture, a single scene; if you set the film in motion in the projector, the individual frames blur into what appears to be a sequence of moving pictures. This is the way to consider the two general approaches to capturing imagination through composition. If your words bring into focus a single impression, or a few closely related impressions in a single scene, you will see it as description. When numerous impressions are created and the impressions are presented in sequence, you will see it as narration. It is easy to distinguish these two kinds of writing if you think of the motion-picture film: Stopped—a picture; in motion—a story.

DESCRIPTION

Since the making of a single picture precedes the completed film, you might begin with descriptive writing. Look first for the single impression, or for the few closely related impressions that make up a single scene.

Start with a brief word picture of some common object. Write a description entitled "Desk."

A desk is a thing on which you write, study, and sometimes sleep. It is usually made of wood and metal with plastic or linoleum for the top. Some desks . . . .

Hold it! You have taken a wrong turn at the crossroads. You are attempting to define and explain "desks." That is an appeal to the intellect, rather than to the imagination, of your reader. Your job is to make a word picture. You cannot make *one* picture of all the desks in the world. If you try to do so, the resulting picture will be a monstrosity.

You may think of many desks at once, but the result is an idea, not a picture. You may have an idea of all the desks in the world rolled into one, but such a combination does not really exist in our world of seeing, feeling, touching, tasting, and smelling.

Now begin again. Use "This Desk" as a title, so you will not get mixed up with things you cannot see or feel.

This Desk

This desk has a green linoleum top and sturdy steel legs. The working surface is two feet by three feet, in a horizontal plane thirty inches above the floor. The legs curve outward, leaving no obstructions along the front. Around the mint-green top is a one-inch strip of unpainted aluminum. A single, narrow metal drawer is recessed under the front edge. No drawer handle is visible; only a lock face interrupts the glossy green surface of the drawer front.

If you wish, you may be less objective when you write descriptions. You may become more personal and bring the feelings of the describer into the word picture.

My Desk

My desk is a slab of linoleum-covered surface, supported by three sturdy, steel legs. The fourth leg is present, but since it is an eighth of an inch shorter than the others, it touches the floor only when it produces a nerve-shattering, thumping sound. The working surface is mint-green, and glossy enough to reflect the rays of the nearest lamp into my eyes. There is a drawer, but unfortunately, it is locked, and I do not know where the key can be found.

Although the second picture of the desk has sacrificed some precision of detail, perhaps you found that it gained in imaginative appeal because it brought the human element into the picture.

Word pictures, like other pictorial representations such as paintings or photographs, must be seen or imagined by a viewer before they are produced. With paintings, and sometimes with photographs, you can speculate about the personality of the painter or photographer by studying the picture for signs of the maker's individualities. Similarly, the maker of word pictures may inject into his description some of his own personality — likes, dislikes, feelings, judgments.

Study these descriptions of the same scene. What does the second version tell you about the writer that is not clearly shown in the first version?

IMPERSONAL DESCRIPTION

From Flintlock Hill one could look south across a rocky, sloping pasture, to the rye fields. Hereford cattle browsed on the slope, all headed in the same general direction. At the foot of the hill, a low stone wall divided the grass from the rye. Parallel to the wall, a narrow wagon road separated the two fields of grain. The rye was beginning to turn from green to yellow. Behind it glossy-leaved cottonwoods formed a dark green border. The heads of the rye bent as the breeze touched them here and there. Sunlight followed the breeze, brushing with gold the crests of shimmering waves that flowed endlessly across the fields.

MORE PERSONAL VERSION

Standing on the summit of Flintlock Hill, we could look southward across McDowell's pasture slope to the Bannon's rye fields and the cottonwood trees beyond. We knew the Little Swan River ran back of the trees, but we couldn't see it from the hilltop, except for one shiny patch of water a mile downstream, at Hardings' Crossing.

The McDowell herd of Herefords was grazing its way across the slope between us and the stone wall that separated the pasture from the rye. The first grain field sloped gently down to the wagon road that set it apart from the second.

We used to run through the fields to the river—downhill through the pasture, then a scramble over the stone wall, leaving the Hereford bull surprised and out-maneuvered. For a minute we were tempted to do the same again, but we restrained our impulse.

The rye fields danced in the sun and wind, their shifting surfaces catching the sun—now here, now there. They reminded us of the waves of a magic ocean that had somehow been transported hundreds of miles inland to flow between Flintlock Hill and the cottonwoods along Little Swan River.

Exercise 2

A. *Select one of the topics listed below and write two brief descriptions, one impersonal, the other personal.*

In the impersonal description, be as scientifically precise as you can. Confine yourself largely to the physical nature of the subject. Use terms, measurements, and standards of judgments with which you believe most of your classmates would agree. Try to create a description from which another person could draw a reasonably accurate sketch. In the more personal description, inject as much of your own personality and individuality into your word picture as is required to illustrate your relationship with the subject. Emphasize the "to-me" quality of your reaction to the subject. Worry less about external measurements, and more about internal reactions. What feelings does it evoke inside you? Do not try to avoid personal judgments.

In each description confine yourself to a single subject (not "Rats," but "Our White Rat, Edgar"). Remember that this description is to create a single impression, or a few closely related impressions which make up a single scene.

The Family Pet
My Favorite Chair
Our Family Car
A Dish of My Favorite Food
A Dish of Food I Dislike
The Classroom That Affects Me Most Strongly
The Most Desirable House on Our Street
The Least Desirable House on Our Street

B. *Study the mail-order catalog description below, or bring to class a comparable catalog entry describing an item you would like to own. After committing all the key details to memory, pretend that you have acquired the item and are writing a letter to a friend in which you will describe the item and your feeling about having it. In your letter speak in friendly, informal terms. Include as much of the factual detail as you wish, but try to make your word picture personal, colorful, and enthusiastic.*

JUNIOR UMBRELLA TENT

- Long-wearing
- No inside poles to rub against fabric
- Outside frame sets up fast; keeps fabric taut without guy ropes
- Nylon screen door and rear window give breezy two-way ventilation
- Double-duty awning ties to door for protection in stormy weather
- Packs in a jiffy into compact carrying case

Stands up on its own. Strong frame of seasoned wood with rust-resistant aluminum joints. Water-repellent, 6.74-oz. drill top and sides; mildew-resistant 5.61-oz. drill floor. 7-ft. sq. base — Sleeps two. 5½ ft. center height.

Color: forest green
Shipping weight: 23 lbs. $23.79
6A7406

Appeals to the Senses. Description has been treated largely in terms of pictures, and will probably continue to be for the sake of simplicity. However, it should be noted that the imagination can be appealed to through all the senses: seeing, hearing, touching, tasting, and smelling.

Sight

Down the dusty road, into the yellow sunset, trudged the bearded man in the flapping Army overcoat.

Sound

The land gave forth a murmur of evening sounds. At the thud of his foot-steps, a lizard rattled off to hide in the sand along the roadside. Crickets plucked untiringly at their one-tone fiddles.

Touch

In his gnarled hand he rolled a river pebble over and over, feeling the smooth surface and its lopsided shape. He could still sense a trace of the coolness of the river bottom where he had found the pebble and lifted it through the swift current.

Taste

As he walked, he thought of the succulent pheasant, sharp with seasonings, that his wife had been preparing when he left the house.

Smell

Now as he approached the doorway of his cabin, he sniffed the air and smiled. Mingled with the scent of roasting fowl was that of fresh bread.

Appeals to the senses through written composition are indirect appeals. As the eye distinguishes marks on a page, the reader is expected to create in his imagination certain sights, sounds, feelings, tastes, or smells that have been described in words. Descriptions involving appeals to the senses can be *external*, dealing with outward appearances; or they may be *internal*, dealing with the emotional reaction of the writer.

How It Looks — How You Feel

Probably the two most common ways of going about constructing a description are through the use of (a) the *spatial approach* and (b) the *dominant impression*. You have already used these approaches in Exercise 2, when you wrote an impersonal description and one of a more personal nature. The distinction will be reinforced here.

The Spatial Approach. Since impersonal physical description deals with objects in relation to the space they occupy, this type of writing is called the *spatial approach*. External characteristics are likely to be stressed: the size and shape of the subject, its length, width, and height, and its location in relation to other objects. These are the details a police officer's description of an accident scene might contain. It is the map maker's approach to his work. It should be the approach of a person who is giving you travel directions, unless he wants you to get lost.

It is important in the spatial approach that the reader be aware at all times of the direction and focus of attention. You should not describe the roof of a car in one sentence and the drive shaft in the next without redirecting the reader's attention. It is a good plan to follow some definite order in your description, and to keep the reader aware of the plan of progression. To follow such a pattern, you might present details as they fit into a certain pattern: from head to foot or foot to head, top to bottom or bottom to top, right to left or left to right, front to back or back to front, clockwise or counterclockwise, near to far or far to near.

The Dominant Impression. To transmit to the reader some vivid impression, the writer must build his description around a central impression which the writer feels is the key to the experience. The *dominant impression approach* is necessarily personal. After the dominant impression has been singled out, all other detail is selected and brought to focus upon that point.

Exercise 3

A. *Indicate which of the passages below are primarily spatial in their approach and which focus upon a dominant impression. Write sentences to explain your choice in each case.*

B. *Select a comparable subject from your own experience. Write one description in which you use the spatial approach. Write another in which you use the dominant impression.*

1. The inside of our car is like the inside of a vacuum-cleaner bag. The dust of a hundred streets has settled in its crevices. Chewing-gum wrappers peek out of every corner, and the ashtrays overflow with everything but ashes. Stubs of pencils, bits of string, ticket stubs, empty matchbooks—all contribute to this litterbag-on-wheels.

2. The flour mill occupies the entire 400 block between Culver Street and Grand Avenue, towering over the single-story buildings which surround it on all sides. Beside its four cylindrical concrete storage tanks is the mill annex, a square five-story building in whose shadow the trucks wait their turns to unload wheat.

3. He was about the saddest-looking dog I ever expect to see. What had been a glossy brown coat was battleship gray, except where it seemed to have been plastered down with used crankcase oil. His underside was a mat of burrs which he tried unsuccessfully to bite loose. When he glanced up, it was with an utterly shamefaced look.

4. To the left of the door in the nine-by-twelve rectangle, which the school has designated as my room, stands a six-foot wardrobe. It smothers that wall and takes three feet of the adjacent wall to boot. What is left of the long wall is given to a lamp and my bed—its foot near the wardrobe. There is a window in the other long wall near the door, and beyond that a chest of drawers. With scarcely an inch to spare, my desk in the corner claims the remaining wall space in my close quarters.

Observing and Selecting Detail

You cannot picture to others what you do not see or imagine. Describing begins with the ability to make careful observations. How much significant detail do you allow your senses to take in? How well can you express to others what you feel? You can test these abilities by comparing notes with some of your friends. After brief exposure to a certain sight, sound, or taste, discuss with your friends what each one has recorded in his senses.

Try to describe all you can see, feel, taste, touch, and smell about some very uncomplicated object placed before you, such as a leaf, a grape, or a walnut. If you run out of things to say before you have filled two or three pages, you probably need more practice in observation.

In any written description, some details will be more important than others. After making the observations, your next problem will be selecting those details which will give the picture you wish to convey. If the approach is spatial, details conveying basic size and shape might be most significant. In the dominant impression method, the principal impression is announced first. Other details are selected as they will best reinforce that basic impression.

Exercise 4   *List the specific actions, gestures, movements that a pre-selected classmate makes from the time he enters the classroom until he sits down at his desk. Notice especially the movements of his head, feet, and hands. Generalize about the way the person entered the room on this occasion; then arrange the items on the list in order of their importance to the dominant impression.*

Descriptive Language

In general, words which name things may evoke the mental picture, or image, of that which they name. The more specific or precise the term is, the clearer the word picture it can create. Compare the type of pictures brought to mind by general and specific terms.

General	Specific
Bell	The Liberty Bell in Philadelphia
Wagon	A child's red wagon
Apple	A Jonathan apple
Bird	A red-winged blackbird

Although figures of speech should be used with caution, they are sometimes helpful in appealing to the reader's imagination. Such expressions usually state or imply a comparison between the unknown object being described and something with which the reader would almost certainly be familiar.

His shoes dug up the flower bed like miniature plows.

Figurative expressions describe, not in terms of what could or does happen, but in terms of what might be imagined to happen. They suggest similarity, on one point of comparison, between things basically dissimilar in literal contexts.

The island had wrapped itself in a cloak of filmy azure.

The ice had frozen smooth; there were three miles of glass between Sand Point and Bell's Landing.

Exercise 5

A. *Suggest ten words that express a vivid impression gained from sight; from hearing; from taste; from touch; from smell.*

B. *Write figurative expressions which might convey, imaginatively, the impressions suggested below.*

the way a very old man might walk
the sound an army tank might make approaching by way of a dry stream bed
the way a cool drink of water might taste to a person just rescued after being lost in the desert
the feel of an icy swim in a mountain pool on a hot day

Try the New, but Say It Clearly

You have been considering techniques that can help you write a good description. You must remember, however, that you can spoil your otherwise good efforts, just by being lazy. You can make your writing far more interesting if you take the time and effort to find ways of expressing your thoughts in some manner that hasn't been used thousands of times before. Also, the trouble it takes to find exactly the right word to make your meaning clear can save you the embarrassment of being misunderstood. Try to avoid the common writing faults discussed below.

Gushing. "The Grand Canyon is indescribable," a student wrote — but she went on to describe it anyway. The words *indescribable, beautiful, glorious, stunning,* and *awe-inspiring* have little, if any, picture-making ability beyond suggesting the reaction or the state of mind of the writer. They have only limited use in personal descriptions, where writers' impressions are basic, and no place whatever in impersonal, or objective, descriptions. One would do better to picture the scene to his reader and allow the reader to make the judgment about its beauty. What is awe-inspiring to one person may seem commonplace to another.

Triteness. If you can finish an expression which another person starts just as he would have finished it, the expression is probably trite and overtired. Such is the case with the worn-out clichés "blind as a bat," "strong as an ox," "happy as a lark."

You can invent your own comparatives: "wet as a tea-taster's mustache," "quick as a lizard's lick," "cold as a gravy sandwich." However, you will probably be more successful in making word pictures if you will get down the specific details that show *how wet, how quick,* or *how cold* the person was.

Was water sloshing and squishing in his shoes, while he left a trail of water across the tiled floor? He was wet, indeed! Could he switch one card for another in a card trick so quickly your eye could not catch the movement? Were his teeth chattering? Was he unable to button his coat because his fingers were too stiff? Did he feel his face stinging when he came indoors?

Specific details will help paint the picture clearly in a reader's mind. You do not have to tell him something is beautiful, or cold, or amusing; you can furnish the details which will show him these things.

Vagueness. Words can convey only a limited amount of information from the writer's mind to the reader's.

After you have written a descriptive passage, read it and imagine yourself in a reader's shoes. How complete would your mental image of the subject be if you had only the information which has been offered? If you doubt its effectiveness, look for ways to (a) substitute precise words for vague words, (b) clarify difficult phrases, or (c) add comparisons to strengthen the sense impressions created by the description.

Character Sketches

The techniques discussed so far in this chapter may be illustrated in descriptions of persons. These descriptions are commonly called character sketches. A review of the descriptive process shows how each technique discussed may be used in writing character sketches.

RELATIVELY IMPERSONAL

Howard Jones is thirty-three years old, six feet tall, and weighs one hundred eighty pounds. He is married and has two children, William, four, and Valerie, two. Mr. Jones is employed by the Farmdale Wickwire Company, where he has worked for seven years. Prior to his work at Farmdale, Jones attended Massachusetts Institute of Technology for five years.

RELATIVELY PERSONAL

Howie Jones is a handsome six-footer of a trim one hundred eighty pounds, who lives near us in Farmdale. He has an important job with the Wickwire

Company. In the seven years since his graduation from M.I.T. he has stayed with one job, getting good raises. He and his wife, Irma, are making a fine home for Billy, a rough, tough four-year-old and Valerie, a sweetheart of two.

EXTERNAL

Wayne is five feet seven and weighs one hundred thirty-five pounds. He has brown eyes and medium brown hair—crew cut. His chin bears a marked cleft, lighter than his otherwise ruddy complexion.

INTERNAL

It is doubtful that Wayne ever told a lie. If confronted with an embarrassing question, he may blush and stammer; but when he finally speaks up, it is always with the truth. He has never been know to go back on his promises.

SPATIAL

Beneath a black derby, a shock of Walter's red hair stood out like a clown's wig. His eyes were watery and his nose sunburned. A faded blue shirt, with a collar too tight for his muscular neck, was tucked into equally faded denim jeans. He was broad of shoulder, narrow of hip, and he walked with an easy, loping stride.

DOMINANT IMPRESSION

Leroy B. was a slight mouse of a man—thin, short, and prematurely gray. Though he seldom spoke above a high-pitched whisper, he never ceased apologizing for being born. If he was early, he apologized for being early; if late, he apologized for his tardiness.

Exercise 6   *Write character sketches about three persons of your acquaintance. In each case emphasize one of the descriptive techniques just illustrated.*

NARRATION

You live in a world that is constantly in motion. The earth turns on its axis while it moves around the sun—which is moving in our galaxy—which moves among other galaxies. Your heart beats. Your breath is taken in and let out. While all these things are in progress, an uncountable number of other motions occur. Let us say that any one of these movements may be considered an event, and that telling the story of any meaningful sequence of events is a *narrative*. This reciting of events is called *narration*. A good story or narrative brings the reader the opportunity to be entertained by experiencing vicariously what the writer may have experienced. In addition, a narrative appeals to curiosity. It answers the question you want to have answered as you read: "What happened?" The narrative may tell you what *did* happen, what *might have* happened, or what *might be only imagined.*

A Selected Sequence of Events

Imagine that a flooding river last night washed away a bridge near your home. When did the event have its beginning? Was it when the bridge struck the water, after a great grinding break from its foundation? Was it the first straining protest from the bridge timbers, or the gentle creaking of timbers in the slowly rising current? Was it the rain falling in the mountains?

Is it possible that all of these actions, and numberless others, are part of the story? Is there any certainty when any series of events began, or when it will end?

List all the actions in which you have participated within the last sixty seconds.

> You looked at this page.
> You scratched your nose.
> You watched a student leave the room.

Are you sure these are all the actions in which you participated? When you looked at this page, did you not incline your head, open your eyelids, focus your eyes, move your eyes to follow the words, blink your eyes?

Why not admit the possibility that no narrative written by man ever told the *whole* story but, instead, focused upon a selected sequence of events. Once you have accepted this assumption, you can stop worrying about whether you are including all the details and relating everything that happened. Instead concentrate on:

> deciding which events to include
> deciding the order of events
> relating the teller to the action
> deciding which event to relate first and which to relate last

Which Events to Include

Study this sample narrative:

> We eased the tired Chevy gingerly back onto the highway and headed west, expecting calamity at every cough of the wheezing engine. Clarence was reading Plato that day. Meanwhile, Harvey couldn't pass up a soft-drink sign. Each time the engine gave a shudder, Sam and I leaned forward as if to keep the car moving by the force of our own momentum. We found New Mexico drier than Texas had been. We stopped twice for gas before

lunch, once where the city gasoline tax was very high, and once where there was no city tax at all. Sam whistled nervously from time to time and mentally, half-audibly, overhauled the carburetor at least seven times before we limped across the Continental Divide. A new carburetor would cost over twenty dollars. Toward evening our fears were realized. On a long, sloping grade among the extinct volcanoes of eastern Arizona, the Chevy sputtered twice and jerked to a halt in the awesome silence of the high, lonesome place.

What do you have—an automobile trip? No, just a segment of such a trip, a record of events that occurred between the time car trouble was expected and the time it arrived. Is the record complete? Were these the only events the boys experienced in this time span? No, a great many things happened that could not be recorded.

How does the writer decide what events to include? Maybe this writer included some details that could have been omitted and left out some that should have been included.

The details selected should not disrupt the direction, the pace, or the basic impression which the narrative seeks to make. Since the sequence involves anxiety ending in car trouble, only those details which have something to add to that anxiety should be included. You can quickly eliminate:

Clarence was reading Plato that day.

Meanwhile, Harvey couldn't pass up a soft-drink sign.

We found New Mexico drier than Texas had been.

We stopped twice. . . .

Having found details included which do not further the narrative, perhaps you should look in the opposite direction, for details which might have strengthened the movement and the basic impression.

Harvey related how his father had been stranded in this area for two days, when his car broke down.

The man who pumped our gas in a New Mexico station shook his head in wonderment and sadness when he listened to the engine, but did not offer any suggestions.

We pooled our money after lunch and found that we had exactly $4.24 left for the trip.

Put these events in what seems to be the most appropriate spot and test them for effect. Do they change the direction of the narrative? Do they interrupt the action? Do they slow the pace or speed it up disadvantageously? Do these details add to the basic impression—anxiety ending in car trouble?

Order of Events

If narration is reciting a selected sequence of events, then the problem of *order* must be faced. You must determine which event to relate *first* and which should follow. In telling about a simple event in everyday life, this may not be a problem, since events happen in one order — or at least seem to. Baby Sarah climbs down from her chair, *then* she begins to run, *then* she stumbles, *then* she falls, *then* she begins to cry. This order — the order in which events actually happen — is called *chronological order.*

In telling a longer narrative, it may be advantageous to rearrange the order to create certain desired effects. Notice how the order of events is reversed in this conversation:

> SAM: What happened to you, Charlie?
> CHARLIE: I hurt myself.
> SAM: I can see that, but how?
> CHARLIE: I fell off Elmer Short's motorcycle.
> SAM: You were riding Elmer Short's motorcycle?
> CHARLIE: He said I could.
> SAM: You mean you asked him if you could?
> CHARLIE: Sure. Why not? I was just hanging around his shop.
> SAM: Why weren't you in school?
> CHARLIE: School was out early because the electricity went off.

Beyond situations like this, writers rarely try to reverse the order of events completely. Written stories are told predominantly in chronological order. You may, however, start relating an incident and then go back in time to supply background information. Often you may prefer to withhold the revelation of what is to happen, in order to create suspense in the narrative.

> At the end of the high board, Harry paused to recall what had brought him to such a predicament. First there was Carl's jibe, at Ann's party. He had overlooked that, but after Carl had questioned his courage, he knew a showdown was inevitable.

Frequently a writer begins his story with some significant happening and then jumps back to an earlier time and brings his story forward from that point. This technique is called *flashback.*

Relation of the Writer to the Action

Compare the narratives below.

> "I'm walking on the dock, alongside a rusty old Argentine freighter, when all of a sudden I hear this funny thumping noise in the stored cargo from the *Lighthorse Harry.*"

"Well," think I to myself, "That's a strange noise for a shipload of type-writers to make."

I was walking on the dock, alongside a rusty old Argentine freighter, when suddenly I heard a strange thumping sound coming from the area where the cargo of the *Lighthorse Harry* was piled.

That's a strange sound for a shipload of typewriters to make, I thought.

In the first narrative the events are told as if they are being related as they happen. In the second narrative, the action appears to have been completed some time before the telling began. Although you may feel that the present tense should give the reader a sense of being on the spot as the action takes place, the writing is likely to be awkward and amateurish. The overwhelming majority of narratives are told in the past tense.

An important question in the writer's relation to the action is whether his place is that of a participant or of an onlooker. In other words, what is his *point of view* as a writer. Notice variations in the following para-graphs about two boys watching an ocean liner come into their Great Lakes port:

1. I wondered what Roger was thinking, as the gigantic oceangoing liner was slowly pushed and jostled into her berth by the tugboats. I knew that I had never seen anything so marvelous at Pier 42 in my four years of ship-watching—but Roger's face showed no feelings at all for the un-usual goings on.

2. He wondered what Roger was thinking, as the gigantic oceangoing liner was slowly pushed and jostled into her berth by the tugboats. He knew that he had never seen anything so marvelous at Pier 42 in his four years of ship-watching. As far as he could see, Roger's face showed no feeling at all for the unusual goings on.

3. Bob wondered what Roger was thinking, as the gigantic oceangoing liner was slowly pushed and jostled into her berth by the tugboats. He had never seen anything so marvelous at Pier 42 in his four years of ship-watching. Roger, however, was no more moved by the docking than if he had watched such incidents every day of his life. He wished the berth-ing would be quick, so he could talk Bob into going to the movies with him.

The writer of the first paragraph appears to have *participated* in the experiences he relates. He was one of the actors in the action that he is reporting. He may have been a major figure in the events, or just a minor one. Only the full context of the story could make that distinction clear.

In the second and third passages, the narrator *observed* what hap-pened to someone else. Whereas the first approach is usually called *first-person point of view*, characterized by pronouns in the first person, the other two are *third-person* narratives.

The first-person narrative is close to the events, a kind of eye-witness report. It may add a tone of truthfulness to the narrative—even when the story is based on imaginary happenings. Since the writer of a first-person story can tell only those things of which the "I" character can logically be aware, he is limited in what he can tell.

The third-person point of view, as it appears in Paragraph 3, extends beyond the limited knowledge of the "I" storyteller. The teller of Paragraph 3 explains how each person felt. Since only a superhuman being could have such insight, this approach is called the *omniscient third-person point of view*—and is generally avoided. Paragraph 2 does not explain Roger's thoughts, but tells only what the "he" (Bob) might know. This approach, known as the *limited third-person point of view*, is widely used in the writing of narratives.

Once you have decided whether you are to be a participant or an on-looker in the story you are telling, you have a definite obligation to maintain that point of view throughout the story. You cannot expect your reader to stay with you if you turn out to be two storytellers—when he had already pigeonholed you *either* as part of the action or as an observer.

Exercise 7   *Bring to class stories in textbooks, newspapers, or magazines, which you have considered in light of their point of view. Remember that point of view deals with these questions:*

> What is the narrator's connection with the events he relates?
>
> Was he in on the events, or did they happen to someone else?
>
> If he tells what happened to someone else, does the writer assume a *limited* knowledge of what happened (as in Paragraph 2), or a superhuman (omniscient) knowledge of the events?

Be prepared to explain to the class devices the writer has used to maintain one point of view throughout.

Thinking About Beginnings and Endings

Imagine that you have a river to cross. There are no bridges. You cannot go around because the headwaters are an impossible distance and the river's mouth is equally inaccessible. Your decision is to *swim* the river. How will you get started?

You could just jump in and start paddling, hoping to reach the opposite bank; but there is a safer way.

You can select your starting point according to the place where you want to land. You always have to enter the water upstream from the landing point you have picked out, and if the water is swift-moving, you have to prepare yourself to be carried with the current accordingly.

Consider storytelling as something like swimming a river. Decide where you expect to land, and select your starting point accordingly. The longer you think it will take you to tell the story, the farther back in time (upstream) you may go to find your starting point. The landing point, or the dramatic highpoint of the story, must be carefully chosen. Without such forethought swimmers and storytellers sometimes drown.

Relating Events to Time

Since narration is a *sequence* of events, the handling of time is very important. The most common consideration of time in any kind of composition is the indication shown by the writer's choice of verb *tense*. Tense shows time relationship between actor and action. Notice the time element in these expressions having to do with the writing of a hypothetical letter:

I write the letter.	I am writing the letter.
I wrote the letter.	I had written the letter.
I have written the letter.	I should have written the letter.

Remember that your choice of tense is made for a definite purpose — to give a general indication of the time an action occurred. Be careful not to shift tenses without definite reason for doing so.

There are devices other than tense for keeping the reader informed about how the events you are describing are related to time. Expressions such as "today," "yesterday," "tomorrow," or "on February 10, 1964" are sample clues to *when it happened.*

Certain expressions show the relationship between events in a narrative. These expressions help carry the reader's attention from one event or incident to another as transitional bridges or simply *transitions.* Some of the words frequently used as transitions are "then," "just then," "while," "meanwhile," "simultaneously."

Record or Story? It is one thing to give a reader a record of what happened and quite another to let him discover what happened by reliving the experience. A skillful writer of narratives makes his characters come alive and act out the story. Note the contrast in the effectiveness of the following passages:

RECORD

Johnny told Maryanne to pick up his bike, or he would tell her father that she had been riding it in the street.

STORY

"You better pick up my bike," called Johnny.

"You get it," Mary said. "It's your bike."

"Sure, but you left it in the street, so you have to pick it up."

"Oh, yeah?"

"Yeah, or I'll snitch on you for riding it in the street. You know what your father said. . . ."

RECORD

Karl walked through the field of Johnson grass. The long stems swished softly as they fell away from his feet.

STORY

Karl brushed through the tall, dry Johnson grass, enjoying the swishing sound of the long stems as they fell away from his feet. The sound reminded him of the small waves that lapped against the lakefront at their summer cottage.

The use of dialogue is the most common device for dramatizing. In the second set of passages, the story was made more vivid by letting the reader in on Karl's thinking. In other words, the reader shares the experience.

Kinds of Narratives

So far the discussion of narratives has been confined to simple stories or sequences of events, whose primary purpose is to entertain the reader. Most of the techniques considered in the discussion of simple narratives will apply readily to short stories, dramatic scripts, or novels.

Many other types of composition are narrative in form, but they have a primary purpose which goes beyond that of entertaining. These narratives — which are considered expositions because they are informative, explanatory, or persuasive in purpose — include such writings as: history, biography, autobiography, journals, and anecdotes. As you study exposition in the following chapter, you will find many occasions to use what you have just learned about telling a story well.

Exercise 8

A. *Select about half the events from the list below. Choose two events appropriate to beginning and ending, and arrange the remainder of the half you selected into some sequence between opening and closing action. Imagine yourself either as a participant or as an onlooker. Use what you have learned in this chapter and write a narrative. Make your presentation as dramatic as possible.*

Ate a meal	Lost something valuable
Walked home	Did not have enough money
Arrived home late	Helped by a stranger
Got the car	Asked Dad for the car
Had trouble	Made someone laugh
Went to a party	Dressed for an occasion
Stopped for gas	Went to an athletic event
Saw the moon	Turned down a chance to race
Ate stale popcorn	Went to a motion picture
Left someone behind	Borrowed money from Jim

B. *Select a short story by a well-known writer—preferably a story you have read recently. Study the way the author has handled: selection of events, order of events, point of view, action-time relationships, transitions, and dramatic devices.*

C. *Recall a memorable event in your past experience. Do the same for some interesting person of your acquaintance. Write a fictional story wherein you relate the experience as if it had happened to that person. Try to merge the character description of the person into the narrative of the experience. Mingle descriptive and narrative details to make story and person come off the page so realistically that you almost begin to believe the incident really happened to that person.*

SUMMING UP

In this chapter you have considered some of the skills involved in writing good description and narration. Description may be thought of as the making of a word picture—the single scene in a motion-picture film. The story that unfolds when the film is set in motion is narrative. The process of telling that story is narration.

The skills developed in writing description are an integral part of the writing of a narrative. The story is told as the description of several single impressions blend into a sequence of events.

Much of your pleasure in life depends on your ability to share with others some of the experiences especially meaningful to you. Describing what you have seen, or imagined, or telling what happened can bring happiness to you as well as to your listeners or readers. Description and narration are necessarily creative processes. The writer uses his skill, just as the artist does, to share his experience and his feelings with others.

Chapter 5

Exposition and Argumentation

A Look Back and a Look Forward

In your experience with description and narration you have probably discovered that to write well you have to exercise considerable mental discipline. If you haven't made this discovery, you should give it some thought. Though you practice writing for many years, it will be necessary for you to continue to plan and organize and to follow the rules of grammar and written expression.

The two types of writing you will experiment with in this chapter require a still further extension of disciplined thought. You will find that you have to think clearly in order to give directions someone else can follow. You may also discover that it takes considerable skill and extra-hard thinking to present a convincing piece of argumentation. The skills you acquire in exposition and argumentation will serve you throughout your lifetime.

RECOGNIZING DIFFERENT KINDS OF WRITING

If a person approaches you and asks, "How do you get to City Hall?" he is probably looking for information. If he says, "How did such a man as Mayor Jones get into City Hall?" he's looking for an argument.

While the first question seems to require an explanation of such things as street markings, directions, landmarks, or distances, the second question requires a statement concerning the reasoning behind particular human actions and attitudes. If you explain how to get to City Hall, your answer is *exposition*. If you respond to the second question by showing that Mayor Jones is worthy of his office, you are answering by *argumentation*. This chapter explores these two kinds of writing.

It is conceivable that in answer to the first question: "How do you get to City Hall?" you might use a descriptive approach. You might say, "See that large brownstone house on the corner? Well, just beyond it is a quaint old tobacco shop whose proprietor is a gentle old man with. . . ."

In reply to "How did such a man as Mayor Jones get into City Hall?" you might use a narrative approach: "Well, once upon a time. . . ."

Generally, however, descriptive and narrative writing do not mix well with exposition and argumentation. Description and narration appeal to the imagination through word pictures and stories. The foundations of exposition and argumentation are ideas and informative statements that appeal to the intellect. Their primary purpose is to make us think.

Exercise 1   *Classify these examples according to the type of writing illustrated. If a word picture seems to be the primary concern, label the passage "D" for description. If an entertaining sequence of events is given, label it "N" for narration. If factual explanation predominates, write "E" for exposition. If reasoning or interpretation prevails, mark the sample "A" for argumentation. Finally, check back to see if those samples marked "D" or "N" seem to appeal more to your feelings or emotions, while those marked "E" or "A" seem to be directed more toward your intellectual side. Which make you think?*

Don't be concerned if there are some differences of opinion over the classification of these samples, as long as you can defend your choice with sensible reasoning.

Example A

That is the real issue. That is the issue that will continue in this country when these poor tongues of Judge Douglas and myself shall be silent. It is the eternal struggle between these two principles — right and wrong — throughout the world. They are the two principles that have stood face to face from the beginning of time, and will ever continue to struggle. The one is the common right of humanity, the other the divine right of kings. . . .

ABRAHAM LINCOLN, The Lincoln-Douglas Debates

Example B

We meet in an hour of grief and challenge. Dag Hammarskjöld is dead. But the United Nations lives on. His tragedy is deep in our hearts, but the task for which he died is at the top of our agenda. A noble servant of peace is gone. But the quest for peace lies before us.

JOHN F. KENNEDY, At the United Nations

Example C

"Here he comes!"

Every neck is stretched further, and every eye strained wider. Away across the endless dead level of the prairie, a black speck appears against the sky, and it is plain that it moves. Well, I should think so! In a second or two it becomes a horse and rider, rising and falling, rising and falling—sweeping us nearer and nearer—growing more and more distinct, more and more sharply defined—nearer and still nearer, and the flutter of hoofs comes faintly to the ear—another instant a whoop and a hurrah from our upper deck, a wave of the rider's hand, but no reply, and a man and a horse burst past our excited faces, and go swinging away like a belated fragment of a storm!

So sudden is it all, and so like a flash of unreal fancy, that but for the flake of white foam left quivering and perishing on a mail sack after the vision had flashed by and disappeared, we might have doubted whether we had seen any actual horse and man at all.

SAMUEL CLEMENS, *Roughing It*

Example D

I have received your polite letter of the 6th of the month and your present of the "Crisis." You will excuse a question or two. . . .

You say, "our divisions began with federalism and antifederalism." Alas! they began with human nature; they have existed in America from its first plantation. In every colony, divisions have always prevailed. In New York, Pennsylvania, Virginia, Massachusetts, and all the rest, a court and a country party have always contended. Whig and Tory disputed very sharply before the revolution, and in every step during the revolution. Every measure of the Congress, from 1774 to 1787 inclusively, was disputed with acrimony, and decided as by small majorities as any question is decided these days. . . .

JOHN ADAMS, a letter to William Keteltas, November 1812

Example E

There is just as much beauty visible to us in the landscape as we are prepared to appreciate—not a grain more. The actual objects which one man will see from a particular hill-top are just as different from those which another will see as the beholders are different. The scarlet oak must, in a sense, be in your eye when you go forth. We cannot see anything until we are possessed with the idea of it, take it into our heads—and then we can hardly see anything else.

HENRY DAVID THOREAU, "The Scarlet Oak"

Example F

"He has been in the habit of lighting his pipe at lamps and gas-jets. You can see that it is quite charred all down one side. Of course a match could not have done that. Why should a man hold a match to the side of his pipe? But you cannot light at a lamp without getting the bowl charred. And it is all on the right side of the pipe. From that I gather that he is a left-handed man. You hold your own pipe to the lamp and see how naturally you, being right-handed, hold the left side to the flame. You might do it once the other way, but not as a constancy. This has always been held so. Then he has bitten through the amber. It takes a muscular, energetic fellow, and one with a good set of teeth, to do that. . . ."

SIR ARTHUR CONAN DOYLE, "The Yellow Face"

EXPOSITION

This discussion is based on the proposition that exposition *explains*. It informs the uninformed who have the desire to find out.

How should you organize the information to be conveyed in an exposition? One logical approach might be to write an explanation based on what a questioner has expressed an interest in knowing.

This approach is fine, but are you sure he has told you exactly what it is he wishes to know? Listen to this conversation:

SON: Will you tell me about cars?

FATHER: What do you want to know about cars?

SON: All about cars.

FATHER: Well, I don't know *all about cars*. Can you say what it is about cars that you want to know all about?

SON: Well, our car has two seats and two doors on each side and a door in the back. Elmer's car has two seats and two doors on each side but none in the back. Elsa's father's car has two seats, but only one door on each side.

FATHER: Oh, you want to know about different *body styles*, is that it?

SON: Yes, that's it!

From the conversation, one might gather that the questioner is not interested, for the moment, in information about various makes, models, colors, or price ranges. His curiosity is focused upon body style, or on numbers of seats and numbers of doors. An explanation which classifies cars as coupés, two-door sedans, four-door sedans, and station wagons will probably satisfy him—until he wants to know about hardtops and convertibles. The nature of his curiosity—once it is focused on a suitable question—helps the informant to establish a *method* for conveying the information. Let's examine some methods of presenting information.

Patterns for Developing Expositions

Consider the following questions:

1. Sam said he needs to replace a grommet in his tent before he can go camping. What is a grommet, anyway?

2. What are the essential parts of a microscope?

3. I heard a television announcer say that a giant observation balloon just lifting off for a flight resembled an exclamation mark. What did he mean?

4. How may football players be classified according to position on the team?

5. How can I make a wastebasket for my room?

6. What are some causes of traffic accidents?

Perhaps these questions strike you as childlike. Perhaps you find them simple to the point of being silly.

Remember, however, that the heart of exposition is a writer who knows a subject and a reader who does not know it but wants to. When a person who is uninformed on a subject asks a question, the question may be awkwardly stated, or it may sound silly to one who knows the subject thoroughly. However, a genius from some nonbaseball-playing land might ask, "What is baseball?" A child who may some day astound the world with his wisdom may ask, "How many legs does a fly have?" These are not silly questions. Rather than laugh at the questions, get busy on the answers. They will be more difficult than you ever imagined.

Remember, too, that what seems like old stuff to you may be unfamiliar territory to your reader. You may wish to have your explanations move from what is simple to what is not so simple. You may find it useful to begin with something you think your reader knows, before moving on to what he does not know. Several approaches to exposition can be illustrated by attempting to supply the information requested above.

Development Through Definition. To answer the first question, you may have to refer to a dictionary.

What is a grommet, anyway?

Your questioner has asked for a definition of an unfamiliar term. It is your job to make the meaning clear. You might answer in this manner:

> According to *Webster's New Students Dictionary,* a grommet may be either "a ring of rope," or "an eyelet of firm material to strengthen or protect an opening." From what I can remember about Sam's tent, I'd say he meant one of those brass rings that comes in two parts and clamps into the canvas like a metal doughnut. It makes an eyelet that will not rip out. Grommets are used on almost anything that laces or ties, such as shoes, boots, leggings, or parachute packs.

This question focuses attention upon a single object or concept. The dictionary gave a good general idea of the information desired. Then a particular knowledge of Sam's tent allowed the writer to surmise about the specific object which had to be replaced. Finally, there is a comment that goes back to the general idea: the *grommet.* This type of eyelet can be used in other situations. Conveying information by focusing attention upon a single idea and upon the word which expresses that idea may be called development through expanded definition or simply development through definition.

Exercise 2   *Answer one of the following questions by developing an exposition through expanded definition. Remember to keep attention focused upon the single concept involved in the question. Consult dictionaries, encyclopedias, and other references. It is not necessary to begin your exposition with a definition from the dictionary, but you should define the central concept by using information from reliable sources.*

1. Who can qualify as a Miss America candidate?
2. What is a Texas tower?
3. What is a grunion run?
4. What is the International Date Line?

Development Through Partition. Question 2 on page 315 requires centering your attention on several subdivisions of the main subject.

What are the essential parts of a microscope?

Some of the essential parts of a microscope are the tube, the adjusting screw, the lenses, the table, and the illuminating mirror. The tube, with the eyepiece lenses at the top and the objective lenses at the bottom, is pointed downward toward the table. A glass slide, on which a specimen has been placed, is positioned on the table for observation. Light is reflected upon the specimen, through the opening in the table, from the illuminating mirror below.

As both the question and the label for this approach indicate, you have focused attention upon how the subject may be partitioned, or broken into several parts. To avoid complicating the picture, you focus attention on the one microscope you are observing. Notice, also, that you have not considered subdivisions of specific parts; there is only one level of breakdown. This helps you concentrate upon the parts as they relate to the whole. If you went beyond one level of breakdown, to talk about the parts of the adjusting screw, you would get into a much more complex set of interrelationships ("Development Through Classification," page 318). The partition method is useful in explaining something when the subject may be considered singly and in terms of a simple breakdown of parts.

Exercise 3   *Use the partition approach to develop a written answer to one of these questions:*

1. What are the major responsibilities of a class president?

2. What are some of the major responsibilities of the President of the United States?

3. What are the ingredients of beef stroganoff?

4. What are the main parts of an air rifle?

5. Explain the meaning of the painted lines on a basketball court.

Development Through Comparison or Contrast. The answer to question 3 on page 315 requires a still different pattern of exposition.

> I heard a television announcer say that a giant observation balloon just lifting off resembled an exclamation mark. *What did he mean?*
>
> If an observation balloon were just beginning its ascent, and you saw it silhouetted at dawn against the eastern sky, it could easily remind you of a gigantic exclamation mark. Its body would be elongated. Since, at takeoff, the gas supporting the balloon would be dense and contracted, it would have filled out only a bubble at the top of the bag. The long folds along the sides, which gradually fill as the gas expands at higher altitudes, would taper downward to a point. Below, like a dot of an exclamation mark, would hang the gondola, or passenger's basket.

In the above example, two quite dissimilar things are compared in terms of a single likeness: under a specific set of circumstances a balloon looks like an exclamation point. Many explanations require more detailed comparison (study of similarities) or contrast (study of differences). It is sometimes possible to use both comparison and contrast in the same explanation.

To consider two common ways of organizing a comparison, say you are to compare items *X* and *Y* on five points, *a, b, c, d,* and *e.* The first method involves discussing points *a, b, c, d,* and *e* of item *X,* before moving over to consider points *a, b, c, d,* and *e* of item *Y.* The second method compares *X* and *Y* on a point-for-point basis. Thus you move from point *a* for *X* and *Y* to point *b* (*X-Y*) to point *c* (*X-Y*), and so on. Both of these methods are effective. The particular situation to be explained may help determine which of these methods should be used.

Exercise 4   *Answer one or more of the following questions by* compari-son, contrast, *or a combination of* comparison *and* contrast:

1. How is an apple different from a pear?

2. How does your football (basketball) team compare with that of the school who played against your team most recently?

3. You are considering purchasing a sweater and find it difficult to decide between *A* and *B.* How does sweater *A* compare with sweater *B?*

Development Through Classification.   At first glance, you might think of trying to answer question 4 on page 315 with the partition approach; but if you try this method, you will find yourself involved in a long and tiresome explanation. A better device is to try grouping the players in some manner.

How may football players be classified according to position on the team?

The eleven players on a football team may be divided rather handily into those in the backfield, called *backs,* and those in the line, called— among other things—*linemen.* The labels by which the players within these two categories are known are apt to vary with the formation being used, but one common set of designations is as follows: In the line, the man who puts the ball in motion to start each play is the *center.* On his left and right are the *left* and *right guards,* respectively. Beyond the guards there is a *tackle* on each side of the line. At each extremity of the line is a player fittingly called the *end.* These seven men make up the forward formation. Meanwhile in the backfield, the player who usually decides what play shall be used and handles the ball from the center is called the *quarterback.* He is supported by two *halfbacks* whose positions in the formation cause them to be designated *right* and *left halfbacks.* The backfield is completed with the *fullback.*

When you arrange items in groups and label the groups, you are classifying. Notice that the discussion of football players, rather than beginning with the eleven *parts*, or players, begins with the group level: the *backs* and the *linemen*. Each of these groups is then subdivided. Such classification gives a picture of each player in relationship to other players.

In explaining by classification, it is wise to limit the explanation to a single consideration or aspect of the subject. The football players were classified only according to the *position* they played. If the discussion had been interrupted to further classify eleven men according to their class in school, their natural-handedness, and the color of their hair, then the already-complicated set of interrelationships which was being explained would have become hopelessly confused.

Exercise 5   *Write an exposition in which you classify one of these subjects into classes and subclasses. Remember to limit your explanation to one aspect of the subject.*

Players on a basketball team
Jobs on the school newspaper
Musical instruments in our school band

Development by Explaining a Process. You undoubtedly have already had the experience of trying to tell somebody else how to make something. Was he able to follow your instructions? If not, was it because he didn't listen, or because you didn't make the process clear? Consider question 5:

How can I make a wastebasket for my room?

If you have wallpaper left over, after your room has been papered, you may use it to make a wastebasket to match the walls. First, you must find a container suitable for covering. This may be a pasteboard box, a cylindrical paper carton, or a plastic container which can be cut to the desired shape — or it may be a wastebasket that is not suitable for the room as it is.

Next, you need to cut the paper to fit both the inside and the outside of the container. Pains should be taken to see that the pattern of the wallpaper will match at the seams. If the container is rectangular, it may be necessary to use five separate sections for the four sides and bottom of the interior. Strips must be cut to cover the top edge and to strengthen the corners. Finally, the sections can be pasted in place. You now have a distinctive wastebasket that goes with your room as though it were made for it — and it was!

When preparing to explain how to make something, your hardest job will be dividing the process into steps. The more complex the process you are explaining, the more carefully you may have to distinguish the steps. This can be done with words like "first, . . ." "second, . . ." if the number of steps is not great. For more clearcut distinctions, however, numbers or letters may be desirable. Such devices may give a passage a formal, "this-is-going-to-be-hard-to-read" appearance. However, if the steps of the process begin to run together in the reader's mind, it is not likely that he will be able to follow them. In more casual situations the numbering or lettering may not be necessary.

Exercise 6   *Answer one or more of the following questions by using the explaining-a-process approach:*

1. How do you make an omelet?

2. What is an easy way to get from my neighborhood to the airport?

3. What route do you follow to get to summer camp?

4. How do you assemble a bicycle, as it comes from the mail-order house?

Development Through Cause and Effect. In answering the last of the six questions introduced earlier, you deal with cause and effect.

What are some causes of traffic accidents?

Auto accidents may be caused by mechanical failure, by human error, or by some combination of these two. When tires blow out or brakes fail, or highways become hazardous without warning, an accident may occur, even though the driver is cautious.

There are many other accidents which reflect directly upon the operator. Drivers sometimes become careless, or permit themselves to be distracted, thereby losing control of the car; or they may fall asleep and run off the road or into the paths of other vehicles.

Many accidents can be traced to a combination of causes. A wreck caused by poor judgment may also be traceable to a problem of the driver's vision. On the other hand, faulty brakes may have been the immediate cause of an accident. If the driver knew his brakes needed repair and failed to have them put in safe condition, his carelessness might be said to have been a significant, though not immediate, cause of the wreck.

In attempting to explain why something happened, you need to be extremely careful. You may fail to take into account all the important factors. The selection above makes several statements in a matter-of-fact way, but judges, lawyers, and juries spend months — sometimes years — trying to get at the causes of a single accident.

In writing exposition, which means "explaining," you should limit yourself to generally accepted, well-verified relationships between events. To whatever degree the assignment of a cause-effect relationship becomes controversial, it moves into the realm of personal opinion, attitude, or belief and becomes a matter for consideration later in this chapter under "Argumentation."

One of the greatest pitfalls in looking for cause-effect relationships involves assuming that since two events occur repeatedly under the same general circumstances, then *one* of the events *must* be causing the *other*. Take into account the fact that certain circumstances may have affected the situation without your knowledge.

Exercise 7   *Answer one or more of the following questions in a brief exposition:*

1. What causes a car to skid?

2. How do bats keep from bumping into unseen things?

3. What causes an eclipse of the sun?

4. What causes water from an artesian spring to flow *up* from the ground?

Selecting a Pattern for Exposition

You have now considered several possible approaches to writing exposition. If you have certain information to convey to a questioner, you would probably select a pattern to make it show (a) what you feel is most important for the reader to know, or (b) what he most wants to know.

To illustrate this point, recall the genius from the nonbaseball-playing land. You could use any one of the patterns of development that have been discussed or a combination of patterns.

You could build your presentation around *what baseball is.* (*Definition*)

You could talk about what *constitutes a team*—a *pitcher*, a *catcher*, and so on. (*Partition*)

You could explain how baseball is like, in certain ways, and unlike, in other ways, a game popular in his country. Of course, you could do so only if you were well versed in both games. (*Comparison or Contrast*)

You could explain that baseball is played on many levels of age and ability: professional or nonprofessional; major league or minor league. (*Classification*)

You could explain play-by-play how a game of baseball is played. (*Process*)

You could tell him about the World Series, especially about how the two opposing teams win the pennant.   (*Cause and Effect*)

Exercise 8   *Pretend that you are attempting to explain what you know about the subjects below either to a child or to someone who is unfamiliar with the specific subject mentioned. Suggest three or four approaches to the subject and indicate which pattern of development you would use in each explanation.*

> Bicycle
> Credit card
> Orchestra
> Internal combustion engine
> Permanent wave
> Communication system

ARGUMENTATION

"You did, too."
"I did not."
"You did, I saw you!"
"No, I didn't."

What you have just read could be the record of a verbal battle, which is generally regarded as an *argument*. However, in written composition or in public speaking, when you speak of *argumentation*, you have something more formal, less warlike, and more effective in mind.

Think back over the past few weeks and try to recall how many times you have found the process of argumentation used. Did you hear a question discussed on a TV panel discussion? Did you hear a politician state why his platform is superior to that of his opponent? Did you read in a magazine or a newspaper a persuasive letter to the editor? Did you discuss with a friend the relative merits of an idea?

The effort to persuade is so much a part of everyday life that you need to think carefully about the techniques of argumentation. The skills you develop in learning to write convincingly will carry over into conversation techniques and improve your ability to make yourself understood in informal discussion. Also, as you become aware of the skills used in argumentation, you will be better equipped to judge the validity of arguments presented by others.

What Makes an Argument Convincing?

Written argumentation will vary in style as the specific situation requires, but certain general principles are basic in making an argument convincing.

1. The writer or speaker should be well informed about the question being discussed.

2. He should state the question clearly.

3. He should follow a definite plan or outline.

4. He should follow a chain of reasoning, making a new point link into the one preceding it.

5. He should back up his statements, supporting them with facts or with opinions given by reliable authorities.

6. He may find it advisable to anticipate counterarguments that may be raised and deal with such questions in advance.

As you read the example of argumentation quoted below, look for ways the writer has, or has not, used the six principles of argumentation we have listed. The excerpt* is from "Sense and Nonsense about Space" by Lee A. DuBridge in Harper's *Magazine*, August, 1959.

> The establishment of human colonies on the Moon or Venus or Mars is certainly an irresistible human dream—a dream whose possibilities should be investigated. However, one can hardly suppose that these places will offer very attractive living conditions to the prospective settler. No place on Earth could conceivably be as unattractive as the airless, waterless, lifeless surface of the Moon. The best that can be said is that it is a good place to get away from other people; and it is a fine place—with its low gravity—for ambitious high jumpers, if it is possible to jump at all in a pressurized space suit with oxygen tank attached.
>
> Furthermore, the difficulties of sending human beings to the Moon are enormous. We might imagine that a man with all the necessary oxygen, space suits, food, water, and instruments could be packed into a vehicle with a total weight of 2,000 pounds. A rocket with a thrust of some 300,000 pounds could project this vehicle into an orbit which would pass near the Moon. But our vehicle must carry along also enough fuel to fire a retrorocket in order to reduce its speed, counter the Moon's gravitational pull, and lower the whole device gently to a suitable spot on the Moon. It seems reasonable to estimate that it would take two or more pounds of fuel for each pound actually landed on the Moon. Thus, 4,000 pounds of fuel would have to be lifted from the Earth in addition to the original 2,000-pound load, making a total load of 6,000 pounds. A total thrust of 900,000 pounds would now be needed.
>
> * Reprinted by permission of the author.

But this would leave our man permanently stranded on the Moon with no fuel to return to Earth. We must then lift from the Earth enough fuel to lift him off the Moon again, and this will multiply our initial thrust requirement by another factor of 3 — to 2,700,000 pounds. And if we want to allow the man and his vehicle to land safely on the Earth again, he will need fuel for that, too — and our initial thrust may climb to 5 million pounds or more.

A single rocket with a thrust of 5 million pounds is far beyond the reach of present technology; large and clumsy (and expensive) clusters of rockets would be needed. Furthermore, we can hardly send one man alone on such a journey. Hence, it has been suggested that such journeys be made in installments, using orbiting space platforms to which fuel and equipment may be transported by many rockets, each bearing a smaller load. Or we can land the men on the moon in one capsule and send the fuel and equipment in others. But the total fuel requirement is not reduced by this technique — rather it will be greatly increased, for all the equipment must still be lifted from the Earth and landed gently and accurately on the Moon.

The technical problems to be met are surely not insoluble — but the expense and effort involved will be colossal, and it is unrealistic to expect the "man on the Moon" mission to be achieved immediately. Sending a man to Mars or Venus or other bodies will be even more difficult — and the price of the journey correspondingly higher.

These considerations suggest that it is hardly realistic to expect that we may someday relieve the congestion of the Earth's rapidly rising population by establishing colonies on the Moon or on other planets. Since the surface area of the Moon is only one-sixteenth, and of Mars only one-quarter, that of the Earth, it would probably be cheaper to build great floating platforms over the surface of all the Earth's oceans (thus multiplying the available "land" area by four) rather than try to transport a few hundred million people, with all their water, oxygen, and food to the Moon or Mars.

Exercise 9   *Evaluate the preceding excerpt by trying to discover how the author has used the techniques of argumentation listed on page 323.*

1. What evidence does the writer give of being well informed about the subject?

2. At what point, or points, does he state the central idea?

3. Make an outline of the excerpted material and decide whether there is evidence that he followed a definite plan.

4. What evidence do you find of a definite chain of reasoning in this discussion?

5. Does he document, or back up, the statements that he makes?

6. Is there an example of handling an anticipated question?

Practice in the Art of Persuasion

Though there are many ways in which argumentation may be used, let's limit ourselves in this discussion to four areas, each fairly close to your own experience. Let us begin with letters to the editor—a device frequently used for airing an opinion.

Exercise 10   *A letter to the editor, in which you express a differing view-point, should observe the principles of argumentation just discussed. If you are disagreeing with an article or an editorial which has appeared earlier, you may wish to follow, point by point, the statements made by the first writer. In any case, you should remember that some persons who will read your letter may not have seen the item to which you are referring.*

1. Write a letter to the editor of your school paper, regarding an issue on which opinion is divided. If you are not well informed about the subject, become informed before you start writing.

2. Think of some subject current in the news in which you are particularly interested, but on which varying opinions are being expressed. Look for comment on this subject in magazines and newspapers and write to the editor.

Exercise 11   *Editorials are not always argumentation. They may be a tribute to some person or to some accomplishment. They may comment on the observation of a certain holiday, or they may caution drivers to be careful on Labor Day weekend. However, the editorial page is the place to look for the editor's expression of his viewpoint, and nine times out of ten he has found something to argue about.*

1. Even if you are not the editor of your school paper, you can imagine that you are. Prepare an editorial that would be appropriate to appear in the next issue. Select a subject on which there is more than one opinion, and remember to refer to the principles of argumentation before you start writing.

2. What local issues are being discussed in your community today? Are you sufficiently informed to take sides on one of the issues? If not, do some digging and ask questions. Be prepared to document the statements you make. Plan an argument on the subject and write an editorial, as if you were the editor of a local daily.

Exercise 12   *While a debate is oral expression, it requires the same type of careful preparation that you should make for a written discourse—perhaps more so, for you have to be ready to think on your feet. The principles of argumentation are fundamental in debating.*

Plan either an affirmative or a negative presentation for a debate on a current topic of controversy in the news. If the class wishes to follow through with oral debate on one of the questions, you will be prepared to participate.

Exercise 13   *With other members of the class, plan a panel discussion, such as you have seen on TV. Select a topic on which different members of the class hold dissimilar opinions. Each member of the panel should prepare a presentation, observing the principles of good argumentation. He should then be prepared to counter the arguments presented by other members of the panel.*

SUMMING UP

After some practice in recognizing the four types of writing—description, narration, exposition, and argumentation—you have centered your attention in this chapter upon the two types of writing primarily designed to make the reader think. You have found that exposition explains; argumentation advances a point of view.

In considering exposition, you have discovered that one of your major problems is finding a way to focus attention upon the specific purpose of the exposition. Several ways of focusing attention have been suggested under the topic "Patterns for Developing Expositions." Your choice of pattern, (a) definition, (b) partition, (c) comparison or contrast, (d) classification, (e) process, (f) cause and effect, will depend upon the primary purpose of your exposition. There is also the possibility that you may find it helpful to combine one or more of these methods in the same exposition.

As you explored the qualities of an effective piece of argumentation, you recognized the importance of being well informed about the subject, of stating the central idea, of being able to back up statements, of following a definite plan, of developing a sound chain of reasoning, and of sometimes being able to anticipate counterarguments.

Chapter 6

Newspaper Writing

A Look Back and a Look Forward

The newspaper plops on your front step every morning. You glance at the headlines, hurry off to school, and perhaps glance at the paper again that night.

Who writes the stories that appear on the front page, the editorials, the special features, the signed columns? How does one learn to write for a newspaper?

We could answer the last question in a flippant manner in just three words: "Through hard work!" But you deserve a better answer than that. In the chapter that follows, we shall try to show you some of the skills involved in writing for a newspaper and help you to discover where your particular abilities lie.

In Chapter 5, you tried your hand at newspaper writing when you wrote editorials in your study of argumentation. Now you will discover other types of newspaper writing and strengthen what you have learned about writing editorials.

EXAMINING NEWSPAPER WRITING

Newscasts on television and radio and news stories in our papers are an important part of our daily lives. In fact, we have so geared our lives to looking at the news, listening to the news, or reading the news that we forget how dependent we are upon thousands of reporters in many parts of the world. We forget, too, that many other persons working in the various forms of mass media — television, radio, magazines, newspapers — are helping to bring the news to us each day. Television engineers, newspaper editors, photographers, workers in news agencies, special writers, and messengers all play their part in keeping the public informed.

The business of getting the news to the people has taken on such proportions that it is highly probable certain members of your class will someday play a part in the distribution of news. You may dream of being a reporter sent to a distant land to describe some dramatic event; or you may hope to become a newscaster who gives a nightly broadcast from a television station. It is quite possible such dreams might materialize, but you are likely to have to prove yourself as a reporter who can get a good story and present it acceptably before you can be considered for either of these fields.

Beginning now, form the habit of studying the structure of important stories that appear in major newspapers and of listening closely to the way a newscaster presents a story on radio or TV. As you study the recommendations made in this chapter about ways to write the news, check these recommendations constantly against the techniques used by writers who handle the news that reaches you each day.

Whether you enter the news field or not, learning to write in a form acceptable to newspapers is an interesting experience. It will give you an appreciation of the way news is presented and will improve your writing skill in other areas. It will help you organize material and present it in an interesting manner.

Even the hasty reading of a reputable newspaper will show you that the paper produces many products for many consumers. Your father may be most interested in one part of the paper; your mother in another. There may be a scramble among the younger members of the family for the comics, the sports page, or the television page. Let us take a look at four types of writing found in the newspaper.

The News Story

A news story is a reporter's account of a current event of interest to many persons. As you read the two examples of news stories that follow, jot down the most important information given in each story.

BERGEN TO BEGIN DIGGING FOR PARK*
Saddle River Park Project
Will Take Two Years
By John W. Slocum
Special to The New York Times

HACKENSACK, N. J., Feb. 29—Work will start soon on excavation for a four-acre lake that will be a feature of the Glen Rock section of the Saddle River County Park, the Bergen County Park Commission announced this week.

About 30 acres will be improved in a three-stage development that will require about two years' work. When finished, the section will be part of a park that stretches for about six miles along the Saddle River and Ho-Ho-Kus Brook from Ridgewood south to Rochelle Park.

Since a great part of the commission's bonded funds are being used for land acquisitions and the development of Overpeck Creek Park in the Hackensack Meadows, work in the Glen Rock section will be accomplished through funds budgeted by the Board of Freeholders. This year's budget allocates $70,000 for the first stage.

Material excavated from the lake site will be used to fill low, swampy ground, James A. McFaul, executive director of the commission, said.

Stage 2 will include a road circling the lake, landscaping, a kidney-shaped play court that can be flooded in the winter for ice skating, two shelters and two parking areas.

The new lake, like others in the county park system, will have facilities for feeding ducks, for fishing by children and for the sailing of model boats.

A path system is planned for stage 3. Mr. McFaul said that ultimately a roadway would permit motorists to drive for about four miles from Ridgewood to Route 4 through the Linear Park.

Long-range plans call for play courts, a fieldhouse and possibly a ballfield area.

The Glen Rock section, which is expected to be open next year, will be entered from Alan Avenue, east to Prospect Street. It will tie in with Dunkerhook Park, which will be improved this year with an extension of a driveway to the north.

Saddle River County Park consists of 540 acres in the Flood Plain of the Saddle River.

Most of the land is swampy and is inundated when the river overflows.

* © 1964 by The New York Times Company. Reprinted by permission.

Jeweled Belle of 800 B. C. Is Found
By U. S. Archeologists in Jordan

By The Associated Press

JERUSALEM, Jordan Sector.

The bejeweled skeleton of a woman lay in the richest tomb ever found in Jordan. Ashes from fires that cooked meals 800 years before Christ still were piled in ovens. Grains of wheat were preserved in storage bins.

American archeologists reported these findings yesterday. They are digging in the ruins of a 5,000-year-old lost city in the Jordan River valley.

Bronze vessels unearthed from the ruins, they said, may be the first ever found of the type used in King Solomon's great Temple.

The 12-man team is headed by Dr. James B. Pritchard of the University of Pennsylvania. The team is excavating at Sa'id Iyeh, 70 miles northeast of Jerusalem.

Dr. Pritchard's archeologists have found a 24-foot thick wall, about half a mile long, running around the iron-age city, and a spectacular camouflaged stone stairway for use in time of war. The city has been deserted since about 800 B. C., Dr. Pritchard said.

Beneath the ruins of the settlement, which Dr. Pritchard said revealed a technological culture more advanced than that of Jerusalem itself, Arab diggers unearthed floors from the early bronze age, 50 centuries ago. Even earlier cities may be buried deeper, he said.

The mound of ruins, more than 700 feet below sea level, may be the Old Testament city of Zarethan, but no evidence has yet been found to confirm this, said the Rev. John E. Huesman, a Jesuit priest from Alma College, Alma, Mich., a member of the expedition.

A scarab bearing an Egyptian seal and other finds indicate the city may have been attacked by the Egyptian Pharaoh Shishak about 900 B. C., Dr. Pritchard said. The city was on the main military and trade route between Egypt and Damascus.

In one tomb was a skeleton coated with bitumen, the first such remains found by archeologists in the Holy Land. It showed a crude attempt to imitate the mummies of the Egyptians.

In the tomb of a woman who, Dr. Pritchard said, may have been a queen, workers found 670 orange carnelian beads, 72 gold beads, four ivory boxes and a set of silver pins and breastplates.

The expedition, with four Americans, one German, one Frenchman, one English artist and five Jordanian experts, began work New Year's Day and has dug through heavy winter rains for two months.*

What similarities in pattern can you discover in the preceding news stories? In what part of each story did you find the most important information? Examine the first paragraph of each story and compare the significance of the facts given there with the significance of the information given later in the same story.

*© 1964, AP Newsfeatures. Reprinted with permission.

The Feature Story

The chief purpose of the feature story is to provide entertainment or to give general information. The feature story is written in a more informal style than the news story and usually deals with topics that are timely but not necessarily current.

The first example given below is an informative science feature. The second is an entertaining feature story hung on a news peg. Had a dog in your town actually learned to talk, such a feature might have appeared in the paper.

The feature stories that follow are of such a widely different nature that you will find more contrast than similarity in their structure. Think about the four types of writing you studied in Chapters 4 and 5 and decide which types of writing are used in these features.

VENUS AT BRIGHTEST
WHEN NEARER EARTH*
By Ken Fitzgerald
Of The Herald Tribune Staff

In the West, after sunset these nights, the planet Venus shines more brightly than any celestial object except the sun and moon.

Like the moon, Venus has phases. These depend on how much of the object's visible disk is lit by reflected sunlight. But unlike the moon, which is brightest at full phase, Venus' light is greatest when only a thin crescent is visible. We cannot see "full" Venus. The planet is then on the other side of the sun and would have an apparent diameter only one-seventh that of her closest approach to earth. Greatest brilliance occurs when Venus is nearer the earth and appears larger in the sky than at other phases.

Venus orbits the sun at a mean distance of 67.2 million miles, the earth at 92.9 million miles. As we watch this spring and summer, Venus will move eastward until April 10, reach greatest brilliancy on May 13, then reverse course to disappear in the sun's glare early in June.

The planet will pass the sun on June 19 to appear in the morning sky late in the month, reach greatest brilliancy on July 26 and be furthest west of the sun on Aug. 29. Moving sunward during the fall and winter, Venus will be behind the sun in April, 1965, then reappear in our evening sky in late summer next year. (*Continued on page 332.*)

*© 1964, New York Herald Tribune, Inc. Reprinted with permission.

Although Venus takes only 225 days to orbit the sun, the earth is also moving. That brings Venus into evening view only once a year. Greatest brilliancy in the evening sky will occur in December, 1965.

Ancient astronomers, with their earth-centered solar system, could not explain this seemingly erratic planet except by supposing it was two planets, one in the morning and one in the evening.

This spring, Venus will be better placed for observation than it has been or will be for years. The path of the planet will take it well above the plane of the solar system. Also the plane, which is called the ecliptic, is higher in the daytime sky in summer because the earth is tilted to it.

Through a 6-inch or larger telescope, experienced observers see Venus as a gray globe with very faint pastel markings of blue, brown, pink and yellow. On the dark or night side of the planet they note an ashen light occasionally. Some amateur astronomers believe Venus can light the dark edge of the crescent moon, something to watch for on March 16 and 17 about 8 P.M. EST.

These phenomena have unknown causes. General belief is that irregularities in Venus' cloud cover vary the amount of light reflected. The markings do not appear permanent. The ashen light may be an electrical storm in the Venusian atmosphere.

Astronomers study Venus in full daylight when the planet is fainter. In contrast with the dark night sky Venus is blinding in a telescope. Venus can be seen with binoculars or a telescope, in the afternoon at 2:50 standard time. Stand in the shadow of a building, face due south and slowly sweep up and down the sky. Venus will look like the glint from a high-flying airplane.

Use the star map by orienting it with the Big Dipper as a guide. With the North Star as center the sky rotates during the night one-eighth of a revolution every three hours. A star map appears the first Sunday of each month.

GREETINGS FROM FIDO

If you should meet Sandy, the Airedale, who lives at 22 East Fifth Street, and he should say "Hello," don't run for the nearest telephone to call a psychoanalyst. Sandy actually talks.

His vocabulary is limited to three words, but with these three attention-getting signals, Sandy manages very well. He can say "Hello!" "Eat!" and "Out!"

Bobby Jamison, who lives where Sandy does, first observed Sandy's aptitude for talking when Sandy clearly said, "Out!" and headed for the door. Within a few weeks Sandy was saying "Eat!" with unmistakable clarity. He reinforced his demand after each signal by pulling his food dish a little farther from the corner. Bobby says that he then decided it was time for him to enter into conversation with Sandy and to teach him to say a few more words. He decided upon the word, "Hello," since that would be a polite way for Sandy to greet visitors, aside from wagging his tail.

He began by saying "Hello" to Sandy, but Sandy only laughed,—so Bobby says,—and thought it was an invitation to play.

Bobby persisted. Each evening before Sandy's dinnertime, he repeated the word, "Hello! Hello! Hello!" Sandy began to be annoyed with all this and tried barking and growling, but Bobby was determined to keep delaying the food until Sandy made some semblance of the sound "Hello."

One night the food was delayed longer than usual. In despair, Sandy began to make strained attempts at bringing forth some strange sound from his throat. Amazingly, the sounds came out in a high, squeaking falsetto—"Ugh oh!" Bobby shrieked for joy and his Mother came running to see what had happened. Sandy explained it to her by proudly saying again, "Ugh oh!"

Needless to say, Sandy had an extra fine dinner that night and has since enjoyed the attention he gets from anyone he meets, when he says in a very genteel and doglike tone, "Ugh oh!"

Bobby is now trying to teach Sandy to say "How are you?" but so far, Sandy seems to think three words from the talk of human beings are enough said.

What is the chief purpose of the feature about the brightness of Venus? What is the chief purpose of the feature about the talking dog? What makes each feature timely? In what ways does each feature embellish the day's news?

The Editorial

An editorial appears on the editorial page. It is generally unsigned and is understood to express the viewpoint of the editor or the publisher. As you read the following editorial, try to decide why the editor thought such an editorial should be written.

WHO ELECTED THE 'PAUL GRANTS'?*

In a student election at Eau Claire State College in Wisconsin, the name of Paul Grant received 38 percent of the votes for freshman treasurer. However, Paul Grant didn't exist. The name was placed on the ballot to study the voting habits of collegians.

Even considering the fact that students could reasonably assume that Paul Grant was a legitimate human being, it is still appalling that 38 percent of them could cast a ballot for someone who was entirely unknown to them. Nothing but the sound of Paul Grant's name helped them to adjudge whether the man they were voting for was a crook, a socialist, a billionaire or a moonshiner.

Granted, if these students were voting in a genuine public election, the bulk of them would have made at least a cursory examination of the record and principles and qualifications of the candidates. Even so, that so many of them were willing to make a mockery of the ballot is an indictment of the citizenship of our young Americans.

These young people attend an institute of higher learning. Presumably they understand that an uninformed vote can be worse than no vote at all. Whether the position of freshman treasurer is an honorary post or a functional one, not a single ballot should have been cast without a firm knowledge of the candidates.

The blame, perhaps, lies in part with the citizenship propaganda of recent years. A great deal has been made of the duty of the American citizen to vote; almost nothing has been made of the fact that he should vote responsibly. The ritualistic act of casting a ballot is only partway citizenship. The unthinking voter may simply help elect his own worst enemy, or an enemy of good government. . . .

There are altogether too many real "Paul Grants" in office, with many names and many purposes. Some of them are undermining the foundations of the republic. Who elected them?

*From the Phoenix *Gazette*. Reprinted with permission.

Make an outline of the editorial above. What do you discover about the structure? Does the editor wish to inform his readers, to influence them, or simply to express his opinion?

The Column

A column appears daily, or at regular intervals, under the columnist's name. It usually centers on a topic in which the writer has a special background, such as politics, music, the theater. Sometimes the columnist has as his chief purpose the entertainment of his readers with comments about topics that present themselves from day to day. Such is the case in the column below.

Each columnist usually has a following. Decide whether you would be likely to follow the writings of this columnist if they appeared in your daily newspaper.

Norton Mockridge
CRACKED WORD GAME GETS MORE PLAYERS*

Never, never, never have I had a response to anything I've written that compares with the reaction to the columns on "Fractured English." Hundreds of people have sent letters and postcards, phoned me at odd hours of day and night and even stopped me on the street to give examples of wounded words and traumatic terminology.

Everybody's asking for more, so far be it from me to skirt my duty or dog the manger.

As you may recall, all this started a few weeks ago when I told how my young son Randy said he had attackled a football player, and this got me to thinking about other classic examples of confused conversation. I am convinced, after reading all this mail, that we're on the verge of a whole new language and that English as we knew it will vanish in a whisk of smoke.

✷   ✷   ✷

Allan Kalmus, who's been collecting muddled clichés for years, says one of his clients contends he's been skating on thin ground and another says his partner always comes up smiling like a rose.

"No one is exempt from this disease," said Allan. Not the ad agency president who said, "You've got to separate the wheat from the shaft," and not even Allan, who admits he caught himself saying: "The proof of the pudding is on the other foot."

Harriet Van Horne is another great collector of malapropisms and she quoted some of them to me "per batem," as a friend of hers often says. "Don't buy any Oriental rugs," says this friend. "They have no resale value and they'll just be a drug on your shoulders."

Harriet's friend also hates apartments where you have to put garbage down the insinuator, she knows a man who blandished a cane, and she described a shy young man as a self-erasing person. (*Continued on page 336.*)

* © 1964, New York *World Telegram and The Sun.*

John Scott Fones has been storing up "Janisms," the say-
ings of his wife, ever since they were married. "Love," she
says, "is a many-splendid thing," but she knows a wife who'll
leave her husband at the slightest prevarication.

❖   ❖   ❖

Several people mentioned Yogi Berraisms, such as "The
Pirates can't get along without Dick Groat; he's the main clog
in their machine," and at least a dozen people said they have
friends who are proud of their sway shoes or sway jackets.

Al LeFaucheur's daughter, Lynne, always called it a heel-
horn instead of a shoehorn (and I think she's got something
there). A lady named Alice said that the auto accident was
caused by a train reaction, and an office worker told Vincent
Redding that she didn't want those papers clustering up her
file.

❖   ❖   ❖

"To sum it up," says Fred Dubrowsky, "those who have
been in this country a long distance, are finally learning to
speak a well United States."

What is the chief purpose of the preceding column? How does the
pattern of this column differ from that of the news stories on pages
329-330?

WRITING FOR THE NEWSPAPER

In the first part of this chapter, you examined examples of the news
story, the feature story, the editorial, and the column. In the second
part, you will try your hand at these four kinds of newspaper writing.

You must bring to newspaper writing the ability to handle sentences
and paragraphs effectively and to express yourself with relatively few
errors in spelling, punctuation, and grammar. You will need the ability
to add the special skills which you will discover as you prepare to write
a news story, a feature story, an editorial, and a column.

PREPARING TO WRITE A NEWS STORY

The news story dominates the newspaper. For this reason alone we
might give our principal consideration to the task of a news reporter,
but there is another reason why the reporter's task is basic to all journalistic writing. Unless you can afford to buy your newspaper and thereby
pick your own job, or unless you have gained a reputation as an authority

in some special area, you are not likely to get a chance to write features, editorials, or columns until you have first established yourself as an expert reporter.

The Reporter as a Fact-Finder

Since a news story is an account of a current happening that interests people, it is the job of the reporter to find the facts and assemble them into appropriate form. He must also be able to recognize what events make news. An editor may anticipate a story and send a reporter to get the facts. The reporter may telephone the information to his office, where the story will be written. However, the fact remains that reporters who rise to the top are those who can, if need be, find the story, get the facts, and write the story themselves.

Fundamental to the reporter's success is his integrity — both in dealing with the persons involved in the story and in recognizing his responsibility to report the story accurately. A reputation for honesty and fairness is the most important asset of a newspaper. The reporter also needs a well-organized mind and the ability to put his story together quickly in time to meet the deadline of his paper.

Probable Sources of News

When an editor learns of a train wreck or a quadruple birth, he does not need to think twice before dispatching his reporters. Many other great and historical events occur on schedule, or happen according to a plan. Reporters are on hand when ships are launched, when presidents are elected and inaugurated, or when important athletic contests are held. But what about the thousands of not-so-earth-shaking events? History may not hinge upon such stories, but they can be informative, humorous, tragic, or heartwarming.

Since there are certain places where newsworthy events are likely to occur, editors usually assign a reporter to cover a certain area, called his *beat*. Courthouses, police stations, hospitals, legislative halls are probable sources of news and are frequently covered by assigned reporters. By anticipating stories in this manner, the editor generally has a reporter ready to gather the information when a story breaks.

Exercise 1   *Discuss some of the possible newsworthy events which might occur on each of these beats:*

1. The City Hall

2. City, county, and state courts

3. Hospitals

4. Firehouses

5. The public library

6. Business enterprises

7. Social functions in a community

8. Your school administrators

9. Your school faculty

10. Your school's athletic program

11. Your school's music program

12. Your school's dramatics program

13. Your school library

14. Other activities at your school

Recognizing Newsworthy Events

The editor of a newspaper once sent a young reporter out to pick up some information, from which a routine story might be written. When the reporter returned, he had to admit that he had failed.

"But you know we needed a story to complete the edition," the editor said. "Why didn't you get a story?"

"I couldn't even get across town," the youth explained. "The bus I was riding in was involved in a big smash-up with some cars. People were hurt and traffic was tied up, so I had to come back without a story."

What was wrong with this reporter?

It is one of the clichés of the newspaper business that a good reporter has a "nose for news." Among all the events taking place within the range of his powers of observation, he must be able to sort out those happenings which, if reported, will capture the interest or imagination of a reading audience. Clearly, the youthful reporter in the story told above had no "nose for news," or he would have recognized that an accident was more newsworthy than the routine story assigned.

The successful reporter and the successful newspaper editor know, almost intuitively, what makes an event worthy of space in the paper. However, there are certain generally recognized standards of news value which will help you decide whether a story is newsworthy. A beginning reporter should check his idea for a story against these questions:

1. Is the event *important* to many persons?

2. Is it *current*?

3. Does the event deal with a *superlative:* the greatest, the fastest, the slowest, the first since . . .?

4. Will the news *benefit* many persons?

5. Should the event be reported in a particular paper because of its *proximity*, or nearness, to the readers?

Exercise 2   *Imagine that you are the editor of a newspaper in your community. Which of the items below should appear on the front page? In other words, which items are most newsworthy? Use the five questions about news value as a guide in making your selection. Then summarize in writing the reasons for your choices.*

1. A bakery truck has overturned on Main Street in your city. The driver is hospitalized and listed in fair condition.

2. A grass fire has been extinguished after burning over twelve acres of uninhabited land near the city dump.

3. The mayor's son and the daughter of a state senator who lives in your city have announced their engagement.

4. The president of a college in your city has resigned.

5. An elderly man has died after an extended illness. He is best known as the father of the driver of the only cross-town bus in your city.

6. A fireman has been scratched while rescuing the city librarian's cat from a tree.

7. Four persons have been injured and three more shaken up when two out-of-state cars were involved in an accident on the highway nine miles from your city. The injured were removed to a hospital in a neighboring town, and the wrecked cars were towed to a garage.

8. A storm has seriously damaged vegetable crops on over four hundred acres of farmland around your city.

9. Your high school basketball team is playing for the state championship tonight.

10. Three railway tank cars have been derailed about a mile from your city.

11. The head football coach at the college has resigned to take a better job, leaving behind him the longest winning streak currently standing in the country.

Distinguishing Fact from Opinion

Notice how the following sets of statements differ:

Group A

John Jones is a man.
John Jones is a married man.
John Jones' wife has brown hair.
Mr. and Mrs. John Jones have four children.

Group B

John Jones will never be President of the United States.
John Jones acts as though he owns the town.
I guess John Jones will quit his job, probably after the first of next year.

The second group of statements cannot be verified, since they are based upon guesses, personal evaluations, and future events — not upon events that can be observed directly. They are *opinions* rather than *facts*.

Covering a news story may involve recording statements of opinion. Guesses or personal evaluations may serve useful purposes, especially when facts are not available. The danger in using such statements in reporting a news story, however, lies in confusing opinion with fact, either in our own minds or in the minds of readers.

As was pointed out earlier, it is the reporter's job to report the facts. He should not write his own opinion into the report. If he includes opinion in his story, he should make clear whose opinion it is:

"Mayor Brown stated that he believes
this is a major advancement."

Exercise 3   *Imagine that the statements below relate to a fire which occurred recently in your town. Some of the statements are clearly someone's opinion and should not appear in a news story unless properly identified as such. Separate fact from opinion by listing the numbers of the statements and writing F or O beside each number. Make a written comment regarding each statement of opinion.*

1. A fire was fought by the Volunteer Fire Department last night at the Ezee Paint Plant.

2. The alarm was received at 11:10 P.M., March 3.

3. Four trucks were dispatched to the scene.

4. The fire was the most spectacular conflagration you ever saw.

5. Four fireman had oxygen administered to them at the scene.

6. The night watchman was unhurt.

7. The cause of the fire is thought to have been internal combustion originating in the paint shed.

8. Paint cans were hurled over a hundred feet from the fire by an explosion which occurred during the blaze.

9. After the blaze was extinguished, a lumberyard and an automobile repair shop were marked by smoke or water.

10. The loss was $30,000.

11. More than a hundred people gathered at the scene within a half hour of the sounding of the alarm.

12. It was a job well done, when the local crews finally subdued the blaze.

13. The town can certainly be proud of its Volunteer Fire Department.

The Structure of the News Story

Unlike the types of writing you have studied earlier, news stories are written according to a definite pattern. The most important information is given first in a sentence or paragraph called the *lead.* Following the lead, other details are given in descending order of importance. The last paragraphs are planned to include the facts of least importance for two reasons: (1) to enable the reader to get the essential facts quickly, (2) to allow the editor to cut the story for space, by chopping off the last paragraphs if necessary.

The structure of the news story may be best understood by contrasting it with the structure of a narrative. A news story begins with what might be the climax in a narrative, then dwindles down to the less important details, while the narrative gradually builds toward a climax.

The Lead. The first sentence or sentences in the story summarize the important information and lead you into the story. Quite naturally, the opening sentences of a news story have become known as the *lead.*

Leads for news stories are planned to answer several of the questions: "Who?" "What?" "Where?" "When?" "Why?" and "How?" Read the news story below and then reexamine its first paragraph to discover which of the five W's and the H are answered in the lead.

SOPH SETS 220 RECORD

Willie Montgomery, last-minute replacement on North High Golden Cyclones, streaked to a new meet record last night at the South High Indoor Track and Field Finals in Baxter Gym. Till yesterday a substitute dash man, he blazed over the Baxter track in 22 seconds, cutting 1.1 seconds from the old record, set in 1961.

On the Cyclone squad, fifteen-year-old Willie's opportunity came after a squad regular, Senior Dennis McCafferty, developed flu symptoms. The victory, which came near the end of the meet, brought the crowd to its feet. An estimated 2000 persons were on hand for the record run.

Although there were many heated matches in the course of the evening, no other records were threatened. The host South team won the meet, with North High tying Bates Preparatory for second place in team standings.

Coach Jerome Brown of the Cyclones admitted that the record-breaking performance of his slender, quiet sophomore had surprised him. "I knew Willie had the potential," Coach Brown said, "but frankly, I didn't think he would be coming along so rapidly. It is obvious, now, that I am going to have to reexamine my squad."

Paragraphs in a News Story.   In the example above, are the paragraphs which follow the lead arranged in descending order of importance? Could the editor cut this story for space without omitting the most essential facts?

Notice that the paragraphs in newspaper stories are generally shorter than those used in description or narration. Since newspaper columns are narrow, the stories are written with short paragraphs. It is easier for the reader to catch the substance of several short paragraphs than to wade through half a column of solid type.

Journalistic Style.   Journalistic style is necessarily brisk and swift-moving. Information must be set down in brief, concise form in an organized pattern that will enable the reader to get the essentials of the story quickly. The writing should be simple and direct, with no effort to impress the reader with the reporter's scholarly vocabulary.

Exercise 4   *Imagine that you are a reporter for the town paper and have jotted down these notes:*

Charlie Jones,   Raced inside a second time
A son of J. J. Jones of 230   Brought out Wilma Baker,
   Oak Street   aged 4

Eighteen years old
A North High senior
Student councilman
Saved lives
Gave an alarm
Summoned help
Broke down a door
Heard a dog barking
Saw smoke
Carried out Barry Baker, aged 2
Questioned a distraught parent.

Yesterday afternoon
April 19, 1965
About 2:15 P.M.
Just after fireman had been summoned elsewhere
Charlie was on his way home
The fire was at 1411 Maple
Near the East Circle Shopping Center
At the residence of Joe Baker

Think for a few minutes about how you should write the lead for your story. You cannot play up with equal importance the Who? What? When? and Where? Which of the W's is most important? With which one will you lead off? Which vital facts will you include in your lead?

Once you have decided upon the answers to these questions, try writing a good lead sentence. It is not as easy as it may seem at first glance. If your first effort produces an awkward sentence, try again—and again. Remember that several bits of information may be combined in the same sentence.

When you have produced a satisfactory lead, try writing the rest of the story, keeping in mind that facts should be arranged in order of descending importance.

Attracting the Reader's Attention. Suppose, in Exercise 4, a member of your class started his story with a lead that ran something like this:

> An eighteen-year-old North High School senior dashed into a flame-swept east-side home yesterday to carry to safety two terrified children who were trapped inside.
>
> Charlie Jones, a son of Mr. J. J. Jones of 230 Oak Street, rescued two youngsters after he heard a dog barking frantically and saw smoke pouring from a house at 1411 Maple, near East Circle Shopping Center.

Notice that the hero of the story is first identified as "an eighteen-year-old," then as a "North High School senior," and finally as "Charlie

Jones, a son of Mr. . . ." You might wonder why the writer didn't come right to the point in the first place and identify the hero as Charlie Jones. However, consider that the prospective reader might not know a "Charlie Jones" but does know several persons who could be referred to as "an eighteen-year-old" or as "a North High School senior." Isn't a person much more likely to keep on reading to find out if this item is about one of his acquaintances?

The first "Who?" is often presented in general terms that will catch the interest of many persons. Look at the news story you have written and see whether you need to revamp the lead to draw the attention of more readers.

WRITING A NEWS STORY

Suppose you are assigned to cover the next major sports event at your school and to prepare a news story for the school paper. How should you go about getting the story?

The event is scheduled so you will have the advantage of being there on time, in a good spot—perhaps the press box. You will also have equipped yourself with pencils and notebook and will probably have the lineup of players for both teams, with names spelled correctly. You will know the rules of the game and the signals used by the umpire or referee. All this preparation will give you background to interpret what happens, but you will also need to be alert for the unexpected.

Once the game begins, you will be busy jotting down information, according to some system that can be read easily later. You will have to get the notes down quickly. Otherwise, you may miss something important while you are bent over your notebook. A word, an abbreviation, or a number may be sufficient to recall a situation—if you are a good reporter.

Now suppose you are a regular reporter on the school paper, always looking for a story to break. You cannot make the careful preparation described above but will have to depend on your nose for news. You must be alert for a reportable event and be ready with pencil and notebook, when it happens. You must observe closely, be able to ask intelligent questions, know what questions to ask, take the trouble to find out how names are spelled, and sense what is important or unusual. The better background you have about a lot of things, the better equipped you will be to cover a story perceptively.

Exercise 5	*Putting into practice what you have learned about reporting, try your hand at these assignments.*

1. Cover the next sports event at your school and write a news story.

2. Find out about some interesting project now being planned or already under way in one of the classes in your school and write a story which would be of interest to other students.

3. Discover some newsworthy event in your community. Get the story and write it, as if it were to appear in the local paper.

PREPARING TO WRITE A FEATURE STORY

Newspaper features help to brighten up the day's news. They are entertaining or informative stories based on actual happenings, but written in a freer style than a news story. Feature stories provide contrast and variety in a newspaper and bring to the attention of the reader many interesting sidelights that might otherwise be missed.

Features are likely to appeal more to the emotions than to the intellect and are based on whatever people find amusing or entertaining or interesting. Favorite areas for features are the humorous, the mysterious, the courageous, the unusual. Stories with emotional appeal that concern children, older persons, or animals appear in almost every newspaper.

Features are often *timely*, rather than *current*. That is, they may focus upon a subject that does not break upon us suddenly, as with news events, but comes to our attention more subtly. A feature might point up the work being carried on regularly by a certain organization. In telling the story of what may seem like everyday happenings, the feature writer plays up one point of interest and develops a story that many persons will enjoy.

From the generally unobserved, the feature writer produces a story that evokes interest, sympathy, surprise, or laughter. He deals with the significant rather than with the apparent.

Ideas for feature stories are everywhere. Many good stories are never told because no one has thought about writing them. In the sample that follows, an interesting feature has been developed for a school paper through a student interview with a new faculty member. Notice how the writer has built the feature on the opening quotation. Note, too, how the direct quotations lend interest to the feature.

NHS IN CHEM TEACHER'S FORMULA
FOR HAPPINESS

By Wayne Ledbetter

"I felt that I had to get back into the classroom to make the fullest use of my training and experience." These are the words of Leo B. Burke, Jr., who this fall joined the Chemistry Department at North High.

"Once I decided to give up the private laboratory for the classroom, the selection of a school was almost automatic," Mr. Burke told *Northerner* interviewers. "North High has always impressed me with its accelerated program in chemistry for seniors. When the opportunity to teach here arose, I jumped at it."

Leo Burke is of medium height and has closely cropped gray hair thinning a bit at the top. When he smiles, his round face gathers into wrinkles around his eyes and mouth.

It is not a hard face, nor is Mr. Burke a hard man, although he has had to be tough. He was an infantry platoon sergeant in combat in Korea. "I am not worried about the softness of young Americans, either in war or in school," Burke says. "I know they will do what they must—if they are properly trained and have leaders they can respect."

After his experiences in Korea, Mr. Burke attended Syracuse University, where he acquired a Master's Degree in Chemistry in 1958. Since that time he has been employed as a research chemist for a number of large corporations. Last year he served as Director of the Hollyfield Laboratories in this city. The Burke family still makes its home near the laboratory, at 2901 East Lawn. Mr. Burke and his wife Mona have four children: Brian 8, Douglas 6, Karen 4 and an infant son Steven.

"Attempting to convey what I know about chemistry and the world to North High students these past few months has been the most satisfying undertaking of my life," Mr. Burke told *Northerner* reporters. "I hope I can continue here indefinitely."

Many of Mr. Burke's chemistry students share his hope.

Unlike the reporter who is sent out on a definite assignment, the feature writer is usually a self-starter who finds his own stories. The basis of a news story is an event. The basis of a feature is likely to be a person, a place, an object, or an idea. How do you suppose the writer of the above feature got his idea for the interview?

Exercise 6   *Imagine that you have been assigned to write a feature for your school paper. List at least five ideas that could be developed into features. A few suggestions are made below, but you should use them only to start your thinking.*

1. Think of three or four persons with whom an interview might provide a basis for a feature story. In each instance, you should have in mind the type of story you hope to draw out.

2. Think of places of interest that would be within your ability to visit. Do any of these places have historical background which would make a good basis for a feature?

3. List at least five feature-worthy objects found in your school. These might be everyday things, so familar that their interesting qualities have been overlooked: an antique typewriter in a classroom, a steam radiator that entertains the class each morning with its own special kind of music.

4. Think of two or three ideas that are current in the news and are being discussed around school. Explore some possible ways these issues could be made the subjects of features. Would you make a survey of student opinion? interview faculty or administrators? summarize comments from radio and TV reports?

WRITING A FEATURE STORY

With a subject in mind, and some notion of an approach to that subject, the feature still has to be written. The purpose of the feature is to surprise the reader, to entertain him, to carry him along into the yarn. The writer therefore frequently adopts a narrative technique and withholds the choice bit of information till the end of the story. Sometimes he uses a modified news style but feels no necessity for revealing the core of the news at the beginning.

Expert feature writers develop their individual techniques. Since you may need to follow a more methodical plan at first, these suggestions may prove to be helpful:

1. Appeal for interest in the opening remarks.
2. Introduce the central point you wish to make or the dominant impression you wish to create.
3. With imaginative details, expand, defend, enlarge upon, illustrate, or otherwise strengthen the central point or dominant impression.
4. Conclude in such a way as to leave the central point or dominant impression clear and fresh in your reader's mind.

Creating Interest in the Opening Remarks. Suppose a recent speaker at your school is a refugee from a foreign land. You have interviewed her and are going to write a feature for the school paper. She came to America after escaping in a hail of bullets from her homeland, from which emigration was forbidden. Her escape with her family represented their fourth try, all made under dangerous and sinister conditions. What a wonderful subject for a feature, but what a shame if this exciting story were hidden behind a dull opening sentence:

> Mary Doe has led a very interesting and exciting life.

Of a far more intriguing nature would be a sentence that sets the mood for the story:

> The fog that hovered in the streets of Warsaw on the morning of February 3, 1942, aided in the escape of . . .

At the opposite extreme is this opening for another feature:

> Does anybody know what happened to the Latin Club's song books?

Not only is the question technique overworked, but the weakness of this opening tries to "pump up" interest in a subject that has no broad basis of appeal (Presuming, of course, that there are no really mysterious aspects of the case of the missing song books — if so, these aspects should have been referred to in the opening.) Except for members of the club and other parties directly involved, a reader's response to the question might be: "Does anybody care what happened to the Latin Club's song books?" If the answer is "No," then the missing books do not rate a feature.

Obviously, an opening sentence should make the widest possible appeal, but the appeal must be made through a point of interest which clearly exists in the story. It is the writer's job to find that point of interest and to present it in fresh, stimulating language in his opening.

Exercise 7   *Imagining further details consistent with what is already given, write five possible openings for the feature on Mary Doe, mentioned earlier on this page. Study your results and rank the five opening sentences from most to least effective. Judge the results on the basis of interest and appropriateness.*

Introducing the Central Point. If you had just one sentence to convey what you want a reader to know or to feel about the subject, what would that sentence say? This is the central point or dominant impression to be made. It is not always stated directly in a feature; sometimes it is only implied through the details that are given. However, for a beginning feature writer, it might be well to state the point directly, bringing it in as smoothly as possible:

> The children in the Hampden Home
> will have no toys this Christmas unless
> outside sources furnish them.

Strengthening the Central Point. All other things in a feature are secondary to that essential information or feeling which the writer most wants to communicate, yet the supporting details are vital to the success of the feature story. Without an interest-catching opening, the reader might stop reading before the central point can be presented to him. By the same token, he might not give serious consideration to a central point, unless that point is supported in such a way as to convince the reader of its validity.

If the subject is a *person*, significant information about the person's actions, attitudes, behavior, appearance, mannerisms, may be needed. If the subject is a *place*, descriptive details, which may convey mood or feeling, may be in order. When the subject is an *object*, the details might involve the unique qualities of the object—its price, value, age, size, speed, efficiency, beauty. Should the subject be an *idea* or an *issue*, then perhaps the details of the controversy, if there is one, would make appropriate support or illustration.

In every case, the supporting detail might be expected to reflect maturity of judgment, as well as imagination and initiative. The writer should be expected to have given more thought to the subject than the average reader has.

Restating the Central Idea. If it is our aim to leave one idea or impression clearly with the reader, then it may be necessary to touch upon that impression or idea—perhaps even to state it again in the concluding passage. This often involves restating the central point in a different way. Freshness of the language in the new expression will allow for reinforcement of the idea without exact repetition.

Exercise 8   Write a feature appropriate for your school paper and based
on one of the ideas suggested below. Try to limit your story
to the space available for such a feature. Seven or eight paragraphs might be a reasonable length.

1. A personality feature based on an interview

2. A feature that gives interesting historical background
   about something in your community

3. A feature story about an animal: the first robin, the mascot
   for the school football team, the wild ducks that have taken
   up residence on a nearby lake

4. A humorous feature about an unexpected turn of events
   that might be of interest to most students in your school

PREPARING TO WRITE AN EDITORIAL

How well acquainted are you with the editorial page of the paper
you read most regularly? It is not usually labeled "Editorials," but you
can easily spot it because the material you find there is *opinion* rather
than news. Most editorials are unsigned but are generally written by
the editor or by some staff writer to whom the editor has assigned the
writing of certain editorials.

The purpose of the editorial writer varies, according to the topics he
feels deserve comment. He may wish to provide extra background for a
certain news story. He may wish to analyze a situation. He may hope to
influence his readers or persuade them. He may simply wish to express
his opinion about some topic of current interest.

Subjects as widely diversified as the news—economics, politics,
matters of social concern, problems of the nation, the world, or the
local community—are likely to be discussed frequently on the editorial
page.

Exercise 9   Collect at least ten editorials from various newspapers.
Label each clipping with the name of the newspaper and the
date on which it appeared.

1. Sort the editorials into categories. You will have to decide
   on the categories needed, but you might try *Politics,
   Economics, Social Welfare,* and *The Cold War* as a beginning.

2. Now select the editorial you think is most effective in its
   purpose and the one you find least effective. Write a

paragraph explaining your reasons for making these selections. Did you base your decision on the strength of the
writer's reasoning? Was writing skill a factor in your
decision?

3. When members of the class have made their independent
evaluations, compare notes. (Undoubtedly several persons
will have selected the same editorials.) Discuss the reasons for thinking that certain editorials are better than
others.

WRITING AN EDITORIAL

Editorials are usually brief. Space limitations seldom allow for more
than three or four paragraphs. Since columns on the editorial page are
frequently wider than those on the news pages, editorial paragraphs can
be a little longer than paragraphs in news stories.

Editorials should be written in a simple direct style. Of chief importance is the writer's ability to present a logical chain of reasoning.
Since space is limited, the writer usually develops his editorial by following a definite *pattern*: (1) a *title*, (2) an *introduction*, in which he
presents the main point, (3) a logically developed *discussion* of that
point, (4) a concluding *punch line*.

Exercise 10   *Using what you have learned about writing editorials in
this chapter and in Chapter 5, test your skill in editorial
writing.*

1. Study the last issue of your school paper, or think over
current issues at your school. What topics present themselves as subjects for editorial opinion? Select a subject
and write an editorial in which you express your views.

2. Think of some happening at your school on which an
editor might write an editorial in a rather humorous vein.
Remembering that it is not the role of a good editor to be
sarcastic but rather, upon occasion, to prick the conscience
of his readers with a bit of wit, write an editorial for your
school paper.

3. Take sides on a current political issue and write a carefully
planned, well-documented editorial in which you try to
influence your readers.

PREPARING TO WRITE A COLUMN

Certain news writers have a regular assignment for turning out a daily column for their papers. Such columns appear under the columnist's name, or *by-line*.

Newspaper readers form the habit of looking to a certain columnist for certain types of information, opinion, or entertaining chatter. Each columnist is usually a specialist in a certain field. Columnist A may be a Washington columnist, keeping the public informed about what is going on in our nation's capital. Columnist B may be a keen political observer whose writings show clearly that he is a Republican—or a Democrat. Columnist C may keep close track of what is going on in the Broadway theaters and fill his daily column with interesting bits of information about actors and new plays. Columnist D may write about sports. Columnist E may discuss business and finance. In any case, the columnist has built up background in a special field. It is his job to keep you up to date in that area.

A columnist usually develops a personal following of readers who anticipate his next offering. Sometimes these readers rejoice in finding a point of view similar to their own. When important events occur, they may look forward to the discussion of those events by their favorite columnist.

WRITING A COLUMN

The columnist's task is not an easy one. He has to grind out a column of a certain length to meet the newspaper's deadline each day. He also has to know considerably more than most of his readers do about his particular field and must keep up to the minute with new developments related to his specialty.

The column reflects the personality of the writer. As might be expected, writing style varies, according to the subject treated and the preferences of the columnist. However, what we have said earlier about journalistic style applies to the column. The columnist's style should be brisk and forceful and—above all—easily understood.

Exercise 11   *From at least two large dailies, clip the columns that appear regularly under columnists' by-lines.*

1. Classify the columns into three categories according to their main purpose: (a) those that inform; (b) those that attempt to influence; (c) those that entertain.

2. Select the writings of one columnist who seeks to influence or inform. After studying his columns carefully, write a paragraph in which you summarize what you have determined about this writer's attitudes on certain issues.

3. Select an area which you feel you are qualified to cover and which will be of interest to students in your school. Prepare a column for your school paper. You may need to review what you have learned about features and editorials in order to make your column distinct from either of these categories.

SUMMING UP

In this chapter you have become acquainted with four types of news writing: the news story, the feature, the editorial, the column. Basic to all news writing is the ability to express yourself clearly and concisely in a well-organized manner, to be able to get the facts and to get them accurately, to be able to work rapidly, in order to meet the deadline of the paper. In addition to this, each type of news writing requires certain special skills.

The news story, which is an account of a current event, is written according to a definite pattern. The lead gives the core of the news; all other details are arranged in descending order of importance.

In the feature story, where the primary purpose is entertainment or enrichment of the news, the structure is more flexible. Frequently the most important information is held until the latter part of the story and the style becomes similar to that of a narrative.

In the editorial, the editor of a newspaper has the opportunity to express his viewpoint on current issues. The structure of an editorial is planned to present a clear, logical development of thinking in a few paragraphs.

Columns are written by specialists in a particular field of interest and appear regularly under the name of the writer. Each columnist develops his own pattern for writing his column within the confines of good journalistic style.

Are You a Newshound?

There is an old saying that if printer's ink sticks to your fingers, you can never get it off. Some of you may already be wishing that you knew more about newspapers and journalists. If such is the case, you will find the research projects on page 354 rewarding.

1. Find out all you can about the way news from abroad reaches a newspaper office in this country. What part in news distribution is indicated by these words or abbreviations: AP, UPI, Tass, Reuters, teletype, telephoto, Telstar, microfilm?

2. Name ten leading newspapers in the United States. Name three important foreign newspapers. Secure samples of as many of these papers as possible.

3. Use the library to find out as much as you can about the life and work of three of these persons. Each of them was a news reporter, although you may recognize the names of some of them more readily for the writer's work in other fields.

    Richard Harding Davis
    Jack London
    William L. Shirer
    Ernie Pyle
    Edward R. Murrow

4. What is the meaning of these expressions as they are used in the newspaper world?

copy	galley
copy editor	legman
cover	proofreader
cub	squib
dateline	syndicate
follow-up	thirty

5. Plan a visit to a newspaper office and try to learn how a story is handled from the time it is assigned until it appears on the printed page.

Composition Workshop

Using the Dictionary

1. Name nine reasons for using a dictionary. If you can't think of nine reasons, turn the page.

2. Label these pairs of words as synonyms or antonyms: 1 delicate-fragile; 2. privilege-right; 3. trustworthy-undependable; 4. emphasize-stress; 5. precede-follow; 6. garrulous-talkative; 7. humane-merciless; 8. abundant-scarce; 9. appropriate-suitable; 10. monotonous-changing. If you need help, turn the page.

3. As you know, many words have various functions. Find five words that function as (a) a noun, (b) a verb, (c) an adjective. Then write a sentence to illustrate each usage. If you need help, turn the page.

Looking at Sentence Structure

1. To prove that you can distinguish between a complex and a compound-complex sentence, combine these simple sentences into (a) complex, (b) compound-complex: *Yesterday we went fishing. We caught only two small trout. The big ones were too clever for us.* For help, turn the page.

2. To prove that you understand the difference between active voice and passive voice, give an example of each. If you do not remember the distinction, turn the page.

3. To prove that you understand verbals, write three sentences to illustrate each, labeling the infinitive, the gerund, and the participle. For help with verbals, turn the page.

4. What is the meaning of parallel structure in the development of a sentence? Write an example. If you need help, turn the page.

5. What is the difference between a loose sentence and a periodic sentence? If you do not recall, turn the page.

Organization and Outlines

1. Explain this statement: "Parallel entries in an outline should be parallel in structure." If you need help, turn the page.

2. What are four ways of developing an outline? If you do not remember, turn the page.

3. Name at least three ways organization and outlining can improve your writing. For help, turn the page.

Helps with Using the Dictionary

1. The dictionary: (1) provides definitions, (2) aids in spelling, (3) aids in pronunciations, (4) indicates word classes, (5) gives abbreviations, (6) provides the origin of words, (7) labels words as obsolete, archaic, and so on, (8) labels words related to special subject areas, (9) provides illustrations.

2. *Synonyms:* 1, 2, 4, 6, 9. *Antonyms:* 3, 5, 7, 8, 10.

3. *Examples of noun, verb, adjective functions:* (1) There's a *spot* on your tie. Did you *spot* the error? Make a *spot* check. (2) What is your favorite *color*? *Color* it red. Some pages have *color* bands. (3) Clip the *hedge*. Why do you *hedge* about your decision? Walk on the *hedge* side of the road. (4) The *forward* on the team is a champion. I will *forward* your mail. What a *forward* child he is! (5) The *spring* is drying up. That pipe may *spring* a leak. What a lovely *spring* day this is!

Helps with Looking at Sentence Structure

1. *Complex:* Yesterday we went fishing but caught only two small trout because the big ones were too clever for us. *Compound-complex:* Yesterday we went fishing, but we caught only three small trout because . . . .

2. *Active:* This morning Sam's dog followed him to school. *Passive:* This morning Sam was followed to school by his dog.

3. *Verbals:* (Infinitive) It is often discouraging *to read* the news. (Gerund) *Camping* is great fun. (Participle) *Having run out of gas,* we had to walk home.

4. Parallel structure is the use of grammatical arrangement of closely related ideas: Jim's aim was to finish high school, to earn a college degree, and to enter his father's business.

5. A loose sentence is one in which the ideas follow in normal sequence in the predicate. A periodic sentence is one in which the main idea falls at the end.

Helps with Organization and Outlines

1. In outlining, the main divisions, such as I, II, and all subdivisions, such as A, B and (1), (2), should be entered consistently in either words, phrases, or sentences.

2. Outlines may be developed from: (1) random association with an idea, (2) logical divisions, (3) a central idea, (4) anticipating questions.

3. Outlining improves your ability to think logically, to retain what you read, and to write more effectively.

Description and Narration

1. What is the main difference between description and narration? If you do not know, turn the page.

2. Distinguish between the spatial approach to descriptive writing and the dominant impression approach. If you do not remember, turn the page.

3. In creating word pictures, description can be in either general or specific terms. Write sentences using these nouns specifically: (1) airplane, (2) flowers, (3) machine, (4) cars. If you need help, turn the page.

4. Descriptive language makes an appeal to the senses. Write a sentence to prove that you understand the appeal made to each sense, labeling the sense you are illustrating. If you need help with your sentences, turn the page.

5. In relating a story, events are usually told in chronological order. What does that statement mean? If you do not remember, turn the page.

6. What is a flashback in narration? If you do not remember, turn the page.

7. From what point of view is a narrative usually related? If you do not remember, turn the page.

8. In what fields of writing is narrative employed other than story-telling? If you need help, turn the page.

Exposition and Argumentation

1. What is the main difference between exposition and argumentation? If you do not recall, turn the page.

2. Why is the proper handling of exposition important? If you do not recall, turn the page.

3. In developing exposition, what six patterns are possible? If you do not remember, turn the page.

4. What are the requisites of a good argument? If you need help, turn the page.

5. Write three suitable topics for a debate. If you cannot think of any, turn the page for suggestions.

Helps with Description and Narration

1. Descriptive writing is used to create pictures of persons, places, and things. Narration is used to tell a story, usually as a means of entertaining.

2. Spatial approach gives external characteristics, such as size. Dominant impression approach presents a vivid conception from a personal point of view.

3. *Specific usage:* (1) The *DC 7* nosedived into the swamp. (2) Jean was wearing a *gardenia*. (3) On the farm last summer, Jim learned how to operate a *tractor*. (4) Look at all the *Fords* in that display window.

4. *Sight:* The snow on the trees glistened in the sun, almost blinding me. *Sound:* After the splash, I waited for the diver's head to appear. *Smell:* As I passed the bakery, I was tempted to forget my diet and buy some freshly baked bread. *Feel:* It was a relief to change from that scratchy woolen dress to a nylon robe. *Taste:* Just the thought of that chocolate cake makes me forget my dinner entirely.

5. Chronological order is the order in which events occur.

6. A flashback is a reference, in narration, to an earlier event, thus breaking the chronological order of the occurrences.

7. A narrative may be related from either the first-person point of view or the third-person point of view.

8. Narrative is employed in such fields as history, biography, journalism, and letter writing.

Helps with Exposition and Argumentation

1. Exposition explains while argumentation presents a point of view.

2. In exposition, it is assumed that the reader or listener needs every detail for a clear picture of the matter under discussion. It is therefore important that no details be omitted.

3. *Patterns:* definition, partition, comparison or contrast, classification, explanation of a process, cause and effect.

4. Argument should be based on information; should be clearly stated and outlined; should follow a chain of reasoning; should support statements with facts; and should anticipate counterarguments.

5. *Suggested topics:* Traffic laws should be more strictly enforced. High school fraternities should be abolished. Saturday night dances should not run past midnight.

Newspaper Writing

1. What is the difference between a news story and a feature story? If you do not remember, turn the page.

2. What purpose for writing has a columnist? In what fields does a newspaper often carry columns? If you do not recall, turn the page.

3. What is the job of the reporter? If you do not know, turn the page.

4. To a reporter, what is a beat? If you need help, turn the page.

5. What is the difference between facts and opinions in news writing? If you do not know, turn the page.

6. In newspaper parlance, what is the lead and what questions should it answer? If you do not remember, turn the page.

7. In what subject areas would a feature writer find material for his feature? If you do not know, turn the page.

8. Since a reporter may present only facts, where in the paper may opinions be expressed? If you do not recall, turn the page.

9. What pattern does an editor follow in developing his editorial? If you do not know, turn the page.

10. Why are the paragraphs of a news story written in descending order of importance? If you do not know, turn the page.

11. In connection with journalistic writing, what is a by-line? If you do not remember, turn the page.

12. In what category would you place each of the following examples of newspaper writing? For help, turn the page.
    (a) Early this morning the police had a call from John Doe, 216 Oak St., urging their help in finding his Seeing Eye, Duchess. Her owner, blinded by a car accident two years ago, sat up until 6 A.M., awaiting the return of his most faithful companion from her romp in the campus opposite his home. Mr. Doe fears she may have . . .
    (b) While Mr. and Mrs. Donald Thorpe were attending the theater last evening, burglars entered their home at 1012 Elm St. and escaped with jewelry and cash valued at over $10,000. Prints outside French doors involve two men, perhaps the very pair . . .
    (c) The young fans of the nation's gift to Hollywood will be gnashing their teeth on hearing that he plans to give up his bachelorhood. It has just been learned that he will shortly be honeymooning with the ingenue . . .
    (d) When will this ridiculous slaughter on our highways cease? How can our citizens force legislation that will help reduce the murders and suicides caused by . . .

Helps with *Newspaper Writing*

1. A news story is an account of an actual recent occurrence. A feature story is one that entertains, often appealing to the emotions and evoking interest, surprise, laughter, or sympathy.

2. A columnist writes to entertain readers with comments on specific topics. The popular columns cover these topics: music, the theater, TV, the movies, politics, food, finances, society, and gossip.

3. A reporter runs down the facts of a news story and then either telephones the information to his editor or writes his story as he wants it to appear in print.

4. A beat is an area to which an editor assigns a reporter to look for news that will interest readers.

5. Facts can be verified, while opinions are based on mere guesses. A reporter should not include his own evaluation of the facts he gathers.

6. A lead is the introductory sentence or sentences of a news story and should answer the questions *who, what, when, where, why,* and *how.*

7. Feature writers usually look for stories of courage, mystery, humor—any subject with an emotional appeal.

8. Opinions may be expressed only in the editorials.

9. *Editorial pattern:* title, introduction, discussion, punch line.

10. In a news story, the important paragraphs come first and dwindle in importance so that the story can be easily cut if it runs too long for the space assigned to it.

11. A by-line is the line carrying the writer's name under the heading of his article.

12. Newspaper categories: (a) feature story; (b) news story; (c) column; (d) editorial.

Supplementary Tests

A NOTE ON THE SUPPLEMENTARY TESTS. The test questions that follow cover the various phases of grammar and composition studied in *Modern Grammar and Composition 2.*

Part I

1. Identify the subject and the predicate in each of the following sentences. Indicate the subject noun (or noun substitute), the predicate verb, and each complement. Label the basic sentence pattern.
   (a) The president of the company addressed the stockholders.
   (b) The beagle that won the blue ribbon belongs to Mr. Stockman.
   (c) The sycamore is a shade tree.
   (d) The man talking to Father offered him a job in Alaska.
   (e) The Republican Party elected Lincoln president.

2. Name and illustrate three structural signals of verbs.

3. Name and illustrate three structural signals of nouns.

4. Write sentences to illustrate the following:
   (a) The use of the past participle form of a five-part irregular verb;
   (b) The use of the past form of a four-part irregular verb;
   (c) Three uses of the plain form of a regular verb.

5. List five different three-part irregular verbs and use all three forms of each verb in a sentence.

6. Write sentences to illustrate the use of a noun clause, an adjective clause, an adverb clause.

7. Analyze the following sentence in terms of headwords and modifiers:
   The ancient volcano, which had long been dormant, spewed out clouds of black smoke which darkened the morning sky.

8. Construct a N-LV-ADJ sentence in which the subject and the complement serve as headwords of a cluster of modifiers.

9. Write pairs of sentences to illustrate the following:
   (a) A word used as a noun and then as the modifier of a noun;
   (b) A word used as a noun and then as a verb;
   (c) A word used as an adjective and then as a verb;
   (d) A word used as an adverb and then as a noun.

10. Write five sentences that illustrate the use of five different noun-modifiers that are ordinarily not thought of as belonging to the adjective word class.

11. List and illustrate five functions of the infinitive or infinitive phrase.

12. Describe the function of each of the underlined verbals or verbal phrases in the following sentences:
    (a) <u>Scaling Mt. Everest</u> is a heroic feat.
    (b) We saw Walt Disney <u>walking along Wilshire Boulevard</u>.
    (c) I like peaches <u>frozen in cream</u>.
    (d) The climbers huddled under a small rock outcropping <u>to conserve body heat</u>.
    (e) They found the revolver <u>buried in the mud</u>.

13. Write sentences to illustrate the following:
    (a) A nonrestrictive appositive;
    (b) An absolute structure;
    (c) A noun clause in apposition with a noun;
    (d) The inflection of personal pronouns for case;
    (e) The third-person, singular, masculine pronoun used as a subject.

14. Correct the sentences that do not conform to standard grammatical usage.
    (a) He is one of those boys who worries about everyone's troubles but his own.
    (b) Jim saw his brother walking along the boulevard in his new sport jacket.
    (c) Dad promised that the final decision would be up to Mother and I.
    (d) My sister along with several friends have gone to Mount Vernon for the week end.
    (e) On the walls of the library are displayed the prize-winning photographs.
    (f) Miss Sills asked Tom and I to make a poster for Book Week.
    (g) Bill Jones is working this summer, which is the best thing that could have happened to him.
    (h) This is the young lady whom we all love and admire.
    (i) Will anyone be taking their car to the game?
    (j) Very often the car what costs the most is expensive to maintain.

Part II

1. Punctuate the following sentences:
   (a) The riot spread through the village army troops finally had to be called out
   (b) George Mother exclaimed weve run out of gas
   (c) The obscure poet MacIntosh wrote a ballad which he called Skating in the Highlands
   (d) This report according to a reliable source tells of a secret attempt to overthrow the current dictator
   (e) If the weather is clear tomorrow well go to the Blue Water Inn for a lobster dinner.
   (f) Mother gave a party for Mrs Smith who is leaving for Denmark tomorrow
   (g) Whos afraid of the big bad wolf joked Uncle Joe as he moved hesitantly toward the shed

2. Write sentences to illustrate the following:
   (a) Parallel structure;
   (b) A loose sentence;
   (c) A periodic sentence;
   (d) A balanced sentence;
   (e) A compound-complex sentence.

3. Write five sentences illustrating the effective use of verbal phrases.

4. Change each example of ineffective passive voice to the active voice:
   (a) A new park will be erected on the south side of town by the city.
   (b) My sister has been taught by experts.
   (c) A twenty-dollar bill was found by Mr. Downs in his overcoat pocket.

5. List and discuss eight different ways in which the dictionary may be of help to the serious student of grammar and composition.

6. Make a detailed outline for a theme on one of the following topics:
   The Game of Baseball
   Baking a Chocolate Cake
   The High School Cafeteria
   The High School Library

7. Describe three different methods of working out an outline.

8. Write a brief description of one of the following:
   My Favorite Food
   The Family Car
   Make the description as personal as possible.

9. What is meant by "point of view" in narration? Describe two different ways in which a story may be told.

10. Describe four effective ways to develop an exposition.

11. List five general principles for making an argument convincing.

12. Write a short theme arguing either for or against a change of menu in the school cafeteria.

13. List four different kinds of newspaper writing. Differentiate between these types.

14. Write a news story reporting some recent event in your school — a basketball game, an accident, the visit of some person of prominence, or some other incident which you consider newsworthy.

The Language of Grammar

One of the problems you have to face in the study of grammar is the acquisition of a working vocabulary of the words and phrases used to describe the structure of language. To help you acquire and master this vocabulary, this section of your text lists alphabetically — with an explanation and with illustrations — the words and phrases essential to an understanding of grammar. Most of the terms used in each explanation have their own entries.

"The Language of Grammar" is intended as a ready reference to the terminology used in Part I of your text. The Index (pages 405-413) will help you find those pages on which most topics are discussed in greater detail.

Absolute Structure

The term *absolute structure* describes a sentence element that apparently does not have a specific function within the sentence.

> The guests having left, we began the disheartening task of cleaning up the living room.

Active Voice

The term *active voice* describes the form of a verb in a N-V-N or N-V-N-N PATTERN in which the subject performs the action communicated by the verb. Active voice is contrasted to the passive voice in which the subject is usually the receiver of the action.

Adjective

The term *adjective* describes a word class. Adjectives can be identified in communication by their form and their function.

Some adjectives have characteristic suffixes: careless, attentive, cautious. Adjectives may be inflected by adding -*er* and -*est* to show degrees of comparison: young, younger, youngest. Words called *intensifiers* are frequently used with adjectives: very young, really pleasant, more beautiful. The intensifiers more and most and less and least are used to show the degree of comparison of some adjectives of two syllables and of all adjectives of three or more syllables.

Adjectives function in the sentence as modifiers, linking-verb complements, and objective complements.

> The rude child glared at Mr. Prince.
> The child was rude.
> Mrs. Prince thought the child rude.

Adjective Clause

The *adjective clause* is one of three kinds of subject-predicate word groups, sometimes called subordinate clauses. The adjective clause modifies a noun or a noun substitute. It follows the noun which it modifies. Adjective clauses are usually introduced by the connectives *who, whose, whom, which,* or *that.*

> I pity people who are always in a hurry.
> Some plants have a mechanism that measures time.

Adverb

The term *adverb* describes a word class. Many words belonging to this class are characterized by suffixes such as *-ly, -ward, -time, -long: happily, sideward, sometime, headlong.* Some adverbs are marked with the prefix *a-: aboard, away, ahead.* There are also several miscellaneous adverbs such as *soon, tomorrow, then, still, north.* Semantically adverbs answer to *where, when, why, how,* and sometimes *how much.*

Adverbs function usually as modifiers of verbs and of predicate adjectives. However, adverbs also modify other adverbs, nouns, and sometimes the whole sentence.

> The shadows stole swiftly across the sand.
> The tide seems unusually low.
> We trained our binoculars directly north.
> The heron took one dainty step forward.
> Suddenly, the gull snapped up three fish.

Adverbs also function as linking-verb complements.

> The contest will be tomorrow.

Adverb Clause

The adverb clause is a subject-predicate word group, sometimes known as a subordinate clause. An adverb clause usually modifies a verb or a predicate adjective, but it may modify an adverb.

> We left when the tide reached the halfway mark.
> It was so cold that we shivered all the way home.
> It was late when the phone rang.

Sometimes an adverb clause introduces a sentence. In this position, the clause usually modifies the whole sentence.

> Although it was not yet dawn, the blackness of the night was perceptibly lessening.

Affixation

The process by which a prefix or a suffix is attached to a root or to a root word is called *affixation.* Suffixes are used primarily as signals of function: *-ion* is a signal that *action* functions as a noun; *-ate* is a signal that *activate* functions as a verb. Prefixes, however, have a lexical function: they change the meaning of the root or the root word to which they are attached. *Postwar,* for example, means something quite different from *prewar.*

Agreement

The bound relationship that exists between subject and verb under certain conditions is called *agreement.* Agreement is expressed by concurrent changes in the form of the subject and the verb. A singular subject is followed by the singular form of the verb. A plural subject is followed by the plain form of the verb.

> My child reads well.
> Some children read poorly.

Analytic Language

An *analytic language* is one that depends on word order, position, and function words rather than on inflectional changes as determiners of function or meaning. English is an analytic language. The term *analytic* is contrasted with *synthetic,* which refers to a language that depends largely on inflection as a signal of function. Latin is a synthetic language.

Antecedent

The *antecedent* is a word or group of words replaced and referred to by a noun substitute. In context, the antecedent precedes the noun substitute.

> Churchill published his memoirs.
> A solitary hermit crab dragged its shell house along the beach.

Apposition (*See also* Close Appositive, Loose Appositive.)

Technically, *apposition* is a side-by-side relationship. An appositive relationship exists ordinarily between nouns or between a noun and a noun clause.

> The cereus, a nocturnal cactus, has large fragrant flowers that open around midnight.
> The fact that most birds see better by day is indisputable.

Auxiliary

The *auxiliary* is commonly called a "helping verb." It serves two main functions. As a function word it serves as a verb marker or signal. In the verb phrase, it serves to communicate shades of meaning in time, attitude, feeling, and condition. Combinations of auxiliaries in a verb phrase give flexibility and lend fine shades of meaning to the English language.

> I can play the piano.
> I should play the piano.
> I might have played the piano.

Basic Sentence Elements

Two *basic elements* of the English sentence are the subject and the predicate.

> The cock / crowed.

The keyword in the subject is a noun or a noun substitute; the keyword in the predicate is a verb. When a verb does not communicate of itself all that the writer or speaker wishes to say, a noun or a noun substitute or an adjective is used in the predicate as a complement.

> The chairman / banged his gavel.
> His words / are always blunt.

The three basic elements of the English sentence, then, are the subject, the predicate, and the complement.

Basic Sentence Patterns

The basic sentence elements communicate meaning in seven basic patterns.

1. N-V
2. N-V-N
3. N-V-N-N
4. N-LV-N
5. N-LV-ADJ
6. The Inverted Sentence
7. The Question

Each of these patterns is described in this glossary under its own entry.

Case Form

Case describes the inflected forms appropriate to certain functions of personal pronouns and of those subordinators known as relative pronouns.

SUBJECT CASE FORM (SUBJECT FUNCTION)
He planned the trip.
We are staying in Oconto on Green Bay.
Here is the man who will guide us.

OBJECT CASE FORM (OBJECT FUNCTION)
Dave met him at the dock.
The guide gave us some good tips.
The guide, for whom Dave developed a keen respect,
    knew all the best fishing grounds.

POSSESSIVE CASE FORM (MODIFYING FUNCTION)
That was our best catch.
Whose catch broke the record for bluefish?

Clause (*See* Subject-Predicate Word Group.)

Close Appositive (*See also* Apposition.)

A *close appositive* is one which has a restrictive, or identifying, relationship to the word with which it is in apposition.

the widow Smith
my neighbor Mulligan
his sister Jean

This type of appositive may be contrasted with the nonrestrictive, or descriptive, relationship of the loose appositive.

Comma Fault

The term *comma fault* describes the unconventional use of a comma instead of a semicolon between two basic sentence patterns that are not joined by a co-ordinator.

The game was over, we had lost again.
                        ∧

Harold has a virus, therefore, he can't pitch in the play-off game.   ∧

Comparative Degree (*See* Comparison of Adjectives and Adverbs.)

Comparison of Adjectives and Adverbs

Comparison is the grammatical device of affixing -*er* or -*est* to a modifier or of putting the intensifiers *more* and *most* or *less* and *least* before a modifier in order to show a different degree of the quality or characteristic indicated by the modifier.

Adjectives (and adverbs) have three degrees of comparison. An adjective in its simplest, or plain form, is in the positive degree: *quick*. An adjective used to compare two persons or things is in the comparative degree: *quicker*. An adjective used to compare more than two persons or things is in the superlative degree: *quickest*. Some adjectives of two syllables and all of three or more syllables are compared by using *more* and *most* or *less* and *least*.

A few adjectives have different words for the comparative and superlative degrees: *good, better, best*. All adverbs ending in *-ly* are compared by using *more* and *most* or *less* and *least*.

Complement

The *complement* is one of the three basic sentence elements. Verbs in certain contexts do not communicate by themselves all that the speaker or writer wishes to say. Such verbs require a noun, an adjective, or another word to complete the sense of the predicate. The complement is usually a direct object, an indirect object, a linking-verb complement, or an objective complement.

The Romans added an extra month to the calendar.
Sosigenes gave Caesar invaluable advice.
Our present calendar is slightly inaccurate.
This inaccuracy will become a problem in 4905.
Many countries considered the adoption of the Gregorian calendar a religious issue.

Complete Subject

The *complete subject* refers to the word group consisting of the subject noun (or noun substitute) and its modifiers.

The fact that man possessed the capacity to rise from bestial savagery to civilization at a time when it had never before been done / is the greatest fact in the history of the universe.   *James Henry Breasted*

The complete subject includes everything to the left of the slash mark.

Complex Sentence

A *complex sentence* is one that includes one or more subordinate clauses. Subordinate clauses are classified as adjective clauses, adverb clauses, and noun clauses.

An expert is a man who has stopped thinking. *Frank Lloyd Wright*

My interest is in the future because I plan to spend the rest of my life there. *Charles Kettering*

What man knows is everywhere at war with what he wants. *Joseph Wood Krutch*

Compound Grapheme (*See* Grapheme.)

Compound Phoneme (*See* Phoneme.)

Compound Predicate

The term *compound predicate* describes two or more predicates joined by a coordinator.

The otters bickered and snarled at one another.

Compound Sentence

A *compound sentence* is one which contains two or more basic sentence patterns joined by a connective. In some compound sentences, a semicolon substitutes for the connective.

Many plans went through Willie's mind, but there was no pleasure connected with any of them.
Gramps was an understanding man; he greeted me without mentioning my unfinished chores.

Compound Subject

The term *compound subject* describes two or more subjects joined by a coordinator.

The big barn and the tumbledown house sprawled among the willows.

Compound-Complex Sentence

A *compound-complex* sentence is a compound sentence which contains one or more subordinate clauses.

> When he reached the clearing, the tiger was still in the bush, and Ramsay could see the consternation on the faces of the villagers.

Conjunction (*See also* Connective.)

A *conjunction* is a connective. Conjunctions that join coordinate elements are called coordinators. Conjunctions that include subordinate clauses within a basic sentence pattern are called subordinators.

> Byron's on a diet, but he visits the Sweet Shoppe regularly.
>
> Byron visits the Sweet Shoppe regularly, although he's supposedly on a diet.

Conjunctive Adverb

Adverbs that function as connectives between coordinate clauses are called *conjunctive adverbs.*

> Byron's on a diet; nevertheless, he visits the Sweet Shoppe regularly.

Connective

A *connective* is a function word that (1) makes a word group or a subject-predicate word group part of a basic sentence pattern and (2) joins two or more basic sentence patterns into a compound sentence. Connectives include prepositions, coordinators, subordinators, and conjunctive adverbs.

Consonant

A *consonant* is a speech sound that is uttered with a complete or partial stoppage of the breath. Consonants are represented in written English by all the letters of the alphabet except *a, e, i, o, u, w, y,* and *h.* The last three are sometimes called *semivowels.* The first five are vowels.

Conventions of Punctuation

The term *conventions of punctuation* describes those standards of punctuated English that are a matter of custom and not of syntax.

Coordinate Adjectives

Two adjectives that modify the same word and have equal semantic value as modifiers are called *coordinate adjectives*. They are separated by a comma.

a shy, awkward girl
an intelligent, interesting conversationalist

Coordination

Coordination is the grammatical process of joining two or more basic sentence patterns either with or without connectives.

The clouds rolled about us, and the wind roared.

Coordinator

A *coordinator* is a connective ordinarily used to join two coordinate clauses in a compound sentence, two nouns or noun substitutes in a compound subject, two verbs in a compound predicate, and so forth.

The otters startled me, and I dropped my can of worms.
Missy and I caught several trout in quick succession.
The sun was past the zenith and began to slide down the western sky.

Cumulative Adjectives

Sometimes an adjective has a very close relationship to the noun it modifies. When a modifier is placed before this combination, it actually serves as a modifier of both the first adjective and the noun. Such modifiers are called *cumulative adjectives*. There is no comma between cumulative adjectives.

the huge old tree
the hardy young tree
the pleasant German woman

Determiner

A *determiner* is a function word that serves as a noun-marker. A determiner always precedes the noun and any single-word modifier or combination of single-word modifiers that comes before the noun.

> the mare
> the skittish mare

Diphthong

A *diphthong* is a compound phoneme $(\backslash \dot{o}i \backslash)$ in which two simple phonemes $(\backslash \dot{o} \backslash + \backslash i \backslash)$ are blended so completely that they may be considered one sound. The compound phonemes $\backslash a\ddot{u} \backslash$ and $\backslash \bar{\imath} \backslash$ $(\backslash a \backslash + \backslash \ddot{u} \backslash$ and $\backslash \ddot{a} \backslash + \backslash i \backslash)$ are also diphthongs.

Direct Object (*See also* Inner Complement.)

In a N-V-N PATTERN, the complement is a *direct object* and the verb is a transitive verb.

> Each cabin accommodates two campers.
> We took the shortest possible route.
> Stoney forced his horse into a spectacular perpendicular rear.

Double-Bar Juncture

Double-bar juncture $(\diagup \parallel \diagup)$ is a terminal juncture accompanied by a rising pitch.

> Are you leaving now?
> 2   3
> Are you leaving now ‖

Double-Cross Juncture

Double-cross juncture is a terminal juncture accompanied by a falling pitch.

> I am leaving now.
> 2   3 1
> I am leaving now #

Feminine Gender (*See* Gender.)

First Person (*See* Person.)

Five-Part Irregular Verb

There are approximately fifty verbs remaining in the English language that are inflected with five forms — the plain form, the singular form, the past form, the present participle, and the past participle.

PLAIN	SINGULAR	PAST	PRESENT PARTICIPLE	PAST PARTICIPLE
go	goes	went	going	gone
throw	throws	threw	throwing	thrown

Five-part verbs have a special form (the past participle) which is used with certain auxiliaries and with combinations of these auxiliaries.

> Michael has gone into town for supplies.
> He has been gone since sunup.

Almost all other verbs, both regular and irregular, use the past form in the function illustrated above.

Form

Morphology, a branch of the study of grammar (structure), deals with form — form of words, affixes, stems. When we speak of characteristics of form, we think of the inflected forms of verbs, nouns, pronouns; we think of the characteristic suffixes that mark nouns, adjectives, adverbs, verbs. Form is contrasted with function which relates to position, or syntax. Function determines meaning, and form usually serves as a signal of function.

> Mary is writing a poem.

The verb is *writing*. Its function, or syntax, is that of predicate verb in a N-V-N PATTERN. We identify *writing* as a verb because of its position between the subject and the complement. However, its form (the -*ing* inflectional suffix) serves to reinforce its position and to signal its function.

Four-Part Irregular Verb

There are approximately sixty four-part irregular verbs in English. These verbs do not have a special form for the past participle as do the five-part irregular verbs. The past form is used in those contexts in which the past participle of a five-part verb would be used.

PLAIN	SINGULAR	PAST	PRESENT PARTICIPLE
keep	keeps	kept	keeping
lay	lays	laid	laying
spend	spends	spent	spending

> I spent five dollars.
> I've spent all my money.

Function

The term *function* describes the way in which a word or a word group communicates within a sentence. The various functions include subject, predicate, complement, modifier, appositive. Position — reinforced by signals of form and by certain function words — is the most important determinant of function.

> The groom has harnessed the team.

The position of *groom* before the verb is the normal position of the subject noun. The determiner *the* is a noun-marker and tends to reinforce the factor of position. The position of the verb between the subject and the complement is the most important signal of predication. Here, position is reinforced by the *-ed* inflectional verb suffix and by the function word *has* which is also a verb-marker. The position of *team* after the verb is the normal position of the complement.

Function Word

The term *function word* describes those words which have no lexical meaning but which give pattern or structure to communication. Function words include connectives, pronouns, auxiliaries, determiners, and particles.

> Byron and Keats were romantic poets.
> We like their poems.
> Jan is reading "Darkness."
> The world is a bundle of hay.   *Lord Byron*
> Please read quietly.

Functional Shift

The term *functional shift* describes the grammatical device whereby a given word may be used in a variety of functions.

> NOUN   The work on the new house is almost finished.
> MODIFIER   The accountant prepared a work sheet.
> VERB   The men won't work on Saturday.

Gender

Gender relates in a general way to sex. In English only the personal pronouns in the third-person singular are inflected for gender.

> MASCULINE   he   him   his
> FEMININE   she   her   hers
> NEUTER   it   its

Gerund

When an *-ing* verbal functions as a noun, it is called a *gerund*.

Seeing is believing.
"I wouldn't dream of spying," said Aunt Wilma.
Oscar dislikes studying.

Gerund Phrase

When a gerund takes a complement or has a modifier, the word group formed is a verbal phrase, or—more specifically—a *gerund phrase*.

Oscar dislikes studying poetry.

Grammar

The word *grammar* is a popular term, not a technical term. It is a term with a number of different meanings. In modern terminology, *grammar* refers to the structure of language or to a description of that structure. As developed in *Modern Grammar and Composition*, grammar is the study of the form and function in communication of the words and word groups that make up sentences. It includes a study of the structure of the words themselves and of the patterns of sound that make up the words. It includes the study of the relation of sound to spelling and of intonation to punctuation.

English is not a static system of language. Twentieth century English is different from nineteenth century English, and nineteenth century English is in turn different from the language of Shakespeare. In the same way, the English of Chaucer's time is difficult for many to understand and the language of Beowulf, although called "Old English," seems to us now as if it were a foreign tongue. It is important to remember, then, that grammar is a description of language as we observe it now, not as it was observed one hundred years ago, two hundred years ago, or several centuries ago.

To many people, grammar is nothing more than a study of what is to be preferred or avoided in inflection and syntax. Although *Modern Grammar and Composition* sets up guidelines for clear and effective communication, its emphasis is on understanding the structure of the English language.

Grapheme

The *grapheme* is the basic unit of the written language. The twenty-six letters of the alphabet are the principal graphemes of English. A single letter that represents a sound is a simple grapheme; two or more letters that represent a sound are a compound grapheme. The *f* in *fake* is a simple grapheme. The *gh* in *laugh* is a compound grapheme. Both the *f* and the *gh* represent the phoneme \f\, one of the basic sounds of our language.

Headword

The *headword* is the nucleus around which clusters of modifiers are built. The headword may be a noun, a verb, an adjective, an adverb, a function word, or a verbal. A noun cluster refers to a noun headword and its modifiers, a verb cluster to a verb headword and its modifiers, and so forth.

The sudden thunder of pounding hoofs broke the silence.

Headword	thunder
Modifiers	sudden
	of pounding hoofs

The foal suddenly trotted off into the gathering dusk.

Headword	trotted
Modifiers	suddenly
	off
	into the gathering dusk

Immediate Constituents

The *immediate constituents* are the largest functioning parts in a structure.

The stallions / fought wildly.

This sentence has two immediate constituents: the subject *The stallions* and the predicate *fought wildly.* The subject in turn has two immediate constituents: the determiner *The* and the subject noun *stallions.* The subject noun consists of two immediate constituents: the morphemes *stallion* and *s,* an inflectional ending. The predicate has two immediate constituents: the verb *fought* and the adverb *wildly.* *Wildly* has two immediate constituents: the morphemes *wild* + *ly.*

Indirect Object (*See also* **Inner Complement.**)

> When the outer complement in a N-V-N-N PATTERN is a direct object, the inner complement is an *indirect object.*
>
> > We handed every senior a copy of the *Tattler.*
> > Dad gave Grandma an electric broom for her birthday.

Infinitive

> The *infinitive* is the plain form of the verb—or the past or past participle form plus auxiliary—introduced by the function word *to.* The infinitive is a verbal that functions in the sentence as a subject, as a complement, as a modifier, or as an appositive.
>
> > To quit now would be madness.
> > Mother likes to weed after a rainstorm.
> > We came to see your prize dahlias.
> > It's exciting to ride the waves.
> > Gramps' dream, to live in Hawaii, just may come true.

Infinitive Phrase

> When an infinitive takes a complement or has a modifier, the word group formed is a verbal phrase, or— more specifically—an *infinitive phrase.*
>
> > The plot to burn down the palace was thwarted by the guard.

Inflection

> *Inflection* refers to the changes in form that a word undergoes in order to mark certain grammatical distinctions.
>
> *Noun:*

SINGULAR	PLURAL	POSSESSIVE
girl	girls	girl's
woman	women	woman's

> *Verb:*

PLAIN	SINGULAR	PAST	PRESENT PARTICIPLE	PAST PARTICIPLE
swim	swims	swam	swimming	swum
talk	talks	talked	talking	

> *Pronoun:*

PERSON		NUMBER	
First	I	Singular	I
Second	you	Plural	we
Third	he		

GENDER		CASE	
Masculine	he	*Subject*	I
Feminine	she	*Possessive*	my, mine
Neuter	it	*Object*	me

Inner Complement

In the N-V-N-N PATTERN, there are two complements, an *inner complement* and an outer complement. These terms describe the position of the complements. In general, two main sentence types conform to this pattern.

I sent Doris a check for fifty-two cents.

In this sentence, the outer complement is a direct object and the inner complement is an indirect object.

The Navy made Uncle Joe a commander.

In this sentence, the outer complement is an objective complement and the inner complement is a direct object.

Intensifier

In modern grammar, words like *very, rather, more, most, less, least* are called intensifiers, not adverbs. *Intensifiers* are function words with little lexical meaning. They are used with adjectives and with adverbs.

very quick	rather weak
most unusual	less forcibly

Intonation

Intonation describes the changes in pitch, stress, and juncture which make up the communication pattern of spoken English. This pattern is unique to English; other languages have their own patterns. Intonation helps us respond to questions and statements. A shift in stress sometimes indicates a change in the function of a word.

Intransitive Verb

The verb form used in the N-V PATTERN is an *intransitive verb*. It does not have a complement.

A crown fire burns through the tops of trees.

A verb may be intransitive in one sentence and transitive in another.

> The raging surface fire burned for three days.
> The fire burned an acre of Christmas trees.

Inverted Sentence

The normal order of the basic sentence elements is: SUBJECT-VERB-COMPLEMENT.

When the position of subject and verb is changed in any way, we describe the change as "inverted order." If the sentence communicates a statement, we think of the sentence as an *inverted sentence*, one of the seven basic sentence patterns.

> There are my uncle and aunt.
> Here is your cheeseburger.

The two preceding sentences illustrate the most common types of inversion. However, inverted sentences are not necessarily limited to these types.

> In the distance rose the jagged peaks of Lonesome Mountain.

Inverted Word Order

When a sentence is written with the normal positions of the subject and verb wholly or partly changed, we speak of the word order as inverted. *Inverted word order* occurs in the inverted sentence, described above, and in the question.

> Were you at the songfest?
> Has this pot been washed?
> When does the next bus leave?

Irregular Verb

The *irregular verbs* are those whose pattern of inflection differs from that of the regular verb.

	PLAIN	SINGULAR	PAST	PRESENT PARTICIPLE
REGULAR VERB	ask	asks	asked	asking
IRREGULAR VERB	bend	bends	bent	bending

There are five-part, four-part, and three-part irregular verbs. The most irregular verb is *to be*; it has eight different forms: *be, am, is, are, was, were, being,* and *been.*

Five-Part Irregular Verb

			PRESENT	PAST
PLAIN	SINGULAR	PAST	PARTICIPLE	PARTICIPLE
grow	grows	grew	growing	grown

Four-Part Irregular Verb

mean	means	meant	meaning

Three-Part Irregular Verb

cost	costs	costing

Juncture

As we speak, we separate our words and word groups with minute pauses. These pauses vary in length and in accompanying pitch. Linguists identify four basic types of separation, or *juncture*: plus juncture ($/+/$), single-bar juncture ($/|/$), double-bar juncture ($/\|/$), and double-cross juncture ($/\#/$). The first type is an internal juncture (between words); the last three are terminal junctures (between word groups).

Language

For many thousands of years, human beings have communicated by means of sounds. These sounds are characteristic of the community and are developed in unique patterns. The patterns are interwoven with changes in pitch, stress, and juncture and are usually accompanied by other noticeable behavior characteristics. *Language* is the name given to the patterned sound system used in communication.

Lexical Meaning

Lexical meaning refers to the definition of a word within the vocabulary of a language — as distinguished from grammatical meaning, which varies from one inflectional form to another. The lexical meaning of the verb *play* is found in the dictionary; the grammatical meaning is defined in terms of number (*we play* as distinguished from *he plays*), of tense (*he played* as distinguished from *he plays*), and so forth.

Linguistics

Linguistics is the name given to the scientific study of language. A linguist, then, is a scholar engaged in this study.

The term *linguist* in the past has been used to refer to a person who has a mastery of a number of languages. While the term is still used for this meaning, discriminating speakers and writers now use the word "polyglot" to describe one who speaks and writes several languages fluently.

Linking Verb

A *linking verb* is one which couples or connects the subject and the complement. When the complement is a noun, it has the same referent as the subject. When the complement is an adjective, the adjective describes the subject. The linking verbs include *to be, seems, appears, becomes, tastes, smells, sounds,* and others.

> In colonial times, oak was the main timber for ships.
> The night suddenly grew cold.

Linking-Verb Complement

The term *linking-verb complement* applies to a noun or an adjective complement following such verbs as *to be, seems, appears, becomes,* and other linking verbs.

> The old mare was a rack of bones.
> All her bones seemed lopsided.

A noun that functions as a linking-verb complement is a predicate noun; an adjective in this function is a predicate adjective.

Loose Appositive (*See also* Apposition.)

A *loose appositive* is one which has a nonrestrictive, or descriptive, relationship to the word with which it is in apposition. Loose appositives are set off with commas.

> The Swiss Alps, a skier's paradise, offer slopes to suit everyone from expert to novice.

This type of appositive may be contrasted with the identifying, or restrictive, relationship of the close appositive.

Masculine Gender (*See* Gender.)

Modifier

A *modifier* may be a word or a word group. A modifier qualifies, limits, or restricts the meaning of the headword which it modifies; it makes communication more exact, more precise. In a sense, a modifier is attached in meaning to its headword and with the headword makes up a cluster.

Snow glistens.
Eternal snow glistens brilliantly on the jagged peaks above the deeply shaded valley.

Headword	snow
Modifier	Eternal
Headword	glistens
Modifiers	brilliantly
	on the jagged peaks above the deeply shaded valley
Headword	peaks
Modifiers	jagged
	above the deeply shaded valley
Headword	valley
Modifier	deeply shaded
Headword	shaded
Modifier	deeply

Morpheme

Morpheme describes the smallest significant unit of grammatical form. A morpheme contains no smaller meaningful units, and the term refers to such parts as prefixes, suffixes, simple words that are words in themselves, and simple words that make up compounds.

reopen	(re+ open)
opening	(open+ ing)
open	(open)
openwork	(open+ work)

Neuter Gender

The personal pronoun *it* is the neuter form of the third-person, singular pronoun. The word *it* designates neither masculine nor feminine and is the only neuter form in English.

Nonrestrictive

Nonrestrictive refers to a modifier that describes but does not identify the word it modifies. Nonrestrictive modifiers are set off by commas.

The Milky Way, <u>which was once thought of as the entire universe,</u> is but one unit in a cluster of galaxies.

Noun

The term *noun* describes a word class. Nouns may be identified in communication by certain signals of form and signals of function.

Nouns are inflected to form the plural, usually by adding *s* or *es*. There are other plural inflections, such as the changes in form from *man* to *men* and *alumnus* to *alumni*. Nouns are inflected to form the possessive by adding *'s* to the singular form or, if the singular form ends in *s*, by adding an apostrophe. If the plural form ends in *s*, an apostrophe is added to form the plural possessive; if the plural form does not end in *s*, an *'s* is added.

Nouns function in the sentence as subjects, as complements, as appositives, and as objects of a preposition. A noun may also function as a noun-modifier.

Many nouns terminate in characteristic suffixes: addition, baker, abandonment, kingdom.

Noun Adjunct

When a noun functions as a noun-modifier, it is called a *noun adjunct*, or an attributive noun.

Mr. Evans is a geometry teacher.
Mr. Love is a trial lawyer.

Noun Clause

The *noun clause* is a subject-predicate word group, or subordinate clause. A noun clause has the same functions as a noun: subject, complement, appositive, object of a preposition.

<u>What we actually saw</u> was a cosmic cloud.
Most astronomers insist <u>that all galaxies are of about the same age.</u>
Gravity is <u>what keeps us all from floating into space.</u>
The theory <u>that space either curves negatively or not at all</u> is upheld by many cosmotologists.
Einstein's prediction of bending starlight was validated by <u>what astronomers observed during an eclipse of the sun.</u>

Noun Cluster

When a number of modifiers cluster about a noun, the word group that results is known as a *noun cluster,* or a noun-headed word group.

Don photographed a small, bright-eyed titmouse whose nest had fallen from a tree.

Headword	titmouse
Modifiers	small
	bright-eyed
	whose nest had fallen from a tree

Noun Suffix

The term *noun suffix* describes certain derivational suffixes that are characteristic of the word class called the *noun.*

N-V Pattern

The N-V PATTERN (NOUN-VERB) is one of the seven basic sentence patterns.

N   V
Seaweed flourishes in greater variety along a rocky coast.
N   V
Stuyvesant yielded to the British.
N   V
Poison sumac grows only in moist ground.

N-V-N Pattern

The N-V-N PATTERN (NOUN-VERB-NOUN) is one of the seven basic sentence patterns. In this pattern, the noun that comes after the verb is the direct object.

N   V   N
The bathyscaphe made five dives in six days.
N   V   N
On the third dive, the *Trieste* found a pile of rubble scattered along the ocean floor.
N   V   N
The captain shouted a last message into the underwater phone.

N-V-N-N Pattern

The N-V-N-N PATTERN (NOUN-VERB-NOUN-NOUN) is one of the seven basic sentence patterns. Both nouns that fall after the verb are complements. When the

outer complement is a direct object, the inner complement is an indirect object.

N   V   N   N
Paula gave Dave her most innocent smile.
N   V   N   N
Paul told Marcia the story of his life.

When the inner complement in a N-V-N-N PATTERN is
the direct object, the outer complement is an objective
complement.

N   V   N   N
The scoutmaster appointed John chief cook for the entire
weekend.

N-LV-N Pattern

In the N-LV-N PATTERN (NOUN-LINKING VERB-NOUN),
one of the seven basic sentence patterns, the noun
after the verb — sometimes referred to as the predicate
noun — is a linking-verb complement.

N   LV   N
Toads are useful creatures.

N-LV-ADJ Pattern

In the N-LV-ADJ PATTERN (NOUN-LINKING VERB-AD-
JECTIVE), one of the seven basic sentence patterns,
the adjective after the verb — sometimes referred to as
the predicate adjective — is the linking-verb complement.

N LV   ADJ
Apparently, salt water is not good for insects.
N
Conditions in the newly opened mining camp at Cripple
LV   ADJ
Creek were terrible.

Number

Nouns, personal pronouns, and verbs are inflected
for *number* to show plural or singular meaning.

Object of a Preposition

A prepositional phrase has the pattern:

PREPOSITION — DETERMINER — NOUN
against   a   wall

A pronoun may be substituted for the noun, and the determiner may be omitted.

> against it

The noun or the pronoun in this pattern is said to be the object of the preposition.

Object Case Form

The *object case form* is the form taken by the personal pronoun when it functions as a direct object, an indirect object, the object of a preposition, or the subject of an infinitive.

> Mother met her for the first time yesterday.
> Nevertheless, Mother offered her a job.
> Then Mother spoke to Dad about her.
> Mother wants her to help with the laundry.

When the subordinator *who* has an object function in its subject-predicate word group, it takes the objective case form *whom*.

> Here is the girl whom we all love.
> This is the girl on whom we're all counting.

Objective Complement (*See also* Complement.)

When the inner complement in a N-V-N-N PATTERN is a direct object, the outer complement is an *objective complement*. The objective complement relates to the direct object and is complementary to it.

> My aunt and uncle named their baby Charles.
> The committee appointed Elsie chairman.

Outer Complement (*See* Inner Complement.)

Parallel Structure

The term *parallel structure* describes the use of the same grammatical structure to express two or more closely related ideas.

> Old Mr. Swensen has time to spare, friends to keep him company, and money to burn.
> The judge told the shamefaced defendant that he would have to get a job and that he would have to support his family.

Participial Phrase

When a participle takes a complement or has a modifier, the word group formed is a verbal phrase, or — more specifically — a *participial phrase.*

We squatted by the jetty, idly tossing pebbles into the black water.

Participle

When an *-ing, -ed,* or *-en* verbal functions like an adjective it is called a *participle.* The participle functions in the attributive or predicative position or as an objective complement.

These frozen peaches are delicious.
The grass in the east meadow looks parched.
Alice considers Edward downright annoying.

Particle

A *particle* is a function word that cannot be placed definitely in the other function word categories: connectives, pronouns, determiners, auxiliaries. Although particles are indeterminate in nature, they are useful in communication. They include the noun substitutes *anybody, nobody, somebody, anything;* the negatives *no* and *not;* the emotional words *indeed* and *oh;* and the salutations *hello* and *good-bye.* Words also known as intensifiers are included in this category.

Parts of Speech

In traditional grammar the word classes are referred to as the *parts of speech.* The parts of speech include nouns, verbs, adjectives, adverbs, pronouns, conjunctions, prepositions, and interjections. The word classes include nouns, verbs, adjectives, adverbs, and function words. Function words include the pronouns, conjunctions, prepositions and interjections of traditional grammar.

Past Form of the Verb

The past form of a regular verb is formed by adding *-ed* to the plain form, frequently with a slight spelling adjustment.

PLAIN	PAST
mix	mixed
stop	stopped
cry	cried

The past form of irregular verbs is formed in a number of different ways.

PLAIN	PAST
drive	drove
bite	bit
go	went
take	took
sting	stung

Three-part irregular verbs do not have a special past form. The plain form is used.

PLAIN	PAST
set	set
bet	bet
burst	burst

Past Participle Form of the Verb

Only five-part irregular verbs have a special form for the past participle.

PLAIN	PAST PARTICIPLE
give	given
wear	worn

The past participle form is used with certain auxiliaries.

I have worn this ski jacket for five seasons.
I have just given it to my favorite charity.

Regular verbs and four-part irregular verbs use the past form in contexts requiring the past participle.

Dad has stopped taking a daily paper.
I've been stung by a used car salesman.

Three-part irregular verbs use the plain form as a past form and therefore repeat this form in contexts requiring a past participle.

Mother has set the table with her best china.
The die has been cast.

Past Tense

Past tense is the verb form that refers to past time. All regular verbs have an inflected past form. All five-part and four-part irregular verbs have an inflected past form. Three-part irregular verbs use the plain form to communicate past time.

PLAIN	PAST
walk	walked
write	wrote
fight	fought
burst	burst

Person

Only personal pronouns are inflected to show *person*. First person relates to the person speaking, second person to the person spoken to, and third person to the person spoken about.

FIRST PERSON	I, me, my, mine, we, us, our, ours
SECOND PERSON	you, your, yours
THIRD PERSON	he, him, his, she, her, hers, they, them, their, theirs, it, its

Personal Pronoun

A *personal pronoun* is a function word that serves as a noun substitute. The personal pronoun has meaning only in relation to its antecedent (the word for which it substitutes). Personal pronouns are useful in communication since they eliminate repetition and unnecessary wordage.

Bud Manzo is visiting his uncle and aunt in Nevada. He hopes to explore the Valley of Fire with them.

Phoneme

Phoneme describes one of the smallest units of significant sound. The \b\ sound in *bin* and the \p\ sound in *pin* are simple phonemes. Phonemes are represented in writing by graphemes, or letters. A compound phoneme is a phoneme in which two simple phonemes are blended so completely that they are considered one sound. The diphthong \aủ\, which is a combination of \a\ + \ủ\ is a compound phoneme.

Phonemics

Phonemics is the study of the significant sounds of English. It is a branch of the science of linguistics.

Pitch

> *Pitch* is one of the vocal effects of intonation. As the voice rises from low through normal and high to very high, we can recognize four levels of pitch. These levels are designated as pitch phonemes and are numbered $/1/$, $/2/$, $/3/$, and $/4/$ from low to high. Pitch communicates emotion and lack of emotion; it also serves to signal the difference between a statement and a question. The common pitch patterns of English sentences are characteristic of our language and are different from the patterns found in other languages.

>   2   3   1
>   I have no money.

Plain Form of the Verb

> The *plain form of the verb* is sometimes known as the infinitive form. The plain form is used in the present tense with a plural subject and with the personal pronouns *I* and *you*. The plain form is also used with such auxiliaries as *can, may, might, must, should, could, shall,* and *will.*

>> Dad wants me to wash the car this weekend.
>> Some people wash their cars every week.
>> I wash ours once a month.
>> We should wash it more often.

Plus Juncture

> *Plus juncture* describes the separations between words. It is represented by the phonemic symbol $/+/$.

>> the +beautiful +bird

Position (*See* Function)

Positive Degree (*See* Comparison of Adjectives and Adverbs)

Possessive Case Form

> The *possessive case form* is the inflected form appropriate to the modifying function of the noun and pronoun. The possessive of the noun is marked by an apostrophe or by an apostrophe and *s*.

>> Ellie 's book
>> Shakespeare 's tragedies
>> a month 's leave

Personal pronouns and the subordinator *who* are inflected for possessive case.

> This is my pen.
> The pen is his. (his pen)
> I wonder whose pen this is.

Predicate (*See also* Complete Subject.)

The *predicate* consists of the verb and its modifiers with a complement, if there is one. The predicate communicates the active or dynamic quality of experience.

> The tree surgeon / whacked off a dozen old limbs.

The predicate includes everything to the right of the slash mark.

Predicate Adjective (*See also* Complement.)

The linking-verb complement in the N-LV-ADJ PATTERN is sometimes referred to as the *predicate adjective*.

> Toads are more terrestrial than frogs.
> The guard seemed exceptionally alert last night.
> The plot sounds exciting.

Predicate Noun (*See also* Complement.)

The linking-verb complement in the N-LV-N PATTERN is sometimes referred to as the *predicate noun*.

> The president is an eager storyteller.
> The cardinal is a great family bird.

Predicate Verb

The term *predicate verb* specifies the verb form contained within the complete predicate.

> The rodeo queen was attended by her ladies-in-waiting.

Prefix

A *prefix* is a letter or a combination of letters attached to the beginning of a word or of a root. Most prefixes change the meaning but not the word class of the words to which they are attached: happy, unhappy.

Preposition

A *preposition* is a connective which joins a certain type phrase to the headword which it modifies. A preposition is a function word and has little lexical meaning except in the context of a sentence.

> There are lots of fish in Lone Tree Creek.
> The trout swim close under the bank at every turn.

Prepositional Phrase

A *prepositional phrase* is a word-group modifier that is included within a basic sentence pattern by means of a preposition.

> Along an old wall in an open field, we found a rare species of edible mushrooms.

Present Participle Form of the Verb

The *present participle form of the verb* is the *-ing* form. It functions as a finite verb only when it is used with some form of *to be* as an auxiliary.

> Peter was sitting with his eyes glued to the TV set.

As a verbal, the present participle form functions as a modifier and as a noun.

> We saw Diablo cantering along with an empty saddle.
> Running out of gas can be dangerous.

Present Tense

The term *present tense* refers to present time. Unlike the past tense, there is no special verb form for the present tense. There are many ways to communicate present time in English. For example, we use the plain form with a plural subject and the singular form with a singular subject.

> The birds sing all day.
> The bird sings all day.

Present time is also communicated by means of auxiliaries used with the present participle form or with the plain form.

> The bird is singing.
> The bird can sing.

Principal Parts of the Verb

The three verb forms from which all the other forms of a verb can be derived are considered the *principal parts*. These forms are the plain form, the past form, and the past participle form.

Pronoun (*See also* Personal Pronoun, Subordinator.)

A *pronoun* is a noun substitute. In modern grammar, we speak of personal pronouns and of relative pronouns (subordinators).

Proper Nouns

Proper nouns are special classes of nouns that are capitalized in English.

Punctuation

Punctuation is the process of using graphic symbols to separate written English into meaningful units of syntax. The graphic symbols include the period, the question mark, the exclamation point, the comma, the semicolon, the colon, the dash, quotation marks, parentheses, brackets, and others.

Question

The *question* is one of the seven basic sentence patterns. Questions are signaled by an inversion of the subject-predicate word order, by the use of auxiliaries, by the use of certain function words, and by a rising pitch.

> Have you any money?
> Do you like football?
> Where are you going?
> You are going to Boston?
> 2   3
> You are going to Boston‖

Reference of Pronouns

A pronoun is a substitute word, a word that gets its exact meaning from the word or words to which it refers — its antecedent. If the reference of a pronoun is not clear, communication becomes ineffective.

> John sold his watch.
> The Wilsons have lost their dog.
> Syl found the book and returned it to Henry.

Reflexive Pronouns

The *-self* pronouns are commonly called *reflexive pronouns*.

SINGULAR	PLURAL
myself	ourselves
yourself	yourselves
himself	
herself	themselves
itself	

A reflexive pronoun may be used as a substitute word or as an intensifier.

Mr. Ames is going into business for himself.
I'll do the job myself, thank you.

Regular Verb

Regular verbs have four inflected forms. The past form is developed by adding the suffix *-ed* to the plain form. The present participle is formed by adding the suffix *-ing* to the plain form. Most English verbs are regular verbs. There are approximately 150 irregular verbs in our language, and more than 5,000 regular verbs.

PLAIN	SINGULAR	PAST	PRESENT PARTICIPLE
deliver	delivers	delivered	delivering

Relative Pronoun(*See* Subordinator)

Restrictive

Restrictive describes a modifier that identifies rather than defines the word it modifies.

Our stretch of beach is occasionally visited by terns <u>that breed along the shores of Newfoundland.</u>

Run-Together Sentence

When two or more basic sentence patterns are written as one sentence without a coordinator or a semicolon, the result is an error known as the *run-together sentence*.

Lightning split the sky suddenly it began to rain.
Correction: Lightning split the sky. Suddenly it began to rain. *Or:* Lightning split the sky; suddenly it began to rain.

Second Person(*See* Person)

Segmental Phonemes

The term *segmental phonemes* describes the vowel sounds and the consonant sounds that form the segments, or small parts, of the stream of speech.

Sentence

A *sentence* is an utterance. In written English, the form of the sentence is standardized. It begins with a capital letter and ends with a mark of terminal punctuation—a period, a question mark, an exclamation point. It has a subject and a finite predicate verb. The normal word order is subject, verb, complement. A subject-predicate word group beginning with a signal of subordination is not of itself a sentence. The written sentence, when it is read aloud, follows the characteristic intonation patterns of English. It terminates with a falling pitch with a fading-off of the voice, or with a rising pitch with a stopping of the voice.

Sentence Fragment

When a word group that does not have the characteristics of a sentence is unintentionally written as a sentence, the error that results is known as a *sentence fragment.*

> One night about midnight I was lying awake. Unable to sleep and listening to the bull bellowing in the meadow.
> *Correction:* Unable to sleep, I listened to the bull bellowing in the meadow.

Sentence-Modifier

A word or a word group which precedes the subject of a sentence is usually considered a *sentence-modifier.*

> Finally, the posse galloped off.
> In the meantime, we reconstructed the accident.

Single-Bar Juncture

Single-bar juncture is a terminal juncture. It separates word groups or units of syntax. It is not accompanied by a change in pitch.

> The colts | raced across the prairie.
> The shrew | a voracious feeder | eats twice its weight daily.

Singular Form of the Verb

The form of the verb used with a singular subject in the present tense is called the *singular form.*

> He plays beautifully.
> Music puts me to sleep.

Standard English

Standard English is the conventional language of writing. It is the kind of language found in newspapers, with the exception of special columns and some sports stories. It is the kind of language found in most magazine articles and published reports. It is the kind of language found in textbooks and taught in schools. Most speeches are written in Standard English. Standard English is well established in the speech and writing of the educated and is readily recognized wherever English is spoken and understood.

Stress

Stress is one of the vocal effects of intonation. It refers to loudness or softness but usually communicates emphasis. According to linguists, there are four degrees of stress. The four stress phonemes are primary, secondary, tertiary, and weak indicated by the symbols $/\,'\,/$, $/\,\hat{}\,/$, $/\,\check{}\,/$, and $/\,\breve{}\,/$.

prèdícămènt

Subject Noun

The *subject noun* is the headword of the word group making up the complete subject.

> A big black iron stove / was set into an alcove at one end of the kitchen.
> In the morning, the room / is flooded with sunshine.
> The drop-leaf cherry table / was covered with a bright cloth.

Subject-Predicate Structure

The basic structure of English is the *subject-predicate structure.* We automatically respond to this structure which is basic to communication and which has been part of our experience since we first learned to talk. Subject-predicate structure occurs in the sentence, in subordinate clauses, and in the two or more patterns that make up a compound sentence.

The noun-verb relationship is the basis of subject-predicate structure. Either the noun or the verb may be expanded indefinitely by modifiers. The verb may have a complement. A pronoun or a word group may substitute for the subject noun. The basic structure of the sentence, however, remains actor-action, noun-verb, subject-predicate.

The dogs/ slept blissfully on the warm dry grass.

Subject-Predicate Word Group (*See*Subordinate Clause.)

Subordinate Clause

In the process of subordination, the subject-predicate word group that is included within the basic sentence pattern is called a *subordinate clause*. Subordinate clauses function as modifiers (adjective clause, adverb clause) and as nouns (noun clause).

Subordination

Subordination is the process of including a subject-predicate word group within a basic sentence pattern. The connectives used are called subordinators. The subject-predicate word group, or subordinate clause, functions either as a modifier (adjective clause, adverb clause) or as a noun (noun clause).

The skunk is a harmless animal that trots around at night in search of food.
Skunks are considered beneficial because they eat insects and catch mice.
A skunk knows where the Snapping Turtle buries its clutches of eggs.

Subordinator

A *subordinator* is a connective used to include a subordinate clause within a basic sentence pattern.

unless	when	as
because	where	while
if	since	whether
until	although	how

Although I have money in the bank, I'm pressed for cash.
If you lend me five dollars, I'll pay you back with interest.

Substitution

The term *substitution* describes the grammatical device of using certain words such as personal pronouns, subordinators, reflexive pronouns, and determiners in place of other words. Effective substitution contributes to economy and flexibility in communication.

Suffix

A *suffix* is an affix attached to the end of a word or of a root. The noun, verb, adjective and adverb suffixes signal these word classes. Some suffixes are signals of inflection. Other suffixes serve as word builders in the extension of vocabulary.

Superlative Degree (*See* Comparison of Adjectives and Adverbs.)

Suprasegmental Phonemes

The *suprasegmental phonemes* are the vocal effects of intonation: the phonemes of pitch, stress, and juncture that accompany, or are super-added to, the segmental phonemes of spoken English. The segmental phonemes are the vowel and consonant sounds that form the segments of the stream of speech.

PITCH	/1/, /2/, /3/, /4/	(low, medium, high, very high)
STRESS	/´/, /ˆ/, /`/, /˘/	(primary, secondary, tertiary, zero)
JUNCTURE	/+/, /|/, /‖/, /#/	(plus, single-bar, double-bar, double-cross)

Syntax

Syntax refers to the way words are put together to form word groups, subject-predicate word groups, and sentences. Syntax also applies to the study of these language patterns in their relation to meaning.

Tense

Tense is a grammatical concept growing out of the inflection of verbs to show time. In English, only the past form of a verb is inflected for tense. In the case of three-part irregular verbs, there is no inflection for tense. A variety of meanings related to time can be communicated by means of combinations of auxiliaries with the verb.

Third Person (*See* **Person.**)

Three-Part Irregular Verb

The *three-part irregular verb* has three forms: the plain form, the singular form, and the present participle.

PLAIN	SINGULAR	PRESENT PARTICIPLE
bet	bets	betting
set	sets	setting

Transitional Adverb

A *transitional adverb* is an adverb that establishes a relationship between two sentences.

The meadow is rich with the leavings of last year's hay. Moreover, the grove of aspen near the creek will provide shelter for the grazing cows.

Transitive Verb (*See also* **Intransitive Verb.**)

A verb that takes a direct object (N-V-N and N-V-N-N PATTERNS) is considered *transitive,* because the action named by the verb goes across from the subject to the object.

Michael carefully inspected the mare.

In the passive construction, the action named by the verb passes over to the subject; such verbs are also considered transitive.

The mare was carefully inspected by Michael.

Usage

Usage refers to the way in which words and word groups are actually used in a language. Conventional usage depends largely on the appropriate choice of language in terms of time, place, and degree of formality. Thus in writing we usually avoid language which is obsolete, dialectal, or colloquial. Grammatical usage depends on the correct choice of language. Thus in writing we avoid the use of a pronoun that has an uncertain antecedent, of a verb form that does not agree with the subject in number, of a verb form incorrectly used with an auxiliary, and so forth.

Verb

The *verb* is the heart of a sentence. It is the chief actor in the drama of communication. Its position in the sentence is fixed and its identification is reinforced by its inflectional forms, by certain characteristic suffixes, and by function words called auxiliaries.

> The hands brought the brood mares up from Castle Rock meadow and moved them through the gorge into the stable pasture.
> The horses were badly frightened by the barbed wire.
> We had been listening for hours for the sudden rustle of an antelope.

Verb Cluster

When a number of modifiers cluster about a noun, the word group that results is known as a *verb cluster*, or a verb-headed word group.

> The miners scrambled wildly into the street when the Concord stage lumbered into town.
>
> Headword scrambled
> Modifiers wildly
> into the street
> when the Concord stage lumbered into town

Verb Phrase

A *verb phrase* refers to the main verb and its auxiliaries.

> This lamp should be rewired.

Verbal

The term *verbal* describes a word whose function has shifted from that of a verb to that of a noun or a modifier. There are three kinds of verbals: the infinitive, the gerund, and the participle. The infinitive functions as a noun or as an adjective or adverb. The gerund functions as a noun. The participle functions as an adjective.

Verbal Phrase

When a verbal takes a complement or has a modifier, the word group formed is called a verbal phrase. There are three kinds of verbal phrases: the infinitive phrase, the gerund phrase, and the participial phrase.

Vowel

The *vowels* are speech sounds made with a clear passage of air through the mouth. In English the letters of the alphabet that represent vowels are *a, e, i, o,* and *u.* Linguists include *h, y,* and *w* as semivowels.

Word Classes

Word classes, in modern grammar, include nouns, verbs, adjectives, adverbs, and function words. The noun, verb, adjective, and adverb word classes, or form classes, include about 93 per cent of all of the different words in the English language. When new words are added, they are either nouns, verbs, adjectives, or adverbs. These are the words that have lexical meaning, as contrasted with function words, words that have little meaning out of context.

Word Group

A *word group* is a phrase, a group of words that does not contain a subject and a verb, as distinguished from subject-predicate word groups.

Word-Group Modifier

A *word-group modifier* is a word group that functions as an adjective or an adverb. The most common type of word-group modifier is the prepositional phrase.

Word Order

Word order is the single most important determiner of meaning in the English language. The normal order of sentence elements is subject, verb, and complement. When this order is changed, meaning is changed or nonsense results. The position of modifiers is largely fixed in English and is also an important factor of meaning. English is called an analytic language since it does not depend on inflections for determining meaning as is the case in a synthetic language such as Latin. Rather, it is position, reinforced by certain function words and sometimes by inflection, which largely determines meaning in English.

> Anne frightened the bull.
> The bull frightened Anne.
>
> Phil sold the cheap car.
> Phil sold the car cheap.

Index